HISTORICAL FICTION GUIDE:

Annotated Chronological, Geographical and Topical List of Five Thousand Selected Historical Novels

by

Daniel D. McGarry
and
Sarah Harriman White

The Scarecrow Press, Inc.
New York 1963

L. C. Card No. 63-7462

FOREWORD

Historical Fiction enjoys justifiable and ever-growing popularity among the reading public. Joining in the admiration for this genre, the compilers of the present Guide -- one a professional historian, the other a homemaker and specialist in English -- have considered it a labor of love and a service to readers to prepare a new, up-to-date Historical Fiction Guide. This work is designed especially for use by adults and by students in high schools, colleges, and universities.

Both authors have long read historical fiction for recreational purposes, and the historian has long required such reading in his introductory survey courses. Thus the authors have become acutely aware of the need for a new general guide. With the increasing demand for historical fiction, the preparation of a new, convenient guide has become ever more imperative. As a stop-gap, some librarians have attempted to accumulate special file cards for historical fiction, to prepare their own typed or mimeographed lists, to assemble historical novels in a separate section of the library, or to mark books of historical fiction with some distinguishing color. Helpful as such measures may be, they do not satisfy the need for a concise, general guide, which may, incidentally, be marked to show the holdings of a particular library, as well as to plan future acquisitions.

Much earlier in the century, general guides to historical fiction were compiled by Jonathan Nield,[1] Ernest Baker,[2] and James R. Kaye,[3] but these, unfortunately, have long been out of date, as well as out of print, although they are still often used for lack of something more recent. A good guide intended mainly for younger persons was prepared by Hannah Logasa in 1927.[4] This has gone through several subsequent editions and revisions,[5] but has continued to be especially useful for juvenile readers.

In recent times, some more specialized introductions to historical fiction in United States history have been appearing. An early instance was a volume by Otis W. Coan and Richard G. Lillard,[6] arranged thematically rather than historically.[7] Another example is Ernest E. Leisy's work on American Historical Fiction,[8] which incorporates extensive summaries of historical novels in its running text. Still another is that of Robert A. Lively,[9] which lists some five hundred novels on the Civil War, most without annotations. A convenient guide to American historical novels by A. T. Dickinson, Jr. was published by Scarecrow Press in 1948.[10] Although valuable for their own purposes, these limited treatises do not satisfy the need for a general guide.

In preparing this _Guide,_ the compilers have followed the view that fiction is historical if it includes reference to customs, conditions, identifiable persons, or events in the past. Thus, a novel concerning the everyday way of life, outlook, mores, and living conditions in fourteenth century France is historical fiction just as much as one which features Charles VII, Edward III, or the Battle of Crècy.

This _Guide_ is also selective, and endeavours to include only _better_ works of historical fiction. Among factors considered are literary excellence, readability, and historical value. Much weight has been attached to opinions of competent reviewers as well as to those of other bibliographers. However, in some categories there is a dearth of historical fiction, and it has been necessary to include less distinguished works. In the final analysis, the entries in this _Guide_ are representative rather than all-inclusive. The book is meant to be a serviceable reference for persons desiring to find generally approved fiction concerning particular periods and fields of history. Poetry and Drama have been excluded as better suited to oral and visual presentation than to silent reading.

For practical purposes the authors have made the year 1900 their terminal date. This is partly because fiction concerning our own twentieth century is so much more abundant and more readily available, and partly because this period is more contemporary than historical. At a future date, coverage may be extended into the present century by a supplement or a revised edition.

Only works available in English have been included, but these are often translations from books written in other languages. Thus many notable works originally written in foreign tongues are listed. Each translated book has been so marked.

Our historical subdivisions as to time and place are those commonly accepted in the historical profession. While to some extent arbitrary, they are generally similar to those followed by the _Guide To Historical Literature._

In making particular entries, the compilers have usually observed the authoritative, accepted practices of the Library of Congress. Where a writer uses a pseudonym, the work is usually listed under the author's real name, with reference and cross-reference to the pseudonym. The exceptions have been where general usage prescribes otherwise, as in the cases of "George Eliot" and "Maurice Druon," and where several authors have collaborated under one pseudonym (for example: Janet, Lillian, _pseud._ for Janet Cicchetti and Lillian Ressler Groom). Where the name under which a book was published differs from the name under which it is listed here, the name that appears on the title page is given after the title (for example: Stephens, Eve. _Anne Boleyn._ by Evelyn Anthony, _pseud._; Turnbull, Francese Hubbard. _The Golden Book of Venice._ by Mrs. Lawrence Turnbull). Where a woman has written under both her maiden and her married names, her latest or most consistently used name is listed for the main entry, with reference and cross-reference to the other (for example: Lenanton, Carola Oman. _Crouchback._ by Carola Oman).

Sometimes a work has appeared under various titles, as is the case where a book has one title in England and another in the United States. In such cases the American, earlier, or more common title is preferred. In all circumstances involving more than one name or title, explanation has been made in the text and cross-references provided in the Index.

Where there have been several editions of a work, as often happens, especially in the case of classics, reference has usually been made to the earlier edition as more indicative of the author's milieu, style, and tendence. Chance has had its part in this matter, so that the editions cited are sometimes, perhaps, not the earliest. Where there have been several publishers, the one listed is likewise fortuitous, since no attempt has been made to choose between them, except that American publishers are usually given preference, since this Guide is initially published in the United States. The Library Of Congress Catalogue has been the main reference here, as being the best yardstick of books available in this country. Publishers are American or English unless otherwise noted.

A common fault of many annotated bibliographies of historical fiction is that they are inclined either to be so diffuse that they tell the story in advance, or so concise as to be satisfied with unadorned entries that give practically no information. An attempt has been made here to trod the middle path. Ordinarily information as to the general time and locale is already given by the chronological and geographical classification. It goes without saying that most of the works included involve exciting action, an element of adventure, and romantic suspense.

Long descriptive sub-titles, so popular in many older novels, have seldom been included unless they provide additional information. In some instances a sub-title has been used for the annotation, in which case it is enclosed in quotation marks.

Although the authors have worked several years and expended much time and money in the preparation of this modest volume, they realize its inevitable limitations. For these they cannot apologize, since they have done their best, and, to quote Martial: "Otherwise, dear Avitus, there would be no book." At the same time they ask any users of the work who have criticisms, suggestions, or constructive comments to advise them. They will regard this as a special favor. Suggestions as to additions, subtractions, or other alterations will, as far as possible, be gratefully incorporated into subsequent editions.

And now we bid farewell to the patient reader: "Happy journeys along the picturesque paths of historical fiction! If this Guide be of any service in lighting your way, it will have fulfilled its purpose."

Notes

1. Jonathan Nield, A Guide to the Best Historical Novels and Tales (London and New York, 1902), which went through five successive, revised editions, the last in 1929.

2. Ernest A. Baker, History in Fiction ... (London and New York, 1907). This reappeared in revised form as A Guide to Historical Fiction in 1914.

3. James R. Kaye, Historical Fiction Chronologically and Historically Related (Chicago, 1920).

4. Hannah Logasa, Historical Fiction Suitable for Junior and Senior High Schools (Philadelphia, 1927).

5. Generally these have been entitled, Historical Fiction and Other Reading References for Classes in Junior and Senior High Schools.

6. Otis W. Coan and Richard G. Lillard, America In Fiction... (Stanford University, 1941; revised in 1945).

7. "Farm and Village Life," "Industrial America," "Politics...," "Religion," etc.

8. Ernest F. Leisy, The American Historical Novel (Norman, Okla., 1950).

9. Robert A. Lively, Fiction Fights the Civil War (Chapel Hill, N. C., 1957).

10. A. T. Dickinson, Jr., American Historical Fiction (New York, 1958).

Table of Contents

INTRODUCTION

> Attempts to reconstruct the past by using the imagination to amplify traditions and other historical evidences are among the oldest and dearest activities of man. Since the earliest times of which we have record, man has taken pleasure in picturing the past in folk-tales, song, epic poems, and dramatic compositions. Although the skeleton of these works is usually historical, their flesh is decidedly fictional.

The great epic poems which have so often constituted the fundamental literature and history of ancient peoples were essentially historical: partly true, partly imaginative. It is accepted as a fact that traditions concerning past events were incorporated into the great epic poems of antiquity, such as Homer's *Iliad* and *Odyssey*, Vergil's *Aeneid*, the early German *Nibelungenlied* (*Song of the Nibelungs*), the French *Chansons de geste* such as the *Song of Roland*, the Spanish *Cid Campeador*, the Byzantine *Digenes Akrites*, and many Scandinavian Sagas and Eddas.

The like may be said of many outstanding dramas of earlier times. Many of the greatest dramatists have composed works on historical themes, for example: Aeschylus, Calderón, Corneille, Racine, and especially Shakespeare. Dramatic presentations of historical subjects still have their attraction, as is evidenced by several recent motion pictures and television presentations.

Thus writers of historical fiction stand in a distinguished company and a great tradition. The main difference is that whereas epic poetry was composed primarily to be recited, and drama to be presented both orally and visually, novels are written simply to be read.

In comparatively recent times, as a result of the increased diffusion of the printed word and public literacy, fiction has become the principal form of literature, and the historical novel the prevailing form of historically oriented belles lettres. Both the art and the popularity of historical fiction were ably promoted in the first half of the nineteenth century by Sir Walter Scott, as well as by other writers such as Alexandre Dumas, the Brontë sisters, James Fenimore Cooper, Nathaniel Hawthorne, Charles Kingsley, and Leo Tolstoy, to mention only a few examples. In our own day we see such figures as Thomas B. Costain, Louis de Wohl, Dmitri Merezhkovsky, Rafael Sabatini, Frank G. Slaughter, and Sigrid Undset among authors of historical fiction.

The same thing draws such writers and their readers to historical fiction as attracted great ancient writers to epic poetry and semi-historical drama. Historical fiction is a powerful medium, which includes at one and the same time, the attractions of fiction and those of history, and it appeals to a broad audience.

One of the charms of fiction is that it seeks "verisimilitude" and clothes itself in the semblance of truth. Historical fiction adds the realistic details and trappings of actuality that belong to a past, often remote time. The task of the author of historical fiction is thus the more difficult and the more exacting, since he must familiarize himself with the facts and features of life in the past as well as the present.

In addition to sharing the values of fiction in general, historical fiction has values all its own. Among shared attributes are the powers to inform and instruct, awaken sympathies and appreciations, communicate experiences and emotions, inspire and uplift, as well as the ability to entertain, amuse, and relax. But over and beyond these things, historical fiction is also an introduction to history: a threshold and a gateway leading into formal history. After reading historical fiction, as after seeing a film version of the story of Samson and Delilah, or Caesar and Cleopatra, for example, one is drawn to consult authentic historical accounts and sources to see how far the presentation has followed the facts.

The famous nineteenth century German historian Leopold von Ranke is said to have been turned to the study of history by reading the novels of Sir Walter Scott. As Robert A. Lively remarks: "The devotee of historical novels moves toward formal history rather than away from it; he rises from excitement at fictions to seek the truth of the matter."[1] And, as the versatile English author, historian, and statesman, Sir John Morley, has forcibly put it: "The great Duke of Marlborough said that he had learnt all the history he ever knew out of Shakespeare's historical plays."[2]

Good historical fiction, besides being an introduction and enticement to history, is itself a form of history. It not only contains many historical elements, but is also a legitimate approach to history. Hervey Allen has observed: "Neither historian nor novelist can reproduce the real past," but by use of his particular art, the novelist may give "the reader a more vivid, adequate, and significant apprehension of past epochs than does the historian."[3]

The conscientious historian has this limitation: he is unable to re-create a full historical picture "in the round" or "in the concrete." Although he may be informed as to the various historical elements which <u>could</u> go to make up a full picture of any past event, he never knows for sure just which of these elements were actually in conjunction at any given time. The hero and heroine might well have been attired thus and so according to the styles of the day, but what did they actually wear on <u>this</u> occasion? What did they actually say? What were the trivial details as well as the more important elements that are essential to construct the living yet accurate picture of any past event? Who can say? Certainly not the historian. By virtue of his profession he is disbarred from simply imagining or improvising; he must stick to ascertained facts. It is here that he must call in his colleague -- and we use the term advisedly -- the historical novelist.

The author of historical fiction is at liberty to reconstruct, with his broader leeway, a detailed, colorful picture of the past as it must have been. He is able to provide "the selective litter of unique detail that ... warms fiction with the breath of reality."[4] As Lively further remarks, "While the historian labors to authenticate each tile he laboriously assembles, the novelist, with broad brush and vivid colors, may capture with a few broad strokes an impression of the age recalled."[5]

In earlier times there was not the distinction that we have today between the historian and the historical novelist. Accordingly, in order to infuse life into his story and create a more striking picture of the past, the historian often acted as an historical novelist, and filled in the details from his imagination or from questionable traditions. In modern times, however, this distinction has been drawn, so that we can now trust the historian to retain his objective accuracy with greater integrity, and, at the same time, enjoy and appreciate the freer picture painted by the historical novelist.

Thomas Carlyle noted that Scott's publication of his absorbing tales known as the Waverley Novels "taught all men this truth ...: that the bygone ages of the world were actually filled by living men, not by protocols, state papers, controversies, and abstractions of men."[6]

In a way, it might even be argued that historical fiction is more truthful than history itself. History supposedly presents all that it records as factual, yet everyone knows that much of what it says is insufficiently proven, doubtful, or even, in many instances, in error, by virtue of the inadequacy of human knowledge. But historical fiction, on the other hand, merely suggests that much of its content is true to life and much fictional, leaving to the discriminating reader the determination of just what is objective and what imaginative. In a broad sense most history is partly fictional, and most fiction is partly true. But whereas history makes claim to thoroughgoing objectivity, historical fiction displays no such presumption. The famous English novelist Thackeray declared, with some exaggeration, over a century ago, that "fiction contains a greater amount of truth in solution than the volume that purports to be all true."[7]

The reading of historical fiction is recreational, and both relaxes and gratifies. But it is also profitable. It leaves us with something to show for our time. While being entertained, we are also instructed. This is to some extent true of all good fiction; but it is doubly true of good historical fiction. The latter adds another dimension to ordinary fiction. As one lady somewhat untactfully, but also with some truth, remarked: "Historical fiction sugar-coats the historical pill." It is a godsend for the tired businessman, the fatigued mother, the weary working girl, laborer, or student, who wish for and need a certain degree of relaxation, but still do not want it to be entirely without profit. They are perhaps not up to digesting a more serious tome of formal history. At the same time, they may not be content with a steady, monotonous diet of television, newspapers, and magazines. For them historical fiction, which can carry them back to the past on a magic carpet, is "just what the doctor ordered." For them the historical novelist may fulfill in modern days the function that used to be performed by epic poets, troubadors, and dramatic authors.

Notes

1. Robert A. Lively, _Fiction Fights the Civil War_ (Chapel Hill, N. C., 1957) p. 190.

2. The quotation is from John Morley, _The Great Commonplaces of Reading,_ quoted in Jonathan Nield, _A Guide to the Best Historical Novels and Tales_ (London, 1929) p. xvi.

3. Hervey Allen, "History in the Novel," in _Atlantic Monthly,_ CLXXIII, No. 2 (1944) 119-120.

4. Lively, _op. cit.,_ p. 72.

5. _Ibid.,_ p. 7.

6. Thomas Carlyle, _Critical and Miscellaneous Essays_ (Century Edition), IV, 77.

7. Quoted in Nield, _op. cit._, p. xvi.

I. Antiquity (to about 400 A. D.)

A. The Near East, Europe, and the Mediterranean Area in Antiquity

1. Ancient Near East (to about 336 B.C.)

a. Ancient Egypt

Bell, Archie. KING TUT-ANKH-AMEN. St. Botolph Soc., 1923. Of the love of the Prince of Hermonthis for a priestess -- and its outcome. 1

Ebers, Georg. AN EGYPTIAN PRINCESS. (tr.) Macmillan, 1887. Romance of Egypt and Persia in the sixth century B. C. with good historical background. 2

--------. UARDA. (tr.) Caldwell, 1877. Life under the powerful Rameses II -- social, military, religious, political-- revolving on a plot of mistaken identity. 3

Eckenstein, Lina. TUTANKH-ATEN. Cape, 1924. Events during monotheistic Aken-aten's reign in fourteenth century B. C. Thebes. 4

Gautier, Théophile. THE ROMANCE OF A MUMMY. (tr.) Lippincott, 1886. About the plagues in ancient Egypt and the Exodus, with details of life based on archeological findings. 5

Glowacki, Aleksander. THE PHARAOH AND THE PRIEST. (tr.) Little, 1902. Conflict between religious and political forces in the reign of Rameses XIII. 6

Grant, Joan. LORD OF THE HORIZON. British Bks., 1948. A vivid story of the Middle Kingdom in Egypt under Amenemhet I. 7

--------. WINGED PHARAOH. Harper, 1938. An Egyptian princess of about 4000 B. C., with ancient culture and ideals as background. 8

Haggard, H. Rider. THE ANCIENT ALLAN. Longmans, 1920. A flash-back transports us to fifth century B.C. Egypt. 9

--------. MORNING STAR. Longmans, 1910. A story of romance and the supernatural in the face of danger with the Pharaoh's daughter as a figure. 10

--------. QUEEN OF THE DAWN. Doubleday, 1925. Romance during King Apepi's rule in the eighteenth century B. C. 11

Hall, Arthur Dana. GOLDEN BALANCE. Crown, 1955. Son of a farmer becomes a member of the Pharaoh's court. 12

Hardy, William George. ALL THE TRUMPETS SOUNDED. Coward, 1942. The story of Moses as adopted Prince of Egypt and as leader of the Hebrews. 13

Kelly, William P. THE STONECUTTER OF MEMPHIS. Dutton, 1904. During the period of animal worship the hero is sentenced to be sold into slavery for killing a sacred cat. 14

McGraw, Eloise Jarvis. PHARAOH. Coward, 1958. Queen Hatshepsut, acting as regent, proclaims herself Pharaoh and rules Egypt. 15

Mann, Thomas. JOSEPH IN EGYPT. (tr.) Knopf, 1938. Joseph's rise from slavery to a position of trust. (followed by JOSEPH THE PROVIDER) 16

--------. JOSEPH THE PROVIDER. (tr.) Knopf, 1944. The height of Joseph's power in Egypt and his reunion with his family. 17

Merezhkovsky, Dmitri. AKHNATON, KING OF EGYPT. (tr.) Dutton, 1924. Association of the Cretan maiden-priestess Dio with the monotheistic Pharaoh Akhnaton (Akenaten). 18

Pier, Garrett Chatfield. HANIT, THE ENCHANTRESS. Dutton, 1921. An archeologist goes back thirty centuries to experience life in Amenhotep's court. 19

Rawlins, Eustace. THE HIDDEN TREASURES OF EGYPT. by R. Eustace, pseud. Stratford, 1926. About the Prophet Moses and his people. 20

Walloth, Wilhelm. THE KING'S TREASURE HOUSE. Gottsberger, 1886. Egypt before the Exodus. 21

Waltari, Mika. THE EGYPTIAN. (tr.) Putnam, 1949. Life in Egypt a thousand years before the coming of Christ. 22

Whisper, A., pseud. KING AND CAPTIVE. Blackwood, 1910. Romance of a monarch and a dancing girl in ancient Thebes. 23

Whyte-Melville, George John. SARCHEDON. Longmans, 1871. Romance of a soldier and a maiden in the time of Semiramis in Egypt and Assyria. 24

Williamson, W. H. THE PANTHER SKIN. Holden, 1924. Set in Egypt during Amenhotep IV's (Akhnaton's) eventful reign. 25

Willis, Anthony Armstrong. THE LOVE OF PRINCE RAMESES. by Anthony Armstrong, pseud. Paul, 1921. Royal romance in Egypt in the twelfth century B. C. 26

--------. WHEN NILE WAS YOUNG. by Anthony Armstrong, pseud. Hutchinson, 1923. Religious conflict in Egypt in the fourteenth century B. C. 27

Wilson, Dorothy Clarke. A PRINCE OF EGYPT. Westminster, 1949. Based on the life of Moses to the time of the Exodus. 28

I. A. 1. b. Ancient Mesopotamia and Persia

Beddoes, Willoughby. A SON OF ASHUR. Sonnenschein, 1905. The glory of Babylon in the days of King Nebuchadnezzar. 29

Crawford, F. Marion. ZOROASTER. Macmillan, 1885. A Persian romance of the time of Daniel--the fall of Babylon and the feast of Belshazzar. 30

Davis, William Stearns. BELSHAZZAR. Doubleday, 1902. "A tale of the fall of Babylon." 31

Gardiner, G. S. RUSTEM, SON OF ZAL. Greening, 1911. Legendary Iranian fighter whose tragedy was unknowningly to kill his son in battle. 32

Jenkins, R. Wade. "O KING, LIVE FOR EVER!" Watts, 1911. A novel of the fall of Babylon. 33

Lofts, Norah. ESTHER. Macmillan, 1950. A warm, human story of Esther, Queen of Persia. 34

Peple, Edward. SEMIRAMIS. Moffat, 1907. Based on the life of the legendary Assyrian queen, Semiramis. 35

Potter, Margaret Horton. ISTAR OF BABYLON: A PHANTASY. Harper, 1902. A fantasy about the moon god's daughter, who takes human form as a beautiful woman. 36

Walker, Agnese Laurie. HADASSAH, QUEEN OF PERSIA. Scott, 1912. Includes a picture of the Persian court and of Esther, whose earlier Jewish name was Hadassah. 37

Weinreb, Nathaniel Norsen. THE BABYLONIANS. Doubleday, 1953. Swift-moving tale of a spy in the household of Nebuchadnezzar. 38

--------. ESTHER. Doubleday, 1955. Based on the Biblical story of the Jewish heroine who became Queen of Persia. 39

Williams, Earl Willoughby. COURT OF BELSHAZZAR. Bobbs, 1918. Liberation of the Jews from Babylon. 40

I. A. 1. c. The Hebrews and Other Peoples of the Ancient Near East

Asch, Shalom. MOSES. (tr.) Putnam, 1951. An impressive retelling of the Biblical tale of Moses and the Exodus. 41

--------. THE PROPHET. (tr.) Putnam, 1955. Isaiah the Prophet at the end of the Babylonian captivity. 42

Ashton, Mark. JEZEBEL'S HUSBAND. Page, 1904. A story which includes the Biblical characters Obadiah, Ahab, Jezebel, and Elijah. 43

Baker, Amy J. TYRIAN PURPLE. Long, 1919. Tyre and Samaria provide the background for this novel of Ahab and Jehu. 44

Bauer, Florence Anne. ABRAM, SON OF TERAH. Bobbs, 1948. Abraham's search for and fidelity to the one true God. 45

Blaker, Richard. THOU ART THE MAN. McBride, 1937. Vivid study of three men of the Bible--Samuel, Saul, and David. 46

Brady, Cyrus Townsend. WHEN THE SUN STOOD STILL. Revell, 1917. A story of the Israelites under the leadership of Joshua. 47

Buchanan, Thompson. JUDITH TRIUMPHANT. Harper, 1905. The siege of Bethulia, based on the Biblical story of Judith. 48

Cabries, Jean. JACOB. Dutton, 1958. Humanizes the Biblical figures of Jacob, Esau, Rachel, Leah, and Joseph. 49

Cahun, Léon. THE ADVENTURES OF CAPTAIN MAGO. Scribner, 1876. Imaginative account of a Phoenician expedition about 1000 B. C. 50

Chinn, Laurene. THE UNANOINTED. Crown, 1959. The heroic fidelity of Joab, David's military commander. 51

Clark, Alfred. LEMUEL OF THE LEFT HAND. Low, 1909. The war between Jerusalem and Syria at the time of Ahab and Obadiah. 52

Davenport, Arnold. BY THE RAMPARTS OF JEZREEL. Longmans, 1903. The invasion of the Syrians into the land of the Jews in the time of Elisha and Ahab. 53

Feuchtwanger, Lion. JEPHTA AND HIS DAUGHTER. (tr.) Putnam, 1958. Jephta's determination to fulfill his rash vow to sacrifice his beloved daughter. 54

Fineman, Irving. JACOB. Random, 1941. Novel presenting the story of Isaac, Jacob, Esau, Rachel, and Joseph, purportedly in the words of Jacob himself. 55

--------. RUTH. Harper, 1949. Fictionalized version of the life of Ruth. 56

Haggard, H. Rider. MOON OF ISRAEL. Longmans, 1918. The Hebrews in Egypt and their Exodus through the Red Sea. 57

-------- and Andrew Lang. THE WORLD'S DESIRE. Longmans, 1891. The flight of the Israelites from Egypt. 58

Ingram, Tolbert R. MAID OF ISRAEL. Broadman, 1955. Portrays slavery and life in the ancient Near East. 59

Kellner, Esther. THE PROMISE. Westminster, 1956. The marriage of Sarah and Abraham and their journey to the Promised Land. 60

Kelly, William P. THE ASSYRIAN BRIDE. Dutton, 1905. Conflict between opposing religions and nationalities in the forbidden marriage of a Jew to a heathen. 61

Ley-Piscator, Maria. LOT'S WIFE. Bobbs, 1954. The wanderings of Abraham, his nephew Lot, and the latter's wife. 62

McLaws, Lafayette, i. e. Emily Lafayette McLaws. JEZEBEL. Lothrop, 1902. A story of Israel when Ahab was king. 63

Mann, Thomas. JOSEPH AND HIS BROTHERS. (tr.) Knopf, 1934. The story of Jacob, Leah, and Rachel and of their sons. (followed by YOUNG JOSEPH) 64

--------. YOUNG JOSEPH. (tr.) Knopf, 1935. Joseph's life from his seventeenth year until he was sold into slavery. (followed by JOSEPH IN EGYPT) 65

Miller, Elizabeth. THE YOKE. Bobbs, 1904. "A romance of the days when the Lord redeemed the children of Israel from the bondage of Egypt." 66

More, E. Anson. A CAPTAIN OF MEN. Page, 1905. About Hiram, King of Tyre, in whose reign Phoenician commerce flourished. 67

Murphy, Edward F. SONG OF THE CAVE. Bruce, 1950. A Biblical novel of the Jewish Naomi and her Moabite daughter-in-law, Ruth. 68

Noller, Ella M. AHIRA, PRINCE OF NAPHTALI. Eerdmans, 1947. Fictional account of the journey of the Hebrews to the land of Canaan. 69

Ormonde, Czenzi. SOLOMON AND THE QUEEN OF SHEBA. Farrar, 1954. Based on the visit of the Queen of Sheba to Solomon. 70

Parker, Gilbert. THE PROMISED LAND. Stokes, 1928. King David and Hebrew life. 71

Penfield, Wilder. NO OTHER GODS. Little, 1954. A search for the one true God, to the time Abraham sets out for the land of Canaan. 72

Pitzer, Robert C. DAUGHTER OF JERUSALEM. Liveright, 1956. Trials of the Jews in the days of the Prophet Jeremias. 73

Schmitt, Gladys. DAVID THE KING. Dial, 1946. Vivid re-creation of the story of David. 74

Slaughter, Frank G. SCARLET CORD. Doubleday, 1956. Story of Rahab, woman of Jericho, told against a well-detailed background of the time. 75

--------. THE SONG OF RUTH. Doubleday, 1954. A novel based on the Biblical story of Ruth. 76

Tandrup, Harald. RELUCTANT PROPHET. Knopf, 1939. The adventures of Jonah--told with a dash of humor. 77

Todres, Max. MAN IN THE ANCIENT WORLD. Meador, 1948. Fictional account concerning the Patriarch Abraham. 78

Watkins, Shirley. THE PROPHET AND THE KING. Doubleday, 1956. Story of the aging prophet Samuel and the young king Saul. 79

Weinreb, Nathaniel Norsen. THE SORCERESS. Doubleday, 1954. Action-filled story of the Hebrew prophetess Deborah. 80

Werfel, Franz. HEARKEN UNTO THE VOICE. Viking, 1938. Life of the Prophet Jeremias presented by way of flash-back. 81

Williams, Jay. SOLOMON AND SHEBA. Random, 1959. The great love and the insurmountable political conflict between King Solomon and Queen Sheba. 82

Wilson, Dorothy Clarke. THE HERDSMAN. Westminster, 1946. Amos, the prophet, who perceived the love as well as the justice of God. 83

I. A. 2. Greece and the Aegean (to about 336 B. C.)

Atherton, Gertrude. THE IMMORTAL MARRIAGE. Boni & Liveright, 1927. Romance of Pericles and Aspasia in the Golden Age of Athens. 84

--------. THE JEALOUS GODS. [En. title: VENGEFUL GODS] Liveright, 1928. Romance and marriage of Alcibiades. 85

Baker, George E. PARIS OF TROY. [En. title: FIDUS ACHATES] Ziff-Davis, 1947. Fictionalized account of the siege and fall of Troy with its Homeric heroes. 86

Bromby, Charles. H. ALKIBIADES. Simpkin, 1905. A story sympathetic to the Athenian demagogue Alcibiades and based on his life. 87

Brun, Vincenz. ALCIBIADES. Putnam, 1935. Life and politics in Athens in the second half of the fifth century B. C. 88

Buchan, John. THE LEMNIAN. Blackwood, 1912. Graphic eyewitness account of the tragic battle of Thermopylae. 89

Davis, William Stearns. A VICTOR OF SALAMIS. Macmillan, 1907. Critical naval battle of Themistocles versus the Persians, with a description of the Isthmian games. 90

De Camp, Lyon. THE BRONZE GOD OF RHODES. Doubleday, 1960. The life of the sculptor of one of the seven wonders of the ancient world--the Colossus of Rhodes. 91

--------. AN ELEPHANT FOR ARISTOTLE. Doubleday, 1958. A story with a sense of humor--Alexander's bizarre gift of an elephant to Aristotle. 92

Dodd, Anna Bowman. ON THE KNEES OF THE GODS. Dodd, 1908. The Peloponnesian War and the impulsive Athenian leader, Alcibiades. 93

Eckstein, Ernst. APHRODITE. (tr.) Gottsberger, 1886. "A romance of ancient Hellas." 94

Erskine, John. THE PRIVATE LIFE OF HELEN OF TROY. Bobbs, 1925. Set in Sparta after the return of Menelaus from Troy with Helen. 95

Gaines, Charles Kelsey. GORGO. Lothrop, 1903. Athens and Sparta during the Peloponnesian War. 96

Gay, Geraldine M. THE ASTROLOGER'S DAUGHTER. Drane, 1906. Set in Athens during its "Golden Age" in the fifth century before Christ. 97

Grazebrook, Owen Francis. NICANOR OF ATHENS. Macmillan, 1947. Imaginary autobiography of a wealthy Athenian in the fifth century B. C. 98

Gudmundsson, Kristmann. WINGED CITADEL. (tr.) Holt, 1940. A good picture of the religion and civilization of early Crete. 99

Hamerling, Robert. ASPASIA. (tr.) Gottsberger, 1882. The activities of a beautiful, intelligent woman, friend of Pericles, Socrates, and Anaxagoras. 100

Harris, Clare Winger. PERSEPHONE OF ELEUSIS. Stratford, 1923. Romance of a soldier during the Persian invasion of Greece. 101

Kelly, William P. THE STRANGER FROM IONIA. Dutton, 1911. The conflict between democracy and aristocracy forbids the marriage of an Athenian girl to a foreigner. 102

Landor, W. Savage. PERICLES AND ASPASIA. Dent, 1836. The romance of Pericles and Aspasia in defiance of Athenian law, which forbade citizens to marry foreigners. 103

Lawrence, Isabelle. NIKO. Viking, 1956. An apprentice to the sculptor Phidias aids in making the figures on the Parthenon. 104

Lytton, Edward Bulwer, *lst. baron.* PAUSANIAS, THE SPARTAN. Routledge, 1873. An unfinished novel concerning Pausanias who, by a tragic mistake, killed the woman he loved. 105

Mauthner, Fritz. MRS. SOCRATES. International Pub., 1926. A tale of the famous philosopher and his spirited wife, Xanthippe. 106

Merezhkovsky, Dmitri. THE BIRTH OF THE GODS. (tr.) Dutton, 1924. The island of Crete about fourteen centuries before Christ as seen by an Egyptian envoy and the Cretan maiden-priestess, Dio. (followed by AKHNATON, KING OF EGYPT) 107

Mitchison, Naomi. CLOUD CUCKOO LAND. Harcourt, 1926. Spartan superiority in the Peloponnesian War. 108

Penfield, Wilder. THE TORCH. Little, 1960. The career of Hippocrates and the practice of medicine in the fourth century B. C. 109

Pick, Robert. THE ESCAPE OF SOCRATES. Knopf, 1954. A delightful story of Socrates based on the writings of Plato. 110

Renault, Mary, pseud. THE KING MUST DIE. Pantheon, 1958. The legendary Greek hero Theseus tells of his eventful youth. 111

--------. THE LAST OF THE WINE. Pantheon, 1956. Athens in the days of Socrates and the Third Peloponnesian War. 112

Schnabel, Ernst. VOYAGE HOME. (tr.) Harcourt, 1958. A novel based, like the ODYSSEY, on the homeward journey of Ulysses. 113

Snedeker, Caroline Dale. THE PERILOUS SEAT. Doubleday, Page, 1923. A priestess in Greece at the time of the Persian invasion in 480 B. C. 114

Stacpoole, Henry de Vere. THE STREET OF THE FLUTE-PLAYER. Duffield, 1912. Athens in the days of Socrates and Aristophanes. 115

Stewart, George Rippey. YEARS OF THE CITY. Houghton, 1955. Chronicle of a Greek colonial city from its founding to its fall. 116

I. A. 3. The Hellenistic (Eastern Mediterranean) World (c. 336-31 B. C.)

Aimery de Pierrebourg, Marguerite. THE LIFE AND DEATH OF CLEOPATRA. (tr.) by Claude Ferval, pseud. Doubleday, Page, 1924. The story of Cleopatra from about her eighteenth year. 117

Beck, Lily Adams. THE LAUGHING QUEEN. by E. Barrington, pseud. Dodd, 1929. A light romance about Cleopatra--part deified queen, part bewitching woman. 118

Dickeson, Alfred. TYCHIADES. Unwin, 1903. The reign of Ptolemy II in Alexandria. 119

Druon, Maurice, pseud. for Maurice Kessel. ALEXANDER THE GOD. Scribner, 1960. Alexander's military victories and his efforts to prove himself semi-divine. 120

Ebers, Georg. ARACHNE. (tr.) Appleton, 1898. Centers around discussions of realism in Hellenistic art. 121

--------. CLEOPATRA. (tr.) Appleton, 1894. The final part of Cleopatra's life. 122

--------. THE SISTERS. (tr.) Gottsberger, 1880. Egypt under the Ptolemy dynasty in the mid-second century B. C. 123

Eiker, Karl V. STAR OF MACEDON. Putnam, 1957. The genius and cruelty of Alexander the Great, told by a slave. 124

Fast, Howard. MY GLORIOUS BROTHERS. Little, 1948. The liberation of Israel from Syrian-Greek overlords. 125

Fisher, Vardis. ISLAND OF THE INNOCENT. Abelard, 1952. "A novel of Greek and Jew in the time of the Maccabees." 126

Fuller, Robert H. THE GOLDEN HOPE. Macmillan, 1905. The victories and dreams of Alexander the Great in the East and Egypt. 127

Gerson, Noel B. THAT EGYPTIAN WOMAN. Doubleday, 1956. Rather frothy account of Julius Caesar and Cleopatra. 128

Haggard, H. Rider. CLEOPATRA. Longmans, 1889. About the last of the Ptolemies, who charmed both Julius Caesar and Mark Anthony. 129

Kirkman, Marshall Monroe. (1) THE ROMANCE OF ALEXANDER THE PRINCE. Simpkin, 1909. (2) THE ROMANCE OF ALEXANDER THE KING (sequel). Simpkin, 1909. (3) THE ROMANCE OF ALEXANDER AND ROXANA (sequel). Simpkin, 1909. A series of novels tracing the life of Alexander. 130

Mitchison, Naomi. THE CORN KING AND THE SPRING QUEEN. Harcourt, 1931. Panoramic view of Greek civilization and religion in the third century B. C. 131

Mundy, Talbot. PURPLE PIRATE. Appleton, 1935. Intrigue involving Cleopatra in the two years after Caesar's death. 132

Payne, Robert. ALEXANDER THE GOD. Wyn, 1954. Alexander the Great from his conquest of Thaissa to his death. 133

Phillpotts, Eden. THE TREASURES OF TYPHON. Richards, 1924. A romance of Athens including the philosopher Epicurus and the poet Menander. 134

Shamir, Moshe. THE KING OF FLESH AND BLOOD. (tr.) Vanguard, 1958. The destructive reign of Alexander Jannaeus, descendant of Simon Maccabeus. 135

Strauss, Frederick. HELON'S PILGRIMAGE TO JERUSALEM. Mawman, 1824. Pictures Judaism just prior to the advent of Christ. 136

I. A. 4. Rome and the Western Mediterranean World (to c. 31 B. C.)

Atherton, Gertrude. DIDO, QUEEN OF HEARTS. Liveright, 1929. The beautiful Queen of Carthage, successful in all things except her love for Aeneas. 137

Bentley, Phyllis. FREEDOM, FAREWELL! Macmillan, 1936. The career of Julius Caesar and a picture of Roman society and politics. 138

Blasco-Ibañez, Vicente. SONNICA. (tr.) Duffield, 1912. Hannibal's bloody, ruthless three-month siege of Saguntum, based on Livy's history. 139

Davis, William Stearns. A FRIEND OF CAESAR. Macmillan, 1900. The "friend" is a young Roman nobleman during Caesar's conquests and the fall of the Republic. 140

Dixon, Pierson. FAREWELL, CATULLUS. British Bks., 1960. Portrays contemporary influences on one of Rome's most famous poets, Catullus. 141

Dolan, Mary. HANNIBAL OF CARTHAGE. Macmillan, 1955. Believable account of Hannibal from the Carthaginian point-of-view. 142

Donauer, Friedrich. SWORDS AGAINST CARTHAGE. (tr.) Longmans, 1932. Campaigns of Scipio Africanus in the Second Punic War. 143

Duggan, Alfred. CHILDREN OF THE WOLF. [En. title: FOUNDING FATHERS] Coward, 1959. The struggle for power in the new city of Rome. 144

--------. THREE'S COMPANY. Coward, 1958. Concerns Lepidus, one of the triumvirate ruling Rome after Caesar's death. 145

--------. WINTER QUARTERS. Coward, 1956. Two young Gallic noblemen join the Roman army to flee the wrath of a goddess. 146

Eckstein, Ernst. PRUSIAS. (tr.) Gottsberger, 1882. This story of Rome tells of Spartacus and the revolt of the slaves and gladiators. 147

Gérard, Francis. SCARLET BEAST. Longmans, 1935. Swift-moving tale of the Second Punic War told with a definite prejudice against Carthage. 148

Gilkes, A. H. KALLISTRATUS. Frowde, 1897. An account of the Second Punic War in autobiographical form. 149

Green, Peter. THE SWORD OF PLEASURE. World Pub., 1958. The memoirs of the illustrious Lucius Cornelius Sulla, Dictator of Rome in Caesar's boyhood. 150

Hardy, William George. CITY OF LIBERTINES. Appleton, 1957. Realistic account of Rome during Caesar's coming to glory. 151

--------. TURN BACK THE RIVER. Dodd, 1938. Roman politics and romance have startling likenesses to those of our own day. 152

Jensen, Johannes Vilhelm. THE CIMBRIANS. (tr.) Knopf, 1923. The author carries the story of civilization through the Stone, Bronze, and Iron Ages, ending with the Cimbrian migration to Italy. (followed by CHRISTOPHER COLUMBUS) 153

Koestler, Arthur. THE GLADIATORS. Macmillan, 1939. The revolt of the gladiators and slaves, led by Spartacus. 154

Lindsay, Jack. ROME FOR SALE. Harper, 1934. A fine narrative of the confusion in Rome which led up to Catiline's rebellion. 155

Mabie, Mary Louise. PREPARE THEM FOR CAESAR. Little, 1949. Caesar's ambitions, conquests, and rise to dictatorial power. 156

Macpherson, Annie Winifred. GATE TO THE SEA. by Bryher, pseud. Pantheon, 1958. The Greek inhabitants of Poseidonia (Paestam), oppressed by the Italic Lucanians, plot to found a city elsewhere in Italy. 157

Marston, William M. VENUS WITH US. Sears, 1932. The human aspects of Julius Caesar against a backdrop of Roman patrician life. 158

Mitchison, Naomi. THE CONQUERED. Harcourt, 1923. The conquest of Gaul by the Romans arouses a tardy sense of Gallic nationalism. 159

Mundy, Talbot. TROS OF SAMOTHRACE. Appleton, 1934. One of the leading lieutenants of Julius Caesar and the first

Roman invasion of Britain. 160

Osborne, Duffield. THE LION'S BROOD. Doubleday, 1901. Hannibal's victory at Cannae and his winter camp at Capua. 161

Radin, Max. EPICURUS MY MASTER. U. of N. C. Press, 1949. The atmosphere of Rome, re-created by Atticus, correspondent of Cicero and follower of Epicurus. 162

Smith, E. M. ANEROESTES THE GAUL. Unwin, 1899. Hannibal's campaigns in the Second Punic War, describing the crossing of the Alps. 163

Waltari, Mika. THE ETRUSCAN. (tr.) Putnam, 1956. The remarkable life of a "semi-divine" pagan woman some twenty-five hundred years ago. 164

Warner, Rex. IMPERIAL CAESAR. Little, 1960. Julius Caesar's recollection, shortly before his death, of the later years of his life. 165

--------. THE YOUNG CAESAR. Little, 1958. Caesar's review of his childhood and rise to power. (followed by IMPERIAL CAESAR) 166

Wilder, Thornton. THE IDES OF MARCH. Harper, 1948. Events leading up to Caesar's assassination told in purportedly ancient documents. 167

I. A. 5. The Roman Empire and Christianity (c. 31 B.C. to 400 A. D.)

a. The Roman Empire at Its Height and Early Christianity (c. 31 B.C. to 180 A. D.)

Abbott, Edwin A. ONESIMUS. Roberts, 1882. The book tells of the ministry of St. Paul. 168

--------. PHILOCHRISTUS. Macmillan, 1878. "The memoirs of a disciple of Christ." 169

--------. SILANUS THE CHRISTIAN. Macmillan, 1906. The changed belief of a Stoic philosopher who became a disciple of Christ. 170

Asch, Shalom. THE APOSTLE. (tr.) Putnam, 1943. A story of the Jewish Roman citizen, Paul, and his preaching, starting seven weeks after the Crucifixion. 171

--------. MARY. (tr.) Putnam, 1949. The love of the Virgin Mary, Mother of Jesus Christ, for her Son. 172

--------. THE NAZARENE. (tr.) Putnam, 1939. The life of Christ told from the viewpoints of a Pharisee's disciple, Judas Iscariot, and a modern Polish Jew. 173

Atherton, Gertrude. GOLDEN PEACOCK. Houghton, 1936. A stirring and exciting account of a girl's part in discovering a plot against Augustus Caesar. 174

Bacheller, Irving. THE TRUMPETS OF GOD. [same as: DAWN] Macmillan, 1927. The spread of Christianity in various areas--Jerusalem, Antioch, Jericho--between 30 and 70. 175

--------. VERGILIUS. Harper, 1904. A patrician in Rome learns of the coming of Christ. 176

Baring-Gould, S. DOMITIA. Stokes, 1898. The unhappy life of Domitian's wife and the deaths of Nero, Vitellius, and Domitian. 177

Bauer, Florence Anne. BEHOLD YOUR KING. Bobbs, 1945. Story of the nephew of Joseph of Arimathea in the last years of Christ's life. 178

Becker, Wilhelm Adolf. GALLUS. (tr.) Longmans, 1838. This novel gives many details of the manners and customs of Augustan Rome. 179

Bekessy, Emery with Andreas Hemberger. BARABBAS. (tr.) Prentice-Hall, 1946. Imaginative portrait of the violent Barabbas and other characters of the time of Jesus. 180

Billings, Edith S. CLEOMENES. by Maris Warrington Billings, pseud. Lane, 1917. Account of Cleomenes, the sculptor of the famous "Medici Venus." 181

Blythe, LeGette. BOLD GALILEAN. U. of N.C. Press, 1948. A compelling portrayal of Christ as He appeared to His contemporaries. 182

Byatt, H. THE TESTAMENT OF JUDAS. Long, 1909. The story of the arch-traitor, Judas Iscariot. 183

Byrne, Donn. BROTHER SAUL. Century, 1927. The spiritual and intellectual growth of St. Paul from youth to death. 184

Carling, John R. THE DOOMED CITY. Clode, 1910. A narrative of besieged Jerusalem culminating in destruction of the temple. 185

Carrel, Frederic. MARCUS AND FAUSTINA. Long, 1904. His pleasure-seeking wife complicates the rule of Stoic Emperor Marcus Aurelius. 186

Carter, Russell Kelso. AMOR VICTOR. by Orr Kenyon, pseud. Stokes, 1902. Gives a picture of the Christians' position in Roman life about 100 A. D. 187

Cooley, William Forbes. EMMANUEL. Dodd, 1889. The ministry of Christ and the labors of His apostles and disciples. 188

Corelli, Marie. BARABBAS. Lippincott, 1893. A story of the betrayal and Crucifixion of Christ, and of the criminal freed in His stead. 189

Costain, Thomas B. THE SILVER CHALICE. Doubleday, 1952. Gripping tale on the Holy Grail theme telling the adventures of Basil, an artist. 190

Couperus, Louis. THE COMEDIANS. Doran, 1926. Informative novel about the decadence of Rome under the despot Domitian. 191

--------. THE TOUR. Dodd, 1920. A young lord tours Egypt to consult oracles about his lost love--and finds a new and better one. 192

Cramp, Walter S. PSYCHE. Little, 1905. Emperor Tiberius appointed the corrupt Sejanus commander of the Praetorian Guards with unhappy consequences. 193

Crockett, Vivian. MESSALINA. Boni & Liveright, 1924. The corrupt wife of Emperor Claudius I, who was executed by him after a serious scandal. 194

Crozier, William Percival. THE FATES ARE LAUGHING. Harcourt, 1945. Life on the senatorial level in the Rome of Tiberius and Caligula. 195

Deamer, Dulcie. THE STREET OF THE GAZELLE. Fisher Unwin, 1922. A story of the Zealots in Jerusalem at the time of Christ. 196

De Ropp, Robert S. IF I FORGET THEE. St. Martins, 1956. Romance in Judaea on the eve of revolt against the Romans. 197

De Wohl, Louis. GLORIOUS FOLLY. Lippincott, 1957. A story about early Christianity featuring St. Paul. 198

--------. THE SPEAR. Lippincott, 1955. Cassius Longinus, the Roman centurion who pierced Christ's Side with his spear. 199

Douglas, Lloyd C. THE BIG FISHERMAN. Houghton, 1948. Account of Peter and his associates in the Christian ministry. 200

Dunscomb, Charles, pseud. BEHOLD, WE LIVE. Houghton, 1956. Cedonius, a slave, comes to believe and follow the doctrines of Christianity. 201

--------. THE BOND AND THE FREE. Houghton, 1955. Account of the beginnings of Christianity told in correspondence. 202

Ebers, Georg. THE EMPEROR. (tr.) Gottsberger, 1881. Concerns the Emperor Hadrian and events in Egypt. 203

Eckstein, Ernst. NERO. (tr.) Gottsberger, 1889. Nero as a man and an emperor, with important people and events of his reign. 204

--------. QUINTUS CLAUDIUS. (tr.) Gottsberger, 1882. Descriptive of social life, political thought, and religious persecution in Domitian's reign. 205

Farrar, Frederick W. DARKNESS AND DAWN. Longmans, 1892. The darkness of pagan immorality contrasted with the dawn of Christian purity. 206

Fast, Howard. SPARTACUS. Citadel, 1952. Revolt of the slaves against their overbearing Roman masters. 207

Feuchtwanger, Lion. (1) JOSEPHUS. (tr.) Viking, 1932. (2)

THE JEW OF ROME. (tr.) Viking, 1936. (3) JOSEPHUS AND THE EMPEROR. (tr.) Viking, 1942. Based on the life of Josephus, Jewish historian--his life in Rome, his search for social justice, his relations with the Emperor Domitian. 208

Fox, Paul H. DAUGHTER OF JAIRUS. Little, 1951. One of Christ's miracles told against the background of Jewish life and customs. 209

France, Anatole (name originally Anatole Thibault). THE PROCURATOR OF JUDAEA. (tr.) Lane, 1908. A sardonic picture of Pilate, who was questioned years later about the death of Christ. 210

--------. THAIS. (tr.) Smith, 1891. Hermit from the desert attempts to convert a libertine beauty, Thais. 211

Frieberger, Kurt. FISHER OF MEN. Appleton, 1954. A novel of the apostle Peter. 212

Frost, Elizabeth H. MARY AND THE SPINNERS. Coward, 1946. About Mary and several of her friends who spent some time as spinners in the Temple. 213

Gibran, Kahlil. JESUS THE SON OF MAN. Knopf, 1928. The story of Jesus as told by people who met Him. 214

Gibson, John, pseud. PATRICIAN STREET. Vanguard, 1940. The brutal persecution of the early Christians by Roman emperors. 215

Goldthorpe, John. THE SAME SCOURGE. Putnam, 1956. The events leading up to the Crucifixion. 216

Graham, John W. NEAERA. Macmillan, 1886. The lavish, dissolute life of the last part of Tiberius' reign. 217

Haggard, H. Rider. PEARL MAIDEN. Longmans, 1902. Vivid account of the destruction of Jerusalem in 70 A. D. 218

Hannah, Ian Campbell. VOADICA. Longmans, 1928. Romance of a Roman patrician and a barbaric princess in occupied Britain. 219

Hartley, J. M. THE WAY. Crowell, 1944. Interest in Palestine concerning the promised Messiah about the year 20

A. D. 220

Hastings, Peter. S. P. Q. R. Holden, 1926. A barbarian gladiator becomes a Praetorian Guard at the time of Domitian and Nerva. 221

Hausrath, Adolf. ANTINOUS. (tr.) by George Taylor, pseud. Gottsberger, 1882. Contrasting principles of Christianity and paganism appear in this story of a page deified by Hadrian. 222

Henkle, Henrietta. AND WALK IN LOVE. by Henrietta Buckmaster, pseud. Random, 1956. A perceptive story of St. Paul. 223

Hobbs, Roe R. THE COURT OF PILATE. Fenno, 1906. Shows the hatred of the Jews for their Roman oppressors personified by Pontius Pilate. 224

Hoppus, Mary A. M. MASTERS OF THE WORLD. Bentley, 1888. The power and glory of Rome in the reign of Domitian with an account of his murder. 225

Ingles, James Wesley. WOMAN OF SAMARIA. Longmans, 1949. The life and marriages of Photina, a woman Christ met in Samaria. 226

Jacobs, Joseph. AS OTHERS SAW HIM. Houghton, 1895. The story of Jesus as told in a letter by one of the Jews who demanded His death. 227

Johnson, Gillard. RAPHAEL OF THE OLIVE. Century, 1913. Jerusalem at the time of the Maccabees, showing their efforts to recover the city. 228

Kelly, William P. THE SENATOR LICINIUS. Dutton, 1909. A desperately worried senator, his daughter's romance, and the ultimate justice of the capricious Caligula. 229

Kingsley, Florence M. VERONICA. Appleton, 1913. A tale of Pilate and his wife, ending at the time of the Crucifixion. 230

Komroff, Manuel. IN THE YEARS OF OUR LORD. Harper, 1942. A novel based on the life and times of Christ. 231

Lagerkvist, Pâr. BARABBAS. Random, 1951. A powerful study of the bandit who was released to the mob instead of Christ. 232

Laut, Agnes C. QUENCHLESS LIGHT. Appleton, 1924. About early Christianity in Ephesus, and a slave boy who became a bishop. 233

Lockhart, John Gibson. VALERIUS. Blackwood, 1821. Descriptive of social life and religious persecution in Rome under Trajan. 234

Loewenstein, Hubertus. THE EAGLE AND THE CROSS. Macmillan, 1947. An Irish prince takes the lance of the Centurion Longinus to Tiberius, Emperor of Rome. 235

Lytton, Edward Bulwer, lst. baron. THE LAST DAYS OF POMPEII. Dutton, 1834. The luxurious life of Pompeii and the destructive eruption of Vesuvius. 236

Mason, Caroline A. THE WHITE SHIELD. Griffith & Rowland, 1904. The persecution to which early Christians were subjected is described in this legend of St. Thekla. 237

Miller, Elizabeth. THE CITY OF DELIGHT. Bobbs, 1908. A romance of the city of Jerusalem during its siege and destruction by Titus. 238

--------. SAUL OF TARSUS. Bobbs, 1906. The Roman Empire in the early days of Christianity, with Mary of Magdala as a character. 239

Mitchison, Naomi. BLOOD OF THE MARTYRS. McGraw, 1948. Nero's persecution of the Christians, who came from all levels of society. 240

Murphy, Edward F. SCARLET LILY. Bruce, 1944. A sympathetic portrait of St. Mary Magdalene--the scarlet lily. 241

Mygatt, Tracy D. and Frances Witherspoon. ARMOR OF LIGHT. Holt, 1930. A thrilling story of the trials of the early Church in the catacombs. 242

Newcomb, Robert T. JANISSA. Destiny, 1943. Egypt and Palestine during the early Christian era. 243

O'Hanlon, Richard. WHAT IF THIS FRIEND. by Richard Hanlon, pseud. Kendall, 1935. Concerns Syria's deputy governor Lucius Vitellius and his Christian wife. 244

Oxenham, John, pseud. for William Arthur Dunkerley. THE SPLENDOR OF THE DAWN. Longmans, 1930. A young Roman's search for knowledge of Christ. 245

Pater, Walter. MARIUS THE EPICUREAN. Macmillan, 1885. Philosophical thought in Marcus Aurelius' time. 246

Perkins, Jacob Randolph. ANTIOCH ACTRESS. Bobbs, 1946. Features pagan attacks on Christianity by means of satirical theatrical presentations. 247

--------. EMPEROR'S PHYSICIAN. Bobbs, 1944. Two physicians meet Jesus and are convinced of His healing powers. 248

Perri, Francesco. THE UNKNOWN DISCIPLE. Macmillan, 1950. Early Christianity in the unrest caused by politics and conflicts with paganism. 249

Petersen, Nis. THE STREET OF THE SANDALMAKERS. (tr.) Macmillan, 1933. The poorer people of Rome in the days of Marcus Aurelius. 250

Roberson, Harriette Gunn. MARY OF MAGDALA. Greening, 1909. Story of Mary Magdalene, supposedly told by St. John. 251

Rosegger, Peter. I. N. R. I. (tr.) Hodder, 1905. A prisoner condemned to death tells the story of Christ's life. 252

Sackler, Harry. FESTIVAL AT MERON. Covici, 1935. Simeon ben Yohai leads a Jewish revolt against Roman persecution. 253

Saunders, W. J. THE NAZARENE. Murray & Evenden, 1915. A first-person narrative by a young man in Pilate's service. 254

Scharlemann, Dorothy Hoyer. MY VINEYARD. Concordia, 1946. Christians and Jews in Palestine at the time of Christ. 255

Schuré, Edouard. THE PRIESTESS OF ISIS. Rider, 1910. Sorcery and religious rites in Pompeii in the year of Vesuvius' eruption. 256

Schuyler, William. HOPE OF GLORY. Four Seas Co., 1916. Christianity in Nero's day as seen in supposed correspondence between a Stoic and a Christian. 257

--------. UNDER PONTIUS PILATE. Funk & Wagnalls, 1906. Letters about Christ from a nephew of Pontius Pilate to a Greek friend. 258

Shore, Maxine. CAPTIVE PRINCESS. Longmans, 1952. Concerns the supposed first Christian Princess of Britain. 259

Siegel, Benjamin. SWORD AND THE PROMISE. Harcourt, 1959. A young Greek physician enslaved by the Romans participates in a Jewish revolt. 260

Sienkiewicz, Henryk. QUO VADIS? (tr.) Little, 1896. A vivid account of the conflict of Imperial Rome and early Christianity. 261

Slaughter, Frank G. THE GALILEANS. Doubleday, 1953. Based on the life of Mary Magdalene. 262

--------. THE THORN OF ARIMATHEA. Doubleday, 1959. A Roman centurion-physician who travels from Judaea to Britain with Joseph of Arimathea and Veronica of the Holy Veil. 263

Solon, Gregory. THE THREE LEGIONS. Random, 1956. Picture of the deterioration which led to the defeat of the Roman army in Germany. 264

Spurrell, Herbert. AT SUNRISE. Greening, 1904. Traders and sun-worshippers in Britain under the Romans. 265

Steinberg, Milton. AS A DRIVEN LEAF. Bobbs, 1940. A second century Jewish rabbi's personal search for truth. 266

Stuart, Frank S. CARAVAN FOR CHINA. Doubleday, 1941. Exciting experiences of a Roman trading expedition to China. 267

Sullivan, Richard. THE THREE KINGS. Harcourt, 1956. The journey of the three Magi who followed the star to find the promised King. 268

Treece, Henry. THE DARK ISLAND. Random, 1952. The Roman armies defeat the barbarian Celtic tribes in Britain. 269

--------. RED QUEEN, WHITE QUEEN. Random, 1958. The rebellion led by Boadicea against the Romans in Britain. 270

Twells, Julia H. ET TU, SEJANE! Chatto, 1904. A romance of the court of Tiberius on the island of Capri. 271

Van Santvoord, Seymour. OCTAVIA. Dutton, 1923. The dark period of Julio-Claudian Rome and the tragic story of Octavia. 272

Wallace, Lew. BEN HUR. Harper, 1880. Hardships of a noble Jew under Roman rule and his conversion to Christianity. 273

Walloth, Wilhelm. EMPRESS OCTAVIA. Little, 1900. A story of Rome in the reign of the infamous Nero. 274

Waltari, Mika. THE SECRET OF THE KINGDOM. (tr.) Putnam, 1961. About a Roman who joined the Jewish followers of Christ after the Crucifixion. 275

Warmington, Gertrude R. KING OF DREAMS. Doran, 1926. Based on the story of the rich young man of the New Testament and located in Palestine and Egypt. 276

Westbury, Hugh. ACTÉ. Bentley, 1890. Illustrates the moral depravity of Nero's court. 277

White, Helen C. FOUR RIVERS OF PARADISE. Macmillan, 1955. The decadence of Rome at the time of Alaric's invasion, seen by a Christian from Gaul. 278

Whyte-Melville, George John. THE GLADIATORS. Appleton, 1863. Roman persecution; the siege of Jerusalem; and a British slave's love for a Roman lady. 279

Williamson, Thames Ross. THE GLADIATOR. Coward, 1948. A gladiator joins the forbidden Christian religion and barely escapes the burning of Rome. 280

Willis, Anthony Armstrong. THE HEART OF A SLAVE-GIRL. by Anthony Armstrong, pseud. Paul, 1922. A tale of Rome when Nero was emperor. 281

Yourcenar, Marguerite. MEMOIRS OF HADRIAN. (tr.) Farrar, 1954. Written as a letter from the Emperor Hadrian to his adopted grandson, Marcus Aurelius. 282

I. A. 5. b. The Later Roman Empire and Christianity (c. 180 to 400)

Albertini, Alberto. TWO YEARS. (tr.) Viking, 1936. Philosophical study of a young Roman who, through prayer, receives a two-year reprieve from death. 283

Armstrong, Martin. DESERT. Harper, 1926. An account of monastic life in Alexandria and the Egyptian desert in the late fourth century. 284

Baring-Gould, S. PERPETUA. Dutton, 1897. A story of the persecution of Christians at Nîmes in 213. 285

Baron, Alexander. QUEEN OF THE EAST. Washburn, 1956. Conflict between Zenobia, Queen of the East, and Aurelian, Emperor of Rome. 286

Baxter, J. Dowling. THE MEETING OF THE WAYS. Greening, 1908. Fighting between Picts and Romans in early Britain, with descriptions of forts. 287

Bickerstaffe-Drew, Francis. FAUSTULA. by John Ayscough, pseud. Benziger, 1912. A girl from a pagan family who, despite her belief in Christianity, was forced to become a vestal virgin. 288

Dahn, Felix. A CAPTIVE OF THE ROMAN EAGLES. (tr.) McClurg, 1902. Story depicting relations between Romans and Germans in the area around Lake Constance. 289

Deeping, Warwick. THE MAN WHO WENT BACK. Knopf, 1940. While recovering from an accident, a man seems to live in the olden days of Roman Britain. 290

De Wohl, Louis. IMPERIAL RENEGADE. Lippincott, 1950.

The career of Julian the Apostate, Emperor of Rome. 291

--------. LIVING WOOD. Lippincott, 1947. Helena, mother of Constantine, and her quest of the True Cross. 292

--------. THE RESTLESS FLAME. Lippincott, 1951. St. Augustine, from his riotous youth to his exemplary old age. 293

Duggan, Alfred. FAMILY FAVORITES. Pantheon, 1961. The brief, notorious reign of adolescent Heliogabalus, who became Emperor at the age of fourteen. 294

Ebers, Georg. HOMO SUM. (tr.) Gottsberger, 1880. A Christian anchorite accepts false accusation and unmerited exile. 295

--------. PER ASPERA. (tr.) Low, 1893. Religious conflict in Alexandria in the early third century. 296

--------. SERAPIS. (tr.) Paul, 1885. The conflict between Christianity and paganism is described in this story of a girl's conversion. 297

Eckstein, Ernst. THE CHALDEAN MAGICIAN. (tr.) Gottsberger, 1886. "An adventure in Rome in the reign of Diocletian." 298

Fidelis, Sister Mary. IN HOLIEST TROTH. Burns & Oates, 1903. "The story of St. Eucratida, one of the martyrs of Saragossa, A. D. 304." 299

Harré, T. Everett. BEHOLD THE WOMAN! Lippincott, 1916. About Mary of Egypt, converted from a life of sin in fourth century Alexandria to a life of penance in the desert. 300

Jeske-Choinski, Teodor. THE LAST ROMANS. Duquesne U., 1936. Pagan revolt against Christianity results in victory for Emperor Theodosius I over Arbogast. 301

Jókai, Maurus. A CHRISTIAN BUT A ROMAN. (tr.) Doubleday, 1900. The Christians in Rome and its vicinity under the Emperor Carinas. 302

Macpherson, Annie Winifred. ROMAN WALL. by Winifred

Bryher, pseud. Pantheon, 1954. A Helvetian outpost of the Roman Empire, and its commander, Valerius. 303

Maurice, C. Edmund. TELEMACHUS. Independent Press, 1927. An heroic monk amidst the conflicting religious and social currents of the late Empire. 304

Merezhkovsky, Dmitri. THE DEATH OF THE GODS. (tr.) Putnam, 1896. The struggle between Christianity and paganism at the time of Emperor Julian. (followed by THE FORERUNNER) 305

Newman, John Henry. CALLISTA. Longmans, 1890. The savage persecution of Christians by the Emperor Decius. 306

Perry, W. C. SANCTA PAULA. Sonnenschein, 1902. A romance of the fourth century with Saints Jerome and Paula well portrayed. 307

Rydberg, Viktor. THE LAST ATHENIAN. (tr.) Petersen, 1883. The end of antiquity and the rise of Christianity in Greece. 308

Schmitt, Gladys. CONFESSORS OF THE NAME. Dial, 1952. Emperor's nephew finds the meaning of life in Christianity. 309

Sherren, Wilkinson. EELEN OF BRINGARD. Palmer, 1923. A romance of Britain toward the end of the fourth century. 310

Tollinton, Bartram. PYRRHO. Williams & Norgate, 1926. A young man's search for religion in the early third century. 311

Ware, William. AURELIAN. Burt, 1838. Emperor Aurelian's persecution of Christians. 312

--------. JULIAN. Estes, 1841. Lavish spectacle of pagan civilization at the time of Julian the Apostate. 313

--------. ZENOBIA. Burt, 1836. A Roman noble describes Zenobia and her court and the destruction of Palmyra. 314

Waugh, Evelyn. HELENA. Little, 1950. The life of Constantine's mother and her search for the True Cross. 315

Westcott, Arthur. THE SUN GOD. Heath Cranton, 1914. Religious conflict in Rome at the time of Emperor Elagabalus (Heliogabalus). 316

White, Edward Lucas. ANDVIUS HEDULIO. Dutton, 1921. A young nobleman, suspected of treason, experiences every facet of Roman life. 317

Wiseman, Nicholas P. FABIOLA. Benziger, 1855. Classic tale of Diocletian's persecution of the Christians, who took refuge in the catacombs. 318

I. A. 6. European and Other Barbarians (to about 400 A. D.)

Adkin, J. H. Knight. THE WOMAN STEALERS. Pitman, 1905. The Celts in Britain in their daily struggles against other tribes and prehistoric animals. 319

Begouen, Max. BISON OF CLAY. (tr.) Longmans, 1926. Magdalenians of the Upper Paleolithic Stone Age in the Pyrenees. 320

Carbery, Mary. CHILDREN OF THE DAWN. Heinemann, 1923. A tale of Druidic Ireland based on ancient legends concerning the coming of sun worshippers from Hellas. 321

Du Chaillu, Paul Belloni. IVAR THE VIKING. Scribner, 1893. Adventures of a Norse boy at the turn of the third to the fourth century. 322

Farrar, Frederick W. GATHERING CLOUDS. Longmans, 1896. Antioch and Constantinople at the time of Alaric and his Goths. 323

Fisher, Vardis. DARKNESS AND THE DEEP. Vanguard, 1943. Primitive man in the period before the development of language. 324

Jensen, Johannes Vilhelm. FIRE AND ICE. (tr.) Knopf, 1923. The first stages in the development of civilization, primitive religion, and use of fire. (followed by THE CIMBRIANS) 325

Kipling, Rudyard. (1) PUCK OF POOK'S HILL. Doubleday, 1906. (2) REWARDS AND FAIRIES (sequel). Doubleday, 1910. The fairy Puck tells of England in ancient times. 326

London, Jack. BEFORE ADAM. Macmillan, 1907. Imaginative tale of life in the Pleistocene or Glacial Age. 327

Roberts, Charles G. D. IN THE MORNING OF TIME. Stokes, 1922. Life and inventions in the early Stone Age. 328

Wallis, Henry M. THE MASTER GIRL. by Ashton Hilliers, _pseud._ Putnam, 1910. Prehistoric man's struggle against animals, hostile tribes, and the elements. 329

I. B. Asia, Africa, and Oceania in Antiquity

Carus, Paul. AMITABHA. Open Court, 1906. Includes a discussion of the philosophies of Buddhism and Brahminism in first century India. 330

Caskie, Jaquelin Ambler. FIGURE IN THE SAND. Am. Library Serv., 1924. Brief romance of North African nomads followed by condemnation to death in a Roman arena. 331

Croly, George. SALATHIEL, THE IMMORTAL. [pub. in 1901 as: TARRY THOU TILL I COME] Funk & Wagnalls, 1827. A tale of the Wandering Jew, rich in Oriental background. 332

France, Anatole (name originally Anatole Thibault). BALTHAZAR. (tr.) Lane, 1909. Based on the Bible story of the Three Wise Men. 333

Gjellerup, Karl. THE PILGRIM KAMANITA. (tr.) Heinemann, 1911. The last years of Buddha's life, his death, and his philosophy. 334

Karney, Evelyn S. THE DUST OF DESIRE. Scott, 1912. The influence and limited appeal of Buddha's philosophy. 335

Merwin, Samuel. SILK: A LEGEND. Houghton, 1923. Imaginary journals concerning life in China about 100 A. D. 336

I. C. The Western Hemisphere in Antiquity

Hyne, C. J. Cutcliffe. THE LOST CONTINENT. Hutchinson, 1900. The supposed disappearance of the flourishing continent of Atlantis. 337

II. The Middle Ages and Early Renaissance (c. 400-1500)

A. Europe, the Near East, and the Mediterranean in the Middle Ages

1. The Early Middle Ages (c. 400-1000)

a. The British Isles (England, Wales, Scotland, Ireland)

Babcock, William Henry. CIAN OF THE CHARIOTS. Lothrop, 1898. A romance of the days of Arthur of Britain and his knights of the Round Table. 338

--------. THE TWO LOST CENTURIES OF BRITAIN. Lippincott, 1890. Britain in the turbulent period after the departure of the Romans. 339

Baker, Amy J. THE KING'S PASSION. Long, 1920. Based on the life of King Edmund, who died in the Danish invasion of 866-70. 340

Bishop, Farnham and Arthur Gilchrist Brodeur. THE ALTAR OF THE LEGION. Little, 1926. Romantic novel of heroism and masquerade during the Saxon invasion of Britain. 341

Breslin, Howard. THE GALLOWGLASS. Crowell, 1958. Irish lords settle their differences and join together to drive the Danes from Dublin. 342

Collingwood, W. G. THE LIKENESS OF KING ELFWALD. Titus Wilson, 1917. Tale of the Viking raids on Northumbria and West Scotland. 343

--------. THORSTEIN OF THE MERE. Arnold, 1895. A saga of the Northmen in Lakeland. 344

Crosfield, Truda H. A LOVE IN ANCIENT DAYS. Mathews, 1907. Romance and warfare in southwestern Britain during the period of the conquering Saxons. 345

Davis, Mrs. M. H. THE WINTER SERPENT. McGraw, 1958. The proud daughter of a Scots chieftain is sold to Vikings by a jealous foster brother. 346

Deeping, Warwick. LOVE AMONG THE RUINS. Cassell, 1904. Picturesque romance of knightly exploits in Avalon. 347

--------. UTHER AND IGRAINE. Outlook, 1903. Purported romance of King Arthur's parents. 348

Donaldson, Mary E. M. THE ISLES OF FLAME. Gardiner, Paisley, 1912. A romance in the Hebrides with St. Columba as a background figure. 349

Du Bois, Theodora M. EMERALD CROWN. Funk, 1955. Faith and superstition, royalty and commoners mingle in this tale of an Irish queen. 350

Duggan, Alfred. CONSCIENCE OF THE KING. Coward, 1952. A witty story of the reputed founder of the West Saxon Kingdom. 351

--------. THE LITTLE EMPERORS. Coward, 1953. About a Roman official stationed in Britain to uphold Roman authority. 352

Erskine, John. GALAHAD. Bobbs, 1926. A clever adaptation of one aspect of the Arthurian legends. 353

Farnol, Jeffery. THE KING LIVETH. Doubleday, 1943. Action galore as Alfred the Great fights the Danes. 354

Forrest, Thorpe. BUILDERS OF THE WASTE. Duckworth, 1899. A romance in Britain during a sixth century Saxon invasion. 355

Griffin, Gerald. THE INVASION. Duffy (Dublin), 1832. Western Ireland in the last part of the eighth century. 356

Keith, Chester. QUEEN'S KNIGHT. Allen, 1920. An Arthurian romance about Britain in the sixth century. 357

Macnicol, Eona K. COLUM OF DERRY. Sheed, 1954. Fictionalized account of the life of St. Columba of Ireland in the sixth century A. D. 358

Macpherson, Annie Winifred. RUAN. by Bryher, _pseud._ Pantheon, 1960. The adventures of Ruan, who prefers the excitement of sea travel to his inherited post as

Druid priest. 359

Reid, J. M. THE SONS OF AETHNE. Blackwood, 1923. Celtic life in west Scotland about the eighth century. 360

Roberts, Dorothy James. LAUNCELOT, MY BROTHER. Appleton, 1954. The Arthurian legend, told by Launcelot's brother, Bors de Ganis. 361

Rooney, Theresa J. THE LAST MONARCH OF TARA. by Eblana, pseud. Gill (Dublin), 1889. Tale of Ireland depicting Irish civilization in the sixth century. 362

Senior, Dorothy. THE CLUTCH OF CIRCUMSTANCE. Macmillan, 1908. About King Arthur and his knights of the Round Table. 363

Sterling, Sara Hawks. A LADY OF KING ARTHUR'S COURT. Jacobs, 1907. Romance of a lady-in-waiting to Queen Guenevere. 364

Taylor, C. Bryson. NIKANOR, TELLER OF TALES. McClurg, 1906. A story of Britain at the close of the Roman period. 365

Treece, Henry. THE GREAT CAPTAINS. Random, 1956. Rich tale of Celtic Britain in the days of King Arthur. 366

Trevor, Meriol. THE LAST OF BRITAIN. St. Martins, 1956. Noble Britons eat, drink, and make merry while the Saxons prepare to invade. 367

White, Terence Hanbury. THE SWORD IN THE STONE. Putnam, 1939. Delightful fantasy based on the Arthurian legends. 368

Williams, Patry. ALFRED THE KING. Faber & Faber, 1951. Story of Alfred the Great, who did so much to prepare England for future greatness. 369

II. A. 1. b. Western and Central Europe

1) Fifth and Sixth Centuries: Ages of Barbarian Invasions and Early Germanic Kingdoms

Costain, Thomas B. THE DARKNESS AND THE DAWN. Doubleday, 1959. Young lovers of a neutral tribe are caught up in the struggle between Attila and Aetius. 370

Dahn, Felix. FELICITAS. (tr.) McClurg, 1883. Germanic invasion of the Danubian regions. 371

De Wohl, Louis. THRONE OF THE WORLD. Lippincott, 1949. The invasion of the Roman Empire by the great Hunnic leader, Attila. 372

Fuller, Roger. SIGN OF THE PAGAN. Dial, 1954. Fifth century Europe with Attila the Hun as a chief figure. 373

Hausrath, Adolf. JETTA. (tr.) by George Taylor, pseud. Paul, 1886. Heidelberg under the Romans of the Later Empire. 374

James, G. P. R. ATTILA. Dutton, 1837. The experiences of a young Roman exile in the camp of Attila the Hun. 375

Pruette, Lorine. SAINT IN IVORY. Appleton, 1927. Touching story of St. Genevieve of Paris and Nanterre in Roman-ruled France. 376

Simon, Edith. TWELVE PICTURES. Putnam, 1955. Colorful fifth century tapestry--part Christian, part pagan. 377

II. A. 1. b. 2) Seventh and Eighth Centuries: Age of Frankish Ascendance

Bennet, Robert Ames. FOR THE WHITE CHRIST. McClurg, 1905. The mighty deeds of Charlemagne against the Moors, Arabs, and Saxons. 378

Hardy, Arthur S. PASSE ROSE. Houghton, 1889. A romance of the semi-barbarian Franks and savage Saxons of Charlemagne's time. 379

Pyle, Katharine. CHARLEMAGNE AND HIS KNIGHTS. Lippincott, 1932. A novel based on stories and legends of Charlemagne. 380

II. A. 1. b. 3) Ninth and Tenth Centuries: Early Feudal Era

Almedingen, Martha E. von. THE GOLDEN SEQUENCE. Westminster, 1949. Peasant and monastic life in and about a French abbey. 381

Bengtsson, Frans Gunnar. THE LONG SHIPS. (tr.) Knopf, 1954. Exploits of Red Orm, a Dane, on land and sea. 382

--------. RED ORM. Scribner, 1943. Red Orm, once a Spanish galley slave, lives in Denmark, later invades and settles in England. 383

Burgess, J. Haldane. THE VIKING PATH. Blackwood, 1894. The wild, violent life of the Vikings. 384

Dasent, George Webbe. THE VIKINGS OF THE BALTIC. Chapman & Hall, 1875. The land and sea adventures of the Vikings of Jomsburg. 385

Eddison, Eric Rucker. STYRBIORN THE STRONG. A & C Boni, 1926. Saga-based account of the attempts of an heir to the Swedish throne to gain his heritage. 386

Gross, Myra Geraldine. THE STAR OF VALHALLA. Stokes, 1907. A romance of early Christianity in Norway and the people's initial resistance to it. 387

Gunnarsson, Gunnar. THE SWORN BROTHERS. (tr.) Knopf, 1921. A rousing story of Vikings in the reign of Harold Fairhair of Norway. 388

Haggard, H. Rider. ERIC BRIGHTEYES. Longmans, 1891. A tale of the Norsemen in Iceland. 389

Hewlett, Maurice. GUDRID THE FAIR. Dodd, 1918. About a Norse girl who fulfills a prophecy. 390

--------. A LOVER'S TALE. Scribner, 1915. A novel based on sagas of ninth and tenth century Iceland, Norway, and Greenland. 391

--------. THORGILS OF TREADHOLT. Scribner, 1917. A tale of adventure in the Scandinavian area in the early Middle Ages. 392

Hough, Clara Sharpe. LEIF THE LUCKY. Century, 1926. "A romantic saga of the sons of Erik the Red." 393

Kamban, Gudmundur. I SEE A WONDROUS LAND. Putnam, 1938. Saga-based novel of Leif Ericsson and his expeditions to Iceland, Greenland, and Labrador. 394

Linklater, Eric. THE MEN OF NESS. Farrar, 1933. A saga of the Vikings of the Orkney Islands. 395

Marshall, Edison. THE VIKING. Farrar, 1951. Story of a Northman based on the Saga of Ogier the Dane, who loved a Welsh princess and sailed toward unknown lands. 396

Myers, Henry. THE UTMOST ISLAND. Crown, 1951. Full of the daring of the Vikings and the clashes of Christianity with pagan mythology. 397

Myers, John. THE HARP AND THE BLADE. Dutton, 1941. An Irish minstrel's strange curse--a compulsion to help everyone. 398

Roth, Richard. KING OTTO'S CROWN. (tr.) Concordia, 1917. Fictional account of Emperor Otto I of Germany and Italy. 399

Scheffel, Joseph Viktor von. EKKEHARD. (tr.) Dutton, 1927. A tale about the Magyar raids of the mid-tenth century. 400

Undset, Sigrid. GUNNAR'S DAUGHTER. (tr.) Knopf, 1936. Saga-like story of a Norwegian girl and an Icelandic youth in the late tenth century. 401

Walton, Evangeline. THE CROSS AND THE SWORD. Bouregy & Curl, 1956. The Northmen and their incursions into tenth century England. 402

Young, Charles. HARALD, FIRST OF THE VIKINGS. Crowell, 1911. About Harold Fairhair, King of Norway. 403

II. A. 1. c. Southern Europe (Iberian Peninsula, Italy, Adjacent Islands) (c. 400-1500)

Collins, Wilkie. ANTONINA. Harper, 1850. The Gothic invasion of Italy and Alaric's first blockade of Rome. 404

Cresswell, Clarice M. MAKING AND BREAKING OF ALMANSUR. Dodd, 1916. The career of an ambitious Moslem in the glorious period of Cordova under the Caliphate. 405

Dahn, Felix. A STRUGGLE FOR ROME. (tr.) Bentley, 1878. The Gothic Kingdom and its collapse after

Theodoric's death; the Roman Empire restored by Justinian. 406

De Camp, Lyon. LEST DARKNESS FALL. Holt, 1941. Fantasy of a present-day archeologist sent back into sixth century Italy by a bolt of lightning. 407

De Wohl, Louis. CITADEL OF GOD. Lippincott, 1959. This novel traces St. Benedict's religious development and the growth of his order. 408

Gallizier, Nathan. THE SORCERESS OF ROME. Page, 1907. The love-story of King Otto III of the Germans and the wife of a Roman senator. 409

Gay, Laverne. THE UNSPEAKABLES. Scribner, 1945. A beautiful Catholic queen of the hated Lombards works for their civilization and conversion. 410

Gissing, George. VERANILDA. Dutton, 1905. Military tactics, heresy, and love during the siege of Rome in the Byzantine War to take Italy. 411

Mann, Thomas. THE HOLY SINNER. (tr.) Knopf, 1951. Story of Pope Gregory I based on an old legend. 412

Park, Mrs. Kendall. RIQUILDA. Murray, 1912. Christian Barcelona and Catalonia during the tenth century Moorish offensive. 413

Pei, Mario Andrew. SWORDS OF ANJOU. Day, 1953. The Moors in Spain--with the Song of Roland as the basis of the story. 414

Raynolds, Robert. THE SINNER OF ST. AMBROSE. Bobbs, 1952. This picture of the decay of the Roman Empire includes Alaric the Goth and Sts. Ambrose and Augustine. 415

II. A. 1. d. Eastern Europe (including the Byzantine Empire, the Balkans, and Russia), the Near East, and North Africa (c. 400-1500)

Butcher, C. H. ARMENOSA OF EGYPT. Blackwood, 1897. The Arab conquest of Egypt in the seventh century. 416

Dahn, Felix. THE SCARLET BANNER. (tr.) McClurg, 1903. The war between the Byzantine General Belisarius and the Vandal King Gelimer. 417

Davis, William Stearns. THE BEAUTY OF THE PURPLE. Macmillan, 1924. A romance about Leo III, the Isaurian peasant who became Emperor of Christian Constantinople. 418

Dumke, Glenn S. TYRANT OF BAGDAD. by Glenn Pierce, _pseud._ Little, 1955. Charlemagne's European court and the opulent splendor of the Moslem East. 419

Ebers, Georg. THE BRIDE OF THE NILE. (tr.) Gottsberger, 1887. A romance of divided Egypt during the period of Moslem conquest. 420

Gallizier, Nathan. THE LOTUS WOMAN. Page, 1922. The court of Constantinople under the semi-barbaric Emperor Nicephorus Phocas. 421

Gordon, Samuel. THE LOST KINGDOM. Shapiro, Vallentine, 1926. A story of the Kingdom of Khazaria, in the Crimean region. 422

Haggard, H. Rider. THE WANDERER'S NECKLACE. Longmans, 1914. Tells of the Empress Irene, widow of the Emperor Leo IV. 423

Harrison, Frederic. THEOPHANO. Harper, 1904. The Byzantine Empire during its great struggle with the Saracens. 424

Kingsley, Charles. HYPATIA. Macmillan, 1853. Clash between the comparatively new Christianity and deep-rooted paganism in fifth century Egypt. 425

Lamb, Harold. THEODORA AND THE EMPEROR; THE DRAMA OF JUSTINIAN. Doubleday, 1952. A detailed picture of life in Constantinople in the sixth century. 426

Masefield, John. BASILISSA. Macmillan, 1940. The amazing Theodora, who became the wife of Justinian I, Emperor of the East. 427

--------. CONQUER. Macmillan, 1941. Dramatic story of a

Byzantine uprising at the time of Justinian and Theodora. 428

O'Connor, Richard. THE VANDAL. Doubleday, 1960. An officer in General Belisarius' army sees the schemings of the Empress and the General's wife. 429

Pottinger, Henry. BLUE AND GREEN. Chapman, 1879. The bloody Nika insurrection of 532 against Justinian proves the courage of his wife, Theodora. 430

Wellman, Paul I. THE FEMALE. Doubleday, 1953. Empress Theodora and sixth century Constantinople are vividly pictured. 431

II. A. 2. The High Middle Ages (c. 1000-1300)

a. The British Isles (England, Wales, Scotland, Ireland

Baring-Gould, S. PABO, THE PRIEST. Stokes, 1899. Henry I's attempt to subdue the Welsh people by weakening their Church. 432

Barnes, Margaret Campbell. THE PASSIONATE BROOD. Macrae Smith, 1945. A story of Richard Plantagenet and the minstrel Blondel. 433

Barringer, Leslie. KAY, THE LEFT-HANDED. Doubleday, 1935. England under John during the absence of Crusader-King Richard Lion-Heart. 434

Bowker, Alfred. ARMADIN. Causton & Sons, 1908. Civil war in the reign of Stephen against the forces of Matilda and Henry of Anjou. 435

Burroughs, Edgar Rice. THE OUTLAW OF TORN. McClurg, 1927. Thrilling action in this story of the Barons' Wars in England. 436

Carlos, Louisa Cooke Don-. A BOTTLE IN THE SMOKE. Fenno, 1908. Benedictine monastic life at the time of Henry II and Richard I. 437

Chidsey, Donald Barr. THIS BRIGHT SWORD. Crown, 1957. Richard Lion-Heart's struggle to regain his throne from his brother John. 438

Costain, Thomas B. BELOW THE SALT. Doubleday, 1957. Panoramic view of England and the Magna Carta in a modern American frame. 439

--------. THE BLACK ROSE. Doubleday, 1945. Travels, adventures, and romance of an Englishman in the Orient. 440

Cunningham, Allan. SIR MICHAEL SCOTT. Colburn, 1828. Based on the career of the famous British scholar and magician at the court of Frederick II. 441

Dane, Joan. PRINCE MADOG, DISCOVERER OF AMERICA. Stock, 1909. Based on the legend that a Welsh prince discovered America in the twelfth century. 442

Davidson, Mary M. EDWARD THE EXILE. Hodder, 1901. Based on the life of Edward the Atheling, son of Margaret of Scotland. 443

Davies, Naunton. THE KING'S GUIDE. Simpkin, 1901. Concerns a period in the life of Prince Llewelyn ap Gruffydd, leader of the thirteenth century Welsh fight for independence. 444

Deeping, Warwick. THE RED SAINT. McBride, 1940. The Barons' Wars in Kent and Sussex, including the Battle of Lewes. 445

Douglas, Donald. THE BLACK DOUGLAS. Doran, 1927. Powerful tale of the daring Black Douglas and of the girl who loved him. 446

Du Bois, Theodora M. LOVE OF FINGIN O'LEA. Appleton, 1957. The adventures and studies of a young doctor who becomes a famous physician. 447

Duggan, Alfred. THE CUNNING OF THE DOVE. Pantheon, 1960. A plausible picture of Edward the Confessor, England's last king before the Norman Conquest. 448

--------. DEVIL'S BROOD. Coward, 1957. Vigorous account of the unpleasant family of Henry II and Eleanor of Acquitaine. 449

--------. LEOPARDS AND LILIES. Coward, 1954. The conflicting loyalties and ambitions of a selfish English noblewoman. 450

Edmondston, C. M. and M. L. F. Hyde. KING'S MAN. Longmans, 1948. Penniless squire who rose to important positions with Henry II, Richard I, and John. 451

Farnol, Jeffery. BELTANE THE SMITH. Little, 1915. Romance of an outlaw and rebel in medieval England. 452

Gerson, Noel B. THE CONQUEROR'S WIFE. Doubleday, 1957. The busy lives of two strong-willed people--William the Conqueror and his consort, Matilda. 453

Gibney, Somerville. JOHN O' LONDON. Ward & Downey, 1887. Some of the researches and experiments of Roger Bacon's early life. 454

Gibson, G. B. DEARFORGIL, THE PRINCESS OF BREFFNY. Hope, 1857. About the little-known abduction of the Princess by Diarmuid MacMurrough. 455

Griffiths, D. Ryles. ELGIVA, DAUGHTER OF THE THEGN. Unwin, 1901. The Welsh border in the time of Edward the Confessor and Harold. 456

Grindrod, Charles F. THE SHADOW OF THE RAGGEDSTONE. Mathews, 1908. About a twelfth century monk; the shadow of the Raggedstone is a sign of death. 457

Gull, C. Ranger. THE SERF. Greening, 1902. The oppression and injustice involved in the feudal system are illustrated. 458

Hall, Hubert. COURT LIFE UNDER THE PLANTAGENETS. Dutton, 1890. A story of twelfth century England based on documents of the period. 459

Harris, Edwin. WILLIAM D' ALBINI. Harris, 1901. The second siege of Rochester castle, an incident in John's dispute with refractory landholders. 460

Hay, Agnes Grant. MALCOLM CANMORE'S PEARL. Hurst & Blackett, 1907. A romance about Malcolm III and his beautiful wife--St. Margaret of Scotland. 461

Hewlett, Maurice. THE FOREST LOVERS. Macmillan, 1898. Romance of a knight and a peasant girl, with good descriptions of medieval customs and ideas. 462

--------. THE LIFE AND DEATH OF RICHARD YEA-AND-NAY. Macmillan, 1900. The pageantry and panoply of the chivalric age. 463

Horne, Roland. THE LION OF DE MONTFORT. Dent, 1909. "A romance of the Barons' Wars." 464

James, G. P. R. FOREST DAYS. Dutton, 1843. England in the period of the Barons' Wars against King John. 465

Kingsley, Charles. HEREWARD THE WAKE. Macmillan, 1874. A saga-like account of the unruly Hereward, who refused to accept the Norman Conquest. 466

Knowles, Mabel Winifred. LET ERIN REMEMBER. by May Wynne, pseud. Greening, 1908. The Norman victory over the unity-lacking Irish in the 1170s. 467

Lenanton, Carola Oman. THE EMPRESS. by Carola Oman. Holt, 1932. The Empress Matilda and her life in England and France. 468

Lytton, Edward Bulwer, 1st. baron. HAROLD, THE LAST OF THE SAXON KINGS. Longmans, 1848. The Norman invasion, the Battle of Hastings, and the fall of the last Saxon king. 469

Maberley, Kate Charlotte. THE LADY AND THE PRIEST. Clarke, 1851. The story is about Henry II, Rosamund, and Thomas á Becket. 470

MacFarlane, Charles. THE CAMP OF REFUGE. Longmans, 1846. Hereward the Wake's famous stand against William the Conqueror. 471

--------. A LEGEND OF READING ABBEY. Dutton, 1904. Conflict between Matilda and the usurper Stephen. 472

Mackay, Charles. LONGBEARD. Routledge, 1841. William FitzOsbert, Longbeard, led the Londoners against the Norman oppressors. 473

Macpherson, Annie Winifred. THE FOURTEENTH OF OCTOBER. by Winifred Bryher, pseud. Pantheon, 1952. Vivid account of the Norman invasion of 1066. 474

Maiden, Cecil. HARP INTO BATTLE. Crowell, 1959. The eventful life of Llewelyn the Great of Wales. 475

Marsh, John B. THE LIFE AND ADVENTURES OF ROBIN HOOD. Dutton, 1875. Based on the career of the legendary outlaw-hero. 476

Marshall, Bernard G. WALTER OF TIVERTON. Appleton, 1923. Heroic exploits in the chivalric days of Richard Lion-Heart. 477

Miller, Thomas. FAIR ROSAMOND. Darton, 1839. Romance of Henry II and his contest with Becket. 478

--------. ROYSTON GOWER. Colburn, 1838. The background of this Robin Hood tale is King John's quarrel with Pope Innocent III. 479

Muddock, J. E. Preston. MAID MARIAN AND ROBIN HOOD. Lippincott, 1892. Opposition to the treacherous John, who seized his crusading brother's throne. 480

Muntz, Hope. THE GOLDEN WARRIOR. Scribner, 1949. Powerful account of the Norman Conquest as vivid as a medieval tapestry. 481

Napier, Charles. WILLIAM THE CONQUEROR. Routledge, 1858. William's preparations for the invasion of England and the Battle of Hastings. 482

O'Byrne, Miss M. L. THE COURT OF RATH CROGHAN. Simpkin, 1887. Disunity among the Irish princes during the Norman Conquest. 483

O'Grady, Standish. THE DEPARTURE OF DERMOT. Talbot Press (Ireland), 1917. King Dermot of Leinster and his departure for Bristol in 1166. 484

O'Hannrachain, Michael. WHEN THE NORMAN CAME. Maunsel (Dublin), 1918. King Dermot of Leinster and his Norman ally Strongbow. 485

Pargeter, Edith. HEAVEN TREE. Doubleday, 1960. This medieval tapestry includes the construction of a Gothic cathedral. 486

Peacock, Thomas Love. MAID MARIAN. Dutton, 1905.

Account of the Robin Hood legend, with some satire. 487

Potter, Margaret Horton. UNCANONIZED. McClurg, 1900. Monastic life in England under King John. 488

Rees, Helen Christina Easson. SING MORNING STAR. by Jane Oliver, *pseud.* Putnam, 1956. Inspiring romance of Malcolm III, King of Scotland, and his saintly wife, Margaret. 489

Reznikoff, Charles. LIONHEARTED. Jewish Pub., 1944. The persecution of the Jews in medieval England. 490

Scott, *Sir* Walter. THE BETROTHED. Lovell, 1885. Warfare on the Welsh border in the reign of Henry II. 491

--------. IVANHOE. Constable, 1821. Scott's most popular book displays the pageantry and romance of the chivalric tradition. 492

Sheppard, Alfred Tresidder. HERE COMES AN OLD SAILOR. Doubleday, 1928. Chronicle of a Kentish family in the reign of King John. 493

Swan, Edgar. THE SWORD AND THE COWL. Digby & Long, 1909. Pictures the Battle of Hastings and domestic life at the time. 494

Talbot, L. A. JEHANNE OF THE FOREST. Melrose, 1914. Vigorous England in the early part of Henry II's reign. 495

Turnbull, Clara. THE DAMSEL DARK. Melrose, 1912. Romance of the reigns of Stephen and Henry II. 496

Walworth, Alice. SHIELD OF HONOR. Doubleday, 1957. One of Simon de Montfort's knights in the struggle for the rights of Englishmen. 497

--------. THE VOWS OF THE PEACOCK. Doubleday, 1955. Isabel of France, Elizabeth, daughter of Warwick, and intrigue surrounding the throne. 498

Ward, Bryan W. THE FOREST PRINCE. Digby & Long, 1903. About the Barons' Wars of the mid-thirteenth century. 499

Weenolsen, Hebe. TO KEEP THIS OATH. Doubleday, 1958.

Pictures mining, medicine, and the conflict between Henry Plantagenet and King Stephen. 500

--------. THE LAST ENGLISHMAN. Doubleday, 1951. Eventful narrative of Hereward's resistance to William the Conqueror. 501

II. A. 2. b. Western and Central Europe

1) France

Addison, Julia de Wolf. FLORESTANE THE TROUBADOUR. Estes, 1903. Southern France and Italy near the end of the thirteenth century, with the artist Cimabue. 502

Aveling, Francis. ARNOUL THE ENGLISHMAN. Herder, 1908. Based on the Paris University debates over such philosophers as Plato and Aristotle. 503

Bailey, H. C. THE FOOL. Dutton, 1927. The Civil War between Stephen and Matilda in England and the exploits of Henry II in France. 504

Barrington, Michael. THE LADY OF TRIPOLI. Chatto, 1910. A romance of Odierna, widow of Raymond I of Tripoli, at the time of the Crusades. 505

Blissett, Nellie K. THE MOST FAMOUS LOBA. Appleton, 1901. The persecution of the Albigenses by Simon de Montfort. 506

Closs, Hannah. HIGH ARE THE MOUNTAINS. Vanguard, 1959. Richly detailed descriptions of medieval scenes and life during the crusade against the Albigenses. 507

Davis, William Stearns. FALAISE OF THE BLESSED VOICE. [later pub. as: THE WHITE QUEEN] Macmillan, 1904. A romance based on the lives of King Louis IX, the Saint, and his Queen, Marguerite of Provence. 508

Hewlett, Maurice. THE HEART'S KEY. Harper, 1905. Romance and revenge under the feudal system in France. 509

James, G. P. R. PHILIP AUGUSTUS. Dutton, 1831. Philip II's quarrel with Innocent III and the case of Arthur

Plantagenet. 510

Lindsey, William. THE SEVERED MANTLE. Houghton, 1910. A tale of the troubadours in twelfth century Provence. 511

Maturin, Charles Robert. THE ALBIGENSES. Hurst & Blackett, 1824. The Civil War in Languedoc which followed Montfort's crusade against the Albigenses. 512

Prescott, Hilda Frances Margaret. SON OF DUST. Macmillan, 1956. A rich tapestry of life in medieval Normandy. 513

--------. UNHURRYING CHASE. Dodd, 1925. The quest for revenge of a young Frenchman who has lost his estates to Richard Lion-Heart. 514

Rawson, Maud Stepney. MORLAC OF GASCONY. Hutchinson, 1915. French plots concerning the Cinque Ports, keys of English maritime defense. 515

Symons, Beryl. PRINCE AND PRIEST. Paul, 1912. Story based on the Albigensian heresy. 516

Waddell, Helen Jane. PETER ABELARD. Holt, 1933. The famous romance of Abelard and Heloise. 517

Webb, Henry B. DEW IN APRIL. by John Clayton, pseud. Kendall & Sharp, 1935. Convent life and daring romance in thirteenth century Provence. (followed by GOLD OF TOULOUSE) 518

--------. GOLD OF TOULOUSE. by John Clayton, pseud. Heinemann, 1932. Brotherly devotion, romance, and sadistic torture in thirteenth century Toulouse. 519

II. A. 2. b. 2) The Empire and Central Europe (including the Germanies, Netherlands, Switzerland, Poland, and Hungary)

Barr, Robert. THE COUNTESS TEKLA. Stokes, 1898. Love affair of the countess with an emperor in disguise in the Rhine area. 520

Conscience, Hendrik. THE LION OF FLANDERS. (tr.) Kelly, 1838. Uprising in Flanders against the French occupation;

the Massacre of Bruges and the Battle of Courtrai. 521

Davis, William Stearns. THE SAINT OF DRAGON'S DALE. Macmillan, 1903. Fantastic tale of the suppression of robber knights in Thuringia by Rudolf I. 522

Ebers, Georg. IN THE TIME OF THE FORGE. (tr.) Low, 1895. Novel of thirteenth century Nuremberg, reflecting life both in and outside of the cloister. 523

James, G. P. R. THE CASTLE OF EHRENSTEIN. Dutton, 1847. The atmosphere of Germany in the early thirteenth century. 524

Josika, Miklos. 'NEATH THE HOOF OF THE TARTAR. (tr.) Jarrold and Sons, 1905. The Mongol invasion of Hungary in the 1240s. 525

Prior, Loveday. A LAW UNTO THEMSELVES. Little, 1934. Robber barons in the Austrian Tyrol in the thirteenth century. 526

Robertson, Frances F. THE WANTON. by Frances Harrod, pseud. Greening, 1909. A romance of the Empire at the time of the conflict between Frederick II and the Papacy. 527

II. A. 2. b. 3) Scandinavia and the Baltic

Drummond, Hamilton. A MAN'S FEAR. Ward & Lock, 1903. A story of Norway when Christian teachings were replacing pagan superstitions. 528

Hewlett, Maurice. FREY AND HIS WIFE. McBride, 1916. A saga of Norway telling of the introduction of Christianity. 529

--------. THE LIGHT HEART. Holt, 1920. Saga of Thormod of the light heart whose loyalty never falters at danger. 530

--------. OUTLAW. Dodd, 1920. A strong, tense saga of a craftsman turned outlaw and a sword which carried a curse. 531

Ingemann, Bernard S. WALDEMAR. Bentley, 1864. A novel

of adventure in thirteenth century Denmark. 532

Kennedy, C. Rann. THE WINTERFEAST. Harper, 1908. A Viking, after twenty years in America, discovers his father had interfered with his romance. 533

Undset, Sigrid. MASTER OF HESTVIKEN. (tr.) Knopf, 1934. [Contains: THE AXE. Knopf, 1928; THE SNAKE PIT. Knopf, 1929; IN THE WILDERNESS. Knopf, 1929; THE SON AVENGER. Knopf, 1930] Exquisite, powerful tetralogy portraying life, love, and violence in Norway. 534

II. A. 2. c. Southern Europe (Iberian Peninsula, Italy, Adjacent Islands)

Alexander, Eleanor. THE LADY OF THE WELL. Longmans, 1906. The adventures and experiences of a troubadour. 535

Bailly, Auguste. THE DIVINE MINSTRELS. (tr.) Scribner, 1909. Based on the lives of St. Francis of Assisi and his companions. 536

Barton, Hester. THE BARON OF ILL-FAME. Paul, 1911. Corso Donati, whose actions won him the unusual nickname of Baron of Ill-Fame. 537

Bickerstaffe-Drew, Francis. SAN CELESTINO. by John Ayscough, pseud. Putnam, 1909. Story of the hermit who became Pope Celestine II for a period of five months. 538

De Wohl, Louis. THE QUIET LIGHT. Lippincott, 1950. Novel based on the life and philosophy of Thomas Aquinas. 539

Drummond, Hamilton. THE BETRAYERS. Dutton, 1919. Stirring account of the struggle for power between Emperor Frederick II and Pope Innocent IV. 540

--------. GREATER THAN THE GREATEST. Dutton, 1917. Frederick II's conflict with Pope Gregory IX. 541

Feuchtwanger, Lion. RAQUEL: THE JEWESS OF TOLEDO. (tr.) Messner, 1955. Alfonso VIII, King of Castile, his

Jewish finance minister, and the latter's daughter, Raquel. 542

Gallizier, Nathan. CASTEL DEL MONTE. Page, 1905. Romantic and political developments attending the coronation of Manfred as King of Sicily. 543

--------. THE HILL OF VENUS. Page, 1913. A young man forced by his father to become a monk. 544

Gifford, Evelyn H. PROVENZANO THE PROUD. Smith & Elder, 1904. Siena during the bitter strife between Guelfs and Ghibellines. 545

Hewlett, Maurice. BUONDELMONTE'S SAGA. Harper, 1905. A tragic romance of Florence. 546

Lee-Hamilton, Eugene. THE LORD OF THE DARK RED STAR. Scott, 1903. "Supernatural influences in the life of an Italian despot of the thirteenth century." 547

Le Fort, Gertrud von. THE POPE FROM THE GHETTO. (tr.) Sheed, 1934. Dramatic story of a Jew who became a Catholic and ruled for a time as anti-Pope Anacletus II. 548

Lewis, Arthur. THE PILGRIM. Blackwood, 1910. A Welsh pilgrim visits Rome during the conflict between Pope Gregory VII (Hildebrand) and Emperor Henry IV. 549

Llewellyn, Richard. WARDEN OF THE SMOKE AND BELLS. Doubleday, 1956. Marco Polo returns from Cathay through thirteenth century Assisi. 550

McCarthy, Justin Huntly. THE GOD OF LOVE. Harper, 1909. A story of the romance between Dante and Beatrice. 551

Osgood, Claude Jack. EAGLE OF THE GREDOS. Reynal, 1942. A Spanish noble fights against Moslem invaders. 552

Schachner, Nathan. THE WANDERER. Appleton, 1944. Dante's undying love for Beatrice. 553

Scollard, Clinton. THE VICAR OF THE MARCHES. Sherman & French, 1911. Padua in the days of Conrad III. 554

Stewart, Newton V. THE CARDINAL. Paul, 1911. Ottaviano Ubaldini is the Cardinal in this novel of thirteenth century Italy. 555

--------. A SON OF THE EMPEROR. Methuen, 1909. Emperor Frederick II's son Enzio and the contention of Guelphs and Ghibellines. 556

Underdown, Emily. CRISTINA. Sonnenschein, 1903. The struggle in Italy between Ghibelline (Imperial) and Guelph (Papal) parties. 557

White, Helen C. BIRD OF FIRE. Macmillan, 1958. The development of Francis of Assisi from a young cloth merchant to the founder of a religious order. 558

--------. NOT BUILT WITH HANDS. Macmillan, 1935. About Matilda, Countess of Tuscany, who attempted to settle the differences between Henry IV and Pope Gregory VII (Hildebrand). 559

--------. A WATCH IN THE NIGHT. Macmillan, 1933. A worldly lawyer becomes a devoted Franciscan. 560

II. A. 2. d. Eastern Europe (including the Byzantine Empire, The Balkans, and Russia), the Near East, and North Africa

Dole, Nathan Haskell. OMAR THE TENTMAKER. Page, 1899. Imaginary romance of the Persian savant, Omar Khayyam, author of the RUBÁIYÁT. 561

Duggan, Alfred. THE LADY FOR RANSOM. Coward, 1953. Informative story of mercenary soldiers in the service of Byzantine emperors. 562

Harrison, Edith. PRINCESS SAYRANE. McClurg, 1910. Mistaken identity and romance in an Egyptian setting. 563

MacFall, Haldane. THE THREE STUDENTS. Knopf, 1926. Based on the life of Omar Khayyam from his student days. 564

Phillpotts, Eden. EUDOCIA. Macmillan, 1921. Intrigues surrounding a Byzantine imperial widow and her reluctant promise not to remarry. 565

Pickthall, Marmaduke. KNIGHTS OF ARABY. Collins, 1917. Tale of adventure in eleventh century Arabia. 566

Weigall, Arthur. THE GARDEN OF PARADISE. Fisher Unwin, 1923. A romance set in the exotic Persia of Omar Khayyam. 567

II. A. 2. e. Overseas Exploration, Enterprise, and Expansion (including the Crusades)

Baerlein, Henry. ON THE FORGOTTEN ROAD. Murray, 1909. Twenty-three years of captivity in Egypt told in a fictional autobiography. 568

Barr, Gladys. CROSS, SWORD, AND ARROW. Abingdon, 1955. A member of the Children's Crusade is captured by the Saracens. 569

Begbie, Harold. THE DISTANT LAMP. Hodder, 1912. Events of the Children's Crusade in France, Egypt, and the Holy Land. 570

Brooke, Teresa. UNDER THE WINTER MOON. Doubleday, 1958. A tapestry of the Middle Ages including romance and crusading. 571

Butcher, C. H. THE ORIFLAMME IN EGYPT. Dent, 1905. The First Crusade of Louis IX of France with initial scenes of English rural life and later of the Coptic Church. 572

Byrne, Donn. CRUSADE. Little, 1928. The capture, escape, and romance of a crusading Irishman. 573

Charques, Dorothy. MEN LIKE SHADOWS. Coward, 1953. A narrative of the Third Crusade to the Holy Land. 574

Crawford, F. Marion. VIA CRUCIS. Macmillan, 1899. The Second Crusade, introducing Bernard of Clairvaux and other religious and political figures. 575

Cronyn, George W. THE FOOL OF VENUS. Covici, 1934. Stirring tale of the Fourth Crusade with Pierre Vidal, troubadour of Provence, as the central character. 576

Davis, William Stearns. GOD WILLS IT. Macmillan, 1902. A tale of the First Crusade--the exploits and romance of a young Norman. 577

Duggan, Alfred. KNIGHT WITH ARMOUR. Coward, 1951. A picture of the feudal way of life including battle scenes. 578

Duncan, David. TRUMPET OF GOD. Doubleday, 1956. Perceptive story of the human aspect of the Children's Crusade. 579

Faust, Frederick. THE GOLDEN KNIGHT. by George Challis, pseud. Greystone, 1937. A tale of Richard I of England as a captive in Austria. 580

Gallizier, Nathan. THE CRIMSON GONDOLA. Page, 1915. Conflict between Venice and Constantinople during the Fourth Crusade. 581

Gay, Laverne. WINE OF SATAN. Scribner, 1949. Vivid account of the First Crusade centering on Bohemond, Prince of Antioch. 582

Haggard, H. Rider. THE BRETHREN. McClure, 1904. Life of Englishmen in Syria preceding the Third Crusade. 583

Jeffries, Graham Montague. WHEN GOD SLEPT. by Peter Bourne, pseud. Putnam, 1956. Picaresque adventures of two Englishmen captured by the Arabs. 584

Johnston, Mary. THE FORTUNES OF GARIN. Houghton, 1915. A young knight, true to the chivalric tradition, sings of a princess but loves a shepherdess. 585

Kossak-Szczucka, Zofja. ANGELS IN THE DUST. (tr.) Roy Pub., 1947. Three Polish brothers, driven from their lands, answer Urban II's call to crusade. 586

--------. BLESSED ARE THE MEEK. (tr.) Roy Pub., 1944. A story concerning the Children's Crusade with St. Francis of Assisi as a character. 587

--------. THE LEPER KING. (tr.) Roy Pub., 1945. The wise reign of Baldwin IV of Jerusalem who played a valiant role despite his leprosy. 588

Lamb, Harold. DURANDAL. Doubleday, 1931. A crusader falls into the hands first of the Saracens and then of the Mongolian horde. 589

Lofts, Norah. THE LUTE PLAYER. Doubleday, 1951. Richard Lion-Heart and the musician who rescued him from a dungeon. 590

Ludlow, James M. SIR RAOUL. Revell, 1905. Diversion of the Fourth Crusade to Constantinople for the benefit of Venice. 591

Mason, Van Wyck. SILVER LEOPARD. Doubleday, 1955. Melodrama of twin brother and sister during the First Crusade. 592

Meakin, Nevill Myers. THE ASSASSINS. Holt, 1902. An Arab is the hero of this novel of the Third Crusade featuring Richard Lion-Heart, Philip Augustus, and Saladin. 593

Myers, Henry. OUR LIVES HAVE JUST BEGUN. Stokes, 1939. The French contingent of the tragic Children's Crusade. 594

Oldenbourg, Zoe. THE CORNERSTONE. (tr.) Pantheon, 1955. Rich panorama of the era of faith and chivalry. 595

--------. THE WORLD IS NOT ENOUGH. (tr.) Pantheon, 1948. A petty knight's home life and crusading. 596

O'Meara, Walter. THE DEVIL'S CROSS. Knopf, 1957. Excitement, romance, and tragedy during the ill-fated Children's Crusade. 597

Scarfoglio, Carlo. THE TRUE CROSS. Pantheon, 1956. Forceful account of the problems of a young Knight Templar. 598

Schoonover, Lawrence. GOLDEN EXILE. Macmillan, 1951. A crusader's attempt to reclaim his lands and end his exile. 599

Scott, *Sir* Walter. COUNT ROBERT OF PARIS. Bazin & Ellsworth, 1833. Concerns romance and dissension among members of the First Crusade. 600

--------. THE TALISMAN. Harper, 1879. About the Third Crusade, with Saladin, Richard Lion-Heart, and Kenneth of Scotland, loyal follower of the King. 601

Shellabarger, Samuel. THE TOKEN. Little, 1955. A silver girdle, symbol of nobility and strength, is the focus of the story. 602

Simpson, Evan John. RIDE HOME TOMORROW. by Evan John, pseud. Putnam, 1951. The atmosphere of the crusades is captured in this narrative. 603

Smith, Arthur D. Howden. SPEARS OF DESTINY. Doran, 1919. Tells of the Fourth Crusade and the capture of Constantinople. 604

Vidal, Gore. SEARCH FOR THE KING. Dutton, 1950. Blondel's search through Europe for the imprisoned Crusader, Richard Lion-Heart. 605

Williams, Jay. THE SIEGE. Little, 1955. Stirring descriptions of battles and of ideal and corrupt aspects of chivalry. 606

Yerby, Frank. THE SARACEN BLADE. Dial, 1952. An Italian armorer's son, on a crusade, finds love with a slave girl in Egypt. 607

Zimmermann, Samuel. SIR PAGAN. by Henry John Colyton, pseud. Creative Age, 1947. A swift-paced adventure story of the crusades. 608

II. A. 3. The Later Middle Ages and Early Renaissance (c. 1300-1500)

a. The British Isles

1) England and Wales

Andrew, Prudence. THE HOODED FALCON. New Authors Guild, 1960. A border baron is torn between loyalty to England or to Wales. 609

Bailey, H. C. THE MERCHANT PRINCE. Dutton, 1929. Concerns the growth of English commerce in the second half of the fifteenth century. 610

Barber, Margaret Fairless. THE GATHERING OF BROTHER HILARIUS. by Michael Fairless, pseud. Murray, 1903. A religious is sent from the monastery to learn the ways of the world during the Black Plague. 611

Barnes, Margaret Campbell. ISABEL THE FAIR. Macrae Smith, 1957. The problems facing the French Princess Isabel who became the wife of Edward II of England. 612

--------. TUDOR ROSE. Macrae Smith, 1953. Elizabeth, consort of Henry VII and mother of Henry VIII. 613

--------. WITHIN THE HOLLOW CROWN. Macrae Smith, 1947. Based on the life of Richard II from his fifteenth year. 614

Begbie, Harold. RISING DAWN. Doran, 1913. A romance of 1377-78 introducing Chaucer, Wycliff, John of Gaunt, and John Ball. 615

Benson, Robert Hugh. RICHARD RAYNAL, SOLITARY. Pitman, 1906. Fifteenth century Quietism in the England of Henry VI and Cardinal Beaufort. 616

Breton, Frederic. GOD SAVE ENGLAND. De la More Press, 1899. England in the latter part of Edward III's reign and at the accession of Richard II. 617

Carleton, Patrick. UNDER THE HOG. Dutton, 1938. Richard III's unscrupulous seizure of the throne and its sequel. 618

Chesson, Nora. FATHER FELIX'S CHRONICLES. Wessels, 1907. A monk's account of the poor living conditions of the people in fifteenth century England. 619

Converse, Florence. LONG WILL. Houghton, 1903. Story of William Langland, author of PIERS PLOWMAN, and other people notable in the Peasants' Revolt. 620

Cooke, J. H. IDA. Mackie, 1912. English monastic life in the reigns of Edward I, II, and III. 621

Cripps, Arthur S. MAGIC CASEMENTS. Duckworth, 1905. Daily life in restless England during the troubled reigns of Henry VI and Edward IV. 622

Deeping, Warwick. THE KING BEHIND THE KING. McBride, Nast, 1914. In southern England at the time of the Peasants' Revolt. 623

--------. THE SHIELD OF LOVE. McBride, 1940. Exciting adventures in England during Richard II's reign. 624

Duros, Edwin. OTTERBOURNE. Bentley, 1832. The Scottish invasion of England and Douglas' defeat of Hotspur at the Battle of Otterbourne. 625

Edmondston, C. M. and M. L. F. Hyde. THE RAGGED STAFF. Longmans, 1932. Romance and adventure during the Wars of the Roses. 626

Ellis, Beth. A KING OF VAGABONDS. Blackwood, 1911. Deals with Perkin Warbeck's contention that he was of royal blood and had a claim to the throne of England. 627

Ellis, Kenneth M. GUNS FOREVER ECHO. Messner, 1941. Yarmouth during the Hundred Years War. 628

Estrange, H. O. M. MID RIVAL ROSES. Selwyn & Blount, 1922. The swift march of events during the Wars of the Roses. 629

Ford, Ford Madox (name originally Ford Madox Hueffer). LADIES WHOSE BRIGHT EYES. Lippincott, 1935. Due to an accident, a twentieth century businessman returns to fourteenth century England. 630

Forster, R. H. IN STEEL AND LEATHER. Long, 1904. The Wars of the Roses, with Henry VI and Queen Margaret's escape to Scotland. 631

--------. THE MISTRESS OF AYDON. Long, 1907. Border clashes in fourteenth century Northumberland. 632

Fullerton, Georgiana. A STORMY LIFE. Bentley, 1867. Written as the journal of Henry VI's queen, Margaret of Anjou. 633

Greener, William. THE MEN OF HARLECH. Ward & Downey, 1896. The scene is laid in Wales during the struggle of Henry VI and Edward IV for the throne. 634

Haggard, H. Rider. RED EVE. Doubleday, Page, 1911. Tells of the disastrous Black Death in England and the decisive Battle of Crécy. 635

Hamilton, Bernard. CORONATION. Ward & Lock, 1902. Events during the reign of Henry V, ending with the decisive Battle of Agincourt. 636

Harding, T. Walter. THE ABBOT OF KIRKSTALL. Heffer, 1926. Features such leaders as John of Gaunt, the Black Prince, and Wycliff. 637

Hardy, Blanche. DYNASTY. Philip Allan, 1925. Romance in England in the time of Henry VII. 638

--------. SANCTUARY. Philip Allan, 1925. Concerns the reign of Richard III and his murder of the little Princes in the Tower. 639

Harwood, Alice. MERCHANT OF THE RUBY. Bobbs, 1950. Romance of a cousin of the Scottish king, and Perkin Warbeck, Pretender to the English throne. 640

Hawtrey, Valentina. IN A DESERT LAND. Duffield, 1915. Traces a family from the early fourteenth century to modern times and includes the Peasants' Revolt and Wycliff's Preachers. 641

Heyer, Georgette. SIMON THE COLDHEART. Small, Maynard, 1925. Life during the thrilling times of Henry IV and Henry V. 642

Hibbert, Eleanor. THE GOLDSMITH'S WIFE. by Jean Plaidy, pseud. Appleton, 1950. Life of a goldsmith's wife at the court of Edward IV. 643

Hudson, H. WILD HUMPHREY KYNASTON, THE ROBBER TROGLODYTE. Paul, 1899. About Kynaston who, outlawed by Henry VII, led a Robin Hood-type life. 644

Hughes, Beatrix. JOAN OF ST. ALBANS. Heath Cranton, 1926. Includes the Yorkist King Edward IV, the printer Caxton, and the second Battle of St. Albans. 645

Jackson, Dorothy V. S. WALK WITH PERIL. Putnam, 1959. A country boy's advance in the service of Henry V at

Agincourt. 646

James, G. P. R. AGINCOURT. Harper, 1844. Concerns Henry V and his victory at Agincourt. 647

--------. THE WOODMAN. Newby, 1849. The scene is England under Richard III, ending with the Battle of Bosworth Field. 648

Jefferis, Barbara. BELOVED LADY. Sloane, 1955. Norfolk manor house life and romance during England's Wars of the Roses. 649

Knowles, Mabel Winifred. THE RED ROSE OF LANCASTER. by May Wynne, pseud. Holden & Hardingham, 1922. Romance of Brittany in which the future Henry VII of England appears. 650

Lawrence, George Alfred. BRAKESPEARE. Routledge, 1868. Battles in England and France in the days of Edward III and the Black Prince. 651

Leary, Francis W. FIRE AND MORNING. Putnam, 1957. The turbulent times of Richard III and the Wars of the Roses. 652

--------. THE SWAN AND THE ROSE. Wyn, 1953. The Wars of the Roses as seen by a young Lancastrian soldier. 653

Lenanton, Carola Oman. CROUCHBACK. by Carola Oman. Holt, 1929. Presents a favorable picture of the controversial character of Richard III. 654

Lewis, Hilda Winifred. WIFE TO HENRY V. Putnam, 1957. Emphasis on the private life of Catherine of Valois. 655

Lindsay, Philip. LONDON BRIDGE IS FALLING. Little, 1934. London citizens defend the city from Jack Cade's rebellion. 656

Lofts, Norah. TOWN HOUSE. Doubleday, 1959. A serf attains freedom by living, undetected, in a walled town for a year and a day. 657

Lytton, Edward Bulwer, 1st. baron. THE LAST OF THE BARONS. Dutton, 1843. Edward IV and Warwick the

King-maker are prominent characters. 658

McChesney, Dora Greenwell. THE CONFESSION OF RICHARD PLANTAGENET. Smith & Elder, 1913. Absorbing defense of the controversial Richard III. 659

Mann, F. O. THE GOLDEN QUILL. Blackwell, 1924. Novel of southern England and London in Chaucer's period. 660

Matthew, Anne Irwin. WARM WIND, WEST WIND. Crown, 1956. Social life in London and adventures of ships which dare to sail far seas. 661

Maude, Sophie. THE HERMIT AND THE KING. Washbourne, 1916. England during the Wars of the Roses seen from a Catholic viewpoint. 662

Maughan, A. Margery. HARRY OF MONMOUTH. Sloane, 1956. Fictionalized account of Henry V and English campaigns in France. 663

Meyer, Annie N. ROBERT ANNYS, POOR PRIEST. Macmillan, 1901. The powerful emotions engendered by the Peasants' Revolt. 664

Minto, William. THE MEDIATION OF RALPH HARDELOT. Harper, 1888. An account of the Peasants' Revolt of 1381. 665

Morris, William. THE DREAM OF JOHN BALL. Longmans, 1888. The awakening of social consciousness in the insurrection that had Jack Ball, Jack Straw, and Wat Tyler as leaders. 666

Muddock, J. E. Preston. JANE SHORE. Long, 1905. A romance of the charming and notorious Jane Shore. 667

Newbolt, Henry. THE NEW JUNE. Dutton, 1909. The reigns of Richard II and Henry IV, ending with the Battle of Shrewsbury. 668

Oakeshott, Ronald. THE MERCHANT AT ARMS. Longmans, 1920. Career of an English merchant in the late fifteenth century. 669

Phelps, Charles Edward. THE ACCOLADE. Lippincott, 1905.

Chaucer's travels on the Continent as an English diplomat. 670

Powers, Anne. RIDE EAST! RIDE WEST! Bobbs, 1947. England and Ireland during the Hundred Years War. 671

Powys, John Cowper. OWEN GLENDOWER. S. & S., 1940. About the famous leader of the Welsh bid for independence. 672

Raine, Allen, pseud. HEARTS OF WALES. Hutchinson, 1905. Events in the period of Owen Glendower and the Welsh rebellion against Henry IV. 673

Rhys, Ernest. THE WHISTLING MAID. Hutchinson, 1900. Pictures South Wales, Lord Mortimer, and Queen Isabella at the time of Edward II. 674

Richings, Emily. IN CHAUCER'S MAYTIME. Unwin, 1902. About Chaucer, his wife, and his sister-in-law, Katherine, wife of John of Gaunt. 675

--------. WHITE ROSELEAVES. Drane, 1912. Court life centering on the queen of Edward IV of York. 676

Schuster, Rose. THE TRIPLE CROWN. Chapman, 1912. Henry VI, his unpopular marriage to Margaret of Anjou, and his insanity. 677

Scott, John Reed. BEATRIX OF CLARE. Lippincott, 1907. Shows Richard III as a strong king in an unsettled era. 678

Seton, Anya. KATHERINE. Houghton, 1954. The romance of John of Gaunt and Katherine Swynford, Chaucer's sister-in-law. 679

Shelley, Mary. THE FORTUNES OF PERKIN WARBECK. Routledge, 1830. About Perkin Warbeck, who claimed to be the lost Duke of York with a right to the English crown. 680

Simon, Edith. THE GOLDEN HAND. Putnam, 1952. Chronicle of the Widowson family in feudal England. 681

Trease, Geoffrey. SNARED NIGHTINGALE. Vanguard, 1958. Youth raised in Italy goes to England to claim an earldom on the Welsh border. 682

Warner, Sylvia Townsend. THE CORNER THAT HELD THEM. Viking, 1948. A tapestry of convent life from the Black Death to the Peasants' Revolt. 683

Woods, William Howard. RIOT AT GRAVESEND. Duell, 1952. Swift, eventful story of Wat Tyler's Rebellion. 684

II. A. 3. a. 2) Scotland and Ireland

Buchan, John. THE RIDING OF NINEMILEBURN. Blackwood, 1912. Involvement of innocent farmers in a Scottish border quarrel. 685

Crockett, Samuel R. THE BLACK DOUGLAS. Doubleday, 1899. Beheading of William, Earl of Douglas, and his brother in the reign of the Scotch boy-king, James II. (followed by MAID MARGARET OF GALLOWAY) 686

--------. MAID MARGARET OF GALLOWAY. Dodd, 1905. The family tragedy of the "Fair Maid of Galloway," wife of the murdered eighth Earl of Douglas. 687

Douglas, William A. LONG JOHN MURRAY. Coward, 1936. Story of the descendants of Long John Murray, a Scotch Presbyterian who settled in Ulster in the time of James I of Scotland. 688

Ferguson, Dugald. THE KING'S FRIEND. Gardner, 1907. The war for Scottish Independence at the time of the early Edwards. 689

Fremantle, Anne. JAMES AND JOAN. Holt, 1948. James I of Scotland spent his youth as a prisoner in England, where he married Joan Beaufort. 690

Galt, John. THE SPAEWIFE. Oliver & Boyd (Scotland), 1823. Tale of the early fifteenth century based on Scottish chronicles. 691

Hamilton, Ernest. THE MAWKIN OF THE FLOW. Unwin, 1898. Romance of a peasant girl in fifteenth century Scotland. 692

Hill, Pamela. MARJORIE OF SCOTLAND. Putnam, 1956.

Concerns a little-known princess, the daughter of Robert the Bruce. 693

Knowles, Mabel Winifred. A KING'S TRAGEDY. by May Wynne, pseud. Long, 1905. The conspiracy of Graham and the assassination of James I of Scotland. 694

Lenanton, Carola Oman. KING HEART. by Carola Oman. Fisher Unwin, 1926. Set in Scotland at the time of James IV. 695

Muddock, J. E. Preston. KATE CAMERON OF BRUX. Digby & Long, 1900. A deadly feud between rival Scottish clans. 696

O'Byrne, Miss M. L. ART MacMURROUGH KAVANAGH, PRINCE OF LEINSTER. Simpkin, 1885. Reaction of an independent Irish chieftain to Richard II's offer of knighthood. 697

Powers, Anne. THE GALLANT YEARS. Bobbs, 1946. Life in Ireland in the fourteenth century. 698

Rees, Helen Christina Easson. THE LION IS COME. by Jane Oliver, pseud. Putnam, 1957. Pictures the life and times of Robert the Bruce, king of Scotland. 699

Scott, Sir Walter. CASTLE DANGEROUS. Munro, 1885. As a condition of marriage, a youth is bidden to defend Douglas Castle, which has changed hands repeatedly. 700

--------. THE FAIR MAID OF PERTH. Munro, 1885. The turbulent Scotland of Robert III, torn by strife of nobles and feuds of clans. 701

Simpson, Evan John. CRIPPLED SPLENDOUR. by Evan John, pseud. Dutton, 1938. James I of Scotland from his imprisonment in England to his assassination in 1437. 702

Willard, Rachel. CATHERINE DOUGLAS. Jarrold & Sons, 1905. Instability in Scotland during the reign of the well-intentioned James I. 703

II. A. 3. b. Western and Central Europe

1) France

Angellotti, Marion Polk. THE BURGUNDIAN. Century, 1912. Concerns international tensions caused by the insanity of King Charles VI. 704

Atkinson, Henry H. THE KING'S FAVOURITE. Allen, 1912. Tale of the French court during the early reign of Louis XI. 705

Bailey, H. C. KNIGHT AT ARMS. Dutton, 1925. Events after the youthful Charles VIII assumed the throne of France. 706

Baring-Gould, S. NOÉMI. Appleton, 1894. Domestic conditions and struggles between England and France in the time of Charles VII. 707

Bowen, Marjorie, _pseud._ for Gabrielle Campbell Long. THE LEOPARD AND THE LILY. Doubleday, Page, 1909. An account of Civil War in Brittany, full of romance and passion. 708

Bray, Anna Eliza. THE WHITE HOODS. Chapman & Hall, 1884. Philip van Artevelde's revolt of 1381-2 against the Count of Flanders. 709

Catherwood, Mary H. THE DAYS OF JEANNE D'ARC. Century, 1897. About Jeanne d'Arc with emphasis on the important years, 1429-31. 710

Comstock, Seth Cook. MARCELLE THE MAD. Appleton, 1906. A feminine counterpart of Robin Hood in the forests of France. 711

Costain, Thomas B. THE MONEYMAN. Doubleday, 1951. Influence of a wealthy merchant, Jacques Coeur, on trade and politics in the reign of Charles VII. 712

Deeping, Warwick. BERTRAND OF BRITTANY. Harper, 1908. Incidents in the life of the clever Bertrand du Guesclin, military leader for Charles V. 713

Deutsch, Babette. ROGUE'S LEGACY. Coward, 1942.

François Villon, the gay thief who brought sensitive poetry out of sordid surroundings. 714

Doyle, Sir Arthur Conan. SIR NIGEL. McClure, 1906. The adventures of an Englishman abroad at the time of the Black Death; the Battle of Poitiers. (followed by THE WHITE COMPANY) 715

--------. THE WHITE COMPANY. Caldwell, 1890. A company of English bowmen fighting in France and Castile. 716

Drummond, Hamilton. CHATTELS. Paul, 1922. The hard lot of French peasants in the reigns of Charles VII-Louis XI. 717

--------. A KING'S SCAPEGOAT. Ward & Lock, 1905. Attempt of the power-greedy Louis XI to seize the heir to Foix and his possessions. 718

--------. A LORD OF THE SOIL. Ward & Lock, 1902. The feudal period, depicting monastic life and conditions among the peasants. 719

--------. THE SEVEN HOUSES. Stokes, 1901. Astrology figures prominently in this story of a girl's life. 720

Druon, Maurice, pseud. for Maurice Kessel. THE IRON KING. (tr.) Scribner, 1956. Romantic, political, religious, and financial conflicts at the court of Philip the Fair. (followed by THE STRANGLED QUEEN) 721

--------. THE POISONED CROWN. (tr.) Scribner, 1957. The ill-fated marriage of Louis X and his consort, Clémence. (followed by THE ROYAL SUCCESSION) 722

--------. THE ROYAL SUCCESSION. (tr.) Scribner, 1958. Manuevering for succession among sons of Philip the Fair and Louis X. (followed by THE SHE-WOLF OF FRANCE) 723

--------. THE SHE-WOLF OF FRANCE. (tr.) Scribner, 1961. The fortunes of Isabella of France, consort of Edward II of England. 724

--------. THE STRANGLED QUEEN. (tr.) Scribner, 1957. Concerns part of the brief reign of the weak Louis X, "the Self-Willed." (followed by THE POISONED CROWN) 725

Hawtrey, Valentina. PERONELLE. Lane, 1904. Compelling story of the common people of Paris in the fifteenth century. 726

--------. SUZANNE. Holt, 1906. A story of France and Flanders including an account of Philip van Artevelde's revolt of 1381. 727

Hewlett, Maurice. THE COUNTESS OF PICPUS. Scribner, 1911. The adventures of Captain Brazenhead, who pretends to be a count. 728

Hugo, Victor. THE HUNCHBACK OF NOTRE DAME. (tr.) [same as NOTRE DAME DE PARIS] Bentley, 1833. The classic, tragic story of Quasimodo, the bellringer of the Cathedral, who loves Esmeralda, a beautiful gypsy girl. 729

James, G. P. R. THE JACQUERIE. Dutton, 1841. The Peasants' Insurrection in France in 1358. 730

James, Grace. JOAN OF ARC. Dutton, 1910. Gives an account of the period and trends which influenced Joan. 731

Kaye, Michael W. THE DUKE'S VENGEANCE. Greening, 1910. The scheming of Louis XI against Charles the Bold and the Dukes of Burgundy and Guienne. 732

Knowles, Mabel Winifred. A MAID OF BRITTANY. by May Wynne, pseud. Greening, 1906. The hatred between Bretons and French is typified in the conflict between the Duchess Anne and Charles VIII. 733

--------. THE TAILOR OF VITRE. by May Wynne, pseud. Gay & Hancock, 1908. A narrative disclosing "the power behind the throne" in Brittany. 734

Lang, Andrew. A MONK OF FIFE. Longmans, 1895. The tale of a Scotsman in France during the period of the valorous Jeanne d'Arc. 735

McCarthy, Justin Huntly. THE FLOWER OF FRANCE. Harper, 1906. Concerns Jeanne d'Arc and her services to France. 736

--------. (1) IF I WERE KING. Harper, 1902. (2) NEEDLES AND PINS (sequel). Harper, 1907. Two light romances loosely based on the career of François Villon, beggar-poet. 737

McComas, Ina Violet. THE MARK OF VRAYE. by H. B. Somerville, pseud. Hutchinson, 1917. Revolt of the nobles against Pierre Landais in Brittany. 738

Morley, Iris. THE PROUD PALADIN. Morrow, 1936. The powerful, lovely Duchess of Montpellier and an English military captain. 739

Neumann, Alfred. THE DEVIL. (tr.) Knopf, 1928. The influence of his barber on superstitious King Louis XI. 740

Potter, Margaret Horton. THE CASTLE OF TWILIGHT. McClurg, 1903. The feudal period in Brittany, showing the status of women. 741

Rickert, Edith. GOLDEN HAWK. Baker & Taylor, 1907. Provence and Avignon during the Avignon residence of the Papacy. 742

Ridding, Laura. BY WEEPING CROSS. Hodder, 1899. Rural life in southern France during the fifteenth century. 743

Schoonover, Lawrence. THE BURNISHED BLADE. Macmillan, 1948. Adventure-packed life of a young Frenchman who witnessed the death of Jeanne d'Arc. 744

--------. THE SPIDER KING. Macmillan, 1954. Pictures Louis XI, the "spider" who reached out for lands on all sides. 745

Scott, Sir Walter. ANNE OF GEIERSTEIN. Harper, 1829. Swiss involvement in the conflict of Louis XI and Charles the Bold. 746

--------. QUENTIN DURWARD. Constable, 1823. A Scottish archer in the service of Louis XI. 747

Stuart, Dorothy M. MARTIN THE MUMMER. Constable, 1910. The court of Burgundy is the scene of a masquerade in the time of Philip the Good. 748

--------. ST. LO. Holden, 1912. Life of a noble at the time of Louis XI, Pope Sixtus IV, and Emperor Maximilian. 749

Symons, Beryl. A LADY OF FRANCE. Paul, 1910. A romance showing life during the reign of Philip the Fair. 750

II. A. 3. b. 2) The Empire and Central Europe (including the Germanies, Netherlands, Switzerland, Poland, and Hungary)

Baker, James. THE CARDINAL'S PAGE. Chapman & Hall, 1898. Henry Beaufort is the Cardinal in this story of the Hussites in Bohemia. (companion volume to THE GLEAMING DAWN) 751

--------. THE GLEAMING DAWN. Chapman & Hall, 1896. Based on the Wycliffite Movement in England and especially the Hussite Wars in Bohemia. (companion volume to THE CARDINAL'S PAGE) 752

Barr, Robert. THE SWORD MAKER. by Luke Sharp, pseud. Stokes, 1910. Germany at the time of Rudolf of Hapsburg's death, showing the power of Prince Roland and the Robber Barons of the Rhine. 753

Bertram, Paul. THE FIFTH TRUMPET. Lane, 1912. The background is the great ecumenical Council of Constance. 754

Crockett, Samuel R. JOAN OF THE SWORD-HAND. Dodd, 1900. Exploits of a north German princess in the fifteenth century. 755

Feuchtwanger, Lion. THE UGLY DUCHESS. (tr.) Viking, 1928. A striking picture of central European life and events, with Margarete of Tyrol as heroine. 756

Fisher, F. Hope. WRITTEN IN THE STARS. Harper, 1951.

A novel of Albrecht Dürer in the city of Nuremberg. 757

Grattan, Thomas C. JACQUELINE OF HOLLAND. Colburn & Bentley, 1831. A tale of Jacoba, countess of Hainault and Holland. 758

Häring, Wilhelm. THE BURGOMASTER OF BERLIN. (tr.) by Wilibald Alexis, pseud. Saunders & Otley, 1843. Frederick's attempts to smooth strained relations between nobles and townspeople. 759

James, G. P. R. MARY OF BURGUNDY. Dutton, 1833. The daughter of Charles the Bold and her marriage to Maximilian of Austria. 760

Kelly, Eric P. FROM STAR TO STAR. Lippincott, 1944. Students at the University of Cracow--one of whom was Copernicus. 761

Kingsley, Henry. OLD MARGARET. Longmans, 1871. Portrays the growth of art and trade in the Netherlands under Philip the Good of Burgundy. 762

Laughlin, Clara Elizabeth. HEART OF HER HIGHNESS. Putnam, 1917. The struggle of Mary of Burgundy for a happy marriage. 763

Lennep, Jacob van. THE ROSE OF DEKAMA. (tr.) Bruce & Wyld, 1847. Set in Holland in the turbulent times of William IV. 764

Maass, Edgar. MAGNIFICENT ENEMIES. Scribner, 1955. Flaring action as the Hanseatic League's power is challenged by merchant seamen. 765

Major, Charles. YOLANDA, MAID OF BURGUNDY. Macmillan, 1905. Tells of Mary, daughter of Charles the Bold, and Maximilian, son of Emperor Frederick. 766

Mellor, Dora. BEWITCHED. Drane, 1922. The German Empire in the troubled days of the Hussites. 767

Reade, Charles. THE CLOISTER AND THE HEARTH. Dodd, 1861. A travelogue of western Europe in the fifteenth century with the father of Erasmus as hero. 768

Rosegger, Peter. THE GODSEEKER. (tr.) Putnam, 1902.

Account of a religious crime with descriptions of pagan ceremonies. 769

Ross, Ronald. THE REVELS OF ORSERA. Murray, 1920. Romantic novel depicting Switzerland in 1495. 770

Sienkiewicz, Henryk. THE KNIGHTS OF THE CROSS. (tr.) Little, 1897. Struggles of Poland and Lithuania against aggressive Teutonic Knights. 771

II. A. 3. b. 3) Scandinavia and the Baltic

Rydberg, Viktor. SINGOALLA. (tr.) Scott, 1904. Sweden at the time of the Black Death, showing survivals of heathenism and superstition. 772

Undset, Sigrid. KRISTIN LAVRANSDATTER. (tr.) Knopf, 1929. [Contains: THE BRIDAL WREATH. Knopf, 1923. THE MISTRESS OF HUSABY. Knopf, 1925. THE CROSS. Knopf, 1927] The dramatic account of a woman's life in fourteenth century Norway. 773

II. A. 3. c. Southern Europe

1) Iberian Peninsula

Ardagh, W. M. THE KNIGHTLY YEARS. Lane, 1912. Spain and the Canary Islands at the time of Ferdinand and Isabella. 774

--------. THE MAGADA. Lane, 1910. A romance of the Spanish conquest of the Canary Islands. 775

Aronin, Ben. THE MOOR'S GOLD. Argus, 1935. A novel of the Spanish Inquisition and its persecution of the Jews. 776

Drummond, Hamilton. THE GRAIN OF MUSTARD. Paul, 1916. A young lady's experiences during the Spanish conquest of Granada. 777

Dumas, Alexandre. AGÉNOR DE MAULÉON. (tr.) Little, 1897. The international conflict over the rule of Pedro the Cruel of Castile. 778

Eça de Queiroz, José María de. OUR LADY OF THE PILLAR.

(tr.) Constable, 1906. Mystery, romance, and passion combine to make a thrilling story. 779

Haggard, H. Rider. FAIR MARGARET. Longmans, 1907. Experiences of a young Jewess with the Inquisition in Spain. 780

Hamilton, Bernard. HIS QUEEN. Hutchinson, 1927. Imaginative account of the friendship between Queen Isabella and Columbus. 781

Humphreys, Jeanne. THE COUNT WITHOUT CASTLES. Duell, 1956. The love of Pedro the Cruel, King of Castile, for María, and her reaction. 782

Kesten, Hermann. FERDINAND AND ISABELLA. Wyn, 1946. Story of the "Catholic Monarchs" who ruled Spain with such success. 783

Lee, Albert. THE BLACK DISC. Digby & Long, 1897. Moorish power in Spain is contested by the armies of Ferdinand and Isabella. 784

Lytton, Edward Bulwer, 1st. baron. LEILA. Dutton, 1838. The Spanish Christian invasion of Moorish Granada. 785

Miller, Elizabeth. DAYBREAK. Scribner, 1915. Romance of a niece of Ferdinand and Isabella with a youth in a voyage led by Columbus. 786

Paterson, Isabel. THE SINGING SEASON. Boni & Liveright, 1924. Spain in the period of Pedro the Cruel of Castile. 787

Richings, Emily. BROKEN AT THE FOUNTAIN. Heath Cranton, 1916. Royal romance and violence in fourteenth century Portugal. 788

Sabatini, Rafael. COLUMBUS, A ROMANCE. Houghton, 1942. A story of Columbus which emphasizes his personality and romance with Beatriz Enriquez. 789

Schoonover, Lawrence. THE QUEEN'S CROSS. Sloane, 1955. Isabella of Spain as a woman and as a queen. 790

Slaughter, Frank G. THE MAPMAKER. Doubleday, 1957. About an actual Venetian mapmaker and the days of Prince

Henry the Navigator. 791

Snaith, John Collis. FORTUNE. Moffatt, 1910. Adventures of an English knight in Spain and France. 792

II. A. 3. c. 2) Italy and Adjacent Islands

Anderson, Arthur J. HIS MAGNIFICENCE. Paul, 1913. Story of Lorenzo de Medici from 1478 to his death in 1492, supposedly told by a contemporary. 793

--------. THE ROMANCE OF FRA FILIPPO LIPPI. Paul, 1909. The romance of the gifted painter and a nun. 794

--------. THE ROMANCE OF SANDRO BOTTICELLI. Paul, 1912. Based on the life of artist Botticelli with some reference to the influence of reformer Savonarola. 795

Andrewes, A. G. IN THE DAYS OF LORENZO THE MAGNIFICENT. Foulis, 1924. Political activities of the powerful Lorenzo de Medici. 796

Andrews, Marian. FELICITA. by Christopher Hare, pseud. Stokes, 1909. A romance of Siena during the time of the Black Death, illustrated with photographs. 797

Bailey, H. C. SPRINGTIME. [same as: UNDER CASTLE WALLS] Appleton, 1906. A romance of Lombardy at the time of Boccaccio--a time of passion and superstition. 798

Borden, Lucille Papin. WHITE HAWTHORN. Macmillan, 1935. Romance in the days of Petrarch and Boccaccio. 799

Bowen, Marjorie, pseud. for Gabrielle Campbell Long. THE CARNIVAL OF FLORENCE. Dutton, 1915. Based on the rise and fall of Savonarola. 800

--------. THE SWORD DECIDES. McClure, 1908. Story of Joanna of Naples and her unfortunate husband, Andrea of Hungary. 801

--------. THE VIPER OF MILAN. Doubleday, 1906. Wars between the Count of Milan and the free towns of northern Italy. 802

Capes, Bernard. BEMBO; A TALE OF ITALY. [same as: A JAY OF ITALY] Dutton, 1906. About a zealous youth who preaches in the court of the cruel Galeazzo Sforza, Duke of Milan. 803

--------. THE LOVE STORY OF ST. BEL. Methuen, 1909. A story of Siena in 1374 with St. Catherine as the central figure. 804

Carter, Barbara Barclay. SHIP WITHOUT SAILS. Dutton, 1934. Based on the life of Dante during his composition of the DIVINE COMEDY. 805

Crawford, F. Marion. MARIETTA: A MAID OF VENICE. Macmillan, 1901. Romance of a glass blower's daughter with one of his workmen. 806

Cronquist, Mabel. BIANCA. Putnam, 1956. Political events during the heyday of the Medici family. 807

De Wohl, Louis. LAY SIEGE TO HEAVEN. Lippincott, 1961. Story of St. Catherine of Siena, one of the fourteenth century's outstanding personages. 808

Drummond, Hamilton. MAKER OF SAINTS. Dutton, 1920. A tale of the peasant-artist Fieravanti, sculptor of saints, at the time of Dante. 809

--------. SIR GALAHAD OF THE ARMY. Paul, 1913. Adventures of a soldier in the army of the French King Charles VIII during his Italian campaign. 810

Eliot, George, <u>pseud.</u> for Mary Ann Evans. ROMOLA. Unwin, 1863. Contrast between good and evil sides of Florentine life during the Renaissance. 811

Faust, Frederick. FIREBRAND. by George Challis, <u>pseud.</u> Harper, 1950. Excitement and adventure in Renaissance Italy. 812

Formont, Maxime. THE SHE-WOLF. Paul, 1913. Features exploits of the capable, ruthless Cesare Borgia. 813

Gallizier, Nathan. THE LEOPARD PRINCE. Page, 1920. A novel filled with political and romantic intrigues. 814

George, Arthur. THE HOUSE OF EYES. Gay & Hancock, 1913.

Intrigues focus on the Lady Valentine Visconti, daughter of the Duke of Milan. 815

Goodwin, Ernest. DUCHESS OF SIONA. Houghton, 1919. A tale of suitors for the hand of the lovely young duchess of an Italian principality. 816

Green, Anne. LADY IN THE MASK. Harper, 1942. A bright panorama of Renaissance Italy with a charming rogue as hero. 817

Grossi, Tommaso. MARCO VISCONTI. (tr.) Macmillan, 1881. Feuds between Guelfs and Ghibellines in Italy in the period of discord between Emperor Frederick II and the Pope. 818

Hewes, Agnes D. SWORDS ON THE SEA. Knopf, 1928. Venetian romance, trade, and warfare in the fourteenth century. 819

Hewlett, Maurice. BRAZENHEAD THE GREAT. Smith & Elder, 1911. About a professional killer in the service of the Duke of Milan. 820

--------. THE LOVE CHASE. Harper, 1905. Three men seek the hand of a lady-in-waiting to the Duchess of Milan. 821

James, G. P. R. LEONORA D'ORCO. Dutton, 1857. Has as background the French King Charles VIII's invasion of Italy and his marriage to Anne of Brittany. 822

James, Katherine. A CITY OF CONTRASTS. Chapman & Hall, 1913. A study of Renaissance Florence where art and culture flourished. 823

Kenny, Louise M. Stacpoole. AT THE COURT OF IL MORO. Long, 1912. Pictures Milanese society under Ludovico Sforza (Il Moro) and includes Leonardo da Vinci. 824

Knowles, Mabel Winifred. THE MASTER WIT. by May Wynne, pseud. Greening, 1911. The creative mind of Boccaccio is at work in a friend's behalf in this romance of Florence. 825

Knowles-Foster, Frances G. JEHANNE OF THE GOLDEN LIPS. Lane, 1910. The magnificent court of Joanna, Queen of Naples and Sicily, where Boccaccio was a visitor. 826

Ladd, Anna Coleman. HIERONYMUS RIDES. Macmillan, 1912. Episodes in the life of a knight and jester at the court of his half-brother, Maximilian. 827

Lance, Rupert. THE CROWNING HOUR. Blackwood, 1910. Romance and adventure in medieval Italy. 828

Livingston, Margaret Vere Farrington. FRA LIPPO LIPPI. by Margaret Vere Farrington. Putnam, 1890. Based on the life of this famous fifteenth century artist. 829

Long, William. SWORD OF IL GRANDE. by Will Creed, pseud. Little, 1948. Politics and swordplay in fifteenth century Florence. 830

Lytton, Edward Bulwer, 1st. baron. RIENZI, THE LAST OF THE TRIBUNES. Macmillan, 1835. The political situation in fourteenth century Italy which did not favor Rienzi's dream of a united Italy. 831

Maugham, H. Neville. RICHARD HAWKWOOD. Blackwood, 1906. Features Lorenzo de Medici and the notorious Pazzi Conspiracy (1477). 832

Muddock, J. E. Preston. THE SCARLET SEAL. Long, n.d. A complicated tale of the notorious Borgia family. 833

Osborne, Duffield. THE ANGELS OF MESSER ERCOLE. Stokes, 1907. Italy in the later fifteenth century at the time of the Umbrian painter Perugino. 834

Rolfe, Frederick W. DON TARQUINIO. Chatto, 1905. Customs, manners, and events in Rome at the time of the Borgias. 835

Sabatini, Rafael. BELLARION. Houghton, 1926. Fast-paced story of a young man's career in and about Milan. 836

--------. CHIVALRY. Houghton, 1935. Interplay of sword and poison in fifteenth century Italy. 837

Samuel, Maurice. WEB OF LUCIFER. Knopf, 1947. Tapestry of Renaissance Italy with Cesare Borgia as villain. 838

Scollard, Clinton. THE CLOISTERING OF URSULA. Page, 1902. Imaginary memoirs of the Marquis of Ucelli in central Italy. 839

--------. A MAN-AT-ARMS. Page, 1898. Gian Galeazzo Visconti, Duke of Milan, and his wars with free Italian cities. 840

Scudder, Vida O. THE DISCIPLE OF A SAINT. Dutton, 1907. This purported biography of her secretary tells of St. Catherine of Siena. 841

Shellabarger, Samuel. PRINCE OF FOXES. Little, 1947. How Cesare Borgia's power affected the lives of many people. 842

Shelley, Mary. VALPERGA. Whittaker, 1823. Romances of Castruccio Castracani, Duke of Lucca. 843

Stowe, Harriet Beecher. AGNES OF SORRENTO. Houghton, 1862. Romance of a pious girl and an irreligious man during the time of Savonarola's preaching. 844

Turnbull, Francese Hubbard. THE ROYAL PAWN OF VENICE. by Mrs. Lawrence Turnbull. Lippincott, 1911. The marriage of Caterina Cornaro of Venice and King James II of Cyprus. 845

Warde, Evelyn B. ELENA. Simpkin, 1910. Cesare Borgia and his sister Lucrezia figure in this tale of the time of Charles VIII's invasion. 846

Williams, Egerton R., Jr. RIDOLFO. McClurg, 1906. Based on the history of the notorious Baglioni family of Perugia. 847

II. A. 3. d. Eastern Europe (including the Byzantine Empire, the Balkans, and Russia), the Near East, and North Africa

Crawford, F. Marion. ARETHUSA. Macmillan, 1907.

Account of life in Constantinople in the late fourteenth century. 848

McCarthy, Justin Huntly. THE DRYAD. Harper, 1905. A fantasy of the romance of a Dryad whose love made her mortal. 849

Motta, Luigi. FLAMES ON THE BOSPHORUS. (tr.) Odhams Press, 1920. Struggle between Turks and Christians culminating in the Ottoman capture of Constantinople. 850

Neale, John Mason. THEODORA PHRANZA. S.P.C.K., 1857. Romance and war during the siege of Constantinople by the Turks. 851

Schoonover, Lawrence. THE GENTLE INFIDEL. Macmillan, 1950. The richness of medieval Turkey and the siege of Constantinople. 852

Waltari, Mika. THE DARK ANGEL. (tr.) Putnam, 1953. The fall of Constantinople with a vivid account of the siege. 853

II. A. 3. e. Overseas Exploration, Enterprise, and Expansion

Blasco-Ibañez, Vicente. UNKNOWN LANDS. (tr.) Dutton, 1929. Features details of shipboard life during Columbus' first voyage to America. 854

Cooper, James Fenimore. MERCEDES OF CASTILE. Lea & Blanchard, 1840. The loves of a companion of Columbus for a Spanish maiden and an Indian princess. 855

Forester, C. S. TO THE INDIES. Little, 1940. The third voyage made by Columbus to America and his career as viceroy of the Indies. 856

Jensen, Johannes Vilhelm. CHRISTOPHER COLUMBUS. (tr.) Knopf, 1924. Vivid re-creation of the famous voyage is the culmination of Mr. Jensen's trilogy of the wanderings of mankind. 857

Johnston, Mary. 1492. [En. title: ADMIRAL OF THE OCEAN SEA] Little, 1922. Christopher Columbus from his first voyage until his death, as seen by one of his sailors. 858

Lytle, Andrew Nelson. AT THE MOON'S INN. Bobbs, 1941. Based on the life and adventures of Hernando de Soto. 859

Street, James Howell. THE VELVET DOUBLET. Doubleday, 1953. From the perils of the Inquisition to the glory of discovery with Columbus. 860

Tourgée, Albion W. OUT OF THE SUNSET SEA. Merrill & Baker, 1893. Supposed story of an English sailor on Columbus' expedition of 1492. 861

II. B. Asia, Africa, and Oceania in the Middle Ages (400-1500)

1. Asia

a. India

Clifford, Hugh. THE DOWNFALL OF THE GODS. Dutton, 1911. Passionate romance combined with religious and political upheaval in the thirteenth century. 862

Potter, Margaret Horton. THE FLAME-GATHERERS. Macmillan, 1904. A story of India before and during the Mohammedan Conquest of 1250. 863

Steel, Flora Annie. KING ERRANT. Stokes, 1912. Based on the life of Baber, founder of the Mogul Empire in India. 864

II. B. 1. b. China

Byrne, Donn. MESSER MARCO POLO. Century, 1921. The travels and exploits of Marco Polo in the Far and Near East, and his love for the daughter of Kublai Khan. 865

Ko lien hua ying. FLOWER SHADOWS BEHIND THE CURTAIN. (tr.) Pantheon, 1959. Version of a classic Chinese novel concerning life in the turbulent fourteenth century. 866

Lane, Kenneth Westmacott. WINTER CHERRY. by Keith West, pseud. Macmillan, 1944. Witty romance of the Emperor's court in China in the eighth century. 867

Marshall, Edison. CARAVAN TO XANADU. Farrar, 1953. Marco Polo's travels to the exotic land of Kublai Khan. 868

Wingate, Lititia Beryl. A SERVANT OF THE MIGHTIEST. by Mrs. Alfred Wingate. Lockwood, 1927. A stirring account of Jenghiz Khan's conquests in China. 869

II. B. 1. c. Japan and Korea

Stacton, David. SEGAKI. Pantheon, 1959. Depicts Buddhist monasticism in fourteenth century Japan. 870

Yoshikawa, Eiji. HEIKÉ STORY. (tr.) Knopf, 1956. A warrior clan, the Heiké, in twelfth century Japan. 871

II. B. 1. d. Other Asiatic Peoples

Caldwell, Taylor (full name: Janet Taylor Caldwell). THE EARTH IS THE LORD'S. Scribner, 1941. The childhood and early career of Jenghiz Khan portraying his skill in uniting the Mongols. 872

Clou, John. CARAVAN TO CAMUL. Bobbs, 1954. The story of a soldier and philosopher in the service of Jenghiz Khan. 873

Kneen, Eleanor. LORDLESS. Putnam, 1936. The life of Tamerlane's youngest wife after his death. 874

II. B. 2. Africa

[No entries in this section. See sections II-A-1-d and II-A-2-d for novels pertaining to North Africa during this period.]

II. B. 3. Oceania

Michener, James A. HAWAII. Random, 1959. A panoramic novel of Hawaii and its successive inhabitants from eleven centuries ago to the present. 875

II. C. The Western Hemisphere in the Middle Ages (400-1500)

Allen, Dexter. JAGUAR AND THE GOLDEN STAG. Coward, 1954. Young Aztec prince of Mexico vies with his uncle to claim his throne. (followed by COIL OF THE SERPENT) 876

Bo'ld, Paul. THE TEMPLE OF DREAMS. Ham Smith, 1912. The civilization of old Peru--its society, religion, mores, and valor. 877

Haggard, H. Rider. THE VIRGIN OF THE SUN. Cassel, 1922. An Englishman's adventures in Peru in the late fourteenth century. 878

III. The Modern World (c. 1500-1900)

A. Europe, the Near East, and the Mediterranean in Modern Times

1. Sixteenth Century: Age of the Reformation and Later Renaissance

a. The British Isles

1) England, Wales, and Scotland

Ainsworth, W. Harrison. CARDINAL POLE. Routledge, 1863. The political, religious, and national controversy over Mary Tudor's marriage. 879

--------. THE CONSTABLE OF THE TOWER. Dutton, 1861. The story of Somerset, the Protector. 880

--------. THE TOWER OF LONDON. Dutton, 1840. The conflicting elements in the struggle for the crown from Henry VIII's death until Lady Jane Grey's execution. 881

--------. WINDSOR CASTLE. Dutton, 1843. Much is told about the castle itself, chiefly during the time of Henry VIII's marriage to Anne Boleyn. 882

Albert, Edward. KIRK O' FIELD. Hodder, 1924. A novel of Scotland and some of the tragic events surrounding Mary Queen of Scots. 883

Anderson, Robert Gordon. THE TAVERN ROGUE. Farrar & Rinehart, 1934. Adventures in London of an outlaw whose life depended on his writing a play Elizabeth liked. 884

Bailey, H. C. BONAVENTURE. Methuen, 1927. Relations between England and Spain in the years just before the attack of the Armada. 885

--------. THE LONELY QUEEN. Methuen, 1911. The people and influences which molded Elizabeth's character in her formative years. 886

--------. THE MASTER OF GRAY. Longmans, 1903. Episodes during the captivity of Mary Queen of Scots, with a deserter of her cause as "hero." 887

Baring-Gould, S. GUAVAS, THE TINNER. Methuen, 1897. Events centering around a tin mine in Dartmoor and a Cornish "foreigner." 888

Barker, Shirley. LIZA BOWE. Random, 1956. Story of a young country maid in London in the days of "Good Queen Bess." 889

Barnes, Margaret Campbell. BRIEF GAUDY HOUR. Macrae Smith, 1949. Life-like picture of Anne Boleyn from the age of eighteen to her trial for her life. 890

--------. KING'S FOOL. Macrae Smith, 1959. The shrewd observations of Henry VIII's jester present a behind-the-scenes view of the court. 891

--------. MY LADY OF CLEVES. Macrae Smith, 1946. Shows the character of Anne of Cleves, fourth wife of Henry VIII. 892

Barrington, Michael. DAVID ARNOT. Crosby Lockwood, 1927. A medical student becomes involved with superstitious beliefs currently popular in Scotland. 893

Beahn, John E. A MAN BORN AGAIN. Bruce, 1954. Fictional autobiography of St. Thomas More. 894

Beck, Lily Adams. ANNE BOLEYN. by E. Barrington, pseud. Doubleday, 1932. Includes some of Henry's letters to the clever woman who, for a time, fascinated him. 895

--------. DUEL OF THE QUEENS. by E. Barrington, pseud. Doubleday, 1930. Competition between Mary Queen of Scots and Elizabeth of England. 896

Beebe, Elswyth Thane. THE TUDOR WENCH. by Elswyth Thane. Harcourt, 1932. A richly colored picture of Elizabeth to the time of her coronation. 897

Benson, Robert Hugh. BY WHAT AUTHORITY? Pitman, 1904. Conflict between conscience and loyalty to the crown over religious issues; hardships of English Catholics. 898

--------. COME RACK! COME ROPE! Hutchinson, 1912. Daring exploits of hunted priests who defied a hostile government to bring religion to Elizabethan England. 899

--------. THE KING'S ACHIEVEMENT. Pitman, 1905. Conflict between brothers over opposing loyalties to Church and Crown under Henry VIII. 900

--------. THE QUEEN'S TRAGEDY. Pitman, 1906. Reports and attempts to explain the harsh methods Mary employed to bring religious unity to England. 901

Beresford-Howe, Constance. MY LADY GREENSLEEVES. Ballantine, 1955. Trials of an aristocratic lady married to a man of the middle class. 902

Borden, Lucille Papin. STARFORTH. Macmillan, 1937. The Starforth family in Tudor England. 903

Boyce, John. THE SPAE-WIFE. by Paul Peppergrass, esq., pseud. Murphy, 1853. Unusual story of a remarkable Scots lady endowed with second sight and involved in royal circles. 904

Brady, Charles Andrew. STAGE OF FOOLS. Dutton, 1953. About Sir Thomas More, called a fool for placing devotion to God before loyalty to Henry VIII. 905

Brookfield, Frances Mary. A FRIAR OBSERVANT. Herder, 1909. A friar observes the closing of the English monasteries and meets Luther. 906

--------. MY LORD OF ESSEX. Pitman, 1907. The expedition of the Earl of Essex to Cadiz against the Spanish fleet. 907

Brophy, John. GENTLEMAN OF STRATFORD. Harper, 1940. A story of Shakespeare with emphasis on the man rather than on his plays. 908

Buchan, John. THE BLANKET OF THE DARK. Houghton, 1931. An attempt to displace Henry VIII from the throne of England. 909

Byrd, Elizabeth. IMMORTAL QUEEN. Ballantine, 1956. Mary Stuart's childhood in France, reign in Scotland, and eventual imprisonment in England. 910

Capes, Bernard. WHERE ENGLAND SETS HER FEET. Collins, 1918. Land and sea adventures of a young Englishman of mysterious birth. 911

Catherine, Sister Mary. STORM OUT OF CORNWALL. by S. M. C., pseud. Kenedy, 1959. A tale of the Prayer-book Rebellion, when Cornishmen fought for freedom of religion. 912

Champion de Crespigny, Rose. THE MISCHIEF OF A GLOVE. by Mrs. Philip Champion de Crespigny. Unwin, 1903. A romance in England in mid-century. 913

Chidsey, Donald Barr. CAPTAIN BASHFUL. Crown, 1955. Efforts of the hero to win his lady love and recover his lands. 914

--------. RELUCTANT CAVALIER. Crown, 1960. A man of good birth becomes an unwilling courier in secret diplomatic negotiations; voyages of Sir Francis Drake. 915

Comstock, Harriet T. THE QUEEN'S HOSTAGE. Little, 1906. Elizabeth's court with emphasis on the theater of the day--Shakespeare, Jonson, the Globe Theater. 916

Cronyn, George W. MERMAID TAVERN. Knight, 1937. Life and adventures of Christopher Marlowe in England during Mary Stuart's time. 917

Cullen, W. R. THE UNWEDDED BRIDE. Long, 1910. Religious dissent in Scotland under Mary Queen of Scots. 918

Curtis, Felicia. UNDER THE ROSE. Sands, 1912. Romance of Elizabethan England features Richard Topcliffe, persecutor of Roman Catholics. 919

Dakers, Elaine. PARCEL OF ROGUES. by Jane Lane, pseud. Rinehart, 1948. A tale of those who opposed Mary Stuart in her reign as Queen of Scots. 920

Delves-Broughton, Josephine. THE HEART OF A QUEEN. [En. title: CROWN IMPERIAL] McGraw, 1949. The loves of Elizabeth--the foremost being her love for England. 921

Eckerson, Olive. MY LORD ESSEX. Holt, 1955. Excellent character portrayal in this romance of Elizabeth and Essex. 922

Ellis, Amanda Mae. ELIZABETH, THE WOMAN. Dutton, 1951. Portrait of Elizabeth against the pageantry, extravagance, and cruelty of Tudor England. 923

Farnol, Jeffery. A JADE OF DESTINY. Little, 1931. Sentimental romance of England during Elizabeth's reign. 924

Filon, Augustin. RENÉGAT. Armand Colin (France), 1894. England's growth in sea power with her defeat of the Spanish Armada. 925

Foote, Dorothy Norris. THE CONSTANT STAR. Scribner, 1959. The story of Frances Walsingham and her marriages, first to Sir Philip Sidney, then to the Earl of Essex. 926

Ford, Ford Madox (name originally Ford Madox Hueffer). THE FIFTH QUEEN AND HOW SHE CAME TO COURT. Rivers, 1906. Henry VIII's reception of Catherine Howard after his disappointing marriage to Anne of Cleves. (followed by PRIVY SEAL) 927

--------. THE FIFTH QUEEN CROWNED. Nash, 1908. Catherine Howard's reign as queen of Henry VIII. 928

--------. PRIVY SEAL. Rivers, 1907. The downfall of Cromwell after he had displeased Henry VIII. (followed by THE FIFTH QUEEN CROWNED) 929

Forster, R. H. THE ARROW OF THE NORTH. Long, 1906. The Battle of Flodden Field is the high point of this story of war between England and Scotland. 930

--------. THE LAST FORAY. Long, 1903. Adventures of one of Cardinal Wolsey's men. 931

--------. MIDSUMMER MORN. Long, 1911. Romance and cattle stealing along the border. 932

Fulton, D. Kerr. THE WITCH'S SWORD. Arnold, 1908. The Battle of Flodden Field and the period following, with a man mistaken for King James IV. 933

Garnier, Russell M. THE WHITE QUEEN. Harper, 1899. The quest for happiness of Mary Tudor, Henry VIII's sister, who contracted a state marriage. 934

Gibbon, Charles. THE BRAES OF YARROW. Harper, 1881. The Regent of Scotland, Queen Margaret Tudor, and the youthful King, James V, after the Battle of Flodden Field. 935

Goudge, Elizabeth. TOWERS IN THE MIST. Coward, 1938. A story of Oxford University with a visit from Queen Elizabeth as a high point. 936

Grant, James. BOTHWELL. Dutton, 1851. The political career of Bothwell and his disastrous romance with Mary Queen of Scots. 937

Gregory, Charles. HIS SOVEREIGN LADY. Melrose, 1919. Drake's search for fame and fortune on the high seas. 938

Gull, C. Ranger. HOUSE OF TORMENT. Greening, 1910. Persecutions in England and Spain in the time of Mary Tudor and Philip II. 939

Hackett, Francis. QUEEN ANNE BOLEYN. Doubleday, 1939. The beautiful, scheming woman who became Henry VIII's second queen. 940

Haggard, H. Rider. THE LADY OF BLOSSHOLME. Hodder, 1909. Time of the closing of the monasteries and the Pilgrimage of Grace in Henry VIII's reign. 941

Hamilton, Ernest. MARY HAMILTON. Methuen, 1901. A romance of Mary Hamilton, lady-in-waiting to Mary Queen of Scots. 942

--------. THE OUTLAWS OF THE MARCHES. Dodd, 1897. Adventures of Liddesdale and the country along the border. 943

Hancock, Sardius. TONFORD MANOR. Unwin, 1903. A

chivalric story of England early in Henry VIII's reign before his break with Rome. 944

Harwood, Alice. THE LILY AND THE LEOPARDS. [En. title: SHE HAD TO BE QUEEN] Bobbs, 1949. The sweet and innocent Lady Jane Grey was sacrificed for her family's ambition for power. 945

--------. SEATS OF THE MIGHTY. Bobbs, 1956. The loyalty of James Stuart, illegitimate half-brother of Mary Queen of Scots. 946

Henham, Ernest George. THE CUSTOM OF THE MANOR. by John Trevena, <u>pseud.</u> Mills & Boon, 1924. England's reaction to Thomas Cromwell's dissolution of the monasteries. 947

Hewlett, Maurice. THE QUEEN'S QUAIR. Macmillan, 1904. A fine romance about the tense period in Mary Queen of Scot's life ending with Darnley's death. 948

Hibbert, Eleanor. THE KING'S PLEASURE. by Jean Plaidy, <u>pseud.</u> Appleton, 1949. Anne Boleyn's swift rise to power and her sudden downfall. 949

Hill, Pamela. KING'S VIXEN. Putnam, 1954. Romance and adventure in the Scotland of James IV. 950

Innes, J. W. Brodie. FOR THE SOUL OF A WITCH. Rebman, 1910. Witchcraft and superstition, based on contemporary documents. 951

Ireland, James. MASTER SECRETARY. Hodder & Stoughton, 1826. The chief character is the politically crafty secretary Sir William Cecil. 952

Irwin, Margaret. ELIZABETH AND THE PRINCE OF SPAIN. Harcourt, 1953. Elizabeth during the precarious period of the marriage of Mary Tudor and Philip II, with her own safety subject to Mary's whims. 953

--------. ELIZABETH, CAPTIVE PRINCESS. Harcourt, 1948. The tense, fateful time from Edward VI's death to the marriage of Queen Mary and Philip II of Spain. (followed by ELIZABETH AND THE PRINCE OF SPAIN) 954

--------. THE GAY GALLIARD. Harcourt, 1942. Romance of Mary Queen of Scots and James Hepburn, Earl of Bothwell. 955

--------. YOUNG BESS. Harcourt, 1944. Elizabeth Tudor in the uncertain days from her twelfth year to the death of her brother, Edward VI. (followed by ELIZABETH, CAPTIVE PRINCESS) 956

James, G. P. R. DARNLEY. Dutton, 1830. Interesting account of the relations between England and France in 1520. 957

James, Miss W. M. COURT CARDS. by Austin Clare, pseud. Unwin, 1904. A story of sheep stealing which involves the court circles of England and Scotland. 958

Johnston, Mary. SILVER CROSS. Little, 1922. The rivalry for worldly glory between two abbeys. 959

Jones, E. Brandram. (1) IN BURLEIGH'S DAYS. Long, 1916. (2) THE SECOND CECIL. Long, 1917. Two historical novels of the Elizabethan period with such literary and political figures as Shakespeare, Bacon, Essex, and Jonson. 960

Jones, Gwyn. GARLAND OF BAYS. Macmillan, 1938. A novel about Robert Greene, poet and playwright, with a realistic Elizabethan background. 961

Kaye-Smith, Sheila. SUPERSTITION CORNER. Harper, 1934. Elizabeth's persecution of Catholics is intensified by the threat of the Armada. 962

Kenyon, Frank Wilson. MARY OF SCOTLAND. Crowell, 1957. The exciting times of Mary Queen of Scots. 963

--------. SHADOW IN THE SUN. Crowell, 1958. Queen Elizabeth loved three men but could not marry any of them. 964

Knight, Charles Brunton. MY LORD CARDINAL. Long, 1924. Cardinal Wolsey in the period of his waning political power. 965

Knipe, John. THE HOUR BEFORE THE DAWN. Lane, 1921.

The tense atmosphere in Scotland about the time of James V's death. 966

--------. THE WATCH-DOG OF THE CROWN. Lane, 1920. A romance of the Tower of London about Sir Henry Talbot and the lovely prisoner Frances Grey in the reign of Edward VI. 967

Knowles, Mabel Winifred. A KING'S MASQUERADE. by May Wynne, pseud. Greening, 1910. Scotland's James V as a young man in the disguise which almost resulted in his death. 968

Lee, Albert. THE GENTLEMAN PENSIONER. Appleton, 1900. Conspiracy to free Mary Queen of Scots from imprisonment and place her on the throne of England. 969

Lenanton, Carola Oman. THE ROAD ROYAL. by Carola Oman. Fisher Unwin, 1924. Mary Queen of Scots' childhood marriage to the French Dauphin and subsequent events in Scotland. 970

Lethbridge, Olive and John de Stourton. THE KING'S MASTER. Paul, 1912. The chief characters are Thomas Cromwell and Queen Anne Boleyn. 971

Letton, Jennette and Francis. ROBSART AFFAIR. Harper, 1956. Tale of the early love of Queen Elizabeth and Robert Dudley--and of Amy Dudley's mysterious death. 972

Lindsay, Philip. HERE COMES THE KING. Little, 1933. The marriage of Henry VIII and Catherine Howard, his fifth wife. 973

Lofts, Norah. HERE WAS A MAN. Knopf, 1936. Romantic novel based on the career of Sir Walter Raleigh. 974

Lusk, Lewis. SUSSEX IRON. Ouseley, 1913. Life in a Sussex village and the defeat of the Spanish Armada. 975

McCarthy, Justin Huntly. HENRY ELIZABETH. Lane, 1920. Elizabethan romance concerning a country boy turned courtier; Dr. Dee is mentioned. 976

McChesney, Dora Greenwell. THE WOUNDS OF A FRIEND. Smith & Elder, 1908. A romance of Raleigh's part in colonizing the New World. 977

MacFarlane, James. THE RED FOX. Lang, 1912. "A story of the Clan Macfarlan." 978

Major, Charles. DOROTHY VERNON OF HADDON HALL. Macmillan, 1902. Based on the legendary romance of Dorothy Vernon. 979

--------. WHEN KNIGHTHOOD WAS IN FLOWER. by Edwin Caskoden, pseud. Bowen-Merrill, 1898. Romance of Mary Tudor, Henry VIII's sister, and Charles Brandon, Duke of Suffolk. 980

Manning, Anne. THE HOUSEHOLD OF SIR THOMAS MORE. Dutton, 1851. Written as the diary of More's daughter Margaret, this pictures the saint as a family man. 981

Mason, A. E. W. FIRE OVER ENGLAND. Doubleday, 1936. England in the uncertain days of the Spanish Armada threat. 982

Mason, Van Wyck. GOLDEN ADMIRAL. Doubleday, 1953. Sir Francis Drake and the Spanish Armada. 983

Mathew, Frank. DEFENDER OF THE FAITH. Lane, 1899. Offers fine characterizations of many people prominent in Henry VIII's reign, including several of his wives. 984

--------. ONE QUEEN TRIUMPHANT. Lane, 1899. The Babington Plot and the execution of Mary Queen of Scots to end her threat to Elizabeth's throne. 985

--------. THE ROYAL SISTERS. Long, 1901. The wary, uneasy relationship between Mary and Elizabeth Tudor. 986

Meadows, Denis. TUDOR UNDERGROUND. Devin-Adair, 1950. Jesuit efforts to keep Catholicism alive although outlawed by the Oath of Supremacy. 987

Michelson, Miriam. PETTICOAT KING. McBride, 1929. Romance in Queen Elizabeth's court. 988

Moubray, Douglas. FAIR HELEN OF KIRKCONNELL LEA. Hayes, 1920. A romance of Scotland in 1565. 989

Muddock, J. E. Preston. FAIR ROSALIND. Long, 1902. London in the stormy reign of Henry VIII. 990

--------. IN THE KING'S FAVOUR. Digby & Long, 1899. A romance of Flodden Field and the weak Scottish King James IV. 991

Mundt, Klara. HENRY VIII AND HIS COURT. (tr.) by Louisa Mühlbach, pseud. Appleton, 1867. The conspiracies and corruption of the English court; Catherine Parr, queen-consort. 992

Nicolls, William Jasper. THE DAUGHTERS OF SUFFOLK. Lippincott, 1910. Lady Jane and Lady Catherine Grey are figures in the battle for royal succession. 993

Oliphant, Margaret O. MAGDALEN HEPBURN. Munro, 1885. Scotland during Mary Stuart's reign, with John Knox as a character. 994

Parry, Edward Abbott. ENGLAND'S ELIZABETH. Smith & Elder, 1904. The dangerous course Elizabeth followed to become and remain Queen. 995

Paterson, Isabel. THE FOURTH QUEEN. Boni & Liveright, 1926. The love of a waiting maid and Fighting Jack Montagu in Elizabeth's court. 996

Pemberton, Max. I CROWN THEE KING. Methuen, 1902. Rebellious elements in England's troubled Tudor period. 997

Power, Edith Mary. A KNIGHT OF GOD. Sands, 1909. The plight of persecuted Catholics in Elizabethan England. 998

Powers, Anne. NO WALL SO HIGH. Bobbs, 1949. Treachery, duels, and the attack of the Spanish Armada. 999

Preedy, George, pseud. for Gabrielle Campbell Long. QUEEN'S CAPRICE. King, 1934. A picture of Mary Queen of Scots at the time of her first meeting with

Darnley. 1000

Prescott, Hilda Frances Margaret. THE MAN ON A DONKEY. Macmillan, 1952. Comprehensive account of English life including the Pilgrimage of Grace during Henry VIII's eventful reign. 1001

Rees, Helen Christina Easson. THE LION AND THE ROSE. by Jane Oliver, pseud. Putnam, 1959. Sympathetic telling of the romance of Mary Queen of Scots and Lord Darnley. 1002

--------. MINE IS THE KINGDOM. by Jane Oliver, pseud. Lippincott, 1937. The life of James I of England (James VI of Scotland), son of Mary Stuart. 1003

Richings, Emily. SIR WALTER'S WIFE. Drane, 1900. Sir Walter Raleigh's romance in the face of royal disapproval. 1004

Robertson, William. THE DULE TREE OF CASSILLIS. Menzies (Scotland), 1904. Fighting over property during the unrest in mid-sixteenth century Scotland. 1005

--------. THE LORDS OF CUNINGHAME. Gardner, 1891. Family feuds in Scotland as related in original documents. 1006

Robinson, Emma. WESTMINSTER ABBEY. Routledge, 1854. An account of London during the religious and moral upheavals of Henry VIII's reign. 1007

Salmon, Geraldine Gordon. THE LOST DUCHESS. by J. C. Sarasin, pseud. Doran, 1927. Romance based on the story of Lady Arabella Stuart, wife of William Seymour. 1008

Saunders, John. A NOBLE WIFE. Jarrold & Sons, 1895. Story of the wife of Archbishop Cranmer. 1009

Scott, Sir Walter. THE ABBOT. Bazin & Ellsworth, 1831. Good picture of Mary Queen of Scots and her flight into England. 1010

--------. KENILWORTH. Bazin & Ellsworth, 1831. Robert Dudley's lavish entertainment for Queen Elizabeth at his home, Kenilworth. 1011

--------. THE MONASTERY. Bazin & Ellsworth, 1830. Set in the border country during the Reformation. (followed by THE ABBOT) 1012

Sheppard, Alfred Tresidder. BRAVE EARTH. Doran, 1925. Confusion caused by the Reformation is reflected in this romance of Henry VIII's reign. 1013

Siegel, Benjamin. A KIND OF JUSTICE. Harcourt, 1960. A Spanish Jew encounters religious persecution in Elizabethan England. 1014

Snaith, John Collis. ANNE FEVERSHAM. [En. title: THE GREAT AGE] Appleton, 1914. Romance of Elizabethan England with Shakespeare appearing prominently. 1015

Stephens, Eve. ALL THE QUEEN'S MEN. [En. title: ELIZABETH] by Evelyn Anthony, pseud. Crowell, 1960. The story involves Queen Elizabeth, Robert Dudley, and Mary Queen of Scots. 1016

--------. ANNE BOLEYN. by Evelyn Anthony, pseud. Crowell, 1957. Convincing portrait of the clever woman who held Henry VIII for ten years. 1017

Stephens, Robert Neilson. CAPTAIN RAVENSHAW. Page, 1901. A romance of London under Elizabeth. 1018

--------. A GENTLEMAN PLAYER. Page, 1899. A comedian in the Lord Chamberlain's company at the time of Shakespeare. 1019

Strode-Jackson, Myrtle B. S. TANSY TANIARD. Scribner, 1945. Romance of Tansy Taniard, whose beautiful red hair made a wig for Queen Elizabeth. 1020

Sutcliff, Rosemary. LADY IN WAITING. Coward, 1957. About Sir Walter Raleigh's wife, who spent many years as a lady-in-waiting. 1021

Sutcliffe, Halliwell. THE CRIMSON FIELD. Ward & Lock, 1916. Relations between England and Scotland ending with the Battle of Flodden Field. 1022

--------. PAM THE FIDDLER. Laurie, 1910. An adventure-romance during the period of Mary Queen of Scots' imprisonment. 1023

Swallow, Henry J. LOVE WHILE YE MAY. Jarrold & Sons, 1907. Based mainly on the Rising of the North in 1569. 1024

Taylor, Mary Imlay. THE HOUSE OF THE WIZARD. McClurg, 1899. The first two marriages of Henry VIII. 1025

Travers, Hettie. A STORMY PASSAGE. Digby & Long, 1913. Queen Catherine Howard in the two years before Henry VIII caused her execution. 1026

Vaughan, Owen. THE SHROUDED FACE. by Owen Rhoscomyl, pseud. Pearson, 1898. The tribal system in effect in turbulent Wales. 1027

Walford, Lucy Bethia. THE BLACK FAMILIARS. Longmans, 1903. Religious intrigue during the early part of Elizabeth's reign. 1028

Walpole, Hugh. THE BRIGHT PAVILIONS. Doubleday, 1940. A romance of the Herries family in Elizabethan England. 1029

Ward, Josephine. TUDOR SUNSET. Longmans, 1932. Persecution of Catholics toward the close of Elizabeth's reign; the Queen's maid, secretly a Catholic. 1030

Westcott, Jan. THE HEPBURN. Crown, 1950. Border war and intrigue in Scotland during the reign of James IV. 1031

--------. THE QUEEN'S GRACE. Crown, 1959. Sweet, sensible Catherine Parr, who had four marriages, including one with Henry VIII. 1032

--------. WALSINGHAM WOMAN. Crown, 1953. Frances Walsingham, whose second husband was Queen Elizabeth's favorite, the Earl of Essex. 1033

Wheelwright, Jere Hungerford. THE STRONG ROOM. Scribner, 1948. Adventures of a young noble twice committed to the Tower of London. 1034

White, Beatrice. ROYAL NONESUCH. Macmillan, 1933. A tapestry of the Tudor court--Henry VIII, his sister Mary, and her husband. 1035

White, Leslie Turner. MAGNUS THE MAGNIFICENT. Crown, 1950. Quest of a pirate for love, fame, and riches. 1036

White, Olive B. THE KING'S GOOD SERVANT. Macmillan, 1936. The last years of Sir Thomas More, who defied his king, Henry VIII, rather than deny his God. 1037

--------. LATE HARVEST. Macmillan, 1940. The Catholic side of the many changes in Elizabeth's time. 1038

Whyte-Melville, George John. THE QUEEN'S MARIES. Longmans, 1864. The romances of four ladies-in-waiting to Mary Queen of Scots. 1039

Wilby, Noel Macdonald. MERRY ETERNITY. Benziger, 1934. Fictional account of the household of Sir Thomas More. 1040

Williams, Jay. THE WITCHES. Random, 1957. Spy investigates a rumored conspiracy of witches against James VI. 1041

Wilson, Mary J. THE KNIGHT OF THE NEEDLE ROCK AND HIS DAYS. Stock, 1905. Written as a family journal of English life. 1042

III. A. 1. a. 2) Ireland

Craig, R. Manifold. THE WEIRD OF "THE SILKEN THOMAS." Moran (Aberdeen), 1900. The customs and traditions of Ireland in the 1530s and the revolt of Lord Thomas Fitzgerald. 1043

Knowles, Mabel Winifred. FOR CHURCH AND CHIEFTAIN. by May Wynne, pseud. Mills & Boon, 1909. Thrilling romance of the Geraldine rebellion in Ireland. 1044

Lawless, Emily. MAELCHO. Appleton, 1894. A sober account of the hard conditions of the Irish under English oppression. 1045

--------. WITH ESSEX IN IRELAND. Lovell, 1890. The expedition led by Essex to put down the Irish Rebellion and win prestige. 1046

Linington, Elizabeth. THE PROUD MAN. Viking, 1955. Shane O'Neill, prince of Ulster, attempts to oust the English. 1047

Machray, Robert. GRACE O'MALLEY, PRINCESS AND PIRATE Stokes, 1898. About a woman whose courage inspired rebellion against English cruelty and oppression. 1048

O'Brien, William. A QUEEN OF MEN. Unwin, 1898. The daring Grace O'Malley, who led her fierce clan in rebellion against English oppression. 1049

O'Byrne, Miss M. L. THE PALE AND THE SEPTS. Gill (Dublin), 1876. A story of rebellious Ireland under English domination in mid-century. 1050

O'Grady, Standish. THE FLIGHT OF THE EAGLE. Sealy & Bryers (Dublin), 1889. Oppression in Ireland in Elizabeth's reign. 1051

Rhys, Grace. THE CHARMING OF ESTERCEL. Dutton, 1913. Northern Ireland during the Irish Rebellion and the English attempt, led by Essex, to quell it. 1052

Sadlier, Mary Anne. MacCARTHY MORE! by Mrs. James Sadlier. Kenedy, 1868. Struggle of an Irish family to retain its religion and possessions during persecution. 1053

Taunton, M. THE LAST OF THE CATHOLIC O'MALLEYS. Kenedy, 1870. Exploits of courageous Grace O'Malley and her resistance to the English. 1054

Walsh, Maurice. BLACKCOCK'S FEATHER. Stokes, 1932. A Scotch-Irish romance during the struggle against Queen Elizabeth. 1055

III. A. 1. b. Western and Central Europe

1) France

Ainsworth, W. Harrison. CRICHTON. [same as: THE

ADMIRABLE CRICHTON] Routledge, 1873. The adventurer James Crichton, son of the Scottish Lord Advocate, at Paris. 1056

Balzac, Honoré de. ABOUT CATHERINE DE MĒDICI. (tr.) Macmillan, 1897. Centers chiefly on Catherine and her relations with other court personages. 1057

Bedford-Jones, Henry. KING'S PARDON. Covici, 1933. A swift-moving adventure story full of swordplay and bloodshed. 1058

Bloundelle-Burton, John. THE KING'S MIGNON. Everett, 1909. Features the assassination of the Duke of Guise and following events. 1059

--------. UNDER THE SALAMANDER. Everett, 1911. Intrigue and romance during France's struggle with Spain. 1060

Bolton, Muriel Roy. THE GOLDEN PORCUPINE. Doubleday, 1947. Story of the Duc d'Orleans, who became Louis XII of France. 1061

Champion de Crespigny, Rose. THE GREY DOMINO. by Mrs. Philip Champion de Crespigny. Nash, 1906. Romance of southern France with scenes at the court of Henry IV. 1062

Clark, Janet M. THE BOURGEOIS QUEEN OF PARIS. Greening, 1910. Life in Paris during the reign of Henry II is marked by dissension between Catholics and Protestants. 1063

Conyers, Dorothea. FOR HENRI AND NAVARRE. Hutchinson, 1911. A romance beginning with the Massacre of St. Bartholomew's Day and featuring Henry of Navarre. 1064

Crockett, Samuel R. THE WHITE PLUMES OF NAVARRE. [same as: THE WHITE PLUME] Dodd, 1906. Henry of Navarre is a central figure in this tale of the French Religious Wars and the Spanish Inquisition. 1065

Curties, Henry. RENÉE. Richards, 1908. A broken state-marriage contract between Austria and France, the battle of Marignano, and the meeting on the Field of the Cloth of Gold. 1066

De La Fayette, Madame. THE PRINCESS OF CLEVES. (tr.) Routledge, 1925. Psychological novel dealing with the French court. 1067

Drummond, Hamilton. THE CUCKOO. White, 1906. A gentle mother and a rough peasant father vie for the control of their son. 1068

--------. (1) FOR THE RELIGION. Smith & Elder, 1898. (2) A MAN OF HIS AGE (sequel). Harper, 1900. Novels of the French Wars of Religion, Coligny's plan to colonize Florida, and the conflicts between Catholics and Huguenots. 1069

--------. A KING'S PAWN. Doubleday, Page, 1901. Adventures of a follower of Henry of Navarre in France and Spain. 1070

--------. LITTLE MADAME CLAUDE. Paul, 1914. The daughter of Anne of Brittany, the Queen of Louis XII. 1071

Dumas, Alexandre. ASCANIO. (tr.) Munro, 1878. Visit of Benvenuto Cellini to the court of Francis I, mecca of artists and authors. 1072

--------. THE PAGE OF THE DUKE OF SAVOY. (tr.) Munro, 1878. Portrays a large number of historic people and events including Emmanuel Philibert, Henry II, Catherine de Medici, and the conflicts at St. Quentin and Calais. 1073

--------. THE TWO DIANAS. (tr.) Munro, 1879. Wars of France during the reigns of Francis I, Henry II, and Francis II; romances of Diana of Poitiers and her daughter, Diana. (followed by THE PAGE OF THE DUKE OF SAVOY) 1074

--------. THE VALOIS CYCLE: (1) MARGUERITE DE VALOIS. (tr.) Routledge, 1857. (2) CHICOT, THE JESTER (sequel). (tr.) [same as: LA DAME DE

MONSOREAU] Munro, 1880. (3) THE FORTY-FIVE (sequel). (tr.) [same as: THE FORTY-FIVE GUARDSMEN] Little, 1889. A series of novels about the French court including Marguerite de Valois, Charles IX, Henry III, Catherine de Medici, Henry of Navarre, the jester Chicot, and Henry III's bodyguard, the Forty-five. 1075

Gobineau, Joseph Arthur, comte de. THE LUCKY PRISONER. (tr.) Doubleday, Page, 1926. A romance having the antagonism between Catholics and Huguenots as background. 1076

Gosse, Edmund. THE SECRET OF NARCISSE. Tait, 1892. Manners, superstitions, and entertainments in court circles. 1077

Hartley, Percy J. THE HAND OF DIANE. Unwin, 1911. A romance of the court of Henry II and of his mistress and her younger sister. 1078

Hibbert, Eleanor. MADAME SERPENT. by Jean Plaidy, pseud. Appleton, 1951. Court life of the merchant's daughter, Catherine de Medici, consort of Henry II. 1079

--------. QUEEN JEZEBEL. by Jean Plaidy, pseud. Appleton, 1953. Catherine de Medici, widow of Henry II, during the Religious Wars in France. 1080

Hope, Jessie. A CARDINAL AND HIS CONSCIENCE. by Graham Hope, pseud. Smith & Elder, 1901. Rivalry between Catholics and Huguenots, with the Cardinal of Lorraine as central figure. 1081

--------. THE GAGE OF RED AND WHITE. by Graham Hope, pseud. Smith & Elder, 1904. The marriage of Jeanne d'Albret and Antoine de Bourbon, parents of Henry of Navarre. 1082

Houston, June Dimmitt. THE FAITH AND THE FLAME. Sloane, 1958. Romance of a Catholic lady-in-waiting to Catherine de Medici with a Huguenot captain. 1083

Isham, Frederic S. UNDER THE ROSE. Bobbs, 1904. An adventure-romance during the reign of Francis I. 1084

James, G. P. R. THE BRIGAND. Dutton, 1841. About an adventurer, with Diane de Poitiers and Henry II of France prominent. 1085

--------. HENRY OF GUISE. Dutton, 1839. The War of the Three Henrys, depicting Henry of Navarre, King Henry III, and Henry Duke of Guise. 1086

--------. THE MAN-AT-ARMS. Dutton, 1840. Religious Wars and the Massacre of St. Bartholomew's Day. 1087

--------. ONE IN A THOUSAND. Harper, 1835. A vivid account of Henry IV's victory in the Battle of Ivry in 1590. 1088

--------. ROSE D'ALBRET. Dutton, 1844. Intrigue and romance in France at the time of the Battle of Ivry. 1089

Johns, Cecil Starr. WITH GOLD AND STEEL. Lane, 1917. Royal-sponsored treasure hunt for a wrecked Spanish galleon. 1090

Johnson, William Henry. (1) THE KING'S HENCHMAN. Little, 1898. (2) UNDER THE SPELL OF THE FLEUR-DE-LIS (sequel). Little, 1899. These stories of France during the Religious Wars depict Henry IV as a romantic hero. 1091

Knowles, Mabel Winifred. HENRY OF NAVARRE. by May Wynne, pseud. Putnam, 1904. A romance of August, 1572, during the Wars of Religion. 1092

--------. THE SILENT CAPTAIN. by May Wynne, pseud. Paul, 1914. Struggle between Catholics and Huguenots, culminating in the Conspiracy of Amboise. 1093

--------. A TRAP FOR NAVARRE. by May Wynne, pseud. Holden, 1922. Intrigue in Henry of Navarre's court. 1094

Levett-Yeats, Sidney. THE CHEVALIER D'AURIAC. Longmans, 1897. The court of Henry of Navarre--romance, intrigue, and petty jealousies. 1095

--------. ORRAIN. Longmans, 1904. The rivalry between

Catherine de Medici, queen of Henry II, and Diane de Poitiers, his mistress. 1096

--------. THE TRAITOR'S WAY. Stokes, 1901. The Conspiracy of Amboise--a scheme aimed at King Francis II. 1097

Lewis, Ada Cook. THE LONGEST NIGHT. Rinehart, 1958. A spirited account of the bloody Massacre of St. Bartholomew's Day. 1098

Lewis, Janet. THE WIFE OF MARTIN GUERRE. Colt, 1941. Romance set in sixteenth century Languedoc. 1099

McComas, Ina Violet. ASHES OF VENGEANCE. by H. B. Somerville, pseud. Hutchinson, 1913. An adventure story of the closing quarter of the century. 1100

--------. RAOUL THE HUNCHBACK. by H. B. Somerville, pseud. Hutchinson, 1921. Love, intrigue, and adventure in sixteenth century Provence. 1101

Macquoid, Katharine S. A WARD OF THE KING. Buckles, 1898. A conspiracy against Francis I, his capture, and his beautiful mistress, the Countess of Chauteaubriant. 1102

Mann, Heinrich. HENRY, KING OF FRANCE. (tr.) Knopf, 1939. Politics and intrigues during the reign of Henry IV. 1103

--------. YOUNG HENRY OF NAVARRE. (tr.) [En. title: KING WREN] Knopf, 1937. The childhood and youth of Henry IV. (followed by HENRY, KING OF FRANCE) 1104

Mérimée, Prosper. A CHRONICLE OF THE REIGN OF CHARLES IX. (tr.) Nimmo, 1889. Depicts a Huguenot's experiences in the St. Bartholomew's Day Massacre and pictures Charles IX, Coligny, Catherine de Medici, and Henry of Navarre. 1105

Montgomery, K. L., pseud. for Kathleen and Letitia Montgomery. THE ARK OF THE CURSE. Hurst, 1906. A romance of the time of Henry III with an appearance by Don Juan of Austria. 1106

Orczy, Baroness Emmuska. FLOWER O' THE LILY. Doran, 1919. Sufferings during the siege of Cambrai led by the Duke of Parma in 1581. 1107

Pater, Walter. GASTON DE LATOUR. Macmillan, 1896. An unfinished though distinguished romance of France's Wars of Religion. 1108

Peterson, Margaret. THE LOVE OF NAVARRE. Melrose, 1915. Henry of Navarre from the War of the League to his Coronation as Henry IV. 1109

Radcliffe, Ann. THE MYSTERIES OF UDOLPHO. Dutton, 1931. A romance of Henry III's reign. 1110

Runkle, Bertha. THE HELMET OF NAVARRE. Century, 1901. A young follower of Henry IV at the latter's entry into Paris in 1594. 1111

Sabatini, Rafael. THE ROMANTIC PRINCE. Houghton, 1929. A French prince chooses between his heritage and a commoner's daughter. 1112

Salmon, Geraldine Gordon. QUEST OF YOUTH. by J. G. Sarasin, pseud. Hutchinson, 1923. A romance of the 1570s with the Duc de Guise prominent. 1113

Shellabarger, Samuel. THE KING'S CAVALIER. Little, 1950. Swordplay and intrigue in a conspiracy against Francis I. 1114

Stephens, Robert Neilson. AN ENEMY TO THE KING. Page, 1898. Struggle for power among Henry III, Henry of Navarre, and Henry of Guise. 1115

Stevenson, Philip L. A GALLANT OF GASCONY. Hurst, 1907. Unhappy marriage of Marguerite de Valois and Henry of Navarre. 1116

--------. LOVE IN ARMOUR. Paul, 1912. Romance of court personages near the end of Charles IX's reign. 1117

--------. THE ROSE OF DAUPHINY. Paul, 1910. Events incident to conspiracies in the Religious Wars concerning the Sieur de Roquelaure, later a trusted aide of Henry

IV. 1118

Stilson, Charles B. A CAVALIER OF NAVARRE. Watt, 1925. The romance of a young couple coincides with Henry of Navarre's rise to the throne. 1119

Walder, Francis. THE NEGOTIATORS. (tr.) McDowell, Obolensky, 1959. The wrangle between Admiral de Coligny and Catherine de Medici over the religion of four towns. 1120

Weyman, Stanley J. THE ABBESS OF VLAYE. Burt, 1904. Peasant unrest in the early part of Henry of Navarre's reign. 1121

--------. COUNT HANNIBAL. Longmans, 1901. Scenes during Charles IX's reign including the St. Bartholomew's Day Massacre. 1122

--------. A GENTLEMAN OF FRANCE. Longmans, 1893. A pleasing mixture of warlike exploits and court romance. 1123

--------. THE HOUSE OF THE WOLF. Longmans, 1890. Vivid picture of the St. Bartholomew's Day Massacre. 1124

Wheelwright, Jere Hungerford. WOLFSHEAD. Scribner, 1949. Adventures of John Aumarie, outlaw and pirate. 1125

III. A. 1. b. 2) Central Europe (including Germany, the Netherlands, Switzerland, Austria, Hungary, Czechoslovakia, and Poland)

Antal-Opzoomer, Adèle Sophia Cornelia von. IN TROUBLED TIMES. (tr.) by A. S. C. Wallis, *pseud.* Sonnenschein, 1883. Account of growing unrest in the Netherlands, chiefly during the regency of Margaret of Parma. 1126

Bailey, H. C. MY LADY OF ORANGE. Longmans, 1901. An Englishman joins William of Orange in opposing the Duke of Alva. 1127

--------. RAOUL: GENTLEMAN OF FORTUNE. Hutchinson, 1907. Romance amid such historic events as the sieges of

Leyden and Antwerp. 1128

Bertram, Paul. THE SHADOW OF POWER. Lane, 1912. The absolute rule of Jaime de Jorquera, representative of Philip II, over the Netherlands, then chafing under Spanish oppression. 1129

Bowen, Marjorie, pseud. for Gabrielle Campbell Long. (1) PRINCE AND HERETIC. Dutton, 1915. (2) "WILLIAM, BY THE GRACE OF GOD." Dutton, 1917. William the Silent, Prince of Orange, and the rebellion of the Netherlands against the Spanish. 1130

Breton, Frederic. TRUE HEART. Dent, 1898. Reflects the religious, political, and intellectual turmoil of the early sixteenth century. 1131

Coleridge, Gilbert and Marion. JAN VAN ELSELO. Macmillan, 1902. Reports, adventures, and schemes of a diplomat in Holland, England, Spain, and France. 1132

Comstock, Seth Cook. MONSIEUR LE CAPITAINE DOUAY. Long, 1904. The cruel Spanish sack of prosperous Antwerp. 1133

--------. THE REBEL PRINCE. Long, 1905. Adventure in the Netherlands during the time of William of Orange and Don Juan of Austria. 1134

Conscience, Hendrik. LUDOVIC AND GERTRUDE. (tr.) Murphy, 1895. Resentment of the people of Antwerp to Spanish rule in the person of Alva. 1135

Cornford, L. Cope. THE MASTER BEGGARS. Lippincott, 1897. The Netherlands following the success of the Beggars' Rebellion. 1136

Davis, William Stearns. THE FRIAR OF WITTENBERG. Macmillan, 1912. A story of Martin Luther from his posting of the Ninety-five Theses. 1137

Dekker, Maurits. BEGGARS' REVOLT. Doubleday, 1938. This novel of rebellion in the Netherlands against Spanish rule encompasses all levels of society. 1138

Ebers, Georg. BARBARA BLOMBERG. (tr.) Appleton, 1897. The German court of Charles V and the passionate, ambitious mother of Don Juan of Austria. 1139

--------. THE BURGOMASTER'S WIFE. (tr.) Macmillan, 1882. The siege of Leyden, the cutting of the dikes, and activities of the revolutionary Dutch "Beggars." 1140

--------. IN THE BLUE PIKE. (tr.) Appleton, 1896. Travellers at the Blue Pike Inn reflect the contemporary ecclestiastical abuses which aroused Luther. 1141

Grattan, Thomas C. AGNES DE MANSFELT. Saunders & Otley, 1835. The Wars of Independence in the Netherlands from mid-sixteenth to mid-seventeenth century. 1142

Haggard, H. Rider. LYSBETH. Longmans, 1901. Sieges of Haarlem and Leyden in the revolt of the Netherlands against Philip II. 1143

Hauff, Wilhelm. LICHTENSTEIN. (tr.) [En. title: MARIE OF LICHTENSTEIN] Bruce & Wyld, 1846. A romance of Swabia describing customs and living standards. 1144

Hausrath, Adolf. KLYTIA. (tr.) by George Taylor, pseud. Munro, 1885. The theological atmosphere of Heidelberg during the dissension between Catholics, Lutherans, and Calvinists. 1145

Hill, Pamela. HERE LIES MARGOT. Putnam, 1958. Margaret of Burgundy, her three state marriages, and her regency for her nephew, Emperor Charles V. 1146

Hocking, Joseph. THE SWORD OF THE LORD. Dutton, 1900. An Englishman in Germany during the Reformation. 1147

Klingenstein, L. GREAT INFANTA. Putnam, 1911. Isabel of Spain, eldest daughter of Philip II, and her role as sovereign of the Netherlands. 1148

Lee, Albert. THE KEY OF THE HOLY HOUSE. Pearson, 1898. The escape of prisoners from the dungeons of the Inquisition and popular opposition to Spanish rule in the Netherlands. 1149

Liefde, Jacob B. de. THE BEGGARS. Scribner, 1868. Fighters for freedom in the Netherlands unite to protest the Inquisition. 1150

Maas, Mabel. THE TWO FLAMES. (tr.) Cape, 1922. Conditions in Leyden and Bruges early in the century. 1151

Mally, Emma Louise. THE TIDES OF DAWN. Sloane, 1949. Sixteenth century Netherlands with a picture of contemporary religious dissension. 1152

Malo, Henri. THE ROMANTIC PASSION OF DON LUIS. (tr.) Harrap, 1925. Life in the Low Countries in the days of the Duke of Parma. 1153

Mason, Caroline A. A LILY OF FRANCE. Griffith, 1901. The career of William of Orange, Dutch revolutionary, and Charlotte de Bourbon, his third wife. 1154

Nietschmann, Hermann Otto. PRINCE ALBRECHT OF BRANDENBURG. German Literary Board, 1907. Features Tetzel, who aroused Luther's opposition by his misuse of indulgences. 1155

Orczy, Baroness Emmuska. LEATHERFACE. Doran, 1916. Story of the "Beggars" following the arrival of the Duke of Alva in the Netherlands. 1156

Sargent, H. Garton. A WOMAN AND A CREED. Blackwood, 1902. Religious persecution in Antwerp. 1157

Sinclair, Kathleen. THE VALIANT LADY. by Brigid Knight, pseud. Doubleday, 1948. Wars between Holland and Spain and emergence of the Dutch Republic. 1158

Stevenson, John P. CAPTAIN GENERAL. Doubleday, 1956. Action against backdrop of Netherlands' resistance to Spain's Philip II. 1159

Walker, Frances M. Cotton. CLOISTER TO COURT. Longmans, 1909. Princess Charlotte leaves a convent to contract marriage with William of Orange. 1160

Weyman, Stanley J. THE STORY OF FRANCIS CLUDDE. Longmans, 1898. A young man embarks on a life of adventure in the Netherlands to escape persecution. 1161

Williams, Jay. THE ROGUE FROM PADUA. Little, 1952. A wandering rascal's adventures in Germany during the Peasants' War. 1162

Zara, Louis. AGAINST THIS ROCK. Creative Age, 1943. The life of the powerful Emperor Charles V. 1163

III. A. 1. b. 3) Scandinavia and the Baltic

Antal-Opzoomer, Adèle Sophia Cornelia von. ROYAL FAVOUR. (tr.) by A. S. C. Wallis, pseud. Sonnenschein, 1884. Story of Goran Person, who becomes Chancellor to the weak and cruel King Eric XIV of Sweden. 1164

Jensen, Johannes Vilhelm. THE FALL OF THE KING. (tr.) Holt, 1933. Adventures of a student who becomes a messenger and friend of Denmark's Christian II. 1165

Jensen, Wilhelm. KARINE. (tr.) McClurg, 1896. A romance of the reign of Gustavus Vasa of Sweden. 1166

Waltari, Mika. THE ADVENTURER. (tr.) Putnam, 1950. A Finn wanders about Europe early in the century, meeting leading characters of the day. (followed by THE WANDERER) 1167

III. A. 1. c. Southern Europe

1) Iberian Peninsula

Blake, Gladys. DOÑA ISABELLA'S ADVENTURES. Appleton, 1928. Gay story of a lady-in-waiting to the Queen and a young soldier, Miguel Cervantes, who later wrote DON QUIXOTE [listed in this section under Cervantes]. 1168

Bloundelle-Burton, John. THE SEA DEVILS. White, 1912. Adventures of a sailor in the Spanish Armada and his later imprisonment and suffering in the Inquisition. 1169

Borton, Elizabeth. THE GREEK OF TOLEDO. Crowell, 1959. The life of El Greco both as a man and a great artist. 1170

Bowen, Marjorie, pseud. for Gabrielle Campbell Long. A KNIGHT OF SPAIN. Methuen, 1913. Successes of Don Juan of Austria at Lepanto and in the Netherlands, which displeased his half-brother, Philip II. 1171

Cervantes Saavedra, Miguel de. DON QUIXOTE DE LA MANCHA. (tr.) Dodd, 1885. An excellent picture of the times is given in this satire on chivalric romances with the hero a would-be knight tilting at windmills. 1172

Crawford, F. Marion. IN THE PALACE OF THE KING. Macmillan, 1900. Suspense-filled story about a romance of Don Juan of Austria which conflicted with the plans of King Philip II. 1173

De Wohl, Louis. THE GOLDEN THREAD. Lippincott, 1952. Story of St. Ignatius Loyola, interwoven with a tale of young lovers. 1174

--------. LAST CRUSADER. Lippincott, 1956. Don Juan of Austria and the Battle of Lepanto. 1175

Frank, Bruno. A MAN CALLED CERVANTES. Viking, 1935. Life-like picture of the creator of DON QUIXOTE [listed in this section under Cervantes], with a vivid account of the Battle of Lepanto. 1176

Hibbert, Eleanor. THE SPANISH BRIDEGROOM. by Jean Plaidy, pseud. Macrae Smith, 1956. Fictionalized effort to penetrate the true character of the enigmatic Philip II. 1177

Hocking, Joseph. A FLAME OF FIRE. Revell, 1903. The hero, during a stay in Spain, obtains information which helps in England's defeat of the Armada. 1178

Kaye, Michael W. FOR BRAGANZA. Greening, 1911. A romance of Portugal under Spanish rule. 1179

Larreta, Enrique. THE GLORY OF DON RAMIRO. Dutton, 1924. Don Ramiro's involvement in a plot for a Moorish uprising. 1180

Moore, H. C. A DEVONSHIRE LASS. Scott, 1908. Adventure in Spain during the Inquisition. 1181

O'Brien, Kate. FOR ONE SWEET GRAPE. [En. title: THAT LADY] Doubleday, 1946. Romance in the court of Philip II involving both the King and his minister. 1182

Sabatini, Rafael. THE HOUNDS OF GOD. Houghton, 1928. The Inquisition, Philip of Spain, and Elizabeth of England figure in this romance of a Spanish gentleman and an English lady. 1183

Schoonover, Lawrence. PRISONER OF TORDESILLAS. Little, 1959. About Juana the Mad of Castile, imprisoned almost fifty years for insanity. 1184

Slaughter, Frank G. DIVINE MISTRESS. Doubleday, 1949. Romance in Spain with art, medicine, and the Inquisition as ingredients. 1185

III. A. 1. c. 2) Italy and Adjacent Islands

Ainsworth, W. Harrison. THE CONSTABLE DE BOURBON. Dutton, 1866. This novel depicts the struggle for Milan between Francis I and Charles V; the bloody sack of Rome. 1186

Astor, William Waldorf. SFORZA, A STORY OF MILAN. Scribner, 1886. Events in Milan in the sixteenth century with Ludovico Sforza, Duke of Milan, prominent. 1187

--------. VALENTINO. Scribner, 1885. Intrigues and exploits of the notorious Cesare Borgia. 1188

Cleveland, Treadwell, Jr. A NIGHT WITH ALESSANDRO. Holt, 1904. Episode in Florence under the last Medici. 1189

Drummond, Hamilton. THE HALF-PRIEST. Paul, 1916. Life in Italy under the powerful and unscrupulous Borgia family. 1190

Faust, Frederick. BAIT AND THE TRAP. by George Challis, pseud. Harper, 1951. Narrative of a man in the service of Duke Cesare Borgia. 1191

Gallizier, Nathan. THE COURT OF LUCIFER. Page, 1910. The complicated entanglements of the Borgias in Rome and the innocence of Lucrezia from involvement. 1192

--------. THE RED CONFESSOR. Page, 1926. Sensational story of political and moral corruption in Rome in mid-century. 1193

Gardner, Edmund G. DESIDERIO. Dent, 1902. A novel of the political dealings of Pope Julius II and King Louis XII. 1194

Godwin, William. ST. LEON. Colburn & Bentley, 1831. Story of a man who gains wealth but finds it does not bring happiness. 1195

Guerrazzi, Francesco D. BEATRICE CENCI. (tr.) Ward & Lock, 1858. The tragic story of Beatrice Cenci, whose father's cruelties drove her to desperate measures. 1196

Hausrath, Adolf. FATHER MATERNUS. (tr.) [same as: PATER MATERNUS] by George Taylor, pseud. Dent, 1911. The visit of two Augustinians from Germany discloses conditions of religious life in Rome in 1511. 1197

Hicks Beach, Susan. A CARDINAL OF THE MEDICI. Macmillan, 1937. Ippolito de Medici, contemporary of Leo X, Clement VII, and Cardinal Bembo. 1198

Kaye, Michael W. THE HONOUR OF BAYARD. Greening, 1912. Attempt to undermine Bayard's defense of a town. 1199

Kelland, Clarence Budington. MERCHANT OF VALOR. Harper, 1947. Italy in the sixteenth century during the period of Medici ascendance. 1200

Levett-Yeats, Sidney. THE HONOUR OF SAVELLI. Appleton, 1895. An adventure story telling of many famous persons--Machiavelli, the Borgia family, Cardinal d'Amboise. 1201

McCarthy, Justin Huntly. THE GORGEOUS BORGIA. Harper, 1908. A thrilling tale of the Borgia family. 1202

Marshall, Rosamond. THE RIB OF THE HAWK. Appleton, 1958.

Romance and conquest in Renaissance Rome. 1203

Merezhkovsky, Dmitri. THE FORERUNNER. (tr.) [also titled: THE RESURRECTION OF THE GODS. LEONARDO DA VINCI; and THE ROMANCE OF LEONARDO DA VINCI] Constable, 1902. The blending of pagan and Christian elements during the Renaissance; a vivid picture of Leonardo da Vinci. (followed by PETER AND ALEXIS) 1204

Montgomery, K. L., pseud. for Kathleen and Letitia Montgomery. THE CARDINAL'S PAWN. McClurg, 1904. A colorful picture of the scheming Medici family of the High Renaissance. 1205

Prokosch, Frederic. A TALE FOR MIDNIGHT. Little, 1955. The murder of Francesco Cenci and his family's trial for the crime. 1206

Pugh, John J. CAPTAIN OF THE MEDICI. Little, 1953. The perilous adventures of the blacksmith captain of the notorious "Black Band." 1207

--------. HIGH CARNIVAL. Little, 1959. Pre-Lentan carnival in prosperous Venice. 1208

Ritson, Arthur. MY LADY LUCIA. Mills & Boon, 1925. Italy at the outset of the century, with a picture of Cesare Borgia. 1209

Robinson, Emma. CAESAR BORGIA. Routledge, 1846. Rome in the days when the Borgias wielded so much power. 1210

Sabatini, Rafael. LOVE AT ARMS. Hutchinson, 1907. Italy during the period of Borgia power early in the century. 1211

--------. THE SHAME OF MOTLEY. Hutchinson, 1908. The Borgia family figures in this novel of the early sixteenth century. 1212

--------. THE SWORD OF ISLAM. Houghton, 1939. Genoese naval action, romance, and captivity mark this typical Sabatini tale. 1213

Sand, George, pseud. for Mme. Dudevant. THE MASTER MOSAIC-WORKERS. (tr.) Little, 1895. Concerns craftsmen who made the beautiful mosaics of St. Mark's Church. 1214

Scollard, Clinton. COUNT FALCON OF THE EYRIE. Page, 1903. Venice and Milan are the setting for this romance. 1215

Spinatelli, Carl J. BATON SINISTER. Little, 1959. Picaresque tale of the natural son of a murdered nobleman. 1216

Stone, Irving. THE AGONY AND THE ECSTASY. Doubleday, 1961. Michelangelo's personal life and career in Florence and Rome. 1217

Tapparelli-D'Azeglio, Massimo. THE CHALLENGE OF BARLETTA. (tr.) Allen, 1880. Dissension between French and Spanish after they jointly invaded Naples. 1218

--------. THE MAID OF FLORENCE. (tr.) Bentley, 1853. Defense of Florence against the army of Emperor Charles V. 1219

Toye, Nina. THE DEATH RIDER. Cassell, 1916. Rome during the time of Pope Julius II. 1220

Turnbull, Francese Hubbard. THE GOLDEN BOOK OF VENICE. by Mrs. Lawrence Turnbull. Century, 1900. Pictures Venice in the period of its dispute with Pope Paul V. 1221

Whiting, Mary B. THE PLOUGH OF SHAME. Dent, 1906. In the background are the accession and conquests of Charles V. 1222

III. A. 1. d. Eastern Europe (including Russia and the Balkans), the Near East, and North Africa

Gogol, Nikolai V. TARAS BULBA. (tr.) Crowell, 1886. The fierce fighting of the Cossacks against the Poles who invaded their territory. 1223

Lindsay, Philip. THE KNIGHTS AT BAY. Loring & Mussey, 1935. The Knights Hospitallers and their fighting against the Turks. 1224

Waltari, Mika. THE WANDERER. (tr.) Putnam, 1951. A Finnish adventurer in North Africa and the Ottoman Empire. 1225

Whishaw, Frederick J. A BOYAR OF THE TERRIBLE. Longmans, 1896. The ruthless Ivan IV, the Terrible, and his diplomatic relations with other countries. 1226

--------. THE TIGER OF MUSCOVY. Longmans, 1904. A lively English girl in Russia at the court of Ivan the Terrible. 1227

White, Leslie Turner. SIR ROGUE. Crown, 1954. Swashbuckling tale of Russia and Ivan the Terrible. 1228

III. A. 1. e. Overseas Exploration, Enterprise, and Expansion

Balfour, Andrew. BY STROKE OF SWORD. Lane, 1897. Adventures in Scotland, England, and on the sea during the troubled times following Mary of Scotland's imprisonment. 1229

Cornford, L. Cope. SONS OF ADVERSITY. Page, 1898. A sea story of England and Holland. 1230

De Wohl, Louis. SET ALL AFIRE. Lippincott, 1953. Compelling account of the dedication and missionary labors of St. Francis Xavier. 1231

Griffith, George. JOHN BROWN, BUCCANEER. White, 1908. Success of English sea power as Spain's national power diminishes. 1232

Haggard, H. Rider. MONTEZUMA'S DAUGHTER. Longmans, 1893. An Englishman seeks his mother's murderer in Spain and Mexico. 1233

Hodgson, W. H. THE BOATS OF THE GLEN-CARRIG. Chapman, 1907. Old mariner's tale of adventures in the South Seas. 1234

Jennings, John. THE GOLDEN EAGLE. Putnam, 1958. A romance of the conquistador De Soto is related along with an account of his explorations. 1235

Johnston, Mary. SIR MORTIMER. Houghton, 1904. The Spanish Main in the time of Drake, when Queen Elizabeth was officially unaware of pirating. 1236

Kingsley, Charles. WESTWARD HO! Macmillan, 1855. Adventures of English seamen who defeated the Spanish Armada and established English naval supremacy. 1237

Raynolds, Robert. THE QUALITY OF QUIROS. Bobbs, 1955. A tale of Spanish and Portuguese exploration in the Pacific. 1238

Sabatini, Rafael. THE SEA-HAWK. Houghton, 1915. Adventures of the lusty sea-rover Sir Oliver Tressilian. 1239

III. A. 2. Seventeenth Century: Age of Absolutism

a. The British Isles

1) England, Wales, and Scotland

Ainsworth, W. Harrison. BOSCOBEL; or, THE ROYAL OAK. Dutton, 1872. The escape of Charles II after the Battle of Worcester. 1240

--------. GUY FAWKES. Dutton, 1841. Causes and failure of the Gunpowder Plot which involved Catholics suffering under harsh penal laws. 1241

--------. JAMES THE SECOND. Carey & Hart, 1848. Includes accounts of the Seven Bishops' Trial and the revolution of 1688. 1242

--------. THE LANCASHIRE WITCHES. Dutton, 1848. A story of the persecution of supposed witches in Lancashire. 1243

--------. THE LEAGUER OF LATHOM. Routledge, 1880. Colorful tale of Lancashire during the Civil War, with the siege of Lathom House and the execution of the Earl of Derby. 1244

--------. OLD ST. PAUL'S. Dutton, 1841. A grocer's family in London during the plague and great fire of mid-century. 1245

--------. OVINGDEAN GRANGE. Dutton, 1860. Charles II's escape to France after his defeat at Worcester. 1246

--------. THE STAR CHAMBER. Dutton, 1854. Activities of the Court of the Star Chamber and general customs of the period of James I. 1247

Anderson, H. M. KELSTON OF KELLS. Blackwood, 1927. Rivalry in Scotland between Episcopalians and Presbyterians. 1248

Arthur, Mary Lucy. THE BATON SINISTER. by George David Gilbert, pseud. Long, 1903. A sympathetic account of the personal life of the Duke of Monmouth. 1249

Bailey, H. C. BEAUJEU. Murray, 1905. A story of the last days of the Stuart dynasty recounting the downfall of James II. 1250

--------. COLONEL GREATHEART. [En. title: COLONEL STOW] Bobbs, 1908. A Civil War story which includes the Battle of Newbury and presents both sides of the conflict. 1251

--------. THE PLOT. Methuen, 1922. Written around the Popish Plot of 1678. 1252

Baker, H. Barton. FOR THE HONOUR OF HIS HOUSE. Digby & Long, 1906. Court life from Monmouth's defeat until James II's downfall. 1253

Bamfylde, Walter. THE ROAD TO ARCADY. Low, 1917. Love surmounts differences of nationality, religion, and political belief. 1254

Baring-Gould, S. URITH. Methuen, 1891. The rough, rugged moor people of Dartmoor during the controversy over Monmouth's movement. 1255

Barnes, Margaret Campbell. MARY OF CARISBROOKE. Macrae Smith, 1956. Royalist intrigue involves a sergeant's daughter in the life of Charles I. 1256

--------. WITH ALL MY HEART. Macrae Smith, 1951. A novel of Catherine of Braganza, consort of Charles II. 1257

Barnes-Austin, Edgar. MARK EMINENCE. by E. Wynton Locke, pseud. McBride, 1947. English life and customs during the rule of Charles II. 1258

Barr, Amelia E. FRIEND OLIVIA. Dodd, 1898. England in the days of Cromwell with events involving Puritans and members of the new Quaker sect. 1259

Barr, Robert. OVER THE BORDER. Stokes, 1903. Adventures of a messenger to the king during the mid-century Civil War. 1260

Barrett, Frank. THE OBLIGING HUSBAND. Chatto, 1907. Tale of a spirited girl whose forced marriage turns out to be successful. 1261

--------. A SET OF ROGUES. Innes, 1896. A company of poverty-stricken actors tours in the country while the plague rages in London. 1262

Barrington, Michael. THE KNIGHT OF THE GOLDEN SWORD. Chatto, 1909. Plots and events during Restoration times with an unsympathetic account of Covenanter activities. 1263

Bayly, Ada. IN SPITE OF ALL. by Edna Lyall, pseud. Longmans, 1901. Vicissitudes of Puritans in England at the time of Charles I. 1264

--------. TO RIGHT THE WRONG. by Edna Lyall, pseud. Harper, 1893. Romance of Civil War England with John Hampden as a chief character. 1265

Beck, Lily Adams. THE GREAT ROMANTIC. by E. Barrington, pseud. Doubleday, 1933. Based on the public and the tumultuous private lives of Samuel Pepys and his lovely French wife, Elizabeth. 1266

Beebe, Elswyth Thane. QUEEN'S FOLLY. by Elswyth Thane. Harcourt, 1937. Four-generation story of a family living in a house presented to an ancestor who had performed a service for Queen Elizabeth. 1267

Benson, Claude E. MILES RITSON. Low, 1925. An adventure tale of the late 1880s with Claverhouse appearing. 1268

Benson, Robert Hugh. ODDSFISH! Hutchinson, 1914. Clever, compelling novel of political and religious intrigue in Restoration England. 1269

Bentley, Phyllis. THE POWER AND THE GLORY. Macmillan, 1940. Inter-relationships between two families--one Royalist and one Puritan. 1270

Berridge, Jesse. THE STRONGHOLD. Melrose, 1926. Stresses the religious aspect of the English Civil War at the time of Cromwell. 1271

Besant, Walter. FOR FAITH AND FREEDOM. Harper, 1888. The plight of the Puritans during the reign of James II. 1272

Binns, Ottwell. THE SWORD OF FORTUNE. by Ben Bolt, pseud. Ward & Lock, 1927. Adventure in England during Monmouth's Rebellion against James II. 1273

Blackmore, R. D. LORNA DOONE. Harper, 1874. Romance of Lorna and her captor, the robber Doone. 1274

Blayney, Owen. THE MacMAHON. Constable, 1898. Novel centering on the Battle of the Boyne. 1275

Blissett, Nellie K. THE SILVER KEY. Smart Set, 1905. The royal families of the English and French courts. 1276

Blyth, James. THE KING'S GUERDON. Digby & Long, 1906. Recounts the naval battle off Lowestaft and the great plague and fire of the 1660s in London. 1277

Bowen, Marjorie, pseud. for Gabrielle Campbell Long. THE GLEN O' WEEPING. McClure, 1907. The Glencoe Pass Massacre of 1692 and the clan feud between Macdonalds and Campbells. 1278

--------. THE GOVERNOR OF ENGLAND. Dutton, 1914. Well-written account of Cromwell's rise to power. 1279

--------. (1) I WILL MAINTAIN. Methuen, 1910. (2) DEFENDER OF THE FAITH. Methuen, 1911. (3) GOD AND THE KING. Methuen, 1911. Political undercurrents during the Revolution and the reign of William III and Mary, with significant people and events. 1280

Braddon, Mary E. IN HIGH PLACES. Hutchinson, 1898. The assassination of the Duke of Buckingham, the English Civil War, and contemporary France. 1281

--------. LONDON PRIDE. Simpkin, 1896. The execution of Charles I and the later restoration of Charles II. 1282

Bray, Claude. A CUIRASSIER OF ARRAN'S. Sands, 1900. Action during the so-called "Glorious" Revolution--the landing of William and the flight of James II. 1283

Brebner, Percy J. THE BROWN MASK. Cassell, 1910. Adventure story of Monmouth's Rebellion and the Bloody Assize with infamous Judge Jeffreys. 1284

Buchan, John. JOHN BURNET OF BARNS. Lane, 1898. University life in Scotland and the Netherlands during persecution of the Covenanters. 1285

--------. WITCH WOOD. Houghton, 1927. The hero's opposition to the persecution of witches incurs abuse and condemnation. 1286

Bunbury, Selina. COOMBE ABBEY. Willoughby, 1843. "An historical tale of the reign of James the First." 1287

Burchell, Sidney Herbert. DANIEL HERRICK. Gay & Hancock, 1900. Romance of a news-writer in London during the plague of 1665. 1288

--------. THE DUKE'S SERVANTS. Little, 1899. A troupe of players in rural England in the period of the Duke of Buckingham's assassination. 1289

--------. THE PRISONER OF CARISBROOKE. Gay & Hancock, 1904. The flight of Charles I to the Isle of Wight. 1290

Burnett, Frances Hodgson. (1) A LADY OF QUALITY. Scribner, 1896. (2) HIS GRACE OF OSMONDE (sequel). Scribner, 1897. The adventurous life of an apparent lady who achieves position and honor. 1291

Caine, Hall. THE SHADOW OF A CRIME. Caldwell, 1885. Exciting murder mystery set in Quaker England. 1292

Carr, John Dickson. THE DEVIL IN VELVET. Harper, 1951. History professor finds a way to return to Restoration

England in this historical fantasy. 1293

--------. MURDER OF SIR EDMUND GODFREY. Harper, 1936. An historical murder-mystery concerning a real crime committed in 1678. 1294

Chalmers, Stephen. WHEN LOVE CALLS MEN TO ARMS. Richards, 1912. Feuds and fighting under James VI of Scotland based on a seventeenth century manuscript. 1295

Charques, Dorothy. DARK STRANGER. Coward, 1957. Combination of romance, religion, politics, and witch-craft in Cromwell's time. 1296

Church, Samuel Harden. PENRUDDOCK OF THE WHITE LAMBS. Stokes, 1902. The daring revolt of Royalists under Colonel Penruddock against Cromwell's forces. 1297

Clark, Justis Kent. THE KING'S AGENT. Scribner, 1958. Sir Ralph Barnard decides his exiled master, James II, has no chance to regain the throne of England. 1298

Cobban, J. MacLaren. THE ANGEL OF THE COVENANT. Fenno, 1898. Montrose and the struggle with the Presbyterians in Scotland. 1299

Cooke, W. Bourne. HER FAITHFUL KNIGHT. Cassell, 1908. The English Civil War as seen by a Roundhead soldier. 1300

Cowen, Laurence. BIBLE AND SWORD. Hodder & Stoughton, 1919. The Cromwells, Charles I, John Milton, and his wife Mary Powell all figure in this story. 1301

Crockett, Samuel R. THE CHERRY RIBBAND. Barnes, 1905. Romance between a Covenanter boy and a girl of a different belief. 1302

--------. THE GRAY MAN. Harper, 1896. Exciting story of feuds and discord in Scotland during the early seventeenth century. 1303

--------. LOCHINVAR. Harper, 1897. Rousing military action and romances of a soldier under both William of Orange and Claverhouse. 1304

--------. THE MEN OF THE MOSS-HAGS. Macmillan, 1895. The sufferings of the persecuted Covenanters. 1305

--------. THE STANDARD BEARER. Appleton, 1898. Persecution and oppression of the Covenanters in Scotland. 1306

Deeping, Warwick. LANTERN LANE. Cassell, 1921. A story of romance and adventure climaxing in a duel. 1307

--------. MAD BARBARA. Cassell, 1908. A murder story set in England at the time of the plague. 1308

--------. ORCHARDS. Cassell, 1922. Life in Royalist England in the seventeenth century. 1309

Defoe, Daniel. MEMOIRS OF A CAVALIER. Macmillan, 1720. A military journal of wars in Germany (under Gustavus Adolphus) and in England (under Charles I). 1310

De Morgan, William. AN AFFAIR OF DISHONOUR. Holt, 1910. Naval warfare between the English-French fleets and the Dutch navy in 1672. 1311

Dexter, Charles. STREET OF KINGS. Holt, 1957. Murder and intrigue in the court of James I. 1312

Dilnot, Frank. MAD SIR PETER. Macmillan, 1932. An action-filled tale of England in the time of William and Mary. 1313

Dix, Beulah M. THE FAIR MAID OF GRAYSTONES. Macmillan, 1905. A young Cavalier prisoner of a Puritan family--his adventures and marriage. 1314

--------. THE FIGHTING BLADE. Holt, 1912. Romantic adventures of a German in the service of Cromwell. 1315

--------. THE LIFE, TREASON, AND DEATH OF JAMES BLOUNT OF BRECKENHOW. Macmillan, 1903. A subaltern assumes the blame for another's act of cowardice. 1316

Dodge, Constance. GRAHAM OF CLAVERHOUSE. Covici, 1937. Religious struggles resulting from Charles II's attempt to establish Episcopacy in Scotland. 1317

--------. THE POINTLESS KNIFE. Covici, 1937. A tale of the MacGregor clan, forbidden to carry any weapons except a pointless knife. 1318

Douglas, Alan. FOR THE KING. Macrae Smith, 1926. Masquerade of a Roundhead as his Cavalier brother leads to danger. 1319

Doyle, Sir Arthur Conan. MICAH CLARKE. Longmans, 1888. Adventure-packed account of the fighting in Monmouth's Rebellion. 1320

Du Maurier, Daphne. FRENCHMAN'S CREEK. Doubleday, 1942. The love of a noble lady for a pirate in the reign of Charles II. 1321

--------. THE KING'S GENERAL. Doubleday, 1946. Cloak and dagger tale of Cornwall during England's Civil Wars. 1322

Eccott, W. J. FORTUNE'S CASTAWAY. Blackwood, 1905. Sympathetic account of the Rye House Plot and Monmouth's Rebellion. 1323

Ellis, Beth. BARBARA WINSLOW, REBEL. Blackwood, 1903. A girl's rebellious activities point up the prejudice and injustice of the latter part of the century. 1324

--------. THE KING'S SPY. Dodd, 1910. A romance of Marlborough's plot to put Anne on the throne of England. 1325

Eyre-Todd, George. ANNE OF ARGYLE. [later pub. as: CAVALIER AND COVENANT] Stokes, 1895. Charles II's exile after the execution of his father; Cromwell's invasion of Scotland. 1326

Fairbairn, Roger. DEVIL KINSMERE. Harper, 1934. A dashing young provincial joins the "secret service" of Charles II. 1327

Farnol, Jeffery. MARTIN CONISBY'S VENGEANCE. Little, 1921. Highly colored adventure story of pirates in seventeenth century England and of the Spanish Inquisition. 1328

Fea, Allan. MY LADY WENTWORTH. Mills & Boon, 1909. Story of Monmouth and the rebellion he led. 1329

Finnemore, John. THE RED MEN OF THE DUSK. Lippincott, 1899. Adventures of a fugitive Cavalier and a band of outlaws. 1330

Fox, Marion. THE HAND OF THE NORTH. Lane, 1911. A story of border warfare which gives a good picture of Essex's plot against the aging Elizabeth. 1331

Galt, John. RINGAN GILHAIZE. Greening, 1899. Stirring account of the Battle of Killiecrankie in the Scottish uprising of 1688. 1332

Garnier, Russell M. HIS COUNTERPART. Harper, 1898. "An historical romance of the early days of John Churchill, first Duke of Marlborough." 1333

Gissingham, James. FOR PRINCE OR POPE. Greening, 1910. Country life in England shortly before the coming of William of Orange. 1334

Gore, Catherine Grace. THE COURTIER. Weldon, 1877. A story of the court of Charles II. 1335

Goudge, Elizabeth. THE WHITE WITCH. Coward, 1957. A "white witch," part gypsy, who used her influence for good in Puritan England. 1336

Grierson, Edward. DARK TORRENT OF GLENCOE. Doubleday, 1960. The feud between the Campbell and Macdonald clans leading to the Massacre of Glencoe in 1632. 1337

Griffin, E. Aceituna. A SERVANT OF THE KING. Blackwood, 1906. Background is the story of Thomas Wentworth's service to Charles I, his trial, and execution. 1338

Griffin, Gerald. THE DUKE OF MONMOUTH. Duffy (Dublin) 1857. The scene is Somerset; the action is Monmouth's Rebellion from his landing to his execution. 1339

Grogan, Walter E. THE KING'S CAUSE. Milne, 1909. Prince Rupert's capture of Bristol. 1340

Hales, A. G. MAID MOLLY. Treherne, 1907. A romance of fighting in Yorkshire--the Battle of Naseby. 1341

Hamilton, John A. CAPTAIN JOHN LISTER. Hutchinson, 1906. Effects of the Civil War on English and Dutch commoners. 1342

--------. THE MS. IN A RED BOX. Lane, 1903. The first successful drainage of the Fens of Lincolnshire by Cornelius Vermuyden. 1343

Hartley, J. Wesley. IN THE IRON TIME. Jennings & Graham, 1908. Adventures of a youthful soldier in Cromwell's service. 1344

Hartley, Percy J. MY LADY OF CLEEVE. Dodd, 1908. Continued plotting of the Jacobites after William's victory. 1345

Hatton, Joseph. THE DAGGER AND THE CROSS. Fenno, 1897. Conditions resulting from the plague of 1665. 1346

Hawkins, Anthony Hope. SIMON DALE. by Anthony Hope, pseud. Stokes, 1897. A romance of Charles II's court with Nell Gwyn as the object of affection. 1347

Heyer, Georgette. THE GREAT ROXHYTHE. Small, 1923. The Marquis of Roxhythe was Charles II's close political friend; his only desire was to serve his king. 1348

--------. ROYAL ESCAPE. Doubleday, 1939. The escape of Charles II from Worcester to France. 1349

Hill, William K. UNDER THREE KINGS. Routledge, 1907. Reflects the political scene in the time of Charles II, James II, and William III. 1350

Hillary, Max. THE BLUE FLAG. Ward & Lock, 1898. Somersetshire during the unrest incident to Monmouth's Rebellion. 1351

Hocking, Joseph. THE CHARIOTS OF THE LORD. Eaton & Mains, 1909. Plots and counter-plots involving James II, Judge Jeffreys, and Monmouth before the landing of William of Orange. 1352

--------. THE COMING OF THE KING. Ward & Lock, 1904. The early years of Charles II's reign and enforcement of the Act of Uniformity. 1353

Hooper, I. HIS GRACE O' THE GUNNE. Black, 1898. Life and adventures of a vagabond thief. 1354

Hope, Elizabeth. MY LADY'S BARGAIN. Century, 1923. A story with a surprise ending set in England during the Protectorate. 1355

Hope, Jessie. THE LADY OF LYTE. by Graham Hope, pseud. Methuen, 1905. Conflict within the court at the time of the Popish Plot of 1678. 1356

--------. MY LORD WINCHENDEN. by Graham Hope, pseud. Elder, 1902. Village life--social and political--during the Restoration period. 1357

Hunt, J. H. Leigh. SIR RALPH ESHER. Colburn, 1832. About the ravages of the Great Plague and sea fights with the Dutch. 1358

Hunter, P. Hay. BIBLE AND SWORD. Hodder, 1905. A story of the Covenanters' fight for freedom from persecution. 1359

Irwin, Margaret. THE BRIDE. Harcourt, 1939. The Stuart cause during the months between the executions of Charles I and the Marquis of Montrose. 1360

--------. THE PROUD SERVANT. Harcourt, 1934. James Graham, first Marquis of Montrose, and his efforts to win Scotland for Charles I. 1361

--------. STRANGER PRINCE. Harcourt, 1937. Prince Rupert, son of Elizabeth of Bohemia, and his part in the English Civil War. 1362

Jahoda, Gloria. ANNIE. Houghton, 1960. The love of a manor house maid and the crippled son of the house's owner. 1363

James, G. P. R. ARABELLA STUART. Dutton, 1844. Romance of William Seymour and Arabella Stuart. 1364

--------. ARRAH NEIL. Dutton, 1845. A romance of the early part of the English Civil War. 1365

--------. THE FATE. Newby, 1851. Social life in the Lincolnshire-Nottinghamshire area of England during

Monmouth's Rebellion. 1366

--------. GOWRIE. Dutton, 1851. Based on the Gowrie Conspiracy of 1600. 1367

--------. HENRY MASTERTON. Colburn & Bentley, 1832. Adventures of a young Cavalier at the Royalist downfall. (followed by LIFE AND ADVENTURES OF JOHN MARSTON HALL) 1368

--------. THE KING'S HIGHWAY. Dutton, 1840. Jacobite conspiracy against William III. 1369

James, Miss W. M. THE CARVED CARTOON. by Austin Clare, pseud. S. P. C. K., 1874. London just after mid-century during the disastrous fire and plague. 1370

Jenkins, Burris Atkins. THE BRACEGIRDLE. Lippincott, 1922. The wooing of Anne Bracegirdle, star of the London theater. 1371

Johnston, Mary. THE WITCH. Houghton, 1914. Life in England under James I, featuring trials of accused witches. 1372

Jones, Dora M. A SOLDIER OF THE KING. Cassell, 1901. Centers on the Royalist defeat at Maidstone. 1373

Jordan, Helen Rosaline. THE SWAN OF USK. Macmillan, 1940. Concerning the life of the poet Henry Vaughan. 1374

Judah, Charles Burnet. CHRISTOPHER HUMBLE. Morrow, 1956. Adventure on two continents as the hero, involved in the Titus Oates Plot, finally returns to Virginia. 1375

Kaye-Smith, Sheila. GALLYBIRD. Harper, 1934. Strange marriage of a widower and a young gypsy. 1376

Keddie, Henrietta. THE WITCH-WIFE. by Sarah Tytler, pseud. Chatto, 1897. A grim story of the witch burnings in Scotland. 1377

Keynes, Helen Mary. HONOUR THE KING. Chatto & Windus, 1914. The scene is Charles I's England, including the Siege of Bristol. 1378

--------. THE SPANISH MARRIAGE. Chatto & Windus, 1913.

Trip of Prince Charles, son of James I, to Madrid in 1623 for a secret discussion of a possible state marriage. 1379

Knowles, Mabel Winifred. HEY FOR CAVALIERS. by May Wynne, pseud. Greening, 1912. The siege of Pontefract Castle. 1380

Lambert, Frederick Arthur. THE ACCUSER. by Frederick Arthur, pseud. Nash & Grayson, 1927. Titus Oates and the Popish Plot from an anti-Puritan viewpoint. 1381

Lance, Rupert. THE GOLDEN PIPPIN. Allen & Unwin, 1917. Plots against Charles II after the Restoration. 1382

Lane, Elinor Macartney. ALL FOR THE LOVE OF A LADY. Appleton, 1906. Romance of a French duke and a Scots lady. 1383

LeGallienne, Richard. THERE WAS A SHIP. Doubleday, Doran, 1930. A light, lyrical novel of romance and search for hidden treasure. 1384

Lewis, Hilda Winifred. WIFE TO GREAT BUCKINGHAM. Putnam, 1960. The Duke of Buckingham's life as recounted by his wife, Catherine. 1385

Linington, Elizabeth. THE KINGBREAKER. Doubleday, 1958. Spying in Oliver Cromwell's household during the English Civil War. 1386

Lorraine, Rupert. THE WOMAN AND THE SWORD. McClurg, 1908. Troubles in England and Germany at the time of the Star Chamber and the Thirty Years War. 1387

Mabie, Mary Louise. THE PALE SURVIVOR. Bobbs, 1934. A disillusioned English lady sails for America and is captured by pirate Henry Morgan. 1388

Macaulay, Rose. THE SHADOW FLIES. Harper, 1932. This novel, written in contemporary language, treats of Herrick, Milton, and other poets of the day. 1389

McCarthy, Justin Huntly. IN SPACIOUS TIMES. Hurst & Blackett, 1916. Romantic tale of Elizabethan England in the last years of the Queen's life. 1390

--------. THE LADY OF LOYALTY HOUSE. Harper, 1904. A light romance of the Civil War period. 1391

--------. THE O'FLYNN. Harper, 1910. Tale of a follower of the deposed James in his search for Irish support in opposition to William III. 1392

McChesney, Dora Greenwell. CORNET STRONG OF IRETON'S HORSE. Lane, 1903. Puritan-slanted story of the battles and sieges of the Civil War. 1393

--------. MIRIAM CROMWELL, ROYALIST. Blackwood, 1897. English society at the time of Oliver Cromwell reflected in the lives of his niece, Miriam, and Royalist Prince Rupert. 1394

--------. RUPERT, BY THE GRACE OF GOD. Macmillan, 1899. The siege of Bristol and an unauthorized plot to make Prince Rupert king are spotlighted. 1395

--------. YESTERDAY'S TO-MORROW. Dent, 1905. Life in Restoration England with an undercurrent of religious unrest. 1396

Macdonald, George. ST. GEORGE AND ST. MICHAEL. Munro, 1875. Romance between a Roundhead and a Royalist and the exploits of Somerset in the Civil War. 1397

MacDonald, Ronald. THE SWORD OF THE KING. Century, 1900. England and Holland under James II and William of Orange. 1398

Mackenna, Robert William. FLOWER O' THE HEATHER. Murray, 1922. A romance which shows the sufferings and the zeal of the Covenanters. 1399

--------. THROUGH FLOOD AND FIRE. Murray, 1925. Romance and adventure in Covenanter times, with a good picture of Claverhouse. 1400

Macmillan, Malcolm. DAGONET THE JESTER. Macmillan, 1886. The story of a jester in Puritan England. 1401

Macpherson, Annie Winifred. THE PLAYER'S BOY. by Winifred Bryher, *pseud.* Pantheon, 1953. A vivid picture of decline in England after Elizabeth's reign. 1402

Macrae, J. A. FOR KIRK AND KING. Blackwood, 1911. Scottish lowland life at mid-century. 1403

Magnay, William. THE AMAZING DUKE. Unwin, 1906. A romance whose central character is the Duke of Buckingham. 1404

Maitland, Alfred L. I LIVED AS I LISTED. Wells Gardner, 1899. An adventure-romance of the road in Restoration England. 1405

Major, Charles. THE TOUCHSTONE OF FORTUNE. Macmillan, 1912. The memoirs of Baron Clyde, who thrived and fell in the reign of Charles II. 1406

Marryat, *Mrs.* F. T. ROMANCE OF THE LADY ARBELL. White, 1899. Story of Arabella Stuart, whose proximity to England's throne endangered her life. 1407

Marryat, Frederick. SNARLEYYOW. Carey & Hart, 1837. The "dog fiend" has a leading role in this tale of smuggler hunters. 1408

Marsh, John B. FOR LIBERTY'S SAKE. Strahan, 1873. A character study of Robert Ferguson, involved in a Jacobite plot. 1409

Martin, A. D. UNA BREAKSPEAR. Clarke, 1926. Reflects religious and political problems of the Commonwealth and Restoration periods. 1410

Mason, A. E. W. THE COURTSHIP OF MORRICE BUCKLER. Macmillan, 1896. Romance-adventure of an Englishman in Monmouth's Rebellion and in Europe in the 1680s. 1411

Mason, Caroline A. THE BINDING OF THE STRONG. Revell, 1908. Turbulent course of the marriage of John Milton and Mary Powell. 1412

Mills, J. M. A. THE WAY TRIUMPHANT. Hutchinson, 1926. Royalist romance of Scotland with the ill-fated Montrose as hero. 1413

Montgomery, K. L., pseud. for Kathleen and Letitia Montgomery. MAJOR WEIR. Unwin, 1904. About Thomas Weir, tried, convicted, and executed as a wizard in Scotland. 1414

Moore, F. Frankfort. NELL GWYN--COMEDIAN. Brentano's, 1901. A romance of the court of Charles II. 1415

Morley, Iris. WE STOOD FOR FREEDOM. Morrow, 1942. Monmouth's Rebellion and the fight for the cause of the common people. 1416

Morrow, Honoré. YONDER SAILS THE MAYFLOWER. Morrow, 1934. A story of the Puritans before they sailed for America. 1417

Munro, Neil. JOHN SPLENDID. Dodd, 1898. War in the highlands with the Royalists under Montrose. 1418

Murdoch, Gladys. MISTRESS CHARITY GODOLPHIN. Murray, 1914. Includes the trial and execution of Lady Alice Lisle, implicated in Monmouth's Rebellion. 1419

Musters, Mrs. Chaworth. A CAVALIER STRONGHOLD. Simpkin, 1890. A romance of the Vale of Belvoir--Nottinghamshire. 1420

Mylechreest, Winifred Brookes. THE FAIREST OF THE STUARTS. Low, 1912. Tells the story of Elizabeth and Henry, two children of James I, and current superstition. 1421

Neill, Robert. ELEGANT WITCH. Doubleday, 1952. Puritan girl comes in contact with witchcraft in Lancashire, England. 1422

--------. REBEL HEIRESS. Doubleday, 1954. Adventure and romance amid Restoration politics. 1423

--------. TRAITOR'S MOON. Doubleday, 1952. Internal strife in England around 1679. 1424

Nepean, Evelyn Maud. (1) LANTERNS OF HORN. Lane, 1923. (2) IVORY AND APES. Bale, Sons & Danielson, 1921. (3) MY TWO KINGS. Dutton, 1918. all by Mrs.

Evan Nepean. A Stuart trilogy of Charles II's reign in which each novel stands as a separate romance although many of the same characters appear in all three. 1425

Orczy, Baroness Emmuska. FIRE IN STUBBLE. Methuen, 1912. An English nobleman and a French tailor's daughter at the time of the Popish Plot. 1426

--------. HIS MAJESTY'S WELL-BELOVED. Doran, 1920. A picturesque romance of the days of Charles II centered on the actor, Thomas Betterton. 1427

--------. THE HONOURABLE JIM. Doran, 1924. Marital discord occasioned by political differences between Roundheads and Cavaliers. 1428

Parker, Katherine. MY LADIE DUNDIE. Gardner, 1926. About the wife of the Scottish Jacobite chieftain, John Graham of Claverhouse. 1429

Paterson, Arthur. CROMWELL'S OWN. Harper, 1899. Cromwell's army in the English Civil War ending with the Battle of Marston Moor. 1430

--------. THE KING'S AGENT. Appleton, 1902. Marlborough's plotting in favor of Anne against William III. 1431

Payne, Robert. ROARING BOYS. Doubleday, 1955. Shakespeare and his players in rowdy Elizabethan England. 1432

Pease, Howard. (1) MAGNUS SINCLAIR. Constable, 1904. (2) OF MISTRESS EVE (sequel). Constable, 1906. Scotland and northern England during the Commonwealth and under Charles II. (followed by THE BURNING CRESSET) 1433

Pilgrim, David, pseud. for John Leslie Palmer and Hilary Aiden St. George Saunders. THE GRAND DESIGN. Harper, 1943. Charles II's natural son travels in Europe on missions for his father. 1434

--------. NO COMMON GLORY. Harper, 1941. Adventure story of England centering on a natural son of Charles II. (followed by THE GRAND DESIGN) 1435

Plant, C. P. THE KING'S PISTOLS. Sonnenschein, 1902. A story about the Court of Common Pleas. 1436

Porter, T. H. A MAID OF THE MALVERNS. Lynwood, 1911. A romance of the Blackfriars Theater in Elizabethan London. 1437

Poynter, H. May. A MERRY HEART. S. P. C. K., 1893. Exile of Lady Grizel Baillie from James II's England and her triumphant return with William. 1438

Quiller-Couch, Arthur T. THE SPLENDID SPUR. by Q., pseud. Scribner, 1889. A messenger of Charles I finds adventure in the performance of his duties. 1439

Raymond, Walter. IN THE SMOKE OF WAR. Macmillan, 1895. Interesting account of Somerset in 1645 and the suffering brought on by the Civil War. 1440

Reid, Hilda S. TWO SOLDIERS AND A LADY. Dutton, 1932. Attempts to obtain an incriminating document in Puritan-ruled England. 1441

Reynolds, George W. M. THE RYE HOUSE PLOT. Dicks, 1884. Based on the Rye House conspiracy of 1683. 1442

Richards, H. Grahame. RICHARD SOMERS. Blackwood, 1911. England during the Civil War and Restoration. 1443

Roberton, Margaret H. A GALLANT QUAKER. Methuen, 1901. Trials of the Quakers under the Stuarts, presenting William Penn and George Fox. 1444

Robertson, William. THE KINGS OF CARRICK. Hamilton, 1890. Historical romance of the feud among the Kennedys of Ayrshire. 1445

Robinson, Emma. WHITEFRIARS. Dutton, 1844. A panoramic view of people and events in the days of Charles II. 1446

--------. WHITEHALL. Mortimer, 1845. Recounts the capture, trial, and execution of Charles I. 1447

Rodenberg, Julius. KING BY THE GRACE OF GOD. (tr.) Bentley, 1871. Characters include Cromwell and other politicians at the time of the King's capture. 1448

Sabatini, Rafael. FORTUNE'S FOOL. Houghton, 1923. A soldier of Cromwell's army in exile after the Restoration, and his return to England. 1449

--------. THE KING'S MINION. Houghton, 1930. The Earl of Somerset and the Countess of Essex become implicated in a murder. 1450

--------. THE STALKING HORSE. Houghton, 1933. Romance and adventure amid Jacobite plotting in England. 1451

--------. THE TAVERN KNIGHT. De la More Press, 1904. A wild, unruly Cavalier condemned to death for his part in Charles II's escape. 1452

Salmon, Geraldine Gordon. THE BLACK GLOVE. by J. G. Sarasin, pseud. Doran, 1925. London and Hampton Court with scenes illustrating the Plague and the fire of 1666. 1453

--------. CHRONICLES OF A CAVALIER. by J. G. Sarasin, pseud. Hutchinson, 1924. Secret missions and spying at the time of the Restoration. 1454

Scott, Thomas. MORCAR. Greening, 1903. A story of hidden treasure and claim to fortune early in the century. 1455

Scott, Sir Walter. THE BRIDE OF LAMMERMOOR. Tauchnitz, 1858. Scottish romance of a couple whose families are enemies of long standing. 1456

--------. THE FORTUNES OF NIGEL. Dean & Munday, 1822. Good picture of James I of England and the young noblemen who followed him from Scotland. 1457

--------. THE LEGEND OF MONTROSE. Lovell, 1885. Story of the Royalists under Montrose in the Scottish Highlands. 1458

--------. OLD MORTALITY. Tauchnitz, 1846. About an old man who wandered about Scotland caring for the graves of the Covenanters slain by Claverhouse. 1459

--------. PEVERIL OF THE PEAK. Dean & Munday, 1823. Complicated plot of romance and revenge during the hostility between Roundheads and Cavaliers. 1460

--------. WOODSTOCK. Constable, 1826. A Roundhead's kind treatment of the fugitive Prince Charles. 1461

Seawell, Molly Elliot. THE HOUSE OF EGREMONT. Scribner, 1900. Jacobite life during and after the Glorious Revolution. 1462

Shorthouse, Joseph Henry. JOHN INGLESANT. Macmillan, 1881. Romance of the English Civil War with some account of diplomatic and religious affairs. 1463

Simpson, Violet A. THE PARSON'S WOOD. Nash, 1905. Religious confusion and controversy in an English village during the 1680s. 1464

Sinnott, Patrick J. SIMON THE FOX. Comet, 1956. Early life of Simon Fraser, Scottish lord and Jacobite intriguer. 1465

Smith, Mrs. Fowler. JOURNAL OF THE LADY BEATRIX GRAHAM. Bell, 1875. Concerned with Montrose and the Covenanters in Scotland. 1466

Smith, Horace. BRAMBLETYE HOUSE. Weldon, 1826. Romance of Cavaliers and Roundheads in Commonwealth and Restoration England. 1467

Snaith, John Collis. MISTRESS DOROTHY MARVIN. Appleton, 1895. A novel with the overthrow of James II as background. 1468

--------. PATRICIA AT THE INN. Dodge, 1906. Events at a coastal inn during the Civil War between Roundheads and Cavaliers. 1469

Speas, Jan Cox. BRIDE OF THE MacHUGH. Bobbs, 1954. Resistance of a Highland clan which refused to give up its sovereignty to James VI. 1470

--------. MY LORD MONLEIGH. Bobbs, 1956. The companion to a Cromwellian must conceal her love for a political enemy. 1471

Steuart, John A. THE RED REAPER. Hodder & Stoughton, 1905. The last fifteen years of Montrose's career. 1472

Stewart, Charlotte. THE SAFETY OF THE HONOURS. by Allan McAulay, pseud. Blackwood, 1906. Desperate efforts to hide the Scottish emblems of royalty during the siege of Dunnottar Castle. 1473

Stucken, Eduard. DISSOLUTE YEARS. (tr.) Farrar, 1935. Love and politics at the court of James I in Stuart England. 1474

Sutcliff, Rosemary. RIDER ON A WHITE HORSE. Coward, 1959. A Baroness and her little daughter accompany her husband as he rides to fight with Cromwell. 1475

--------. SIMON. Oxford, 1953. Vivid description of battles during the English Civil War. 1476

Sutcliffe, Halliwell. THE WHITE HORSES. Ward & Lock, 1915. Sieges and fighting during the English Civil War. 1477

Syrett, Netta. LADY JEM. Hutchinson, 1923. The atmosphere of plague-stricken London pervades this romance. 1478

Tanqueray, Mrs. Bertram. THE ROYAL QUAKER. Methuen, 1904. Religious conflict of a natural daughter of the Duke of York, later James II. 1479

Taunton, Winefrede Trafford-. THE ROMANCE OF A STATE SECRET. Simpkin, 1910. Intrigue in London after the restoration of Charles II. 1480

Taylor, Mary Imlay. MY LADY CLANCARTY. Little, 1905. Describes many prominent people and their activities in the closing years of the century. 1481

Teague, John J. THE BROKEN SWORD. by Morice Gerard, pseud. Hodder, 1910. The revolution against Catholic James II. 1482

--------. CHECK TO THE KING. by Morice Gerard, pseud. Hodder, 1906. Set during the revolution of the English people against James II. 1483

--------. THE KING'S SIGNET. by Morice Gerard, pseud. Hodder, 1909. The Restoration of Charles II and the part played by George Monk. 1484

--------. PURPLE LOVE. [Formerly titled: LOVE IN THE PURPLE] by Morice Gerard, pseud. Hodder, 1908. Courtship of William of Orange and the Stuart Princess Mary. 1485

Thomas, H. Elwyn. THE FORERUNNER. Lynwood, 1910. The calling and romance of a young Welsh evangelist. 1486

Thynne, Arthur Christopher. SIR BEVILL. Lane, 1904. Account of life in Cornwall, particularly among the lower classes. 1487

Tremlett, C. H. CIVIL DUDGEON. Blackwood, 1914. Historical allusions abound in this novel of the Popish Plot and Rye House Plot period. 1488

Vallings, Harold. BY DULVERCOMBE WATER. Macmillan, 1902. Shows the discontent that prompted rebellion in James II's reign. 1489

--------. THE LADY MARY OF TAVISTOCK. Milne, 1908. Life of the people showing the advent of a plague and the punishment of criminals. 1490

Vance, Wilson. BIG JOHN BALDWIN. Holt, 1909. A Roundhead fights in Ireland and settles in America. 1491

Vaughan, Owen. BATTLEMENT AND TOWER. by Owen Rhoscomyl, pseud. Longmans, 1896. Events in north Wales during the English Civil War recounting the siege of Conway. 1492

--------. SWEET ROGUES. by Owen Rhoscomyl, pseud. Duckworth, 1907. Disappearance of an important message after the Battle of Naseby. 1493

Walpole, Hugh. KATHERINE CHRISTIAN. Doubleday, 1943. The Herries family from Queen Elizabeth's death (1603) to the outbreak of the Civil War at mid-century. 1494

Walsh, Maurice. THE DARK ROSE. Chambers, 1938. Rescues of two women during the revolt in Scotland against the Covenanters (1644-45). 1495

Watson, H. B. Marriott. CAPTAIN FORTUNE. Methuen, 1904. Adventure and romance during the Civil War. 1496

--------. (1) GALLOPING DICK. Lane, 1895. (2) THE HIGH TOBY (sequel). Methuen, 1906. (3) THE KING'S HIGHWAY (sequel). Mills & Boon, 1910. The entertaining adventures of a likable rogue--Dick Ryder. 1497

--------. THE REBEL. Harper, 1900. The corrupt, brittle way of life of Charles II's court. 1498

Watson, John. GRAHAM OF CLAVERHOUSE. by Ian Maclaren, pseud. Cupples, 1908. The Jacobite Claverhouse, his wife Lady Jean Cochrane, and William of Orange are prominent figures. 1499

Weyman, Stanley J. SHREWSBURY. Smith & Elder, 1898. Deals with the Jacobite conspiracy led by Fenwick and Robert Ferguson. 1500

White, Leslie Turner. HIGHLAND HAWK. Crown, 1952. Resistance to Cromwell results in Scottish guerrilla warfare. 1501

Whyte-Melville, George John. HOLMBY HOUSE. Longmans, 1860. Describes the battles of Newbury and Naseby and the trial of Charles I. 1502

Williamson, Hugh Ross. JAMES, BY THE GRACE OF GOD. Regnery, 1956. The intermingling of religious intolerance and political intrigues in the Glorious Revolution. 1503

Wood, Lydia C. FOR A FREE CONSCIENCE. Revell, 1905. Trials of Quakers in England, resulting in the colonization of Pennsylvania. 1504

Woodruffe-Peacock, Dennis Max Cornelius. THE KING'S ROGUE. [En. title: COLONEL BLOOD] by Max Peacock, pseud. Macrae Smith, 1947. A dispossessed Irish landowner attempts to steal the English crown jewels. 1505

Yeoman, William Joseph. A WOMAN'S COURIER. Chatto, 1896. Based on the plot of Jacobites Fenwick and

Charnock. 1506

Young, Margaret. THE WREATHED DAGGER. Cassell, 1909. Features Cromwell's siege of Thirlsby House in 1648. 1507

III. A. 2. a. 2) Ireland

Banim, John. THE BOYNE WATER. Duffy (Dublin), 1826. A vivid account of the Jacobite Rebellion and the siege of Limerick. 1508

--------. THE DENOUNCED. Harper, 1830. Protestant persecution of Irish Catholics after the Williamite Wars. 1509

Blake-Forster, Charles F. THE IRISH CHIEFTAINS. Whittaker, 1874. Accurate, comprehensive account of Ireland during and following the Williamite Wars. 1510

Burchell, Sidney Herbert. MY LADY OF THE BASS. Gay & Hancock, 1903. The seizure and holding of the Bass Rock by four dauntless Jacobites. 1511

Butt, Isaac. THE GAP OF BARNESMORE. Smith & Elder, 1848. "A tale of the Irish highlands and the Revolution of 1688." 1512

Canning, Albert S. BALDEARG O'DONNELL. Marcus Ward, 1881. Story of an Irish leader who joined the English enemy. 1513

Carleton, William. REDMOND, COUNT O'HANLON, THE IRISH RAPPAREE. Duffy (Dublin), 1862. Exploits of an Irish outlaw whose fortune was ruined by the English Revolution. 1514

Church, Samuel Harden. JOHN MARMADUKE. Putnam, 1889. Describes Cromwell's taking of Drogheda in 1649. 1515

Field, Louise. ETHNE. by Mrs. E. M. Field. Wells Gardner, 1888. Diary of an Irish girl caught in the upheavals caused by Cromwell's invasion. 1516

Finlay, T. A. THE CHANCES OF WAR. Gill (Dublin), 1877. The Catholic Confederation of Kilkenny and the wars in Ireland, 1648-49. 1517

Fitzpatrick, Thomas. THE KING OF CLADDAGH. Sands, 1899. A story of the Cromwellian occupation of Galway and its attending cruelties. 1518

Hinkson, Henry A. SILK AND STEEL. Chatto & Windus, 1902. Fighting, politics, and secret orders in the wars of Charles I. 1519

Le Fanu, J. Sheridan. THE FORTUNES OF COLONEL TORLOGH O'BRIEN. Routledge, 1847. Shows the bitter feuds and rivalries current during the Wars of King James. 1520

McChesney, Dora Greenwell. KATHLEEN CLARE. Blackwood, 1895. Story of Thomas Wentworth, Lord-Deputy of Ireland under Charles I. 1521

McDonnell, Randal. MY SWORD FOR PATRICK SARSFIELD. Gill (Dublin), 1907. Exploits of a cavalry colonel in the Jacobite War in Ireland. 1522

--------. WHEN CROMWELL CAME TO DROGHEDA. Gill (Dublin), 1906. Military account of Cromwell's subjugation of Ireland. 1523

Macken, Walter. SEEK THE FAIR LAND. Macmillan, 1959. One man's quest for freedom after Cromwell's ruthless subjection of Ireland. 1524

MacManus, Francis. STAND AND GIVE CHALLENGE. Loring & Mussey, 1935. The oppression of Irish peasants by absentee landlords. 1525

McManus, Miss L. NESSA. Sealy & Bryers (Dublin), 1904. The Cromwellian Settlement causes the quartering of Puritan soldiers in resentful County Mayo. 1526

--------. THE WATER, or, IN SARSFIELD'S DAYS. Buckles, 1906. The siege of Limerick in 1690 and the midnight cavalry action led by Sarsfield. 1527

Mathew, Frank. LOVE OF COMRADES. Lane, 1900. A romantic tale of adventure during Wentworth's service in Ireland. 1528

Moore, F. Frankfort. (1) CASTLE OMERAGH. Appleton, 1903. (2) CAPTAIN LATYMER (sequel). Cassell, 1907. Conditions in the west of Ireland during and after Cromwell's taking of Drogheda. 1529

O'Byrne, Miss M. L. LEIXLIP CASTLE. Gill (Dublin), 1883. Religious friction and the flight of James II, with various battles and sieges. 1530

--------. LORD ROCHE'S DAUGHTERS OF FERMOY. Sealy & Bryers (Dublin), 1892. Account of the wars following the Catholic Confederation of Kilkenny. 1531

O'Grady, Standish. IN THE WAKE OF KING JAMES. Dent, 1896. Jacobite activities in the years after James II was driven from Ireland. 1532

--------. ULRICK THE READY. Dodd, 1896. Feuds among the clans, the siege of Dunboy, and general unrest. 1533

Sadlier, Mary Anne. THE CONFEDERATE CHIEFTAINS. by Mrs. James Sadlier. Gill (Dublin), 1860. Owen Roe O'Neill and his part in the Irish Rebellion of 1641. 1534

--------. THE DAUGHTER OF TYRCONNELL. by Mrs. James Sadlier. Kenedy, 1863. The story of Mary Stuart O'Donnell, who fled Ireland to avoid marriage outside her religion. 1535

III. A. 2. b. Western and Central Europe

1) France

Achard, Amédée. BELLE-ROSE. (tr.) Street & Smith, 1895. A Dumas-type novel of romance, fighting, and adventure. 1536

--------. THE GOLDEN FLEECE. (tr.) Page, 1900. Romance and adventure set amid the Turkish Wars of Louis XIV's early reign. 1537

Andrews, Marian. IN THE STRAITS OF TIME. by Christopher Hare, pseud. Cassell, 1904. Depicts the conditions under which the Huguenots pursued their religion in southern France. 1538

Barr, Robert. CARDILLAC. Stokes, 1909. Blois is the locale of this romance of Louis XIII's early reign, showing influences of his mother, Richelieu, and Luynes. 1539

Beattie, William B. THE WEREWOLF. Paul, 1910. A lord's cruel treatment of his peasants in the time of Mazarin and Anne of Austria. 1540

Bedford-Jones, Henry. D'ARTAGNAN; THE SEQUEL TO THE THREE MUSKETEERS. Covici, 1928. The author completes an unfinished manuscript by Dumas. 1541

Bloundelle-Burton, John. THE CLASH OF ARMS. Methuen, 1897. General Turenne's brilliant work in Louis XIV's wars for more territory. 1542

--------. FATE OF HENRY OF NAVARRE. Lane, 1911. A story leading up to and including the tragic death of King Henry of Navarre. 1543

--------. IN THE DAY OF ADVERSITY. Appleton, 1895. The dueling, imprisonment, and military service of a youth whose inheritance is threatened. 1544

--------. KNIGHTHOOD'S FLOWER. Hurst & Blackett, 1906. The fifteen-month siege of La Rochelle over the issue of religious freedom. 1545

--------. TRAITOR AND TRUE. Long, 1906. Based on a plot to bring about a Dutch invasion and remove Louis XIV from power in France. 1546

--------. WITHIN FOUR WALLS. Milne, 1909. An assassination attempt against Henry of Navarre is revealed to his wife by a maid-of-honor. 1547

Brebner, Percy J. GALLANT LADY. Duffield, 1919. The treachery and intrigues of Louis XIV and his courtiers. 1548

Bungener, Louis F. THE PREACHER AND THE KING. (tr.) Lothrop, 1853. A story of the reign of Louis XIV, dealing with religion, written by a Protestant. 1549

Caldwell, Taylor (full name: Janet Taylor Caldwell). THE ARM AND THE DARKNESS. Scribner, 1943. Politics, intrigue, and religious strife in Richelieu's time. 1550

Chatfield-Taylor, H. C. FAME'S PATHWAY. Chatto, 1910. Has Molière as hero and Corneille as a prominent character. 1551

Coryn, Marjorie. SORROW BY DAY. Appleton, 1950. Royal romance featuring La Grande Mademoiselle, Louise de Bourbon. 1552

Courtney, Etta. CHECKMATE. Arnold, 1904. Diplomatic scheming under Louis XIV at Versailles. 1553

Doyle, _Sir_ Arthur Conan. THE REFUGEES. Harper, 1891. Rivalry at court between Madame de Maintenon and the Marquise de Montespan, and the flight of oppressed Huguenots to Canada. 1554

Drummond, Hamilton. THE GREAT GAME. Paul, 1918. The carefully planned schemes of French War Minister Louvois provide the background. 1555

Dumas, Alexandre. THE D'ARTAGNAN ROMANCES, the many daring adventures of three guardsmen, Porthos, Athos, and Aramis, and their Gascon companion, D'Artagnan. (1) THE THREE MUSKETEERS. (tr.) Little, 1888. The feud between Richelieu and Queen Anne. (2) TWENTY YEARS AFTER (sequel). (tr.) Munro, 1878. In the service of Mazarin; the Fronde; the execution of Charles I in England. (3) THE VICOMTE DE BRAGELONNE (sequel). (tr.) [same as: TEN YEARS LATER] Routledge, 1857. The time of Louis XIV's increasing power, with the son of Athos as hero; contains the story of the "Man in the Iron Mask." 1556

--------. THE WAR OF WOMEN. (tr.) Little, 1895. The end of the second Fronde and Mazarin's defeat of Condé, stressing the part played by the latter's wife. 1557

Eccott, W. J. A DEMOISELLE OF FRANCE. Blackwood, 1910. Dashing adventure in this novel featuring an Abbé and relating the downfall of Finance Minister Fouquet. 1558

--------. HIS INDOLENCE OF ARRAS. Blackwood, 1905. A romantic tale of Louise de la Valliere and the Marquise de Montespan, court favorites of Louis XIV. 1559

--------. THE RED NEIGHBOUR. Blackie, 1908. A romance which has Louvois, Minister of War under Louis XIV, as the leading character. 1560

Frischauer, Paul. SHEPHERD'S CROOK. Scribner, 1951. The daughter of a Huguenot martyr flees court to join fellow religionists in hiding in the mountains. 1561

Gallet, Louis. CAPTAIN SATAN. [same as ADVENTURES OF CYRANO DE BERGERAC] Fenno, 1900. A story of the swaggering Cyrano de Bergerac. 1562

Gautier, Théophile. CAPTAIN FRACASSE. (tr.) Page, 1897. Daring exploits in a romance which pictures travelling actors and the homes of nobles. 1563

Gay, _Madame_ Sophie. MARIE DE MANCINI. (tr.) Lawrence & Bullen, 1898. A story of mid-century court life reflecting military and political developments. 1564

Golon, Sergeanne, _pseud._ for Anne and Serge Golon. ANGÉLIQUE. (tr.) Lippincott, 1958. Historical romance of the spectacular court of Louis XIV. (followed by ANGÉLIQUE AND THE KING) 1565

--------. ANGÉLIQUE AND THE KING. (tr.) Lippincott, 1960. The heroine becomes a favorite of the "Sun King," Louis XIV. 1566

Grant, James. ARTHUR BLANE. Dutton, 1858. The Scottish Guard in France in the third decade of the century. 1567

Hill, Pamela. THE CROWN AND THE SHADOW. Putnam, 1955. Social life at the time of Louis XIV centered on Madame de Maintenon. 1568

Hooper, I. THE SINGER OF MARLY. Methuen, 1897. The slave market is featured in this story which embraces events in France, Ireland, and Martinique. 1569

Irwin, Margaret. ROYAL FLUSH. Harcourt, 1932. A moving story of the royal houses of France and England in the age of Louis XIV. 1570

James, G. P. R. THE HUGUENOT. Dutton, 1838. The persecutions that resulted when the Edict of Nantes was revoked. 1571

--------. LIFE AND ADVENTURES OF JOHN MARSTON HALL. Dutton, 1834. The exploits of an adventurous Scotsman in France during the first Fronde outbreak. 1572

--------. RICHELIEU. Dutton, 1829. Based on the career of Richelieu, with emphasis on the Cinq-Mars Conspiracy. 1573

Jordan, Humfrey. MY LADY OF INTRIGUE. Blackwood, 1910. Court intrigues involve Louis XIII, Richelieu, Marie de Rohan, and Anne of Austria. 1574

Kaye, Michael W. THE CARDINAL'S PAST. Greening, 1910. Tells of plotting against France's great politician, Cardinal Richelieu. 1575

Kenny, Louise M. Stacpoole. LOVE IS LIFE. Greening, 1910. The exiled soldier, Sarsfield, in the employ of Louis XIV. 1576

Lee, Albert. THE FROWN OF MAJESTY. Hutchinson, 1902. French court and village life when Madame de Maintenon was most influential. 1577

Lewis, Janet. GHOST OF MONSIEUR SCARRON. Doubleday, 1959. Louis XIV punishes a bookbinder for possessing a pamphlet attacking the king's scandalous behavior. 1578

Maass, Edgar. A LADY AT BAY. (tr.) Scribner, 1953. The Marquise de Brinvilliers, notorious poisoner, at the court of Louis XIV. 1579

McCarthy, Justin Huntly. THE DUKE'S MOTTO. Harper, 1908. Adventure story of the time of Louis XIII and Richelieu. 1580

MacDougall, Sylvia B. A DUCHESS OF FRANCE. by Paul Waineman, pseud. Hurst & Blackett, 1915. Court of Louis XIV at Versailles up to the time of the revoking of the Edict of Nantes. 1581

MacGrath, Harold. THE GREY CLOAK. Bobbs, 1904. France during the period of Cardinal Mazarin, successor to Richelieu. 1582

Macquoid, Katharine S. HIS HEART'S DESIRE. Hodder, 1903. A story based on the career of Cardinal Richelieu, with Louis XIII portrayed. 1583

Mann, Millicent E. MARGOT, THE COURT SHOEMAKER'S CHILD. McClurg, 1901. A romance of the time of Louis XIV. 1584

Manning, Anne. JACQUES BONNEVAL. Dodd, 1869. The days of the Dragonnades under Louis XIV. 1585

Meeker, Arthur. IVORY MISCHIEF. Houghton, 1942. Two sisters are the heroines of this French romance. 1586

--------. THE SILVER PLUME. Knopf, 1952. The Duc de Rohan's fight to prove his right to his title. 1587

Melbury, John. MONSIEUR DESPERADO. Murray, 1924. Includes the submission of Huguenot La Rochelle to Richelieu. 1588

Mundt, Klara. PRINCE EUGENE AND HIS TIMES. (tr.) by Louisa Mühlbach, pseud. Appleton, 1869. European politics and warfare during the years from about 1680 to 1718. 1589

O'Shaughnessy, Michael. MONSIEUR MOLIÈRE. Crowell, 1959. French theater and theatrical society in Molière's time. 1590

Pemjean, Lucien. CAPTAIN D'ARTAGNAN. (tr.) Doubleday, 1933. Adventures of D'Artagnan from the death of his beloved Irene to his trip to England. 1591

--------. WHEN D'ARTAGNAN WAS YOUNG. (tr.) Doubleday, 1932. Based on the life in Paris of the historical figure, D'Artagnan. (followed by CAPTAIN D'ARTAGNAN) 1592

Sabatini, Rafael. ST. MARTIN'S SUMMER. Hutchinson, 1909. Domestic life in a feudal chateau early in the century. 1593

Smith, Albert. THE MARCHIONESS OF BRINVILLIERS. Bentley, 1846. A novel based on the activities of an infamous poisoner. 1594

Stilson, Charles B. THE ACE OF BLADES. Watt, 1924. The extraordinary swordsmanship of an untitled lad is his key to success. 1595

Taylor, Mary Imlay. THE CARDINAL'S MUSQUETEER. McClurg, 1900. Contest for power between Marie de Medici and Cardinal Richelieu. 1596

Tessin, Brigitte von. THE BASTARD. (tr.) McKay, 1959. Relations between a man and his three sons against a background of religious warfare. 1597

Thompson, E. Perronet. A DRAGOON'S WIFE. Greening, 1907. Features Louis XIV's Dragonnades and an escaped Huguenot. 1598

Vigny, Alfred Victor, comte de. CINQ-MARS. (tr.) Low, 1847. Attempt to assassinate the despotic Richelieu. 1599

Weyman, Stanley J. THE MAN IN BLACK. Longmans, 1894. Adventure-romance during the time of Louis XIII and Richelieu. 1600

--------. UNDER THE RED ROBE. Longmans, 1894. A spy in the service of Cardinal Richelieu struggles with his conscience. 1601

III. A. 2. b. 2) Central Europe (including Germany, the Netherlands, Switzerland, Austria, Hungary, Czechoslovakia, and Poland)

Auerbach, Berthold. SPINOZA. Holt, 1882. The development of Spinoza's philosophy, his romance, interest in Christianity, and break with Judaism. 1602

Bailey, H. C. KARL OF ERBACH. Longmans, 1903. Adventures during the Thirty Years War reflecting Richelieu's masterly diplomacy. 1603

Brebner, Percy J. THE TURBULENT DUCHESS. Little, 1915. Romance involving the Duchess of Podina. 1604

Crockett, Samuel R. THE RED AXE. Harper, 1898. Lawlessness and violence in seventeenth century Germany. 1605

DeQuincy, Thomas. KLOSTERHEIM. Black, 1896. A mysterious apparition unsettles a superstitious man who holds power in the palace unjustly. 1606

Dumas, Alexandre. THE BLACK TULIP. (tr.) Munro, 1877. Struggles of the rising Dutch Republic; William of Orange and the De Witt brothers; the tulip industry craze. 1607

Durych, Jaroslav. DESCENT OF THE IDOL. (tr.) Dutton, 1936. Romance and adventure during the Thirty Years War. 1608

Eccott, W. J. THE MERCENARY. Blackwood, 1913. A Scotsman in the Thirty Years War in Germany and Austria. 1609

Gerson, Noel B. THE QUEEN'S HUSBAND. by Samuel Edwards, pseud. McGraw, 1960. The course of the political marriage of Holland's William of Orange and England's Mary II. 1610

Hamilton, Cosmo. HIS MAJESTY THE KING. Doubleday, Page, 1926. Charles II during the final period of his exile in the Low Countries. 1611

Harsányi, Zsolt. LOVER OF LIFE. (tr.) Putnam, 1942. The compelling personality and great work of artist Peter Paul Rubens. 1612

Hay, Marie. THE WINTER QUEEN. Houghton, 1910. Concerns the daughter of James I of England who, as wife of Frederick V the Elector Palatine, was briefly Queen of Bohemia. 1613

Innes, Norman. MY LADY'S KISS. Rand McNally, 1908. Hardships, destruction, and tensions during the Thirty Years War. 1614

James, G. P. R. HEIDELBERG. Smith & Elder, 1846. The beautiful district of Heidelberg, the court of Frederick I, King of Bohemia and Elector Palatine. 1615

Jókai, Maurus. (1) 'MIDST THE WILD CARPATHIANS. (tr.) Page, 1894. (2) THE SLAVES OF THE PADISHAH. (tr.) Jarrold & Sons, 1902. The feudal, semi-barbaric society of Transylvania at the time of warfare between Turks and Hungarians. 1616

--------. PRETTY MICHAL. (tr.) Doubleday, 1892. The state of affairs in Hungary under Turkish rule. 1617

Koerner, Herman T. BELEAGUERED. Putnam, 1898. "A story of the uplands of Baden." 1618

Kossak-Szczucka, Zofja. THE MEEK SHALL INHERIT. (tr.) Roy Pub., 1948. An aristocrat lives among the poor in seventeenth century Poland-Lithuania. 1619

Lons, Hermann. HARM WULF. (tr.) Minton, Balch, 1931. The much-oppressed peasants fight back against both sides in the Thirty Years War. 1620

McCarthy, Justin Huntly. A HEALTH UNTO HIS MAJESTY. Doran, 1912. The life of Charles II during his exile in Holland. 1621

Mason, A.E.W. KÖNIGSMARK. Doubleday, Doran, 1939. Picturesque novel of the small German state of Celle. 1622

Meinhold, Wilhelm. MARY SCHWEIDLER, THE AMBER WITCH. (tr.) Scribner, 1844. An interesting account of a witchcraft trial assertedly based on a manuscript by the accused's father. 1623

--------. SIDONIA THE SORCERESS. (tr.) Reeves & Turner, 1894. Vivid account of the woman who supposedly destroyed the reigning ducal house of Pomerania by black magic. 1624

Molander, Harald. THE FORTUNE-HUNTER. (tr.) Heinemann, 1905. Experiences during the Thirty Years War including the siege of Magdeburg. 1625

Orczy, Baroness Emmuska. (1) THE LAUGHING CAVALIER. Doran, 1914. (2) THE FIRST SIR PERCY (sequel). Doran, 1921. The Netherlands in the early years of their hard-won independence. 1626

Pick, John B. LAST VALLEY. [En. title: FAT VALLEY] Little, 1960. A wandering philosopher's influence on mercenary soldiers in the Thirty Years War. 1627

Purtscher, Nora. WOMAN ASTRIDE. Appleton, 1934. International adventures of a German noblewoman who fought in the Thirty Years War. 1628

Sienkiewicz, Henryk. THE DELUGE. (tr.) Little, 1891. The Swedish invasion of Poland in the third quarter of the century. (followed by PAN MICHAEL) 1629

--------. ON THE FIELD OF GLORY. (tr.) [same as: THE FIELD OF GLORY] Little, 1906. Unfinished romance of Poland at the time of King John Sobieski and the Turkish invasions. 1630

--------. PAN MICHAEL. (tr.) Little, 1893. Domestic life in Warsaw and the invasion of 1672-73. 1631

--------. WITH FIRE AND SWORD. (tr.) Little, 1890. An uprising of the Cossacks on the Dnieper. (followed by THE DELUGE) 1632

Stevenson, Philip L. THE BLACK CUIRASSIER. Hurst & Blackett, 1906. Adventures of an Irish hero in the Thirty Years War, featuring Wallenstein. 1633

Vansittart, Robert. JOHN STUART. Murray, 1912. Adventures of John Stuart, who claimed to be a son of Charles II. 1634

Wassermann, Jacob. THE TRIUMPH OF YOUTH. (tr.) Boni & Liveright, 1927. Experiences of a youth in Germany confronted by superstition and fanaticism. 1635

Weyman, Stanley J. THE LONG NIGHT. McClure, 1903. Chiefly concerns the attack of the Savoyards on Geneva, 1602. 1636

--------. MY LADY ROTHA. Longmans, 1899. Shows the Thirty Years War with the countryside overrun by soldiers and bandits. 1637

Zangwill, Israel. THE MAKER OF LENSES. Harper, 1898. A novel based on the career of Spinoza. 1638

III. A. 2. b. 3) Scandinavia and the Baltic

Jacobsen, Jens Peter. MARIE GRUBBE. (tr.) Knopf, 1925. A Danish tragic novel of romance, warfare, and high politics. 1639

Lewis, Janet. TRIAL OF SOREN QUIST. Doubleday, 1947. Tragic drama rooted in an old folk tale of seventeenth century Denmark. 1640

Stephan, Ruth. THE FLIGHT. Knopf, 1956. Purported autobiography of Queen Christina of Sweden, who was converted to Catholicism. (followed by MY CROWN, MY LOVE) 1641

III. A. 2. c. Southern Europe

1) Iberian Peninsula

Ainsworth, W. Harrison. THE SPANISH MATCH. Routledge, 1865. Charles Stuart and Buckingham go to Madrid in quest of a royal Spanish bride. 1642

Burr, Amelia Josephine. A DEALER IN EMPIRE. Harper, 1915. Statesmanship and diplomacy in Spain under the youthful Philip IV. 1643

Drummond, Hamilton. LOYALTY. Nash, 1921. Maneuverings at the Madrid court of Philip IV. 1644

Hunt, Frederick. ROYAL TWILIGHT. by John Fitzgay, pseud. Roy Pub., 1946. International intrigue centered on Maria Luisa, consort of the idiot Carlos II. 1645

III. A. 2. c. 2) Italy and Adjacent Islands

Candler, Pat. TESTORE. Dutton, 1916. Story of a fiddle-maker of Milan. 1646

Cotton, Albert Louis. THE COMPANY OF DEATH. Blackwood, 1905. Neopolitan revolt against strict Spanish rule. 1647

Crawford, F. Marion. STRADELLA. Macmillan, 1909. Elopement and flight of musician Alessandro Stradella. 1648

Harsányi, Zsolt. THE STAR-GAZER. (tr.) Putnam, 1939. Galileo's teachings, inventions, discoveries, and trouble with the Inquisition. 1649

Manzoni, Alessandro. THE BETROTHED. (tr.) Macmillan, 1875. Obstacles to a peasant marriage are met and overcome in a story descriptive of Milan. 1650

Montgomery, K. L., pseud. for Kathleen and Letitia Montgomery. 'WARE VENICE. Hutchinson, 1927. Exciting adventure based on the Spanish Conspiracy of 1618. 1651

Stephan, Ruth. MY CROWN, MY LOVE. Knopf, 1960. Christina of Sweden in the period after she relinquished her crown and joined the Catholic faith. 1652

III. A. 2. d. Eastern Europe (including Russia and the Balkans), the Near East, and North Africa

Groseclose, Elgin Earl. THE CARMELITE. Macmillan, 1955. Contrast of the simplicity and austerity of Fray Juan to the Persian pageanty which surrounded him. 1653

Knowles, Mabel Winifred. A PRINCE OF INTRIGUE. by May Wynne, pseud. Jarrolds Ltd., 1920. Mazeppa and his relations with Russia's Peter the Great and Sweden's Charles XII. 1654

Taylor, Mary Imlay. ON THE RED STAIRCASE. McClurg, 1896. Confusion and intrigue in Russia following Czar Feodor's death. 1655

--------. THE REBELLION OF THE PRINCESS. McClure, 1903. The heroine is Sophia, sister of Peter the Great and regent of Russia. 1656

Tolstoi, Alexei N. PETER THE GREAT. (tr.) Covici, 1932. Account of Peter I from boyhood to young manhood. 1657

Whishaw, Frederick J. MAZEPPA. Chatto, 1902. A story of Mazeppa and the Cossasks. 1658

--------. NATHALIA. Digby & Long, 1913. Depicts Moscow court life, the romance of Peter the Great's parents, and his questioned birth. 1659

--------. A SPLENDID IMPOSTOR. Chatto, 1903. An impostor claims to be the murdered son of Ivan the Terrible. 1660

III. A. 2. e. Overseas Exploration, Enterprise, and Expansion

Bailey, H. C. THE GENTLEMAN ADVENTURER. Doran, 1915. The hero, a sort of gentleman pirate, has many thrilling experiences in the West Indies. 1661

Bullen, Frank T. SEA PURITANS. Hodder, 1904. The navy of the Puritan Commonwealth and the career of Admiral Blake. 1662

Costain, Thomas B. FOR MY GREAT FOLLY. Putnam, 1942. English piracy in the Mediterranean under the dashing John Ward. 1663

Farnol, Jeffery. BLACK BARTLEMY'S TREASURE. Little, 1920. Adventures of an English nobleman on the high seas in quest of vengeance and treasure. (followed by MARTIN CONISBY'S VENGEANCE) 1664

Forbes, George. ADVENTURES IN SOUTHERN SEAS. Dodd, 1920. Voyages in search of treasure, based on the journeys of the Dutch navigator, Hartog. 1665

Ford, Ford Madox (name originally Ford Madox Hueffer). THE HALF MOON. Doubleday, Page, 1909. Harsh conditions under James I led to such expeditions as Henry Hudson's voyage to the New World. 1666

Heyer, Georgette. BEAUVALLET. Longmans, 1930. Pirating on the Spanish Main and the capture of an explosive Spanish girl. 1667

Hyne, C. J. Cutcliffe. PRINCE RUPERT THE BUCCANEER. Stokes, 1900. Prince Rupert's voyage to the West Indies and his adventures with Caribbean buccaneers. 1668

Judah, Charles Burnet. TOM BONE. Morrow, 1944. Slave trading, a romantic triangle, and plenty of action. 1669

Masefield, John. CAPTAIN MARGARET. Lippincott, 1908. Combines romance and adventure on the Spanish Main. 1670

--------. LOST ENDEAVOUR. Nelson, 1910. Buccaneering on the Spanish Main at the end of the seventeenth century. 1671

Niven, Frederick. THE ISLAND PROVIDENCE. Lane, 1910. Experiences of an Englishman on the Spanish Main and as a prisoner at Cartagena. 1672

Orcutt, William Dana. ROBERT CAVALIER. McClurg, 1904. LaSalle's experiences in Old World and New, crowned by his exploration of the Mississippi. 1673

Parrish, Randall. WOLVES OF THE SEA. McClure, 1918. A sea story about a man who had been condemned to slavery in Virginia. 1674

Quiller-Couch, Arthur T. THE BLUE PAVILIONS. by Q., *pseud.* Scribner, 1891. Tale of a youthful orphan and two old sea captains who were once his mother's suitors. 1675

Reach, Angus B. LEONARD LINDSAY. Routledge, 1850. Exploits of English and Scottish buccaneers in the West Indies near the end of the century. 1676

Sabatini, Rafael. CAPTAIN BLOOD. Houghton, 1922. A tale of buccaneering with an Irishman who was doctor, slave, pirate, and politician. 1677

Van Zile, Edward Sims. WITH SWORD AND CRUCIFIX. Harper, 1900. Exploration of the Mississippi Valley by La Salle and Jesuit missionaries. 1678

Vaughan, Owen. THE JEWEL OF YNYS GALON. by Owen Rhoscomyl, *pseud.* Longmans, 1895. The infamous pirate, Sir Henry Morgan, is the leading character. 1679

Westerman, Percy F. THE QUEST OF *THE GOLDEN HOPE*. Blackie, 1911. The sea adventures of a fugitive from Monmouth's Rebellion. 1680

Williams, R. MEMOIRS OF A BUCCANEER. Mills & Boon, 1909. A tale of pirating and naval warfare between English and Spanish. 1681

Wilson, R. A. A ROSE OF NORMANDY. Little, 1903. Explorations of La Salle and De Tonty in the Mississippi Valley. 1682

III. A. 3. Eighteenth Century: Age of Enlightenment and Revolution

a. The British Isles

1) England, Wales, and Scotland

Ainsworth, W. Harrison. BEAU NASH. Dutton, 1880. Social life in the resort town of Bath. 1683

--------. THE MISER'S DAUGHTER. Wilson, 1842. A tale of London society in 1744. 1684

--------. PRESTON FIGHT. Dutton, 1877. Romance at the

time of the Jacobite Rebellion of 1715. 1685

--------. ROOKWOOD. Dutton, 1931. The notorious highwayman, Dick Turpin, is the inspiration here. 1686

--------. THE SOUTH SEA BUBBLE. Routledge, 1868. The wild speculation of investors in the South Sea Company and the eventual results. 1687

Allardyce, Alexander. BALMORAL. Blackwood, 1893. Elopement of a young couple in Scotland at the beginning of the Jacobite Rebellion. 1688

Andrews, Robert. BURNING GOLD. Doubleday, 1945. Surgeon's adventures as ship's doctor with a crew of pirates. 1689

Arblay, Frances Burney. EVELINA. by Fanny Burney. Lowndes, 1791. A series of letters discloses the gay social whirl of late eighteenth century London. 1690

Arthur, Mary Lucy. TO MY KING EVER FAITHFUL. by George David Gilbert, pseud. Nash, 1909. The love story of Maria Fitzherbert, whose marriage to the Prince of Wales (George IV) was declared illegal when he married Caroline of Brunswick. 1691

Ashton, Blair. DEEDS OF DARKNESS. Little, 1957. A fashionable London gentleman is, secretly, a dashing highwayman. 1692

Bailey, H. C. THE GOLDEN FLEECE. Methuen, 1925. Jacobite plans and romances in mid-century. 1693

--------. THE HIGHWAYMAN. Dutton, 1918. A tale of the open road in the reign of Queen Anne, told with a backdrop of Jacobite scheming. 1694

Baker, Emily. PEGGY GAINSBOROUGH, THE GREAT PAINTER'S DAUGHTER. Griffiths, 1909. Social life of artistic and literary families, the Gainsboroughs and Sheridans, in London and Bath. 1695

Balfour, Andrew. TO ARMS! Page, 1898. Experiences of a Scottish medical student who views the prisons of Paris and is involved in the Scottish rebellion of 1715. 1696

Balfour, Melville. THE BLACKBIRD. Hodder & Stoughton, 1925. A story of the Old Pretender and intrigues and schemes surrounding the throne. 1697

Banks, G. Linnaeus. FORBIDDEN TO WED. Heywood, 1883. A story of Manchester in the late 1700s showing the social and economic status of the tradespeople. 1698

--------. GOD'S PROVIDENCE HOUSE. Paul, 1865. Growing sentiment to free the slaves results in the Emancipation Act of 1833. 1699

Baring-Gould, S. BLADYS OF THE STEWPONEY. Methuen, 1897. About such diverse characters as a highwayman, a hangman, an innkeeper's daughter, and a woman condemned to death by fire. 1700

--------. THE BROOM-SQUIRE. Stokes, 1895. A story of murder and violence in Hindhead in 1786. 1701

Barker, Shirley. SWEAR BY APOLLO. Random, 1958. A doctor from the American colonies goes to Edinburgh to learn new medical techniques. 1702

Barr, Amelia E. BERNICIA. Dodd, 1895. Social and political life following the Jacobite Rebellion of 1745, showing influence of the Methodist Revival. 1703

Barrington, Michael. THE REMINISCENCES OF SIR BARRINGTON BEAUMONT, BART. Richards, 1902. This supposed autobiography affords glimpses of cultured and corrupt society in England and France during the French Revolution. 1704

Beck, Lily Adams. THE CHASTE DIANA. by E. Barrington, _pseud._ Dodd, 1923. About the actress Lavinia Fenton, star of THE BEGGAR'S OPERA. 1705

--------. THE DIVINE LADY. by E. Barrington, _pseud._ Dodd, 1924. The historic romance of Lord Nelson and Lady Hamilton, with her life before she met him. 1706

--------. THE EXQUISITE PERDITA. by E. Barrington, _pseud._ Dodd, 1926. Theatrical and private life of Mary Robinson, an actress who worked with Sheridan and

Garrick. 1707

--------. THE IRISH BEAUTIES. by E. Barrington, *pseud.* Doubleday, 1931. The Irish Gunning sisters take a brilliant place in the social whirl of London. 1708

Bennett, Alice Horlock. THE PRINCE'S LOVE AFFAIR. Longmans, 1926. The romance and illegal marriage of the Prince of Wales (later George IV) and Marie Fitzherbert. 1709

Bentley, Phyllis. MANHOLD. Macmillan, 1941. Features a cloth manufacturer in the Yorkshire district of eighteenth century England. 1710

Besant, Walter. DOROTHY FORSTER. Chatto, 1884. A view of Northumberland noble society during the tumultuous first part of the century. 1711

--------. A FOUNTAIN SEALED. Stokes, 1897. George II and George the Prince of Wales in the closing months of the king's reign. 1712

--------. THE LADY OF LYNN. Dodd, 1901. Romance of an English beauty in the late 1740s. 1713

--------. NO OTHER WAY. Dodd, 1902. The desperate actions of a debt-ridden lady reflect conditions of the lowest levels of London society. 1714

--------. THE ORANGE GIRL. Dodd, 1899. Theatrical life in London in the 1760s with glimpses of taverns, mansions, and prisons. 1715

--------. ST. KATHERINE'S BY THE TOWER. Harper, 1891. The activities of the Jacobin Clubs just before the close of the century. 1716

-------- and James Rice. THE CHAPLAIN OF THE FLEET. Chatto, 1881. Manners and customs of London and Epsom in the middle of the century. 1717

Blackmore, R. D. THE MAID OF SKER. Burt, 1872. Thrilling events in the life of a well-born girl raised as a foundling. 1718

--------. MARY ANERLEY. Burt, 1880. Characters are

people along the Yorkshire coast; events include smuggling and naval service. 1719

Blake, Bass. A LADY'S HONOUR. Appleton, 1902. Chiefly a character study of John Churchill, first Duke of Marlborough. 1720

Bleackley, Horace. A GENTLEMAN OF THE ROAD. Lane, 1911. Adventure-romance of the road between Portsmouth and London in the early part of George III's reign. 1721

Bloundelle-Burton, John. DENOUNCED. Appleton, 1896. Followers of Stuart Prince Charlie in England and France after his defeat. 1722

--------. FORTUNE'S MY FOE. Appleton, 1899. Adventure on shipboard in action between British and French. 1723

--------. THE INTRIGUERS' WAY. Religious Tract Soc., 1908. Implication of an innocent man in a conspiracy to assassinate George I shortly before his coronation. 1724

Blundell, Mary E. NOBLESSE OBLIGE. by M. E. Francis, *pseud.* Long, 1909. The exile of French *émigrés* to London during the early part of the French Revolution. 1725

Bodkin, M. McDonnell. LORD EDWARD FITZGERALD. Chapman & Hall, 1896. Career of an English soldier who served in the American Revolution, in Ireland, and in Canada. 1726

Bone, Florence. THE MORNING OF TO-DAY. Eaton & Mains, 1907. Reaction of the people to Methodist preaching. 1727

Bowen, Marjorie, *pseud.* for Gabrielle Campbell Long. THE RAKE'S PROGRESS. Rider, 1912. A light romance of highly fashionable society. 1728

Bowles, Emily. AURIEL SELWODE. Sands, 1908. The story of an Oxford scholar and his niece, Auriel, with scenes at Queen Anne's court. 1729

Braddon, Mary E. THE INFIDEL. Simpkin, 1900. Reflects English thought and feeling during the Methodist Revival led by the Wesley brothers. 1730

--------. MOHAWKS. Simpkin, 1886. Life in London in the early eighteenth century. 1731

Brady, Cyrus Townsend. THE ADVENTURES OF LADY SUSAN. Moffat, 1908. Experiences of a lady who crosses the Atlantic fleeing from her husband. 1732

--------. THE TWO CAPTAINS. Macmillan, 1905. Conflict between Nelson and Bonaparte in the Mediterranean. 1733

Brandane, John. MY LADY OF AROS. Duffield, 1910. Depicts Jacobite plotting in Scotland as much as ten years after their defeat at Culloden. 1734

Brandreth, Charles A. THE HONOURABLE ROGER. Hutchinson, 1926. A picture of Methodists, Jacobites, Whigs, and Tories in Lincolnshire at mid-century. 1735

Bray, Anna Eliza. HARTLAND FOREST. Chapman & Hall, 1871. A domestic tragedy of western England in the rebellious early eighteenth century. 1736

Briton, E. Vincent. SOME ACCOUNT OF AMYOT BROUGH. Seeley, 1884. A romance of England which includes an account of James Wolfe and the taking of Quebec in Canada. 1737

Broster, Dorothy K. (1) THE FLIGHT OF THE HERON. Dodd, 1926. (2) THE GLEAM IN THE NORTH. Coward, 1931. (3) THE DARK MILE. Coward, 1934. Series of three books dealing with the unrest in Scotland during the Jacobite Rebellion and the fierce loyalty of the Highlanders to the cause of Bonnie Prince Charlie. 1738

Buchan, John. A LOST LADY OF OLD YEARS. Lane, 1899. The Jacobite period in Scotland with Lord Lovat and Murray of Broughton pictured. 1739

--------. MIDWINTER. Doran, 1923. Dr. Johnson and General Oglethorpe appear in this story of the Jacobite unrest. 1740

Burchell, Sidney Herbert. THE MISTRESS OF THE ROBES. Hurst, 1905. The court of Queen Anne. 1741

Byng, N. W. THE LAWLESS LOVER. Methuen, 1926. Story of an English highwayman about the middle of the eighteenth century. 1742

Calthorp, Dion Clayton. LITTLE FLOWER OF THE STREET. Hodder & Stoughton, 1923. Romance of eighteenth century London. 1743

Campbell, Grace MacLennan. TORBEG. Duell, 1953. The daily life of loyal Scots who aided Bonnie Prince Charlie. 1744

Capes, Bernard. JEMMY ABERCRAW. Brentano, 1910. A well-born youth's career as a highwayman. 1745

--------. OUR LADY OF DARKNESS. Dodd, 1899. A novel using the French Revolution as background. 1746

Carey, Wymond. (1) MONSIEUR MARTIN. Blackwood, 1902. (2) FOR THE WHITE ROSE (sequel). Blackwood, 1903. Jacobite activities in England and on the Continent between 1700 and 1720. 1747

Carmichael, Miss E. M. THE HOUSE OF DELUSION. Melrose, 1925. Pictures Lord Lovat and the Rebellion of '45 in Scotland. 1748

Castle, Agnes and Egerton. (1) THE BATH COMEDY. Stokes, 1900. (2) INCOMPARABLE BELLAIRS. Stokes, 1904. (3) LOVE GILDS THE SCENE, AND WOMEN GUIDE THE PLOT. Smith & Elder, 1912. Accounts of society life in these three romances of Bath are supposedly based on fact. 1749

--------. FRENCH NAN. Smith & Elder, 1905. A comedy of manners in the London of George II. 1750

--------. PAMELA POUNCE. Appleton, 1921. Life at court and in high society. 1751

Champion de Crespigny, Rose. THE ROSE BROCADE. by Mrs. Philip Champion de Crespigny. Nash, 1905. The court of George I at Leicester House and a surprising marriage. 1752

Charles, Elizabeth. DIARY OF MRS. KITTY TREVELYAN. Nelson, 1864. The manners, customs, and thought of the time reflected in this tale of Cornish domestic life. 1753

Chidsey, Donald Barr. HIS MAJESTY'S HIGHWAYMAN. Crown, 1958. A youth mistakenly captured as a highwayman escapes and joins the bandits until he can clear his name. 1754

Cobbold, Richard. THE HISTORY OF MARGARET CATCHPOLE. Frowde, 1845. Experiences of a woman jailed for stealing a horse and later transported to Australia. 1755

Compton, Herbert. THE INIMITABLE MRS. MASSINGHAM. Chatto, 1900. Story of an actress in London, with scenes on a convict ship and at the Botany Bay colony. 1756

Cooke, H. Robswood. ALTURLIE. Hodder & Stoughton, 1925. A Jacobite tale of France and Scotland. 1757

--------. OUTLAWED. Hodder & Stoughton, 1924. Adventures of a man who was outlawed following the Battle of Culloden. 1758

Cooper, Henry St. John. THE GALLANT LOVER. Low, 1926. An adventure story in Queen Anne's reign. 1759

Creswick, Paul. THE RING OF PLEASURE. Lane, 1911. About Lady Emma Hamilton before her romance with Lord Nelson. 1760

Crockett, Samuel R. (1) THE RAIDERS. Macmillan, 1893. (2) THE DARK O' THE MOON (sequel). Macmillan, 1902. Pathos, romance, and adventure in Scotland in the 1720s. 1761

Dakers, Elaine. MADAME GENEVA. by Jane Lane, pseud. Rinehart, 1946. Effect on Londoners of the bursting of the South Sea Bubble and the importation of cheap, poisonous gin. 1762

Dampier, E. M. Smith. INEFFECTUAL FIRES. Melrose, 1913. Artistic circles in London and Florence with

Sir Joshua Reynolds a figure. 1763

--------. OIL OF SPIKENARD. Melrose, 1911. A picture of manners and character in the reign of George II. 1764

Dawson, A. J. THE FORTUNES OF FARTHINGS. Harper, 1904. Contrasts peaceful life in rural Dorset with hardships of a Christian slave of the barbaric Moors. 1765

Deane, Mary. THE ROSE-SPINNER. Murray, 1904. English life during the unrest caused by Jacobite activity and South Sea Bubble speculation. 1766

Dearmer, Mabel. THE ORANGERY. Smith & Elder, 1904. Portrays London society--its parties, clubs, and gambling rooms. 1767

Deeping, Warwick. BESS OF THE WOODS. Harper, 1906. English country life in the mid-eighteenth century. 1768

Dickens, Charles. BARNABY RUDGE. Chapman & Hall, 1849. Dramatic account of the Gordon Riots of 1780 against modifying the penal laws against Catholics. 1769

Dill, Bessie. MY LADY NAN. Hurst, 1907. A light novel of society life in resort areas. 1770

--------. THE SILVER GLEN. Digby & Long, 1909. Schemes of the Jacobites and Hanoverians with a portrait of the Old Pretender. 1771

Dudley, Ernest. PICAROON. Bobbs, 1953. An engaging Irish pickpocket mixes theft and romance in London. 1772

Duke, Winifred. HEIR TO KINGS. Stokes, 1926. The Young Pretender's attempts to attain the English throne. 1773

--------. SCOTLAND'S HEIR. Chambers, 1925. Prince Charlie is the central figure in this novel. 1774

Dundas, Norman. CASTLE ADAMANT. Murray, 1927. The adventures, imprisonment, and escape of a Jacobite hero. 1775

Eccott, W. J. THE HEARTH OF HUTTON. Blackwood, 1906. A squire uses his knowledge of his own region to serve the Young Pretender. 1776

Ellis, Beth. THE MOON OF BATH. [same as: THE FAIR MOON OF BATH] Dodd, 1907. Romance and Jacobite conspiracy in the resort town of Bath. 1777

Elvin, Harold. STORY AT CANONS. Roy Pub., 1952. Spirited story of the Dukes of Canons. 1778

Everett, Mrs. H. D. WHITE WEBS. by Theo. Douglas, pseud. Secker, 1912. An imaginative romance of Henry Stuart and Margaret Hay. 1779

Falkner, J. Meade. MOONFLEET. Arnold, 1898. A tale of smuggling along the coast of England. 1780

Farnol, Jeffery. OUR ADMIRABLE BETTY. Little, 1918. A London belle and her train of admirers. 1781

Field, Bradda. BRIDE OF GLORY. [En. title: MILEDI] Greystone, 1942. The romances of Emy Lyon, the blacksmith's daughter who became Lady Hamilton. 1782

Fielding, Henry. THE HISTORY OF TOM JONES, A FOUNDLING. Millar, 1749. A novel of manners concerning mid-century life with pictures of all levels of society. 1783

Findlater, Jane Helen. A DAUGHTER OF STRIFE. Methuen, 1897. Domestic life in Scotland early in the century. 1784

--------. THE GREEN GRAVES OF BALGOWRIE. Methuen, 1896. A charming story of family life in Scotland. 1785

Findlay, J. T. A DEAL WITH THE KING. Digby & Long, 1901. "A tale of the period of the Jacobite Rebellion of 1715." 1786

Fleming, Guy. OVER THE HILLS AND FAR AWAY. Longmans, 1917. Land and sea adventures in the area of England, Ireland, and Scotland. 1787

Fletcher, Joseph S. I'D VENTURE ALL FOR THEE! Nash, 1913. Adventures of a Jacobite on the Yorkshire coast in 1746. 1788

Ford, Ford Madox (name originally Ford Madox Hueffer). THE PORTRAIT. Methuen, 1910. Social life of fashionable young dandies and their club activities. 1789

Forster, R. H. THE LITTLE MAISTER. Long, 1913. A tale of Northumberland which includes an account of Prince Charlie in Carlisle. 1790

--------. STRAINED ALLEGIANCE. Long, 1905. Romance during the Jacobite Rebellion of 1715. 1791

Foster, Elizabeth. CHILDREN OF THE MIST. Macmillan, 1961. An actual romantic scandal, the parties to which all lived in the same house. 1792

Fox, Marion. THE BOUNTIFUL HOUR. Lane, 1912. A pleasing account of late eighteenth century life having light touches of humor. 1793

Francillon, Robert E. ROPES OF SAND. Munro, 1885. Life in North Devon at the end of the century. 1794

Francis, Marian. WHERE HONOUR LEADS. Hutchinson, 1902. Domestic life in confused mid-eighteenth century England. 1795

Frye, Pearl. A GAME FOR EMPIRES. Little, 1950. Admiral Lord Nelson and his rousing naval victories. 1796

Galt, John. THE ANNALS OF THE PARISH. Dutton, 1820. The manners and thought-patterns of Scottish village life. 1797

Gaskell, Elizabeth C. SYLVIA'S LOVERS. by Mrs. Gaskell. Scribner, 1863. A romance of the closing years of the century during the war with France. 1798

Gaskin, Catherine. BLAKE'S REACH. Lippincott, 1958. A young woman, attempting to rebuild the family manor, becomes involved in smuggling. 1799

Gilchrist, R. Murray. THE GENTLE THESPIANS. Milne, 1908. A troupe of travelling actors in the country areas of England. 1800

Godwin, William. THINGS AS THEY ARE. Robinson, 1794. An expression of the author's protest against eighteenth century English penal laws. 1801

Goldring, Maude. DEAN'S HALL. Murray, 1908. English Quaker life from a sympathetic point-of-view. 1802

Goldsmith, Oliver. THE VICAR OF WAKEFIELD. Newbery, 1766. The life of a vicar and his family in a small rural community. 1803

Goodridge Roberts, Theodore. CAPTAIN LOVE. by Theodore Roberts. Page, 1908. Thrilling incidents and romances in the company of gamblers and highwaymen. 1804

Goodwin, Maud W. VERONICA PLAYFAIR. Little, 1909. Based on the literary, political, and social life of George I's time with Beau Nash as a figure. 1805

Gough, George W. YEOMAN ADVENTURER. Putnam, 1917. A farmer turns soldier in the Jacobite cause. 1806

Graham, Winston. THE RENEGADE. Doubleday, 1951. Defiance of conventions in the colorful Cornwall countryside, 1783-1787. 1807

Grant, James. LUCY ARDEN. Dutton, 1859. A romance of persons involved in the Jacobite rising of 1715. 1808

Harrison, Herbert. DICK MUNDAY. Low, 1923. An adventure story of London and Kent. 1809

Hayes, Frederick W. (1) A KENT SQUIRE. Hutchinson, 1900. (2) GWYNETT OF THORNHAUGH (sequel). Hutchinson, 1900. (3) THE SHADOW OF A THRONE (sequel). Hutchinson, 1904. A series of adventures in England and France during the disturbed eighteenth century. 1810

Hector, Annie French. THE HERITAGE OF LANGDALE. by Mrs. Alexander, pseud. Hutchinson, 1877. A story of southern England during the Jacobite Rebellion. 1811

Heyer, Georgette. THE BLACK MOTH. Houghton, 1921. High society life in fashionable English places at mid-century. 1812

Hinkson, Henry A. THE KING'S DEPUTY. McClurg, 1899. Ireland during the viceroyalty of the Duke of Rutland, featuring social customs and traditions. 1813

Hocking, Joseph. THE BIRTHRIGHT. Dodd, 1897. Exciting

adventures, including smuggling, in mid-century Cornwall. 1814

--------. MISTRESS NANCY MOLESWORTH. Doubleday, 1898. Daily life and Jacobite activities in Cornwall at mid-century. 1815

Hocking, Silas K. THE STRANGE ADVENTURES OF ISRAEL PENDRAY. Warne, 1899. A didactic novel of Cornwall in the time of Wesley. 1816

Innes, Norman. PARSON CROFT. Nash, 1907. Social life early in the century. 1817

Jacob, Naomi Ellington. THEY LEFT THE LAND. Macmillan, 1940. Yorkshire yeomen leave the land for London but their descendants return to the country. 1818

Jacob, Violet. FLEMINGTON. Murray, 1911. Adventures of a spy in the Jacobite Rebellion of '45. 1819

James, G. P. R. THE SMUGGLER. Dutton, 1845. The contest between smugglers and customs men in Kent. 1820

Jeffery, Walter. THE KING'S YARD. Everett, 1903. The attempt of an American to set fire to the Portsmouth Dockyard at the outbreak of the American Revolution. 1821

Johnston, Mary. FOES. Harper, 1918. Boyhood friends become enemies due to their love for the same girl. 1822

--------. THE LAIRD OF GLENFERNIE. Harper, 1919. Adventures of the hero in Scotland and abroad in Jacobite times. 1823

Kaye-Smith, Sheila. STARBRACE. Dutton, 1926. Life in the English countryside. 1824

--------. THE TRAMPING METHODIST. Dutton, 1922. The mission of an itinerant preacher. 1825

Keddie, Henrietta. FAVOURS FROM FRANCE. by Sarah Tytler, _pseud._ Long, 1905. A Scottish Jacobite family in exile after 1745. 1826

--------. INNOCENT MASQUERADERS. by Sarah Tytler,

pseud. Long, 1907. Domestic life in English villages. 1827

--------. LADY BELL. by Sarah Tytler, pseud. Chatto, 1885. The entertainments of noble society in the reign of George III and Queen Charlotte. 1828

--------. LADY JEAN'S SON. by Sarah Tytler, pseud. Jarrold & Sons, 1897. A novel of manners set in Scottish society. 1829

--------. THE MacDONALD LASS. by Sarah Tytler, pseud. Chatto, 1895. Flora MacDonald's part in the rescue and escape of Bonnie Prince Charlie. 1830

--------. THE POET AND HIS GUARDIAN ANGEL. by Sarah Tytler, pseud. Chatto, 1904. The literary circle at Olney, with the poet Cowper as chief figure. 1831

Keeling, Elsa d'Esterre. THE QUEEN'S SERF. Unwin, 1898. A romance of England in Queen Anne's reign. 1832

King-Hall, Magdalen. LOVELY LYNCHS. Rinehart, 1947. Drawing room society in Ireland, England, and France as it appears in the lives of two sisters. 1833

Kirk, James Prior. FORTUNA CHANCE. by James Prior, pseud. Constable, 1910. Rural life on the secluded western border of Sherwood Forest, affected little by current events. 1834

Knowles, Mabel Winifred. THE GIPSY COUNT. by May Wynne, pseud. McBride, 1909. Based on the adventures of Bamfylde Moore Carew, known as "king of the gypsies." 1835

--------. HONOUR'S FETTERS. by May Wynne, pseud. Paul, 1911. The search of a young French girl for her brother, a prisoner-of-war in England. 1836

--------. MISTRESS CYNTHIA. by May Wynne, pseud. Greening, 1910. Romance involving Jacobite intrigues with Spain and France. 1837

Laing, Jan. PRISCILLA. Putnam, 1951. Story of a girl left in the London Foundling Hospital. 1838

Lambert, Frederick Arthur. THE GREAT ATTEMPT. by Frederick Arthur, pseud. Murray, 1914. Jacobite activity in northern England in the 1730s. 1839

Lane, Elinor Macartney. NANCY STAIR. Appleton, 1905. Romance and murder figure in this story of Nancy Stair and Robert Burns. 1840

Lee, Albert. THE BARONET IN CORDUROY. Appleton, 1903. Pictures English life from noble homes to prisons. 1841

Legge, Clayton Mackenzie. HIGHLAND MARY. Clark, 1906. The story of Robert Burns and his romances with Mary Campbell and Jean Armour. 1842

Lenanton, Carola Oman. PRINCESS AMELIA. by Carola Oman. Duffield, 1924. Tragic romance of Princess Amelia at the court of her father, George III. 1843

Lever, Charles. SIR JASPER CAREW, KNIGHT. Hodgson, 1855. The early days of the Irish Parliament in the unrest preceding the open rebellion of 1798. 1844

Linington, Elizabeth. MONSIEUR JANVIER. Doubleday, 1957. A cloak-and-sword story of revenge and romance. 1845

Lofts, Norah. AFTERNOON OF AN AUTOCRAT. Doubleday, 1956. Two separate romances are told in this enjoyable picture of manor and village life. 1846

--------. COLIN LOWRIE. Knopf, 1939. The varied life and loves of a Scotsman driven from his home by the Jacobite Rebellion. 1847

Lyell, W. D. THE JUSTICE-CLERK. Hodge, 1923. Social and political life in high legal circles in Edinburgh. 1848

Lytton, Edward Bulwer, 1st. baron. DEVEREUX. Dutton, 1829. Based on activities of Lord Bolingbroke with literary figures introduced. 1849

--------. EUGENE ARAM. Harper, 1832. Study of a murderer, giving the man credit for his good points. 1850

McCarthy, Justin Huntly. THE KING OVER THE WATER. Harper, 1911. A romance of the Old Pretender, James

Stuart, and Princess Clementina Sobieska. 1851

McFadden, Gertrude Violet. HIS GRACE OF GRUB STREET. Lane, 1918. Dependence of Grub Street writers on their rich and powerful patron. 1852

Machray, Robert. SIR HECTOR. Constable, 1901. Shows the influence of the Rebellion of '45 on financial matters. 1853

McIlwraith, Jean. THE CURIOUS CAREER OF RODERICK CAMPBELL. Constable, 1901. Thrilling adventures of a man involved in the Rebellion of '45. 1854

Mackenzie, Compton. THE PASSIONATE ELOPEMENT. Lane, 1911. The gay life and light entertainments of a resort town at the turn of the century. 1855

Mackenzie, William Cook. THE LADY OF HIRTA. Gardner, 1905. The kidnapping and imprisonment of Lady Grange, involved in Jacobite plotting. 1856

Maclean, Norman. HILLS OF HOME. Hodder, 1906. The search for Jacobites in hiding after the Battle of Culloden. 1857

McLennan, William. SPANISH JOHN. Harper, 1898. A Spanish lieutenant sent by the king of Spain to the Young Pretender arrives after the Battle of Culloden. 1858

Macquoid, Katharine S. CAPTAIN DALLINGTON. Arrowsmith, 1907. Adventures of highwaymen and campaigns of Marlborough. 1859

Malling, Matilda. THE IMMACULATE YOUNG MINISTER. (tr.) Constable, 1913. Centers around the career of William Pitt the Younger and reflects politics and court life. 1860

Markham, Virgil. THE SCAMP. Macmillan, 1926. The fortunes of Francis Talbot and his friends during the reign of George I. 1861

Marsh, Frances. A ROMANCE OF OLD FOLKESTONE. Fifield, 1906. Romance of an English admiral and a god-daughter of Marie Antoinette. 1862

Marshall, Edison. THE UPSTART. Farrar, 1945. The streets of London and the provincial theaters are the setting. 1863

Mason, A. E. W. and Andrew Lang. PARSON KELLY. Longmans, 1899. Based mainly on the Jacobite plot in which Bishop Atterbury was involved. 1864

Middleton, Ellis. THE ROAD OF DESTINY. Mills & Boon, 1923. Gambling and Jacobite activities in eighteenth century England. 1865

Milne, James. THE BLACK COLONEL. Lane, 1921. Adventures of a Jacobite after the Rebellion. 1866

Montgomery, K. L., pseud. for Kathleen and Letitia Montgomery. COLONEL KATE. Methuen, 1908. A Scots girl resolves, against her husband's wishes, to arouse her clan to Prince Charlie's cause. 1867

Moore, F. Frankfort. FANNY'S FIRST NOVEL. Doran, 1913. A novel based on the acceptance of Fanny Burney's first novel, EVELINA [listed in this section under Frances Burney Arblay]. 1868

--------. THE JESSAMY BRIDE. Hutchinson, 1897. Oliver Goldsmith and Mary Horneck are the central figures in this novel of cultured circles. 1869

--------. A NEST OF LINNETS. Appleton, 1901. The courtship and marriage of Elizabeth Linley and the playwright Sheridan. 1870

--------. SIR ROGER'S HEIR. Hodder, 1905. A novel of manners with characters such as those in Addison and Steele's SPECTATOR PAPERS. 1871

Morrow, Honoré. LET THE KING BEWARE! Morrow, 1936. Depicts the English government during Franklin's negotiations concerning the American Revolution. 1872

Muddock, J. E. Preston. FOR THE WHITE COCKADE. Long, 1905. A tale of the double-dealing Simon Fraser during the 1740s. 1873

--------. THE LOST LAIRD. Long, 1898. The search for hiding rebels after the Battle of Culloden. 1874

Munro, Neil. DOOM CASTLE. Dodd, 1901. The French hero searches for a traitor in western Scotland after Culloden. 1875

--------. THE NEW ROAD. Blackwood, 1914. Scotland in the 1740s. 1876

--------. THE SHOES OF FORTUNE. Dodd, 1901. A romance concerning the Young Pretender ten years after his defeat at Culloden. 1877

Murray, David Leslie. COMMANDER OF THE MISTS. Knopf, 1938. Charles Edward, the Young Pretender, and the valiant Scots who tried to help him. 1878

Neill, Robert. BLACK WILLIAM. Doubleday, 1955. Romance and details of life in bleak, austere Northumberland. 1879

--------. HANGMAN'S CLIFF. Doubleday, 1956. Exciting tale of smuggling and murder on the English Channel coast. 1880

--------. MILLS OF COINE. Doubleday, 1959. The troubled, depressed times just before the Industrial Revolution. 1881

O'Riordan, Conal. YET DO NOT GRIEVE. Scribner, 1928. Conditions under George III are reflected in the life of a loyal subject. 1882

Ormerod, Frank. THE TWO-HANDED SWORD. Simpkin, 1909. Jacobite and Methodist influences on English thought and action. 1883

Overton, John. HAZARD: A ROMANCE. Melrose, 1920. A love story with Jacobite elements in George II's time. 1884

Pearce, Charles E. MADAM FLIRT. Paul, 1922. A romantic novel about actress Lavinia Fenton. 1885

Pease, Howard. THE BURNING CRESSET. Constable, 1908. Lord Derwentwater and his associates in the Rising of

'15. 1886

Peck, Theodora. THE SWORD OF DUNDEE. Duffield, 1908. Adventures of a girl who assisted Bonnie Prince Charlie. 1887

Pemberton, Max. SIR RICHARD ESCOMBE. Harper, 1908. High society circles in mid-century Warwickshire. 1888

Pinkerton, Thomas A. BLUE BONNETS UP. Long, 1901. The time when Jacobite hopes were centering on the claim of the Young Pretender--about 1730. 1889

Ponsonby, Doris. IF MY ARMS COULD HOLD. Liveright, 1947. "A vivid and colorful romance of Bath in the time of Beau Nash." 1890

Quiller-Couch, Arthur T. HETTY WESLEY. Dutton, 1931. Tragic life of Hetty, sister of the famous John and Charles Wesley. 1891

Raymond, Walter. JACOB AND JOHN. Hodder, 1905. Rural life in Somerset at the time of South Sea Bubble speculation. 1892

--------. NO SOUL ABOVE MONEY. Longmans, 1899. A domestic tragedy of village life in which murder figures. 1893

Reade, Charles. PEG WOFFINGTON. Scribner, 1853. Based on the life of a Covent Garden actress, Margaret Woffington. 1894

--------. THE WANDERING HEIR. Chatto, 1882. The journeys and romance of a young heir. 1895

Rhys, Ernest. THE MAN AT ODDS. Hurst, 1904. Smuggling and piracy in Lundy and Wales. 1896

Richardson, Samuel. THE HISTORY OF CLARISSA HARLOWE. Dutton, 1748. Sentimental portrait of a young lady at mid-century. 1897

--------. THE HISTORY OF SIR CHARLES GRANDISON. Dutton, 1753. Realistic story of a gentleman at mid-century. 1898

Ritchie, Anne Thackeray. MISS ANGEL. by Anne Thackeray. Harper, 1875. The cultural life of Venice and London with the painter Angelica Kauffmann as the main figure. 1899

Robertson, Frances F. THE TAMING OF THE BRUTE. by Frances Harrod, pseud. Methuen, 1905. A young lady's attempts to instill the social graces in her uncouth cousin. 1900

Robertson, William. THE STONE OF DUNALTER. Gardner, 1901. Set in Scotland during the turbulence of 1745. 1901

Rogers, Garet, pseud. LANCET. Putnam, 1956. Practice of medicine in London by two very different men in a swift-moving drama. 1902

Sabatini, Rafael. THE GATES OF DOOM. Paul, 1924. Adventures of a Jacobite agent during the Atterbury Plot. 1903

--------. THE LION'S SKIN. Appleton, 1911. Domestic crisis after the bursting of the South Sea Bubble. 1904

Salmon, Geraldine Gordon. THE RED CURVE. by J. G. Sarasin, pseud. Hutchinson, 1927. A romance of many historic events in Scotland at mid-century. 1905

Schumacher, Henry. THE FAIR ENCHANTRESS. Hutchinson, 1912. The life of Emma, Lord William Hamilton's wife, before her marriage to him. (followed by NELSON'S LAST LOVE) 1906

Scott, Sir Walter. THE ANTIQUARY. Tauchnitz, 1845. Lives of gentry and fisherfolk on the coast of Scotland at the end of the century. 1907

--------. THE BLACK DWARF. Lovell, 1885. A dwarf is the central character in this tale of Scotland before the Rebellion of 1715. 1908

--------. GUY MANNERING. Bazin & Ellsworth, 1829. Lawlessness, smuggling, and a gypsy's curse in Galloway. 1909

--------. THE HEART OF MIDLOTHIAN. Tauchnitz, 1858.

Jeanie Deane walks from Edinburgh to London to petition Queen Caroline to pardon her sister. 1910

--------. THE PIRATE. Parker, 1822. Concerns a pirate in the Shetland and Orkney Islands and pictures the life and customs of the time. 1911

--------. REDGAUNTLET. Constable, 1824. A Scottish romance which tells of the Young Pretender's farewell. 1912

--------. ROB ROY. Bazin & Ellsworth, 1817. Robert MacGregor, Highland robber-outlaw, in the beautiful Loch Lomond area. 1913

--------. WAVERLEY. Tauchnitz, 1845. Scotland during the Jacobite Rebellion of 1745. 1914

Sheldon, Gilbert. BUBBLE FORTUNE. Dutton, 1911. A story of the development and fate of the South Sea Company. 1915

Shellabarger, Samuel. LORD VANITY. Little, 1953. Elegant and artificial mid-century English society is pictured here. 1916

Shepard, Odell and Willard Odell Shepard. JENKINS' EAR. Macmillan, 1951. Concerns the results of the War of Jenkins' Ear. 1917

Silberrad, Una L. SAMPSON RIDEOUT, QUAKER. Nelson, 1911. Peaceful life of a Quaker merchant in rural England. 1918

Sladen, Douglas. THE ADMIRAL. Pearson, 1898. Romance of Lord Nelson and Lady Hamilton. 1919

Smith, Arthur D. Howden. CLAYMORE. Skeffington, 1918. A young man with Prince Charlie at Derby and Culloden. 1920

Smith, Frederick R. THE COMING OF THE PREACHERS. by John Ackworth, pseud. Hodder, 1901. The Methodist Revival in northern, rural England. 1921

Snaith, John Collis. THE WAYFARERS. Ward & Lock, 1902. London social life in the time of novelist Henry Fielding. 1922

Stephens, Robert Neilson. THE FLIGHT OF GEORGIANA. Page, 1905. Northern England is the scene for these events following the Battle of Culloden. 1923

-------- and George Hembert Westley. CLEMENTINA'S HIGHWAYMAN. Page, 1907. A gentleman turned highwayman for a lark rescues a damsel in distress. 1924

Steuart, Catherine. BY ALLAN WATER. Elliot (Edinburgh), 1901. Recounts meetings held in a certain house in '15 and '45. 1925

--------. RICHARD KENNOWAY AND HIS FRIENDS. Methuen, 1908. A preacher and his associates at the turn of the century. 1926

Stevenson, Robert Louis. (1) KIDNAPPED. Scribner, 1886. (2) DAVID BALFOUR (sequel). [En. title: CATRIONA] Scribner, 1892. The exciting travels of two young Scots and conditions in Scotland after the Rebellion of 1745. 1927

--------. THE MASTER OF BALLANTRAE. Scribner, 1889. The tragic story of a fighting Scots family involved in the Jacobite troubles of mid-century. 1928

Stewart, Charlotte. POOR SONS OF A DAY. by Allan McAulay, pseud. Nisbet, 1902. A tale showing the sufferings and heartbreak incident to the Rebellion of '45. 1929

--------. THE RHYMER. by Allan McAulay, pseud. Scribner, 1900. A Scottish romance concerning an episode in Robert Burns' life. 1930

Strain, Euphans H. A PROPHET'S REWARD. Blackwood, 1908. Political unrest in Scotland before and during the French Revolution. 1931

Sutcliffe, Halliwell. THE LONE ADVENTURE. Doran, 1911. Reflects the attitude of the squire and yeoman classes during the disturbances of '45. 1932

--------. THE OPEN ROAD. Ward & Lock, 1913. In a case of mistaken identity the hero is taken for Prince

Charlie. 1933

--------. RICROFT OF WITHENS. Appleton, 1898. A violent story of the country folk of Yorkshire around 1745. 1934

--------. WILLOWDENE WILL. Pearson, 1901. Exploits of a highwayman in Cornwall during the '45 Rebellion. 1935

Tarbet, W. G. A LOYAL MAID. Arrowsmith, 1908. A picture of Galloway during Prince Charlie's scheming. 1936

Tarkington, Booth. MONSIEUR BEAUCAIRE. McClure, 1900. Complications arise when a nobleman disguised as a barber falls in love with an aristocratic lady. 1937

Teague, John J. A ROSE OF BLENHEIM. by Morice Gerard, _pseud._ Hodder, 1907. The successful campaign of Marlborough at Blenheim. 1938

Thackeray, William Makepeace. THE HISTORY OF HENRY ESMOND, ESQUIRE. Harper, 1879. Noted English literary figures appear in this story of the era of Queen Anne. (followed by THE VIRGINIANS) 1939

Tunstall, Beatrice. THE LONG DAY CLOSES. Doubleday, 1934. An ancestral estate in the Midlands during the time of Bonnie Prince Charlie. 1940

Tynan, Katharine. ROSE OF THE GARDEN. Constable, 1912. The story of Lady Sarah Lennox, with whom George III had a brief romance. 1941

Walpole, Hugh. JUDITH PARIS. Doubleday, 1931. A dramatic tale of the fun-loving daughter of Rogue Herries' old age. 1942

--------. ROGUE HERRIES. Doubleday, 1930. The Herries come to live in the family castle in Keswick. 1943

Ward, Mary Augusta. FENWICK'S CAREER. by _Mrs._ Humphry Ward. Harper, 1906. Romantic tragedy involving artists George Romney and Benjamin Haydon. 1944

Ware, _Mrs._ Hibbert. THE KING OF BATH. Skeet, 1879. A novel of manners at the fashionable resort. 1945

Watson, H. B. Marriott. THE HOUSE DIVIDED. Harper, 1901. English social life of the nobility with scenes at court and in London. 1946

Watson, William L. SIR SERGEANT. Blackwood, 1899. Adventures of a French sergeant who had served the Jacobites until their defeat. 1947

Watt, Lauchlan Maclean. EDRAGIL, 1745. Hodder, 1907. Western Scotland at the time of Bonnie Prince Charlie's landing. 1948

Wentworth, Patricia. QUEEN ANNE IS DEAD. Melrose, 1915. London at the time of Queen Anne's death. 1949

Weyman, Stanley J. THE CASTLE INN. Longmans, 1898. Adventures of travellers on mid-century English roads. 1950

Whitelaw, David. THE LITTLE LADY OF ARROCK. Chapman & Hall, 1921. Domestic tragedy in Jacobite times in Scotland. 1951

Whyte-Melville, George John. KATERFELTO. Longmans, 1875. A sportsman's story with a vivid description of stag hunting. 1952

Wilkins, William Vaughan. CROWN WITHOUT SCEPTRE. Macmillan, 1952. Romance in England and Italy during the 1770s. 1953

Wingfield, Lewis Strange. LADY GRIZEL. Bentley, 1877. Society life at Bath in mid-century. 1954

Winstanley, L. THE FACE ON THE STAIR. Hutchinson, 1927. Mystery and adventure in England's Lake District. 1955

Woods, Margaret L. ESTHER VANHOMRIGH. Murray, 1891. Portrays Jonathan Swift and many of his associates. 1956

--------. A POET'S YOUTH. Chapman & Dodd, 1923. Wordsworth's school days in England, his tours of the Continent, and his romance with Annette Vallon. 1957

Yoxall, James Henry. SMALILOU. Hutchinson, 1904. Gypsy life in English rural areas. 1958

III. A. 3. a. 2) Ireland

Alexander, Miriam. THE HOUSE OF LISRONAN. Melrose, 1912. Ireland under William III and in Anne's reign, showing the harshness of the Penal Laws. 1959

--------. THE PORT OF DREAMS. Putnam, 1912. Romance of Irish Jacobites. 1960

Arthur, Mary Lucy. THE ISLAND OF SORROW. by George David Gilbert, pseud. Long, 1903. Account of Ireland at the close of the century centers around the career of Robert Emmet. 1961

Banim, John and Michael. THE CROPPY. Duffy (Dublin), 1828. An Irishman's view of the excesses of the Rebellion of 1798. 1962

Bennett, Louie. A PRISONER OF HIS WORD. Maunsel (Dublin), 1908. An Englishman, motivated by love of an Irish girl, joins the Irish cause for which he has little sympathy. 1963

Bodkin, M. McDonnell. IN THE DAYS OF GOLDSMITH. Long, 1903. Pictures members of mid-eighteenth century literary circles. 1964

--------. THE REBELS. Ward & Lock, 1899. Politics, capture, and imprisonment in the Irish Rebellion of 1798. 1965

Bowen, Marjorie, pseud. for Gabrielle Campbell Long. DARK ROSALEEN. Houghton, 1933. A tragic story of Ireland's unrest and rebellion in the late eighteenth century. 1966

Buckley, William. CROPPIES LIE DOWN. Duckworth, 1903. A realistic account of the more severe aspects of the 1798 Rebellion. 1967

Burnett, William Riley. CAPTAIN LIGHTFOOT. Knopf, 1954. Exploits of a youthful highwayman who wanders through Ireland and Scotland. 1968

Byrne, Donn. BLIND RAFTERY AND HIS WIFE HILARIA. Century, 1924. Marriage of an Irish poet and a Spanish lady in the Connaught hills. 1969

Carleton, William. WILLIE REILLY AND HIS DEAR COLLEEN BAWN. Dutton, 1855. Portrays the hunting and persecuting of priests in mid-century. 1970

Crosbie, W. J. DAVID MAXWELL. Jarrold & Sons, 1902. A Loyalist view of the Rebellion of 1798. 1971

Edgeworth, Maria. CASTLE RACKRENT. Dutton, 1800. The reminiscences of an old family retainer depict Irish life and character. 1972

Faly, Patrick C. 'NINETY-EIGHT. Downey, 1897. Life in Dublin during the 1798 Rebellion. 1973

Froude, James Anthony. THE TWO CHIEFS OF DUNBOY. Longmans, 1889. Shows Ireland chafing under the yoke of English oppression. 1974

Gilbert, Rosa Mulholland. O'LOGHLIN OF CLARE. by Rosa Mulholland. Kenedy, 1916. Catholic suffering under the harsh Penal Laws. 1975

Gogarty, Oliver St. John. MAD GRANDEUR. Lippincott, 1941. How the decay of the aristocracy and the desperation of the peasants led to revolt. 1976

Gwynn, Stephen. JOHN MAXWELL'S MARRIAGE. Macmillan, 1903. Conflict between Protestants and Catholics involving forced marriage and political schemes. 1977

Hannay, James Owen. THE NORTHERN IRON. by George A. Birmingham, pseud. Maunsel (Dublin), 1909. Pictures intense political feelings at the end of the century. 1978

Hinkson, Henry A. THE POINT OF HONOUR. McClurg, 1901. The restless Irish at mid-century. 1979

--------. UP FOR THE GREEN. Lawrence & Bullen, 1898. Based on the experiences of a man captured by the United Irishmen in their uprising of 1798. 1980

Kerr, Archibald W. M. BY THE POOL OF GARMOYLE. Northern Whig (Ireland), 1925. Jacobite schemings in the early 1700s. 1981

Knowles, Mabel Winifred. FOR THE SAKE OF CHARLES THE ROVER. by May Wynne, pseud. Fenno, 1909. Adventures of a follower of Prince Charlie after the Rebellion of 1745. 1982

Lepper, John Heron. A TORY IN ARMS. Richards, 1916. Wool smuggling and other activities in Ireland. 1983

Lever, Charles. MAURICE TIERNAY. Harper, 1852. The capture and death of Wolfe Tone during the Irish Rebellion of 1798, and French attempts on Ireland. 1984

--------. THE O'DONOGHUE. Routledge, 1845. Conflict between Irish and French at the end of the century. 1985

Lover, Samuel. RORY O'MORE. Dutton, 1837. A novel of the Rebellion of 1798 blaming a desperate few for the horrors committed. 1986

McDonnell, Randal. ARDNAREE. Gill (Dublin), 1911. An English girl in Connaught during the Rebellion of 1798. 1987

--------. KATHLEEN MAVOURNEEN. Sealy & Bryers (Dublin), 1898. The Irish Rebellion and attempted intervention of France in the 1790s. 1988

Mathew, Frank. THE WOOD OF THE BRAMBLES. Lane, 1896. Events during the Rebellion of 1798. 1989

Maxwell, William H. O'HARA, 1798. Andrews, 1825. Dealings with the United Irishmen imperil a landowner. 1990

Murphy, James. THE HOUSE IN THE RATH. Sealy & Bryers (Dublin), 1909. Negotiations with France shortly before the Irish Rebellion of 1798. 1991

--------. THE SHAN VAN VOCHT. Gill (Dublin), 1883. Diplomatic and military relations between France and Ireland in 1798. 1992

Newcomen, George. A LEFT-HANDED SWORDSMAN. Smithers, 1900. Social life in Dublin in the unsettled years before the Rebellion of 1798. 1993

O'Hannrachain, Michael. A SWORDSMAN OF THE BRIGADE. Sands, 1914. An adventure-romance in Ireland and Flanders. 1994

O'Neill, Egan. THE ANGLOPHILE. [En. title: PRETENDER] Messner, 1957. Handsome Irish rebel falls in love with his English wife--jeopardizing his cause and his life. 1995

Orpen, Mrs. CORRAGEEN IN '98. New Amsterdam Bk. Co., 1898. A description of atrocities committed during the 1798 Rebellion. 1996

Parker, Gilbert. NO DEFENCE. Lippincott, 1920. A novel of Ireland, England, and Jamaica including the French attack on Ireland. 1997

Pender, Mrs. M. T. THE GREEN COCKADE. Downey, 1898. Northern Ireland during the Rebellion of '98. 1998

Sadlier, Mary Anne. THE FATE OF FATHER SHEEHY. by Mrs. James Sadlier. Duffy (Dublin), 1845. A parish priest is accused of involvement in a murder. 1999

Sheehy-Skeffington, Francis. IN DARK AND EVIL DAYS. Duffy (Dublin), 1919. The United Irishmen Movement in the Rebellion of 1798. 2000

Sillars, John. THE McBRIDES. Blackwood, 1922. Smuggling and adventure on the Isle of Arran. 2001

Thackeray, William Makepeace. THE MEMOIRS OF BARRY LYNDON, ESQ. Lippincott, 1871. Exploits of an Irish scoundrel who travels about Europe. 2002

Tynan, Katharine. A KING'S WOMAN. Hurst, 1900. A Quaker lady's view of the Irish Rebellion of 1798. 2003

III. A. 3. b. Western and Central Europe

1) France

Ainsworth, W. Harrison. JOHN LAW, THE PROJECTOR. Chapman & Hall, 1864. About John Law and his disastrous speculation, the Mississippi Bubble. 2004

Atkinson, Eleanor. MAMZELLE FIFINE. Appleton, 1903. "A romance of the girlhood of the Empress Josephine on the island of Martinique." 2005

Aubry, Octave. THE LOST KING. (tr.) Stokes, 1927. Report of a retired secret agent relating his attempts to trace the Lost Dauphin, Louis XVII. 2006

Austin, F. Britten. FORTY CENTURIES LOOK DOWN. Stokes, 1937. Napoleon's Egyptian campaign and his suspicions about Josephine's loyalty. 2007

--------. THE ROAD TO GLORY. Stokes, 1935. Napoleon's view of his first Italian campaign. (followed by FORTY CENTURIES LOOK DOWN) 2008

Bailey, H. C. BARRY LEROY. Dutton, 1920. About a spy for Napoleon who changes loyalties and serves the British. 2009

--------. THE GOD OF CLAY. Brentano, 1908. Napoleon's career from the time he was a Lieutenant until he became First Counsul. 2010

--------. STORM AND TREASURE. Methuen, 1910. The Reign of Terror in provincial France--the Vendean Rebellion and Carrier's wholesale drownings at Nantes. 2011

Balzac, Honoré de. THE CHOUANS. (tr.) Little, 1896. Royalist activities and Fouche's far-flung spy system. 2012

Baring-Gould, S. IN EXITU ISRAEL. Macmillan, 1870. Relations between Church and State in 1788-89, when revolution was imminent. 2013

Beck, Lily Adams. THE EMPRESS OF HEARTS. by E. Barrington, pseud. Dodd, 1928. Sympathetic portrayal of the young queen, Marie Antoinette, and the trouble caused by a costly diamond necklace. 2014

Bedford-Jones, Henry. RODOMONT. Putnam, 1926. "A romance of Mont St. Michel in the days of Louis XIV." 2015

--------. SAINT MICHAEL'S GOLD. Putnam, 1926. A young American involved in the politics of the Revolution. 2016

Belloc, Hilaire. THE GIRONDIN. Nelson, 1911. The experiences of an adventurer impressed into the army of the Republic. 2017

Bloundelle-Burton, John. A FAIR MARTYR. Everett, 1910. Story of a child during the plague at Marseilles. 2018

--------. THE FATE OF VALSEC. Methuen, 1902. Family dissent in the Revolution--a judge's disowned son loves the daughter of a woman condemned by the judge. 2019

--------. THE RIGHT HAND. Everett, 1911. The Battle of Dettingen is an important event in this tale of a dispute over the right to a title. 2020

--------. THE SCOURGE OF GOD. Appleton, 1898. Romance of the daughter of Baville, who figured in the insurrection of the Camisards for religious freedom. 2021

--------. SERVANTS OF SIN. Methuen, 1900. Marseilles during the plague; the banishment of a girl as a criminal and her rescue. 2022

--------. A WOMAN FROM THE SEA. Nash, 1907. An actress in England serves as a spy of the revolutionary French government. 2023

--------. THE YEAR ONE. Dodd, 1901. Adventures of a lady whose husband has joined the Revolutionists; the massacre of the Swiss Guards. 2024

Bowen, Marjorie, pseud. for Gabrielle Campbell Long. THE BURNING GLASS. Dutton, 1920. Paris at the time of the Encyclopaedists. 2025

--------. MR. MISFORTUNATE. Collins, 1919. Bonnie Prince Charlie's life in Paris and elsewhere on the Continent. 2026

--------. THE QUEST OF GLORY. Methuen, 1911. Sophisticated Parisian society life and the War of Austrian Succession. 2027

--------. THE THIRD ESTATE. Dutton, 1918. The rise to power of representatives of the French people. 2028

Brebner, Percy J. A GENTLEMAN OF VIRGINIA. Macmillan,

1910. A story of French life, which continued as usual in many places despite the Revolution. 2029

Brinton, Selwyn J. THE JACOBIN. Besant, 1936. Activities of the leftist Jacobins during the early part of the French Revolution. 2030

Broster, Dorothy K. SIR ISUMBRAS AT THE FORD. Murray, 1918. Includes the kidnapping of a small child during the French Revolution. 2031

-------- and G. W. Taylor. CHANTEMERLE. Murray, 1912. Romance dealing with the suppression of religious orders in revolutionary France at the start of the Terror. 2032

Capes, Bernard. ADVENTURES OF THE COMTE DE LA MUETTE DURING THE TERROR. Dodd, 1898. This tale of revolutionary Paris includes scenes of prison life. 2033

Carey, Wymond. "NO. 101." Blackwood, 1906. A spy of Louis XV's court during the War of Austrian Succession. 2034

Champion de Crespigny, Rose. FROM BEHIND THE ARRAS. by Mrs. Philip Champion de Crespigny. Unwin, 1902. Life of a young lady of the upper class. 2035

Cleugh, Sophia. ANNE MARGUERITE. Houghton, 1932. Romantic adventures of an aristocratic young lady during the early French Revolution. 2036

Coryn, Marjorie. ALONE AMONG MEN. Appleton, 1947. Napoleon and Josephine in the month between his return from Egypt and his becoming First Consul. 2037

--------. GOOD-BYE, MY SON. Appleton, 1943. Napoleon's mother, the engaging Letizia Bonaparte, and her amazing children. (followed by THE MARRIAGE OF JOSEPHINE) 2038

--------. INCORRUPTIBLE. Appleton, 1943. Compelling story of Robespierre in the last five months of his life. 2039

--------. THE MARRIAGE OF JOSEPHINE. Appleton, 1945. Beautiful Josephine de Beauharnais and her marriage to Napoleon. (followed by ALONE AMONG MEN) 2040

Crockett, Samuel R. FLOWER O' THE CORN. McClure, 1902. The insurrection of the Camisards under Jean Cavalier, a movement of people greatly stirred by religious fervor. 2041

Cuninghame, Lady Fairlie. THE LITTLE SAINT OF GOD. Hurst, 1901. A heroine of the Red Terror in Brittany during the French Revolution. 2042

Dale, Mrs. Hylton. CROWNED WITH THE IMMORTALS. Nichols, 1896. Romance based on the life of journalist-revolutionary Camille Desmoulins. 2043

Davis, Harold Lenoir. HARP OF A THOUSAND STRINGS. Morrow, 1947. Novel of the French Revolution and the period immediately following. 2044

Davis, William Stearns. THE WHIRLWIND. Macmillan, 1929. The passionate, widespread excesses in Paris and at Court during the Revolution. 2045

Dehon, Theodora. HEROIC DUST. Macmillan, 1940. The lovely Normandy countryside is the locale for this tale of the Chouan revolt of 1792. 2046

Delderfield, Ronald Frederick. FAREWELL THE TRANQUIL. Dutton, 1950. Adventures of an English smuggler who takes part in the French Revolution. 2047

Dickens, Charles. A TALE OF TWO CITIES. Chapman & Hall, 1859. Classic tale of the French Revolution's Reign of Terror. 2048

Dumas, Alexandre. ANDREE DE TAVERNEY. (tr.) Peterson, 1862. Centering on the executions of Louis XVI and his queen, this novel introduces many noted revolutionary personages. 2049

--------. (1) THE CHEVALIER D'HARMENTAL. (tr.) [same as: THE CONSPIRATORS] Little, 1891. (2) THE REGENT'S DAUGHTER (sequel). (tr.) Harper, 1845.

The conspiracy to overthrow Louis XV and his regent is foiled by Dubois, French foreign minister. 2050

--------. THE MARIE ANTOINETTE ROMANCES, a chronicle of history and court life from 1770 to 1793. (1) MEMOIRS OF A PHYSICIAN. (tr.) Little, 1893. Supposed memoirs of the swindler, Cagliostro, showing the decline of Louis XV's disastrous reign. (2) THE QUEEN'S NECKLACE (sequel). (tr.) Munro, 1877. Louis XVI's early reign; the scandal of the diamond necklace. (3) ANGE PITOU, or THE TAKING OF THE BASTILLE (sequel). (tr.) [same as: SIX YEARS LATER] Little, 1890. The attack on the Bastille, where state political prisoners were kept. (4) LA COMTESSE DE CHARNY (sequel). (tr.) Little, 1890. The king and queen's flight; their capture at Varennes; the king's execution. (5) THE CHEVALIER DE MAISON-ROUGE (sequel). (tr.) Little, 1890. The queen's imprisonment; unsuccessful attempts to rescue her; her execution. 2051

--------. MONSIEUR DE CHAUVELIN'S WILL. (tr.) Munro, 1900. This novel of the end of Louis XV's life depicts his decadent court and his death by smallpox. 2052

--------. SYLVANDIRE. (tr.) Little, 1897. Versailles during the ascendancy of Madame de Maintenon toward the closing part of Louis XIV's reign. 2053

--------. (1) THE WHITES AND THE BLUES. (tr.) Little, 1894. The period of the Directory and Napoleon's seizure of power. (2) THE COMPANIONS OF JEHU (companion volume). (tr.) Little, 1894. The Chouan conspiracy, a Royalist movement against Napoleon. 2054

--------. THE WOMAN WITH THE VELVET COLLAR. (tr.) Munro, 1900. A scene from the Reign of Terror including the execution of Madame du Barry. 2055

Dunlap, Katharine. GLORY AND THE DREAM. Morrow, 1951. The romance of an actress and a soldier. 2056

Edwards, Matilda Betham. A ROMANCE OF DIJON. Macmillan, 1894. The feelings of the peasant class just before the outbreak of the Revolution. 2057

--------. A STORM-RENT SKY. Hurst & Blackett, 1898. Provincial life in eastern France with a picture of Danton's execution in Paris. 2058

Ellis, Beth. THE KING'S BLUE RIBBAND. Hodder, 1912. A swift-paced novel of intrigue in Louis XIV's court at Versailles. 2059

Erckmann-Chatrian, pseud. for Emile Erckmann and Alexandre Chatrian. MADAME THÉRÈSA. (tr.) Scribner, 1869. Daily life in a Vosges village in 1793 and the effect of the political turmoil in France. 2060

--------. THE STORY OF A PEASANT. (tr.) Dutton, 1915. Illustrates the lot of peasants during the Revolution and their attempts to prosper at the expense of the monarchy. 2061

Everett, Mrs. H. D. A GOLDEN TRUST. by Theo. Douglas, pseud. Smith & Elder, 1905. The storming of the Tuileries; massacre in the prisons; and the brutal murder of a friend of the queen. 2062

Eversleigh, E. G. THE ROSE OF BÉARN. Paul, 1925. Romance in Paris at the start of the Revolution. 2063

Feuchtwanger, Lion. PROUD DESTINY. (tr.) Viking, 1947. Benjamin Franklin's stay in France seeking aid for the American Revolution. 2064

--------. 'TIS FOLLY TO BE WISE. (tr.) Messner, 1953. Revolutionary France between the death of Rousseau and his re-burial in Paris. 2065

Fezandié, Hector. KNIGHT OF THE THIRD ESTATE. Kyle, 1938. Romance of a lovely aristocrat during the Revolution. 2066

Fitchett, William H. A PAWN IN THE GAME. Eaton & Mains, 1908. A narrative about the attack on the Tuileries, the Reign of Terror, and Napoleon's campaigns in Egypt and

Syria. 2067

Forbes, Eveline Louisa. LEROUX. by Mrs. Walter R. D. Forbes. Greening, 1908. Career of a soldier of the Republic who becomes a general. 2068

France, Anatole (name originally Anatole Thibault). AT THE SIGN OF THE QUEEN PÉDAUQUE. (tr.) Gibbings, 1912. The Abbé Coignard figures in this satiric picture of a Paris inn. 2069

--------. THE GODS ARE ATHIRST. (tr.) Lane, 1913. Adventures of a patriotic Parisian artist at the time of the downfall of Marat and Robespierre. 2070

Gaulot, Paul. THE RED SHIRTS. (tr.) Greening, 1894. A novel based on the Batz Conspiracy of 1794. 2071

Gerson, Noel B. MOHAWK LADDER. Doubleday, 1951. A group of Americans fight against Louis XIV in the War of Spanish Succession. 2072

Gibbs, Willa. SEED OF MISCHIEF. Farrar, 1953. A novel of the Lost Dauphin, Louis XVII of France. 2073

--------. TELL YOUR SONS. Farrar, 1946. This story emphasizes Napoleon's personal magnetism for those around him. 2074

--------. TWELFTH PHYSICIAN. Farrar, 1954. The conflict of a young doctor in the turbulent time of Napoleon. 2075

Gorman, Herbert Sherman. THE MOUNTAIN AND THE PLAIN. Farrar, 1936. An excellent picture of the French Revolution seen through the eyes of a young American. 2076

Gras, Felix. (1) THE REDS OF THE MIDI. (tr.) Appleton, 1899. (2) THE TERROR (sequel). (tr.) Appleton, 1898. (3) THE WHITE TERROR (sequel). (tr.) Appleton, 1899. Three novels of the Revolution covering the introduction of "The Marseillaise," Marat in power, Louis XVI's execution, and Napoleon's battles at Marengo, Austerlitz, Moscow, and Waterloo. 2077

Green, Anne. THE SILENT DUCHESS. Harper, 1939. The

story of a French duchess during the Revolution. 2078

Grierson, Edward. HASTENING WIND. Knopf, 1953. Efforts to restore the Bourbons to the throne during Napoleon's rule. 2079

Haggard, Andrew C. P. THÉRÈSE OF THE REVOLUTION. White, 1921. A countess uses her influence to save many from execution during the Revolution. 2080

Hamilton, Bernard. THE GIANT. Hutchinson, 1926. An account of Danton as a boy and in the Revolution. 2081

Harding, Bertita. FAREWELL 'TOINETTE. Bobbs, 1938. Light-hearted tale of Marie Antoinette's wedding journey from Vienna to Versailles. 2082

Heard, Adrian. ROSE IN THE MOUTH. Ward & Lock, 1927. Tells of many prominent figures in the Revolution, including the Dauphin, Robespierre, and Marie Antoinette. 2083

Heyer, Georgette. THESE OLD SHADES. Small, Maynard, 1926. Light romance of court life under Louis XV. 2084

Holland, Clive. THE LOVERS OF MADEMOISELLE. Hurst & Blackett, 1913. The French Revolution provides the background for this romance, which includes an attack on a chateau. 2085

Hood, Arthur. DRAGON'S TEETH. Cassell, 1925. Record of a nobleman of France during the Revolution, compiled from diaries and papers. 2086

Hough, Emerson. THE MISSISSIPPI BUBBLE. Bobbs, 1903. John Law's scheme to colonize and exploit the Mississippi Valley for the French. 2087

Hugo, Victor. NINETY-THREE. (tr.) Little, 1900. A romantic account of the Royalist struggle in Brittany. 2088

Isham, Frederic S. THE LADY OF THE MOUNT. Bobbs, 1908. The efforts of a young lord to regain his inheritance, taken by an unprincipled governor. 2089

James, G. P. R. THE ANCIENT RÉGIME. Longmans, 1841. The corrupt court of Louis XV with a picture of the French police system. 2090

James, Henry. GABRIELLE DE BERGERAC. Boni & Liveright, 1918. Courageous French girl who dared marry "beneath" her is caught up in the Reign of Terror. 2091

Jennings, Edward W. UNDER THE POMPADOUR. Brentano's, 1907. Embraces English-French smuggling and the court of Louis XV. 2092

Jessop, George H. DESMOND O'CONNOR. Long, 1914. Love story of Louis XIV's ward and a captain in the Irish Brigade. 2093

Johnson, Owen. IN THE NAME OF LIBERTY. [En. title: NICOLE] Macmillan, 1905. Some of the grimmer aspects of the Reign of Terror. 2094

Jones, Dora M. CAMILLA OF THE FAIR TOWERS. Melrose, 1920. A story of revolutionary Paris and southern England with Madame Roland and Tom Paine. 2095

Kaye, Michael W. THE KING'S INDISCRETION. Paul, 1920. A romance of Louis XV, with a plan for France to invade England. 2096

--------. A PATRIOT OF FRANCE. Paul, 1909. Fighting in the Revolution and the attempted rescue of Louis XVI. 2097

--------. A ROBIN HOOD OF FRANCE. Paul, 1912. Having earned the displeasure of the powerful Madame de Pompadour, the hero becomes another Robin Hood. 2098

Keddie, Henrietta. CITOYENNE JACQUELINE. by Sarah Tytler, pseud. Routledge, 1865. "A woman's lot in the great French Revolution." 2099

Kenyon, Frank Wilson. MARIE ANTOINETTE. Crowell, 1956. A novel of the unfortunate queen. 2100

--------. ROYAL MERRY-GO-ROUND. Crowell, 1954. The gay, extravagant court of Louis XV. 2101

Kingsley, Henry. MADEMOISELLE MATHILDE. Longmans,

1868. Life in England and France during the perilous time of the Revolution. 2102

Knowles, Mabel Winifred. A BLOT ON THE 'SCUTCHEON. by May Wynne, pseud. Mills & Boon, 1910. The spreading of revolutionary ideas in England and France. 2103

--------. KING MANDRIN'S CHALLENGE. by May Wynne, pseud. Paul, 1927. A wild-living nobleman incurs Madame de Pompadour's wrath, leaves the court, and turns outlaw. 2104

--------. THE RED FLEUR-DE-LYS. by May Wynne, pseud. Paul, 1911. A story of the White Terror, the opposition of aristocrats to revolutionists in 1791. 2105

--------. THE REGENT'S GIFT. by May Wynne, pseud. Chapman & Hall, 1915. Brittany and Paris during Orleans' regency for Louis XV. 2106

--------. THE SPENDTHRIFT DUKE. by May Wynne, pseud. Holden & Hardingham, 1920. The French court with Louis XV, Madame de Pompadour, and the Duc de Choiseul. 2107

Lambert, Frederick Arthur. THE MYSTERIOUS MONSIEUR DUMONT. by Frederick Arthur, pseud. Murray, 1912. A woman disguised as a man during and after the Revolution's Reign of Terror. 2108

Landau, Mark Aleksandrovich. THE NINTH THERMIDOR. (tr.) by M. A. Aldanov, pseud. Knopf, 1926. Travels in Europe of a diplomatic messenger. 2109

Levy, Barbara. ADRIENNE. Holt, 1960. The celebrated actress, Adrienne Lecouvreur, is the central figure; Voltaire appears as a character. 2110

Luther, Mark Lee. THE FAVOUR OF PRINCES. Macmillan, 1899. Exciting adventure in Louis XV's France. 2111

Maass, Edgar. IMPERIAL VENUS. Bobbs, 1946. A story of one of Napoleon's sisters, Pauline. 2112

McCarthy, Justin Huntly. SERAPHICA. Harper, 1907. The French court during the regency of Orleans when

John Law was much in favor. 2113

Mahner-Mons, Hans. SWORD OF SATAN. by Hans Possendorf, pseud. McKay, 1952. About Charlot, hangman of Paris. 2114

Martin, Sylvia. I, MADAME TUSSAUD. Harper, 1957. Concerns Madame Tussaud's famous waxworks in France during the Revolution and afterwards in England. 2115

Mitchell, S. Weir. THE ADVENTURES OF FRANÇOIS. Century, 1898. Adventures of the wily hero during the Revolution. 2116

Mundt, Klara. THE EMPRESS JOSEPHINE. (tr.) by Louisa Mühlbach, pseud. Appleton, 1867. A sympathetic portrait of Josephine including Napoleon, the royal family, and national events. 2117

--------. MARIE ANTOINETTE AND HER SON. (tr.) by Louisa Mühlbach, pseud. Appleton, 1867. The fate of the queen and the supposed escape of the Dauphin. 2118

Openshaw, Mary. THE LOSER PAYS. Laurie, 1908. The writer of the stirring "Marseillaise" of the revolutionists is the hero. 2119

Orczy, Baroness Emmuska. PETTICOAT RULE. [En. title: PETTICOAT GOVERNMENT] Doran, 1910. The influence of women, especially Madame de Pompadour and the finance minister's wife, on public affairs. 2120

--------. (1) THE SCARLET PIMPERNEL. Putnam, 1920. (2) I WILL REPAY. Lippincott, 1906. (3) THE ELUSIVE PIMPERNEL. Dodd, 1908. (4) THE LEAGUE OF THE SCARLET PIMPERNEL. Doran, 1919. (5) THE TRIUMPH OF THE SCARLET PIMPERNEL. Doran, 1922. (6) LORD TONY'S WIFE. Doran, 1917. (7) ELDORADO. Doran, 1913. (8) SIR PERCY HITS BACK. Doran, 1927. (9) ADVENTURES OF THE SCARLET PIMPERNEL. Doubleday, 1929. (10) WAY OF THE SCARLET PIMPERNEL. Putnam, 1934. (11) CHILD OF THE REVOLUTION. Doubleday, 1932. An Englishman, whose wife is French, heads a group engaged in the hazardous enterprise of rescuing innocent victims of the Revolution. 2121

Oxenham, John, pseud. for William Arthur Dunkerley. QUEEN OF THE GUARDED MOUNTS. Lane, 1912. English involvement in the Vendean revolt provides background for romance and adventure. 2122

Parker, Gilbert. THE BATTLE OF THE STRONG. Harper, 1898. The French invasion of Jersey during the revolutionary period. 2123

Pemberton, Max. MY SWORD FOR LAFAYETTE. Dodd, 1906. "Episodes in the wars waged for liberty in France and America." 2124

Pickering, Sidney. PATHS PERILOUS. Chapman, 1909. This story of life in revolutionary France includes scenes in the prisons of Paris. 2125

Potter, Margaret Horton. THE HOUSE OF DE MAILLY. Harper, 1901. This romance contrasts life in New England with life in Louis XV's court. 2126

Praed, Rosa Caroline. THE ROMANCE OF MLLE. AISSÉ. by Mrs. Campbell Praed. Long, 1910. The court life of a Circassian chief's daughter who had been captured by Turks, later educated in France. 2127

Preedy, George, pseud. for Gabrielle Campbell Long. GENERAL CRACK. Dodd, 1928. The varying successes of a bold adventurer in politics and love. 2128

Rowsell, Mary C. THE FRIEND OF THE PEOPLE. Marshall, 1894. Efforts of an illegitimate son to have his brother guillotined. 2129

--------. MONSIEUR DE PARIS. Chatto, 1907. A story of Madame du Barry and her fate. 2130

Sabatini, Rafael. THE GAMESTER. Houghton, 1949. Dramatic account of John Law and his fantastic financial manipulations. 2131

--------. MASTER-AT-ARMS. Houghton, 1940. French fencing master returns from London to take part in the Revolution. 2132

--------. THE NUPTIALS OF CORBAL. Houghton, 1927. Exciting romance of Paris and provincial France. 2133

--------. SCARAMOUCHE. Houghton, 1921. Brilliant romance of the French Revolution with a dashing and eloquent hero. 2134

--------. THE TRAMPLING OF THE LILIES. Hutchinson, 1906. A picture of Picardy at the start of the Revolution. 2135

Sage, William. ROBERT TOURNAY. Houghton, 1900. Danton and Robespierre figure prominently in this novel of the Revolution. 2136

Savage, Charles Woodcock. A LADY IN WAITING. Appleton, 1906. About one of Marie Antoinette's attendants, who lost her family to the guillotine. 2137

Seawell, Molly Elliot. FRANCEZKA. Bobbs, 1902. A novel introducing the philosopher Voltaire, the actress Adrienne, and Marshal Saxe. 2138

--------. THE LAST DUCHESS OF BELGARDE. Appleton, 1908. A duke and duchess at Louis XVI's court and during the Reign of Terror. 2139

Selinko, Annemarie. DÉSIRÉE. Morrow, 1953. About Désirée, early love of Napoleon, later wife of Bernadotte, and her relations with the Bonaparte family. 2140

Shay, Edith and Katharine Smith. PRIVATE ADVENTURE OF CAPTAIN SHAW. Houghton, 1945. Experiences of a Cape Cod sea captain during the Reign of Terror. 2141

Sheean, Vincent. A DAY OF BATTLE. Doubleday, 1938. The battle between French and English at Fontenoy in 1745. 2142

Sheehan, Patrick A. THE QUEEN'S FILLET. Longmans, 1911. Concerns Marie Antoinette, Louis XVI, and the slaughtering of the Swiss Guard during the Revolution. 2143

Simpson, Evan John. KINGS' MASQUE. by Evan John, <u>pseud.</u>

Dutton, 1941. Marie Antoinette of France and Gustav III of Sweden are central characters. 2144

Sinclair, Edith. HIS HONOUR AND HIS LOVE. Blackwood, 1911. Pictures many prominent people of the nobility at the court of Louis XV. 2145

Spender, Harold. AT THE SIGN OF THE GUILLOTINE. Merriam, 1895. Robespierre and his activities in the Reign of Terror. 2146

Spillman, J. VALIANT AND TRUE. Sands, 1905. "Adventures of a young officer of the Swiss Guards at the time of the French Revolution." 2147

Stacpoole, Henry de Vere. MONSIEUR DE ROCHEFORT. Hutchinson, 1914. The hero becomes involved in politics at Louis XV's court. 2148

--------. THE ORDER OF RELEASE. Hutchinson, 1912. Concerns Versailles and attempts to free a man unfairly imprisoned in the Bastille. 2149

Stair, Grace. A LADY OF FRANCE. Stokes, 1930. About the lovely Louise de Lamballe, ill-fated attendant to Marie Antoinette. 2150

Stevenson, Burton E. AT ODDS WITH THE REGENT. Lippincott, 1900. A story of the Cellamare Conspiracy, which occurred during the regency of the Duke of Orleans. 2151

Sue, Eugène. THE SWORD OF HONOR. N. Y. Labor News, 1910. A tale of the Revolution including the fall of the Bastille. 2152

Theuriet, André. THE CANONESS. Nelson, 1893. Eastern France during the Revolution with an account of the Battle of Valmy. 2153

Trollope, Anthony. LA VENDÉE. Chapman, 1850. The struggles and success of the Vendean insurgents during the Revolution. 2154

Vansittart, Robert. PITY'S KIN. Murray, 1924. Conflicting feelings and ideas of the people in Nantes during the Revolution. 2155

Wagnalls, Mabel. THE PALACE OF DANGER. Funk & Wagnalls, 1908. The great influence of the king's mistress, Madame de Pompadour. 2156

Ward, Mary Augusta. LADY ROSE'S DAUGHTER. by Mrs. Humphry Ward. Harper, 1903. A novel of manners based on actual events in Louis XV's France. 2157

Watson, Frederick. SHALLOWS. Dutton, 1913. Jacobite intrigues in France, England, and Scotland, with Prince Charles Edward and the philosopher Condillac. 2158

Wentworth, Patricia. A MARRIAGE UNDER THE TERROR. Putnam, 1910. A marriage is performed to save the bride from the guillotine. 2159

Weyman, Stanley J. THE RED COCKADE. Longmans, 1895. Revolutionary activity recounted by an aristocrat sympathetic with the commoners. 2160

Wheelwright, Jere Hungerford. DRAW NEAR TO BATTLE. Scribner, 1953. The exploits of an American in Napoleon's army. 2161

White, Helen C. TO THE END OF THE WORLD. Macmillan, 1939. The work of a priest to support religion during the Reign of Terror in the French Revolution. 2162

White, Leslie Turner. MONSIEUR YANKEE. Morrow, 1957. Youthful American doctor becomes enmeshed in espionage during the French Revolution. 2163

Whyte-Melville, George John. CERISE. Appleton, 1866. France during the last days of Louis XIV and the regency for Louis XV. 2164

Wilkins, William Vaughan. A KING RELUCTANT. Macmillan, 1953. The story of the Lost Dauphin, Louis XVII. 2165

--------. LADY OF PARIS. St. Martin's, 1957. Madame Tallien, later Princesse de Chimay, against a backdrop of the French Revolution and the Reign of Terror. 2166

Williams, Hugh Noel. THE HAND OF LEONORE. Harper, 1904. Adventure-romance of a poor Englishman and a wealthy lady, telling of the Battle of Rossbach. 2167

Williams, Valentine. THE RED MASS. Houghton, 1925. An English soldier goes as a spy to revolutionary France. 2168

Winwar, Frances. THE EAGLE AND THE ROCK. Harper, 1953. A fresh story of Napoleon and the people around him. 2169

Yerby, Frank. THE DEVIL'S LAUGHTER. Dial, 1953. A bold, brilliant lawyer in the French Revolution. 2170

III. A. 3. b. 2) Central Europe (including Germany, the Netherlands, Switzerland, Austria, Hungary, Czechoslovakia, and Poland)

Ammers-Küller, Jo van. THE HOUSE OF TAVELINCK. (tr.) Farrar, 1938. Holland at the time of the French Revolution, including a Dutch boy's exploits in France. 2171

Auerbach, Berthold. POET AND MERCHANT. Holt, 1877. The time in which Mendelssohn lived. 2172

Bailey, H. C. THE GAMESTERS. Dutton, 1919. The exciting adventures of owners of European gambling houses--the haunts of nobility. 2173

--------. HIS SERENE HIGHNESS. Dutton, 1922. Two Englishmen on a trip through the Continent. 2174

Bett, Henry. THE WATCH NIGHT. Paul, 1912. Religious thought, mainly in Germany, at mid-century, with John Wesley prominent. 2175

Bloundelle-Burton, John. ACROSS THE SALT SEA. Stone, 1898. Marlborough's victory at Blenheim in the War of the Spanish Succession. 2176

--------. THE SWORD OF GIDEON. Cassell, 1905. A story of the Netherlands during the War of the Spanish Succession. 2177

Casserley, Gordon. THE RED MARSHAL. Clode, 1923. The liberation of a small Austrian state. 2178

Castle, Agnes and Egerton. THE PRIDE OF JENNICO. Macmillan, 1898. Memoirs of an Englishman who inherited Moravian estates. 2179

Conscience, Hendrik. VEVA. (tr.) Burns & Oates, 1853. The French taking of Belgium and the uprising of the peasants against their rule. 2180

Feuchtwanger, Lion. POWER. (tr.) [same as JEW SUSS and JUD SUSS] Viking, 1926. Political and religious forces at work on mid-European history. 2181

Grant, James. SECOND TO NONE. Dutton, 1864. Action-filled story of military service in Hanover under the Duke of Cumberland. 2182

Grun, Bernard. GOLDEN QUILL. Putnam, 1956. A story of Mozart as seen through his sister's diary. 2183

Innes, Norman. THE GOVERNOR'S DAUGHTER. Ward & Lock, 1911. Adventures of an Austrian spy in the Seven Years War. 2184

--------. THE LONELY GUARD. Ward & Lock, 1908. A story of the Austro-Bavarian border giving the Austrian attitude toward Frederick the Great's ambitions. 2185

Jókai, Maurus. THE STRANGE STORY OF RAB RABY. (tr.) Jarrold & Sons, 1909. Social reform in Hungary under Emperor Joseph II. 2186

Knowles, Mabel Winifred. FOES OF FREEDOM. by May Wynne, pseud. Chapman & Hall, 1916. The revolt of the Belgian provinces against Joseph II of Austria. 2187

--------. THE KING OF A DAY. by May Wynne, pseud. Jarrolds Ltd., 1918. Stanislaus I and the War of Polish Succession. 2188

Kraszewski, Jósef I. THE COUNTESS COSEL. (tr.) Downey, 1901. The court of Augustus the Strong, Elector of Saxony. 2189

Lowe, Charles. A FALLEN STAR. Downey, 1895. A story of Scots who saw action with Frederick the Great in the Seven Years War. 2190

Major, Charles. A GENTLE KNIGHT OF OLD BRANDENBURG. Macmillan, 1909. The domestic life and diplomatic relations of Frederick William I of Prussia. 2191

Mundt, Klara. GOETHE AND SCHILLER. (tr.) by Louisa Mühlbach, pseud. Appleton, 1868. Romantic story based chiefly on the life of Schiller. 2192

--------. (1) OLD FRITZ AND THE NEW ERA. (tr.) Appleton, 1868. (2) FREDERICK THE GREAT AND HIS COURT. (tr.) Appleton, 1866. (3) BERLIN AND SANS SOUCI; or, FREDERICK THE GREAT AND HIS FRIENDS (sequel). (tr.) Appleton, 1867. (4) FREDERICK THE GREAT AND HIS FAMILY (sequel). (tr.) Appleton, 1867. (5) THE MERCHANT OF BERLIN. (tr.) Appleton, 1867. all by Louisa Mühlbach, pseud. A series of novels concerning the court of Frederick the Great and contemporary social, political, and economic activities. 2193

Porter, Anna Maria. THE HUNGARIAN BROTHERS. Lippincott, 1807. Hungary, Austria, and Italy during the wars against the French in Italy, 1797 ff. 2194

Porter, Jane. THADDEUS OF WARSAW. Routledge, 1803. Poland's struggle for survival inspired by the heroism of Kosciusko. 2195

Ramuz, Charles F. WHEN THE MOUNTAIN FELL. (tr.) Pantheon, 1947. Tragic avalanche in the Swiss Alps. 2196

Sabatini, Rafael. BIRTH OF MISCHIEF. Houghton, 1945. Rise of Prussia during the reigns of Frederick William I and Frederick II, the Great. 2197

Sand, George, pseud. for Mme. Dudevant. (1) CONSUELO. (tr.) Ticknor, 1846. (2) THE COUNTESS OF RUDOLSTADT (sequel). (tr.) Ticknor, 1847. The career of a woman singer in Europe. 2198

Schuster, Rose. THE ROAD TO VICTORY. Chapman & Hall, 1913. The relationship between Frederick William I and his son Frederick II, the Great. 2199

Sheppard, Alfred Tresidder. THE RED CRAVAT. Macmillan, 1905. An Englishman's adventures at the eccentric court of Frederick William I. 2200

Stevenson, Philip L. A GENDARME OF THE KING. Hurst, 1905. Frederick the Great's battles in the Seven Years War. 2201

Stewart, Charlotte. BEGGARS AND SORNERS. by Allan McAulay, pseud. Lane, 1912. Scottish and Jacobite influences in Amsterdam. 2202

Yoxall, James Henry. THE COURTIER STOOPS. Smith & Elder, 1911. Based on the life and romance of Goethe. 2203

Zschokke, Heinrich. THE ROSE OF DISENTIS. (tr.) Sheldon, 1873. Romance in Switzerland during the war between France and Austria. 2204

III. A. 3. b. 3) Scandinavia and the Baltic

Brogger, Mae. LINDEMAN'S DAUGHTERS. by Synnove Christensen, pseud. Doubleday, 1958. Norwegian country life, an unhappy marriage, and a forbidden love. 2205

Caine, Hall. THE BONDMAN. Appleton, 1890. Iceland and the Isle of Man at the outset of the Napoleonic Wars. 2206

Coleridge, Mary E. THE KING WITH TWO FACES. Arnold, 1897. Relations between Sweden and France with Gustavus III a central figure. 2207

Freuchen, Peter. WHITE MAN. Rinehart, 1946. Couple finds a new life in Greenland in a Danish settlement peopled largely by former convicts. 2208

Heidenstam, Verner von. THE CHARLES MEN. American-Scandinavian Foundation, 1897-98. A powerful novel with Charles XII of Sweden as chief character. 2209

Hesekiel, J. G. L. TWO QUEENS. (tr.) Sonnenschein, 1869. Queen Caroline Matilda of Denmark and Queen Marie Antoinette of France. 2210

Hornborg, Harald. PASSION AND THE SWORD. Appleton, 1941. Attempts of a pastor in Finland to win over the people of his parish. 2211

Hunt, Frederick. ROYAL PHYSICIAN. by John Fitzgay, pseud. Roy Pub., 1947. Secret intrigue and tangled plots in the Danish court of King Christian VII. 2212

Maass, Edgar. QUEEN'S PHYSICIAN. Scribner, 1948. The court of Christian VII of Denmark, his lovely queen, and the royal physician. 2213

Neumann, Robert. THE QUEEN'S DOCTOR. Knopf, 1936. Struensee, the doctor who had great influence, personally and politically, with Christian VII and his wife. 2214

Nisser, Peter W. RED MARTEN. (tr.) Knopf, 1957. The hard lot of the peasants during the Swedish-Russian (Northern) War. 2215

Pontoppidan, Henrik. (1) EMMANUEL, or, CHILDREN OF THE SOIL. Dent, 1892. (2) THE PROMISED LAND. Dent, 1896. A Danish pastor espouses the cause of the peasants by vocation and by marriage. 2216

Sand, George, pseud. for Mme. Dudevant. THE SNOW MAN. (tr.) Little, 1871. A dispute over inheritance provides the plot for this story of winter life in Sweden. 2217

Undset, Sigrid. MADAME DORTHEA. (tr.) Knopf, 1940. Vicissitudes of a Norwegian family left without a father. 2218

III. A. 3. c. Southern Europe

1) Iberian Peninsula

Bloundelle-Burton, John. THE LAST OF HER RACE. Milne, 1908. The contest among Austria, France, and England in the War of the Spanish Succession. 2219

Capes, Bernard. A CASTLE IN SPAIN. Hutchinson, 1903. An adventurer attempts to take the French Lost Dauphin, Louis XVII, from a Spanish convent where he is allegedly hiding. 2220

Feuchtwanger, Lion. THIS IS THE HOUR. (tr.) Viking, 1951. A novel of the eventful life of Goya, famous Spanish painter. 2221

Griffiths, Arthur. THRICE CAPTIVE. White, 1908. Adventures of an Englishman in Spain during the campaigns of the capable, restless general, Peterborough. 2222

Knowles, Mabel Winifred. A GALLANT OF SPAIN. by May Wynne, pseud. Paul, 1920. Jacobites in Spain during Philip V's reign. 2223

Mackay, Margaret. THE WINE PRINCES. Day, 1958. Two cousins, named Prince, go to Portugal to learn the wine business. 2224

White, Charles William. IN THE BLAZING LIGHT. by Max White, pseud. Duell, 1946. Novel concerning the life and love of Francesco Goya. 2225

III. A. 3. c. 2) Italy and Adjacent Islands

Calvino, Italo. BARON IN THE TREES. (tr.) Random, 1959. An Italian baron fulfills his youthful vow of never setting foot on the ground. 2226

Capes, Bernard. THE POT OF BASIL. Constable, 1913. A romance centering on state marriage plans between Italy and Austria. 2227

--------. A ROGUE'S TRAGEDY. Methuen, 1906. A rogue, Cartouche, undertakes to destroy a secret political society. 2228

Dumas, Alexandre. (1) THE NEAPOLITAN LOVERS. (tr.) Brentano's, 1917. (2) LOVE AND LIBERTY. (tr.) Peterson, 1874. Naples during the French Revolutionary period, featuring Lord Nelson. 2229

Eaton, Evelyn. IN WHAT TORN SHIP. Harper, 1944. The liberation of Corsica from the Genoese by Pasquale Paoli. 2230

Forbes, Helen E. HIS EMINENCE. Nash, 1904. A Cardinal in an Italian town under threat of invasion by Napoleon. 2231

Hewlett, Maurice. THE FOOL ERRANT. Macmillan, 1905. Adventures of an English gentleman who gives up rank and wealth to do "penance" in Italy. 2232

Lambton, Arthur. THE SPLENDID SINNER. Nash, 1911. A conspiracy against Queen Caroline's prime minister, Sir John Acton. 2233

McManus, _Miss_ L. LALLY OF THE BRIGADE. Page, 1899. The French service of an Irish brigade in Italy during the War of the Spanish Succession. 2234

Mason, A. E. W. CLEMENTINA. Stokes, 1901. Marriage in Rome of the Old Pretender of England and Princess Clementina Sobieski of Poland. 2235

Nievo, Ippolito. THE CASTLE OF FRATTA. Houghton, 1958. The fading days of the aristocracy during the time of Napoleon. 2236

Pemberton, Max. BEATRICE OF VENICE. Dodd, 1904. Account of Napoleon's Italian campaign. 2237

--------. PAULINA. Cassell, 1922. "A story of Napoleon and the fall of Venice." 2238

Pickering, Edgar. KING FOR A SUMMER. Hutchinson, 1896. An exciting tale of rebellion in Corisca in 1735. 2239

Pickering, Sidney. THE KEY OF PARADISE. Macmillan, 1903. Romance of an English soldier and a girl married to an Italian prince. 2240

Quiller-Couch, Arthur T. SIR JOHN CONSTANTINE. by Q., pseud. Scribner, 1906. "Memoirs of his adventures at home and abroad, and particularly in the island of Corsica." 2241

Radcliffe, Ann. THE ITALIAN; or, THE CONFESSIONAL OF THE BLACK PENITENTS. Cadell & Davies, 1811. The Inquisition in and about Naples. 2242

Rodocanachi, Emmanuel. TOLLA THE COURTESAN. (tr.) Heinemann, 1905. Life and manners at Rome featuring Tolla Boccadileone and Prince Constantine Sobieski. 2243

Salmon, Geraldine Gordon. CORSICAN JUSTICE. by J. G. Sarasin, pseud. Doran, 1927. Adventure in Italy, with Napoleon's military activities as the background. 2244

Schumacher, Henry. NELSON'S LAST LOVE. Hutchinson, 1913. Lady Hamilton's life in Naples, showing especially her friendships with Queen Maria Caroline and Nelson. 2245

Sheean, Vincent. SANFELICE. Doubleday, 1936. Colorful account of the unsuccessful Revolution of 1799 in Naples. 2246

Stewart, Charlotte. THE EAGLE'S NEST. by Allan McAulay, pseud. Lane, 1907. Napoleon as a young man in Corsica. 2247

Wharton, Edith. THE VALLEY OF DECISION. Scribner, 1902. Gives an insight into European thought prior to the French Revolution. 2248

III. A. 3. d. Eastern Europe (including Russia and the Balkans), the Near East, and North Africa

Alexander, grand duke of Russia. EVIL EMPRESS. Lippincott, 1934. A novel based on the career of Catherine the Great. 2249

Almedingen, Martha E. von. YOUNG CATHERINE. Stokes, 1938. A novel of Russia's Catherine the Great telling of her childhood and tragic marriage. 2250

Beddoe, David M. THE LOST MAMELUKE. Dutton, 1913. Fall of the Mameluke influence in Egypt and events of Napoleon's Egyptian campaign. 2251

Chevigny, Hector. LOST EMPIRE. Macmillan, 1937. Nikolai Rezánov's dream of an empire in Siberia is stirringly told. 2252

Danilevski, Grigovii P. THE PRINCESS TARAKANOVA. (tr.) Sonnenschein, 1891. A threat to the throne of Catherine the Great by a supposed daughter of the preceding Empress, Elizabeth. 2253

Dickson, Harris. SHE THAT HESITATES. Bobbs, 1903. Chiefly about the marriage of the unscrupulous Alexis of Russia and Charlotte of Brunswick. 2254

Drummond, Hamilton. SHOES OF GOLD. Paul, 1909. A French diplomat's assignment to win Russia's friendship by charming Catherine the Great. 2255

Durand, Henry Mortimer. NADIR SHAH. Dutton, 1908. A romance of the great conqueror, Nadir Shah, against a rich background of Persian customs. 2256

Gerson, Noel B. THE SCIMITAR. by Samuel Edwards, pseud. Farrar, 1955. An Englishman's adventures in the Near East, told in a light vein. 2257

Helps, Arthur. IVAN DE BIRON. Isbister, 1874. The place in Russian government held by the German, Biron, a favorite of Empress Anna Ivanovna. 2258

Hope, Jessie. THE TRIUMPH OF COUNT OSTERMANN. by Graham Hope, pseud. Holt, 1903. The blending of Eastern and Western civilizations in Russia during Peter the Great's reign. 2259

Jókai, Maurus. HALIL THE PEDLAR. (tr.) Jarrold & Sons, 1901. A poor peddler who led a rebellion in Turkey and eventually became Prime Minister. 2260

Jones, Maurice Bethell. PETER, CALLED THE GREAT. Stokes, 1936. The cruelty, ability, and madness of Peter I, Emperor of Russia. 2261

Merezhkovsky, Dmitri. PETER AND ALEXIS. (tr.) Putnam, 1905. The unhappy relationship between Peter the Great and his son Alexis. 2262

Price, Jeramie. KATRINA. Farrar, 1955. Russian life during the time of Peter I and his peasant wife, Catherine. 2263

Pushkin, Alexander S. THE CAPTAIN'S DAUGHTER. (tr.) Müller, 1846. A story of the peasants' insurrection led by Pougachev. 2264

River, Walter Leslie. THE TORGUTS. Stokes, 1939. Mass migration of a southeastern Russian tribe to China. 2265

Stephens, Eve. REBEL PRINCESS. by Evelyn Anthony, pseud. Crowell, 1953. Young Catherine II overthrows her half-wit husband, Peter III, to become a great Empress. 2266

--------. ROYAL INTRIGUE. by Evelyn Anthony, pseud. Crowell, 1954. Cruelty and intrigue in the Russia of Catherine the Great and her son, Paul. 2267

Swan, Edgar. THE MARK OF THE CROSS. Digby & Long, 1911. Elizabeth, daughter of Peter the Great, came to the throne through a series of plots. 2268

Taylor, Mary Imlay. AN IMPERIAL LOVER. McClurg, 1897. A French diplomat at the court of Peter the Great and his secretary's romance with the future Catherine I. 2269

Underwood, Edna. WHIRLWIND. Small, Maynard, 1918. Catherine the Great's inexorable climb to ultimate power in Russia. 2270

Whishaw, Frederick J. AT THE COURT OF CATHERINE THE GREAT. [En. title: MANY WAYS OF LOVE] Stokes, 1899. Court of Catherine and Peter III telling of his accession and murder. 2271

--------. AN EMPRESS IN LOVE. Paul, 1910. The reign of Catherine the Great who was more successful as a ruler than as a wife. 2272

--------. A FORBIDDEN NAME. Chatto, 1901. A story of the child Czar Ivan VI who was imprisoned by the Empress Elizabeth and later executed. 2273

--------. HER HIGHNESS. Long, 1906. The Empress Catherine as a bride. 2274

--------. NEAR THE TSAR, NEAR DEATH. Chatto, 1903. Peter the Great's disappointment in his son Alexis. 2275

III. A. 3. e. Overseas Exploration, Enterprise, and Expansion

Allen, Hervey. ANTHONY ADVERSE. Farrar, 1933. Young man travels all over the world in quest of adventure. 2276

Besant, Walter. THE WORLD WENT VERY WELL THEN. Harper, 1886. Naval adventures on the Thames River and the South Seas. 2277

Chambers, Robert W. THE MAN THEY HANGED. Appleton, 1926. Sympathetic account of the notorious Captain Kidd. 2278

Chamier, Frederick. TOM BOWLING. Dutton, 1839. A tale of sea action in the English war with France. 2279

Defoe, Daniel. LIFE, ADVENTURES, AND PIRACIES OF CAPTAIN SINGLETON. Macmillan, 1720. Exciting career of an eighteenth century pirate. 2280

Garstin, Crosbie. (1) THE OWL'S HOUSE. Stokes, 1924. (2) HIGH NOON. Stokes, 1925. (3) THE WEST WIND. Stokes, 1926. Far-flung adventures of smugglers, gypsies, and privateers. 2281

McIntyre, John Thomas. STAINED SAILS. Stokes, 1928. An early romance of John Paul Jones, slave trader, later American naval hero. 2282

Marryat, Frederick. THE KING'S OWN. Dutton, 1834. Sea adventures, fighting, and mutiny on shipboard. 2283

Stevenson, Robert Louis. TREASURE ISLAND. Lovell, 1886. Classic tale of pirates and buried treasure. 2284

III. A. 4. Nineteenth Century: Age of Nationalism and Liberalism

a. The British Isles

1) England, Wales, and Scotland

Ainsworth, W. Harrison. MERVYN CLITHEROE. Dutton, 1857. Manchester in the time of industrial upheaval after the war with the French. 2285

Alington, Argentine. GENTLEMEN--THE REGIMENT! by Hugh Talbot, pseud. Harper, 1933. Story of two military families in England during the Crimean War. 2286

Ashton, Helen. FOOTMAN IN POWDER. Dodd, 1954. The time of King George IV as seen by the royal servants. 2287

Ashton, Winifred. HE BRINGS GREAT NEWS. by Clemence Dane, pseud. Random, 1945. A British naval lieutenant brings the news of Trafalgar and of Nelson's death back to England. 2288

Austen, Jane. (1) EMMA. Murray, 1816. (2) MANSFIELD PARK. Egerton, 1814. (3) NORTHANGER ABBEY. Carey & Lea, 1833. (4) PERSUASION. Bentley, 1848. (5) PRIDE AND PREJUDICE. Egerton, 1813. (6) SENSE AND SENSIBILITY. Egerton, 1813. Six separate novels of quiet country life containing excellent character studies and pictures of the morals and customs of the times, and of the preoccupation of young ladies with appropriate marriages. 2289

--------. THE WATSONS. (a fragment continued and completed by John Coates) Crowell, 1958. Typical Austen story of a family of girls concerned with achieving good marriages. 2290

Banks, G. Linnaeus. BOND SLAVES. Griffith & Farran, 1893. The riots of the Luddite Society, an organization of workers in Yorkshire. 2291

--------. CALEB BOOTH'S CLERK. Simpkin, 1878. An escaped convict and his sister insinuate their way into a respectable Lancashire household. 2292

--------. THE MANCHESTER MAN. Heywood, 1895. A detailed picture of the Manchester region in the first quarter of the century. 2293

Baring-Gould, S. CHEAP JACK ZITA. Methuen, 1893. Conspiracy, rioting, and fear in England during the period of the decisive Battle of Waterloo. 2294

--------. EVE. Appleton, 1888. A romance of the moors, rampant in supersitition, with a convict's escape from Dartmoor Prison. 2295

--------. IN DEWISLAND. Methuen, 1904. Country folks' rebellion against the unpopular increase in highway tolls. 2296

--------. KITTY ALONE. Dodd, 1894. About Kitty and her uncle, a man who commits arson to collect insurance money. 2297

--------. RED SPIDER. Appleton, 1888. A realistic picture of life in the village areas of England. 2298

--------. ROYAL GEORGIE. Methuen, 1901. A story of the Prince Regent, later George IV, with a glimpse of Dartmoor. 2299

Barr, Amelia E. BETWEEN TWO LOVES. Harper, 1886. Rural life in England. 2300

--------. A DAUGHTER OF FIFE. Dodd, 1886. Romantic novel of life in a Scottish fishing village. 2301

--------. I, THOU, AND THE OTHER ONE. Dodd, 1899. Domestic scene at the time of the controversial Reform Bill agitation. 2302

--------. JAN VEDDER'S WIFE. Dodd, 1885. Domestic life in the Shetland Islands. 2303

--------. A KNIGHT OF THE NETS. Dodd, 1896. Marriage of a landed youth and a poor girl in a village in Fifeshire. 2304

--------. MASTER OF HIS FATE. [same as IN SPITE OF HIMSELF] Dodd, 1888. A man who marries an heiress finds happiness when he works for a living. 2305

--------. THE PAPER CAP. Appleton, 1918. The introduction of the factory system into England. 2306

--------. PAUL AND CHRISTINA. Dodd, 1898. Life and hardships of the simple fisherfolk of the Orkneys. 2307

Barrett, Frank. PERFIDIOUS LYDIA. Chatto, 1910. The runaway marriage of a rebellious girl. 2308

Bartram, George. LADS OF THE FANCY. Duckworth, 1906. Concerns English sports-fanciers and features thrilling accounts of prize-fighting. 2309

--------. THE LONGSHOREMEN. Arnold, 1903. A tale of smuggling told from the viewpoint of those who tried to prevent it. 2310

Beaconsfield, Benjamin Disraeli, 1st. earl of. CONINGSBY. Colburn, 1844. Political and social life of England in the 1830s. 2311

Beck, Lily Adams. THE GLORIOUS APOLLO. by E. Barrington, pseud. Dodd, 1925. The political, social, and romantic life of Lord Byron, and three women who were prominent in it. 2312

Bellasis, Margaret. MRS. BETSEY. by Francesca Marton, pseud. Coward, 1955. Period piece of the Victorian era, reminiscent of Jane Austen. 2313

Bennett, Arnold. THE OLD WIVES' TALE. Doran, 1908. Life in the English midlands during the Victorian period. 2314

Bentley, Phyllis. INHERITANCE. Macmillan, 1932. Long struggle between capital and labor in the Yorkshire district of England. 2315

Besant, Walter. BY CELIA'S ARBOUR. Chatto, 1878. A girl receives a mistaken report of her sweetheart's death in the Crimean War. 2316

Bickerstaffe-Drew, Francis. HURDCOTT. by John Ayscough, pseud. Herder, 1911. Country life in England from a Catholic viewpoint, with glimpses of Hazlitt as well as Charles and Mary Lamb. 2317

Blackmore, R. D. ALICE LORRAINE. Burt, 1875. A romance in England and some events in Spain during the Peninsular War. 2318

--------. PERLYCROSS. Harper, 1894. Scenes of village life in eastern Devon. 2319

--------. SPRINGHAVEN. Harper, 1887. Southern England under threat of invasion by Napoleon. 2320

Bleackley, Horace. A HUNDRED YEARS AGO. Nash, 1917. Reflects some of the problems resulting from an increasingly mechanized industry. 2321

--------. THE MONSTER. Doran, 1921. The "monster" is the English factory system, which was so cruel and demanding of employees. 2322

Blundell, Mary E. LYCHGATE HALL. by M. E. Francis, pseud. Longmans, 1904. Life in a haunted country mansion. 2323

--------. YEOMAN FLEETWOOD. by M. E. Francis, pseud. Longmans, 1900. A yeoman falls in love with a girl of higher social status, and becomes involved in a Regency court romance. 2324

Blyth, James. A HAZARDOUS WOOING. Ward & Lock, 1907. Set amidst the exploits of daring highwaymen. 2325

--------. NAPOLEON DECREES. White, 1914. Adventures of a French spy in England. 2326

Bonnet, Theodore. THE MUDLARK. Doubleday, 1949. About Queen Victoria's palace, Disraeli, the mudlark (a slum urchin), and the Queen's unconventional bodyguard, Brown. 2327

Brebner, Percy J. A ROYAL WARD. Little, 1909. Time is 1813 when there was still some fear of French invasion. 2328

Brontë, Charlotte. JANE EYRE. Harper, 1848. The classic story of a governess who falls in love with her employer. 2329

--------. SHIRLEY. Derby, 1856. Centers on the curtailment of trade caused by the Napoleonic Wars and shows the contemporary position of women. 2330

Brontë, Emily. WUTHERING HEIGHTS. Harper, 1848. Story of terror and hatred in the Yorkshire moors. 2331

Broster, Dorothy K. "MR. ROWL." Doubleday, Page, 1924. The imprisonment in England of a young Frenchman early in the nineteenth century. 2332

--------. SHIPS IN THE BAY! Coward, 1931. An Englishman in Wales, involved with French foes and Irish rebels, defends himself against a charge of treason. 2333

Buchan, John. THE FREE FISHERS. Houghton, 1934. Rescue operations of a group of Scottish fishermen organized to do espionage during the Napoleonic Wars. 2334

Capes, Bernard. THE SECRET IN THE HILL. Smith & Elder, 1903. Adventure story of smuggling and treasure hunting. 2335

Carey, Alfred E. SIR WATERLOO. Selwyn & Blount, 1920. Life in the period of early railway development around Sussex and London. 2336

Castle, Agnes and Egerton. WROTH. Macmillan, 1908. Dramatic romance in aristocratic Regency society. 2337

Castle, Egerton. THE LIGHT OF SCARTHEY. Macmillan, 1895. The tense Hundred Days are the time and a lighthouse the place for this tale of smuggling and adventure. 2338

Chalmers, Stephen. A PRINCE OF ROMANCE. Small, Maynard, 1911. Unusual romance of Jacobite Scotland around 1812. 2339

--------. THE VANISHING SMUGGLER. Clode, 1909. Attempts of customs officials to apprehend smugglers countered by the latters' efforts to elude capture. 2340

Chamier, Frederick. BEN BRACE: THE LAST OF NELSON'S AGAMEMNONS. Routledge, 1835. Naval story based on the career of Lord Nelson's servant, Allen. 2341

Cleland, Robert. INCHBRACKEN. Wilson & M'Cormack (Glasgow), 1883. The effect on a Highland parish of the secession of the Free Church from the Church of Scotland. 2342

Cobban, J. MacLaren. THE KING OF ANDAMAN. Methuen, 1895. Interesting story of Scottish life in young

Victoria's time. 2343

Compton, Herbert. THE PALACE OF SPIES. Treherne, 1903. Intrigue in the court of Caroline of Brunswick and the Prince Regent, later George IV. 2344

--------. THE QUEEN CAN DO NO WRONG. Chatto, 1904. Exciting romance of the court of Queen Caroline. 2345

Conrad, Joseph. THE NIGGER OF THE NARCISSUS. Heinemann, 1897. A sailing ship's stormy voyage from India to England. 2346

Cooper, Lettice U. THE OLD FOX. Hodder & Stoughton, 1927. Southern England when French smuggling and talk of French invasion were rampant. 2347

Cornish, Francis Warre. SUNNINGWELL. Dutton, 1899. Social life of villagers active in the church in Victoria's reign. 2348

Costain, Thomas B. RIDE WITH ME. Doubleday, 1944. Sir Robert Wilson--a general in the Napoleonic Wars--and a crusading newspaper publisher. 2349

--------. THE TONTINE. Doubleday, 1955. Narrative of two families entangled in the annuity-lottery-insurance scheme. 2350

Cowper, Edith E. LADY FABIA. S. P. C. K., 1909. "A story of adventure on the south coast" in the first decade of the century. 2351

Craigie, _Mrs._ Pearl Mary. ROBERT ORANGE. by John Oliver Hobbes, _pseud._ Stokes, 1900. About an Englishman who becomes a Catholic and a Member of Parliament. 2352

Craik, Dinah Maria. JOHN HALIFAX, GENTLEMAN. Harper, 1856. The rise of a poor man to a position of wealth through the Industrial Revolution. 2353

Crockett, Samuel R. THE BANNER OF BLUE. McClure, 1903. A romance of Galloway with religious disturbances in the background. 2354

--------. THE MOSS TROOPERS. Hodder & Stoughton, 1912. Romance and smuggling in the second decade of the century. 2355

--------. STRONG MAC. Dodd, 1904. A story of conditions in the rough lowlands of Scotland and the siege of San Sebastian. 2356

Crouch, Archer Philip. NELLIE OF THE EIGHT BELLS. Long, 1908. A story of naval life centering in a Portsmouth tavern popular with English sailors. 2357

Deeping, Warwick. THE HOUSE OF SPIES. McBride, 1938. A French spy in southern England during the threat of Napoleonic invasion. 2358

De Morgan, William. JOSEPH VANCE. Holt, 1906. A romance of Victorian life and manners. 2359

Dickens, Charles. DAVID COPPERFIELD. Bradbury & Evans, 1850. The famous cast of characters includes Aunt Betsy Trotwood, Peggotty, Steerforth, Barkis, and Uriah Heep. 2360

--------. HARD TIMES. Harper, 1883. Pictures life in a manufacturing town and reflects Carlyle's criticism of contemporary conditions. 2361

--------. LITTLE DORRIT. Bradbury & Evans, 1857. Satirizes the civil service and depicts prison life in mid-nineteenth century England. 2362

--------. NICHOLAS NICKLEBY. Chapman & Hall, 1839. The hero is first a teacher in a severe school, then an actor in a provincial company. 2363

--------. OLIVER TWIST. Bentley, 1838. Corruption of a youth in an environment of crime and poverty. 2364

Dixon, W. Wilmott. THE ROGUE OF RYE. Chatto, 1909. The escape of many English people caught in France by the Napoleonic Wars. 2365

Dodd, Catherine. CLAD IN PURPLE MIST. Jarrolds Ltd., 1926. Middle class life on the Isle of Man, in Liverpool, and in Australia. 2366

Doyle, Sir Arthur Conan. RODNEY STONE. Appleton, 1896. A novel which deals with social life and prize fighting. 2367

Dudeney, Alice. THE BATTLE OF THE WEAK. by Mrs. Henry Dudeney. Dillingham, 1906. Village life on England's southern coast at the beginning of the century. 2368

--------. THE STORY OF SUSAN. by Mrs. Henry Dudeney. Heinemann, 1903. A deep, true love underlies the frivolous actions of a girl who delights in parties and gaiety. 2369

Du Maurier, Daphne. MARY ANNE. Doubleday, 1954. Story of the author's ancestress, a clever woman reminiscent of Thackeray's Becky Sharp [see VANITY FAIR by William Makepeace Thackeray]. 2370

Eden, Emily. THE SEMI-ATTACHED COUPLE. Mathews & Marrat, 1860. English manners and life in nineteenth century high Whig circles. 2371

Edwards, Matilda Betham. THE LORD OF THE HARVEST. Hurst & Blackett, 1899. Farm life in Suffolk. 2372

--------. MOCK BEGGARS' HALL. Hurst & Blackett, 1902. Suffolk farm life before the repeal of the Corn Laws. 2373

--------. A SUFFOLK COURTSHIP. Hurst & Blackett, 1900. Romance of the farm people of Suffolk. 2374

Eliot, George, pseud. for Mary Ann Evans. ADAM BEDE. Harper, 1859. Detailed account of village and country life with the romance of a carpenter and a dairymaid. 2375

--------. DANIEL DERONDA. Harper, 1876. Social life and Jewish character at mid-century. 2376

--------. FELIX HOLT, THE RADICAL. Harper, 1866. A working man marries into a "higher class" during the social upheaval of the 1832 Reform Bill. 2377

--------. MIDDLEMARCH. Harper, 1872-3. A panoramic picture of everyday village happenings in the lives of two families. 2378

--------. THE MILL ON THE FLOSS. Blackwood, 1860. The results of emotional conflict between a brother and a sister. 2379

--------. SILAS MARNER. Dutton, 1861. Novel of village life in which a miserly weaver is rehabilitated by love for a child. 2380

Everett, Mrs. H. D. COUSIN HUGH. by Theo. Douglas, pseud. Methuen, 1910. A tale of traffic in the escape of French prisoners and the importation of false coins. 2381

Farnol, Jeffery. THE AMATEUR GENTLEMAN. Low, 1913. An innkeeper's son inherits a fortune and enters English society. 2382

--------. THE BROAD HIGHWAY. Little, 1911. A youth scorns an inheritance conditioned on a certain marriage. 2383

--------. HERITAGE PERILOUS. McBride, 1947. A brave sailor endeavors to claim an inherited title and fortune. 2384

--------. THE HIGH ADVENTURE. Little, 1926. Conspiracy, adventure, and prize fighting in southeast England. 2385

--------. THE LORING MYSTERY. Little, 1925. A tale dealing with murder in Sussex. 2386

Ferrier, Susan. DESTINY. Macmillan, 1831. A picture of

Scottish life and manners early in the century. 2387

Findlater, Jane Helen. THE STORY OF A MOTHER. Nisbet, 1903. The everyday life of a Scots family. 2388

Foreman, Stephen. THE FEN DOGS. Long, 1912. Two soldiers from the Fens in the Battle of Waterloo and in their rugged life at home. 2389

Forrest, Charles E. ALL FOOLS TOGETHER. Collins, 1925. Poaching, politics, and other elements of English country life about 1820. 2390

Fothergill, Jessie. PROBATION. Fenno, 1880. The cotton shortage of 1863 caused by the American Civil War; the struggle for women's rights. 2391

Frye, Pearl. SLEEPING SWORD. Little, 1952. Concerns Lord Nelson, Lady Hamilton, and Nelson's naval warfare. 2392

Galt, John. THE GATHERING OF THE WEST. Johns Hopkins, 1939. Features George IV's first visit to Edinburgh. 2393

Garnett, Martha. THE INFAMOUS JOHN FRIEND. by Mrs. R. S. Garnett. Holt, 1909. A tale of London and Brighton in 1805, with the hero a spy for Napoleon. 2394

Gaskell, Elizabeth C. MARY BARTON. by Mrs. Gaskell. Dutton, 1848. Set in industrial Manchester during the early Victorian period. 2395

--------. NORTH AND SOUTH. by Mrs. Gaskell. Dutton, 1855. Contrasts the "manufacturing north" and the "rural south" of the Industrial Revolution. 2396

Goudge, Elizabeth. DEAN'S WATCH. Coward, 1960. An old clockmaker and a cathedral dean demonstrate the power of love and respect to change human lives. 2397

Graber, George Alexander. THE RAPE OF THE FAIR COUNTRY. by Alexander Cordell, pseud. Doubleday, 1959. Wales in the 1830s when mine owners controlled economics and thus whole families. (followed by THE ROBE OF HONOUR) 2398

--------. THE ROBE OF HONOUR. [En. title: HOSTS OF REBECCA] by Alexander Cordell, pseud. Doubleday, 1960. The Rebecca Movement in Wales in the 1830s and 1840s. 2399

Grant, James. UNDER THE RED DRAGON. Dutton, 1872. Another vivid picture of life during the Crimean War. 2400

Griffiths, Arthur. A ROYAL RASCAL. Unwin, 1905. The story of a career soldier who saw action in many campaigns. 2401

--------. THE THIN RED LINE. Macqueen, 1900. A story of the Crimean War. 2402

Gunn, Neil. HIGHLAND NIGHT. Harcourt, 1935. Eviction of Scots peasants from their homes to make way for lucrative sheep raising. 2403

Hall, Evelyn Beatrice. BASSET: A VILLAGE CHRONICLE. [En. title: EARLY VICTORIAN] by S. G. Tallentyre, pseud. Moffat, 1910. A peaceful scene of village life early in Victoria's reign. 2404

--------. MATTHEW HARGRAVES. by S. G. Tallentyre, pseud. Putnam, 1914. The early years of Queen Victoria's reign and the changing social and industrial conditions. 2405

Hamley, William G. TRASEADEN HALL. Blackwood, 1882. Pictures both English country life and military life during the Peninsular War. 2406

Hardy, Thomas. THE TRUMPET-MAJOR. Harper, 1879. A soldier in the war with Bonaparte and his brother in the merchant service. 2407

Harwood, Alice. THE STRANGELING. Bobbs, 1954. The often misunderstood adventures of a well-meaning but impractical daughter of a missionary. 2408

Hewlett, Maurice. BENDISH: A STUDY IN PRODIGALITY. Scribner, 1913. The literary and political circles of the 1830s with several historical figures introduced. 2409

--------. MAINWARING. Dodd, 1920. An Irish-born adventurer, after much wandering, becomes a member of the English Parliament. 2410

--------. THE STOOPING LADY. Dodd, 1907. Romance of high society life with its heroine wooed by a worthy butcher. 2411

Heyer, Georgette. BATH TANGLE. Putnam, 1955. A novel of manners with Regency Bath as background. 2412

--------. COTILLION. Putnam, 1953. Light-hearted tale of romance in Regency England. 2413

--------. THE FOUNDLING. Putnam, 1948. Adventure and romance in Regency England. 2414

--------. FRIDAY'S CHILD. Putnam, 1946. High society romance with a light-hearted approach. 2415

--------. THE GRAND SOPHY. Putnam, 1950. Forthright girl, educated on the Continent, comes to live with conservative London relatives. 2416

--------. RELUCTANT WIDOW. Putnam, 1946. An impoverished governess is married, through a mistake in indentity, to a wealthy, but dying, man. 2417

--------. SPRIG MUSLIN. Putnam, 1956. A light and lively tale of love in Regency England. 2418

--------. SYLVESTER. Putnam, 1958. The tangled love affair of an improbable pair has a happy ending. 2419

--------. THE TOLL-GATE. Putnam, 1954. A veteran of the Napoleonic Wars finds toll-gate keeping in England anything but dull. 2420

--------. UNKNOWN AJAX. Putnam, 1960. A lively story of young love with an incidental picture of the new textile industry. 2421

--------. VENETIA. Putnam, 1959. A charming and sensible woman circumvents a planned marriage. 2422

Holt, Victoria. MISTRESS OF MELLYN. Doubleday, 1960. The young governess to the child of a widowed Cornish manor lord. 2423

Hope, Matilda. BECAUSE OF THE ANGELS. Longmans, 1883. The early story of the Irvingite Church in Scotland. 2424

Hunt, Dorothy Alice Bonavia. PEMBERLEY SHADES. Dutton, 1949. A sequel to Jane Austen's PRIDE AND PREJUDICE [q.v.] giving an account of Elizabeth and Darcy's marriage after three years. 2425

Hutchinson, Horace G. CROWBOROUGH BEACON. Smith & Elder, 1903. A tale of quiet country life early in the century. 2426

--------. A FRIEND OF NELSON. Longmans, 1902. An account of Nelson's Baltic campaign of 1801. 2427

Jacob, Naomi Ellington. TIME PIECE. Macmillan, 1937. A Yorkshire squire and his family in the second half of the century. 2428

Jacob, Violet. THE HISTORY OF AYTHAN WARING. Dutton, 1908. Thrilling activities of an outlaw band. 2429

--------. THE INTERLOPER. Heinemann, 1904. The effects of a young laird's learning that there is some question about his birth. 2430

--------. THE SHEEP STEALERS. Putnam, 1902. Events connected with the Highway Acts and resultant Turnpike Riots in Welsh border regions. 2431

Jameson, Storm. LOVELY SHIP. Knopf, 1927. The two marriages of the niece of a shipyard owner in a mid-century shipbuilding town. 2432

Jesse, F. Tennyson. SECRET BREAD. Doran, 1917. A novel of domestic affairs in the last half of the century showing the influence of religious and political developments. 2433

Jones, Margam. THE STARS OF THE REVIVAL. Long, 1910. Religious feeling in Wales in the first quarter of the century. 2434

Kaye, Michael W. DEVIL'S BREW. Paul, 1912. Social unrest caused by economic insecurity following Waterloo. 2435

Kaye-Smith, Sheila. THE CHALLENGE TO SIRIUS. Dutton, 1918. Life in Sussex during the Crimean War and the American Civil War. 2436

--------. SUSSEX GORSE. Knopf, 1916. Depicts Sussex rural life and makes many allusions to politics and public events. 2437

Keddie, Henrietta. A DAUGHTER OF THE MANSE. by Sarah Tytler, <u>pseud</u>. Long, 1905. The plight of pastors whose financial security was affected by the break in the Church of Scotland. 2438

--------. LOGAN'S LOYALTY. by Sarah Tytler, <u>pseud.</u> Long, 1900. A family rift is caused by a daughter's elopement with a man of her low-born mother's class. 2439

--------. SIR DAVID'S VISITORS. by Sarah Tytler, <u>pseud.</u> Chatto, 1903. A novel of Kensington during the Regency. 2440

Kennedy, Margaret. A NIGHT IN COLD HARBOR. Macmillan, 1960. A picture of English village life. 2441

--------. TROY CHIMNEYS. Rinehart, 1952. A refreshing method of story telling depicts a young man's dual personality. 2442

Kenyon, Frank Wilson. GOLDEN YEARS. Crowell, 1959. A romantic novel of the life and loves of poet Percy Bysshe Shelley. 2443

Kingsley, Henry. RAVENSHOE. Longmans, 1802. Recounts University life, political discussions, and scenes from the Crimean War. 2444

Kirk, James Prior. FOREST FOLK. by James Prior, pseud. Dodd, 1901. The character and life of farm people affected by the spread of industrialization. 2445

Leslie, Doris. FULL FLAVOUR. Macmillan, 1934. A family chronicle of the Victorian and Edwardian eras. 2446

--------. ROYAL WILLIAM. Macmillan, 1941. Lively fictionalized biography of William IV, England's "Sailor King." 2447

Linklater, Eric. THE HOUSE OF GAIR. Harcourt, 1954. Suspense on the Scottish moors. 2448

Linton, Lynn. LIZZIE LORTON OF GREYRIGG. Ward & Lock, 1866. A dedicated young minister finds his new parish rough and supersitition-ridden. 2449

Llewellyn, Richard. HOW GREEN WAS MY VALLEY. Macmillan, 1940. Life of a coal-mining family in southern Wales. 2450

Lofts, Norah. THE BRITTLE GLASS. Knopf, 1943. About an embittered woman who is left a business at her father's death. 2451

--------. CALF FOR VENUS. Doubleday, 1949. Smuggling and coffee house life early in the century. 2452

--------. THE GOLDEN FLEECE. Knopf, 1944. Diverse events in an English inn during a day and night of 1817. 2453

--------. TO SEE A FINE LADY. Knopf, 1946. Rise of an ambitious dairy-maid on a farm in post-Napoleonic Essex. 2454

Lucas, Audrey. OLD MOTLEY. Macmillan, 1938. Centers on a Quaker community in London in the 1830s. 2455

Lysaght, Sidney Royse. ONE OF THE GRENVILLES. Macmillan, 1899. Adventures of an Englishman who is, for a time, a prisoner of the Arabs. 2456

Lytton, Edward Bulwer, 1st. baron. THE CAXTONS. Dutton, 1849. True-to-life novel of society in Victorian England. 2457

--------. KENELM CHILLINGLY. Dutton, 1873. A country squire lives as a worker and discovers the contrast between luxury and poverty. 2458

McCarthy, Justin. THE WATERDALE NEIGHBOURS. Chatto, 1867. How two men met the challenge of personal profit versus political loyalty. 2459

McCrone, Guy. RED PLUSH. Farrar, 1947. Fictional chronicle of a Scots family, the Moorhouses, 1870-1881. 2460

McFadden, Gertrude Violet. THE HONEST LAWYER. Doran, 1916. A novel of Wareham and Dorchester in the first half of the century. 2461

--------. MAUMBERY RINGS. Doran, 1921. A rural horse-stealing episode in the time of George IV. 2462

--------. PREVENTIVE MAN. Lane, 1920. A government agent comes to the Dorset coast in search of smugglers. 2463

--------. THE ROMAN WAY. Doran, 1925. The local color of the Dorchester district in the late eighteenth and early nineteenth centuries. 2464

--------. SHERIFF'S DEPUTY. Lane, 1924. A romance during the time of the Machinery Riots in the Dorchester district. 2465

--------. SO SPEED WE. Doran, 1926. Social life in Dorsetshire in the early nineteenth century. 2466

--------. THE TURNING SWORD. Lane, 1923. Presents people of the picturesque market town and seaport of Poole in 1833. 2467

Mackenzie, Agnes Mure. THE QUIET LADY. Doubleday, Page, 1926. The Outer Hebrides in the early nineteenth century. 2468

Marriage, Caroline. THE LUCK OF BARERAKES. Heinemann, 1903. About the rugged people who inhabit the Yorkshire moors. 2469

Marshall, Edison. THE INFINITE WOMAN. Farrar, 1950. An Irish adventuress determines to become a countess. 2470

Meade, L. T., pseud. THE WITCH MAID. Nisbet, 1903. The persecution of a young girl accused of witchcraft. 2471

Meredith, George. BEAUCHAMP'S CAREER. Scribner, 1876. Mid-century politics in the period of Carlyle's influence. 2472

Montgomery, K. L., pseud. for Kathleen and Letitia Montgomery. THE GATE-OPENERS. Long, 1912. A tale of the Turnpike Riots and of some unusual Welsh customs. 2473

Munro, Neil. CHILDREN OF TEMPEST. Blackwood, 1903. Customs, life, and romance among rural Catholics. 2474

--------. GILIAN THE DREAMER. Dodd, 1899. Highland village life just after Napoleon's defeat at Waterloo. 2475

Newbolt, Henry. TAKEN FROM THE ENEMY. Chatto & Windus, 1892. A tale of London and the sea concerned with an attempt to rescue Napoleon from St. Helena. 2476

Ollivant, Alfred. DEVIL DARE. Doubleday, 1924. The story of a traitor in the conflict between Nelson and Napoleon. 2477

--------. THE GENTLEMAN. Macmillan, 1908. Attempt of a Napoleonic spy to capture Nelson shortly before the

Battle of Trafalgar. 2478

O'Neil, George. SPECIAL HUNGER. Liveright, 1931. Depicts the tragic life of the poet Keats. 2479

Oxenham, John, pseud. for William Arthur Dunkerley. LAURISTONS. Methuen, 1910. A London banking house during the suspense-laden Hundred Days and at the news of Waterloo. 2480

Parker, Gilbert. THE JUDGMENT HOUSE. Harper, 1922. England in the period towards the end of the Boer War in South Africa. 2481

Pearce, Charles E. CORINTHIAN JACK. Paul, 1920. A tale of prize fighting in Bristol, Bath, and London about 1823. 2482

Peard, Frances M. CATHERINE. Harper, 1893. Romance in a normally peaceful English countryside upset by the threat of Napoleon's ambition. 2483

Phillpotts, Eden. THE AMERICAN PRISONER. Macmillan, 1904. Pictures a harsh English prison where many Americans were held during the War of 1812. 2484

--------. FAITH TRESILION. Macmillan, 1916. Smuggling and adventure in nineteenth century Cornwall. 2485

--------. MINIONS OF THE MOON. Macmillan, 1935. Dartmoor prison and the problem of escaping from it. 2486

Pinkerton, Thomas A. THE FRENCH PRISONER. Sonnenschein, 1894. Piracy and smuggling during the threatened invasion by Napoleon. 2487

Poynter, H. May. SCARLET TOWN. S. P. C. K., 1894. The tale of a young naval officer who escapes Napoleon's imprisonment. 2488

Quiller-Couch, Arthur T. THE ADVENTURES OF HARRY REVEL. Scribner, 1903. The youth of a foundling in England and his adventures in the Peninsular Wars. 2489

--------. THE MAYOR OF TROY. Scribner, 1905. Exploits of the Troy Volunteer Artillery when English civilians were preparing for Napoleonic invasion. 2490

--------. POISON ISLAND. Scribner, 1907. Shows influences of the Napoleonic Wars and the War of 1812. 2491

--------. THE WESTCOTES. Coates, 1902. Pathetic romance of an English spinster who falls in love with a much younger French prisoner. 2492

-------- and Daphne du Maurier. CASTLE DOR. Doubleday, 1962. A tragic romance in Cornwall is a modern counterpart of the Tristan and Iseult legend. 2493

Rawson, Maud Stepney. THE APPRENTICE. Hutchinson, 1904. Life in the shipbuilding town of Rye in the 1820s. 2494

--------. A LADY OF THE REGENCY. Harper, 1900. The unhappy life of Queen Caroline is shown in this story of one of her ladies. 2495

Raymond, Walter. TWO MEN O' MENDIP. Doubleday, 1899. Strained relations between farmers and lead miners in the Cheddar area. 2496

Reade, Charles. FOUL PLAY. Estes, 1869. A novel which treats of social conditions in a realistic manner. 2497

--------. HARD CASH. Estes, 1863. A realistic account of the status of the insane; financial panic in early railroad development. 2498

--------. IT IS NEVER TOO LATE TO MEND. Scribner, 1856. An attack on the harsh and unreasonable prison system. 2499

--------. PUT YOURSELF IN HIS PLACE. Estes, 1870. A serious treatment of the Trade Union question. 2500

Rives, Hallie Erminie. THE CASTAWAY. Bobbs, 1904. A sympathetic novel based on the life of the poet

Byron. 2501

Roberts, Morley. A SON OF EMPIRE. Lippincott, 1899. Vigorous adventures of a soldier and explorer. 2502

Russell, W. Clark. AN OCEAN FREE-LANCE. Macmillan, 1881. A tale of privateering in the War of 1812. 2503

--------. THE YARN OF OLD HARBOUR TOWN. Jacobs, 1905. Nelson's naval operations in the English Channel. 2504

Sagon, Amyot, _pseud._ WHEN GEORGE III WAS KING. Sands, 1899. Mystery story involving smugglers in Cornwall and London. 2505

Scott, _Sir_ Walter. ST. RONAN'S WELL. Bazin & Ellsworth, 1832. Local customs and manners at a small watering place in Scotland. 2506

Sheppard, Alfred Tresidder. RUNNING HORSE INN. Lippincott, 1906. A soldier returns from war to find his brother marrying his sweetheart. 2507

Simpson, Violet A. THE BONNET CONSPIRATORS. Smith & Elder, 1903. Smuggling on the Sussex coast during the Napoleonic Wars. 2508

--------. THE SOVEREIGN POWER. Smith & Elder, 1904. A romance set during the threat of Napoleonic invasion. 2509

Snowden, James K. THE PLUNDER PIT. Methuen, 1898. Thrilling story of Yorkshire early in Victoria's reign. 2510

Stephens, Eve. VICTORIA AND ALBERT. by Evelyn Anthony, _pseud._ Crowell, 1958. The one-sided love of the famous royal couple. 2511

Stevenson, Robert Louis. ST. IVES. Dutton, 1934. Adventures of a French gentleman held at Edinburgh during the Napoleonic Wars. 2512

--------. WEIR OF HERMISTON. Scribner, 1896. Unfinished romance, based on fact, concerning the unhappy relations between a father and his son. 2513

Stewart, Charlotte. BLACK MARY. by Allan McAulay, pseud. Unwin, 1901. A half-caste girl plagued by the accident of her birth. 2514

Sutcliffe, Halliwell. MISTRESS BARBARA. [En. title: MISTRESS BARBARA CUNLIFFE] Crowell, 1901. Pictures wool and cotton producers on the Yorkshire moors. 2515

--------. SHAMELESS WAYNE. Dodd, 1900. A bloody feud between two respected Yorkshire families. 2516

--------. THROUGH SORROW'S GATES. Unwin, 1904. Folklore and superstition on the Yorkshire moors. 2517

Sykes, J. A. C. MARK ALSTON. Nash, 1908. Based on the personal life of the writer Ruskin. 2518

Teague, John J. A GENTLEMAN OF LONDON. by Morice Gerard, pseud. Nash, 1908. About a man who becomes Lord Mayor of London early in the century. 2519

Tearle, Christian. HOLBORN HILL. Clode, 1909. Pictures the locality and the people of Holborn, Highgate, and Kent. 2520

Thackeray, William Makepeace. THE HISTORY OF PENDENNIS. Harper, 1850. Portrait of a typical young man about mid-century. 2521

--------. THE NEWCOMES. Harper, 1855. Good picture of English social life in the first half of the century. 2522

--------. VANITY FAIR. Bradbury & Evans, 1848. Classic novel of society with an account of the Battle of Waterloo and society's attitude toward it. 2523

Thirkell, Angela. CORONATION SUMMER. Oxford, 1937. Panorama of ceremonies and celebrations during Victoria's coronation. 2524

Thomas, R. M. TREWERN. Unwin, 1901. The uncertainty and change of political thought at the time of the Reform Act of 1832. 2525

Tilsley, Frank. MUTINY. Reynal, 1959. The discontentment of mistreated sailors aboard the H. M. S. REGENERATE. 2526

Trollope, Anthony. CHRONICLES OF BARSETSHIRE: (1) THE WARDEN. Munro, 1885. (2) BARCHESTER TOWERS. Munro, 1881. (3) DOCTOR THORNE. Munro, 1882. (4) FRAMLEY PARSONAGE. Smith & Elder, 1861. (5) SMALL HOUSE AT ALINGTON. Dodd, 1904. (6) LAST CHRONICLE OF BARSET. Smith & Elder, 1867. Separate but related novels of quiet country life around the cathedral town of Barchester, containing numerous fine character studies. 2527

--------. (1) PHINEAS FINN. Ward & Lock, 1869. (2) PHINEAS REDUX. Ward & Lock, 1874. The social side of political life in the 1860s. 2528

--------. THE WAY WE LIVE NOW. Chatto, 1875. An account of contemporary English society. 2529

Trollope, Frances. LIFE AND ADVENTURES OF MICHAEL ARMSTRONG. Colburn, 1840. Illustrates the conditions of child labor in factories. 2530

Wallis, Henry M. DEMI-ROYAL. by Ashton Hilliers, _pseud._ Methuen, 1915. The social and religious life of the early part of the century in England and on the Continent. 2531

Walpole, Hugh. THE CATHEDRAL. Doran, 1922. Life in an English cathedral city at the end of the nineteenth century. 2532

--------. THE FORTRESS. Doubleday, 1932. A feud between Judith Paris and Walter Herries, whose family had grown rich in commerce after Waterloo. 2533

Ward, Mary Augusta. THE MARRIAGE OF WILLIAM ASHE. by Mrs. Humphry Ward. Harper, 1905. Romance in cultured circles in Regency England. 2534

--------. ROBERT ELSMERE. by Mrs. Humphry Ward. Macmillan, 1888. Centers on English intellectual life and the Oxford Movement. 2535

Warry, C. King. THE SENTINEL OF WESSEX. Unwin, 1904. Gaiety and uncertainty in London during the Napoleonic Wars. 2536

Watson, H. B. Marriott. CHLORIS OF THE ISLAND. Harper, 1900. Dilemma of a youth who loves an Irish girl but differs politically with her family. 2537

--------. THE HOUSE IN THE DOWNS. Dent, 1914. Smuggling, naval activities, and threat of invasion in the Napoleonic era. 2538

--------. TWISTED EGLANTINE. Appleton, 1905. Vivid society romance of the Regency period. 2539

Watson, Helen H. ANDREW GOODFELLOW. by Mrs. Herbert Watson. Macmillan, 1906. Romance of a lieutenant in Nelson's service with an account of Trafalgar. 2540

Watson, Margaret. DRIVEN. Unwin, 1905. Economic problems before the repeal of the hated Corn Laws. 2541

Webb, Mary. PRECIOUS BANE. Cape, 1924. Welsh border life and ways at the beginning of the nineteenth century. 2542

Weyman, Stanley J. THE GREAT HOUSE. Longmans, 1919. Centered on the controversies caused by the Corn Laws and their repeal. 2543

--------. OVINGTON'S BANK. Longmans, 1922. The Welsh border after the Napoleonic Wars and during the development of industry. 2544

--------. STARVECROW FARM. Longmans, 1905. A young girl's romances amidst social injustices in England early in the century. 2545

White, William Hale. THE REVOLUTION IN TANNER'S LANE. by Mark Rutherford, pseud. Dodd, 1887. Unrest of the lower middle classes in the first half of the century. 2546

Wilkins, William Vaughan. AND SO--VICTORIA. Macmillan, 1937. Plots and intrigue about the throne in the years before Victoria's accession. 2547

--------. CONSORT FOR VICTORIA. [En. title: HUSBAND FOR VICTORIA] Doubleday, 1959. Plot to discredit Albert and force Victoria to relinquish the throne. 2548

Wilson, Margaret. THE VALIANT WIFE. Doubleday, 1934. A young wife goes to England to be near her husband, a prisoner at Dartmoor in the War of 1812. 2549

Wilson, Theodora Wilson. JACK O' PETERLOO. Labour Pub., 1924. Shows social injustice and unrest in England at the outset of the century. 2550

--------. MOLL O' THE TOLL BAR. Hutchinson, 1911. The rugged, sometimes illegal pursuits of the Cumberland country folk. 2551

Wright, Constance. SILVER COLLAR BOY. Dutton, 1935. Tells the story of a little Negro page in the age of Queen Anne. 2552

Wright-Henderson, R. W. JOHN GOODCHILD. Murray, 1909. Life in England during Victoria's reign. 2553

III. A. 4. a. 2) Ireland

Ashton, Helen. HEDGE OF THORNS. Dodd, 1958. The tragic failure of the potato crop in Ireland in 1846. 2554

Banim, Michael. CROHOORE OF THE BILL-HOOK. Duffy (Dublin), 1825. Savage revolt of the down-trodden peasants against their oppressors in the first quarter of the century. 2555

--------. FATHER CONNELL. Newby, 1840. An Irish priest and his flock in Kilkenny. 2556

Bodkin, M. McDonnell. TRUE MAN AND TRAITOR. Duffy (Dublin), 1910. Robert Emmet's college career, romance, and political involvement with Napoleon as well as with the Irish rebellion. 2557

Byrne, Donn. THE FIELD OF HONOR. Century, 1929. The love story of a young Irishman in the service of the English minister, Castlereagh. 2558

Carleton, William. THE BLACK PROPHET. Sadlier, 1847. The suffering and endurance of the Irish people during the dread famine. 2559

--------. RODY THE ROVER. Duffy (Dublin), 1845. Exploits of a Ribbonite agent. 2560

--------. THE TITHE-PROCTOR. Duffy (Dublin), 1849. Somewhat biased account of the tithe rebellion of the Irish peasants. 2561

Colum, Padraic. CASTLE CONQUER. Macmillan, 1923. Conditions centering around the Land Question of the 1870s and 1880s. 2562

Dowsley, William George. TRAVELLING MEN. Stokes, 1926. Entertaining tale of two Irish students which shows the depressed conditions following the Battle of Waterloo. 2563

Du Maurier, Daphne. HUNGRY HILL. Doubleday, 1950. Feud between two families--one proud and haughty, the other reckless and vicious. 2564

Edgeworth, Maria. THE ABSENTEE. Macmillan, 1812. Trials of the tenant farmers left by absentee landlords to the mercy of unscrupulous agents. 2565

--------. BELINDA. Macmillan, 1801. Contrasts between the rich and the poor in their daily lives. 2566

--------. ORMOND. Macmillan, 1817. Tenant farmers abandoned to their own resources by absentee landlords who pursue gay and frivolous lives. 2567

--------. VIVIAN. Dent, 1893. The luxury of the rich in contrast to the hardships of the poor. 2568

Gilbert, Rosa Mulholland. ONORA. by Rosa Mulholland. De la More Press, 1900. A girl's pathetic life during the Land League evictions. 2569

Gwynn, Stephen. ROBERT EMMET. Macmillan, 1909. Events leading up to and resulting from the rising in Ireland in 1803 led by Robert Emmet. 2570

Hackett, Francis. THE GREEN LION. Doubleday, 1936. The childhood and schooling of Gerald Coyne, who became, at seven, a follower of Parnell. 2571

Hall, Anna Marie. THE WHITEBOY. by Mrs. S. C. Hall. Routledge, 1845. An attempt to improve conditions of impoverished peasants. 2572

Hannay, James Owen. THE BAD TIMES. by George A. Birmingham, pseud. Methuen, 1908. Political experiences of a landlord who advocates home rule in the tense 1870s. 2573

Hartley, May. ISMAY'S CHILDREN. Macmillan, 1887. The conditions of the poverty-stricken peasants and the military activities of the Fenians. 2574

Johnson, Myrtle. THE RISING. Appleton, 1938. Irish resistance to the English culminates in the Fenian uprising of 1867. 2575

Keary, Annie Maria. CASTLE DALY. Macmillan, 1875. The anti-English feelings of the starving Irish peasants. 2576

Kelly, Peter Burrowes. THE MANOR OF GLENMORE. Butt, 1839. The actual conditions of the Irish peasants, sympathetically told. 2577

Kickham, Charles J. KNOCKNAGOW. Benziger, 1879. A character novel illustrating the arbitrary power of eviction exercised by landlords in mid-century. 2578

King, Richard Ashe. THE WEARING OF THE GREEN. by Basil, pseud. Harper, 1885. A romance with the revolutionary Fenian Brotherhood in the background. 2579

Lawless, Emily. HURRISH. Methuen, 1886. A strong story of the peasants' attitude toward the land reform issue. 2580

Leslie, Shane. DOOMSLAND. Chatto & Windus, 1923. Life and politics in the late nineteenth century. 2581

Lever, Charles. JACK HINTON. Little, 1841. A tale of early century life abounding in humorous character sketches. 2582

--------. THE KNIGHT OF GWYNNE. Routledge, 1847. Irish life, politics, and character in the first quarter of the century. 2583

--------. ST. PATRICK'S EVE. Munro, 1877. The cholera epidemic and the general discontent of the Irish tenant farmers form the background. 2584

McCarthy, Justin. A FAIR SAXON. Sheldon, 1873. A member of Parliament finds his career threatened by involvement with the Fenians. 2585

--------. MONONIA. Chatto, 1901. Combines accounts of a romance and the attempted insurrection of 1848. 2586

MacManus, Seumas. A LAD OF THE O'FRIELS. Digby & Long, 1903. A rather more cheerful than usual picture of the poor peasants' lot. 2587

Merry, Andrew. THE HUNGER. Melrose, 1910. Realistic story based on actual records of the severe famine of the 1840s. 2588

Moran, James J. THE DUNFERRY RISIN'. Digby & Long, 1894. A sympathetic report of the Irish Republican Brotherhood, the Fenians. 2589

Morgan, Sydney Owenson. THE O'BRIENS AND THE O'FLAHERTYS. by Lady Morgan. Colburn, 1827. A young patriot flees Ireland to escape harsh political and religious laws. 2590

--------. O'DONNEL. by Lady Morgan. Colburn, 1814. About a poor, but proud, Irish aristocrat much oppressed by the cruel penal laws. 2591

--------. THE WILD IRISH GIRL. by Sydney Owenson. Routledge, 1805. Romance between two young people whose families have been feuding for centuries. 2592

O'Brien, Kate. WITHOUT MY CLOAK. Doubleday, 1931. An Irish family of the Victorian era sacrifices freedom for position. 2593

O'Brien, R. B. THE D'ALTONS OF CRAG. Duffy (Dublin), 1882. Shows the desperate situation of the people during the great famine. 2594

O'Brien, William. WHEN WE WERE BOYS. Longmans, 1890. Account of the Fennian-Nationalist conflict, written from a jail cell. 2595

O'Flaherty, Liam. FAMINE. Random, 1937. The potato famine in Ireland during the 1840s. 2596

Reade, Amos. NORAH MORIARTY. Blackwood, 1886. Gladstone's advocacy of Irish land reform and home rule. 2597

Rhys, Grace. THE PRINCE OF LISNOVER. Methuen, 1904. A romance of Ireland during the Fenian Movement. 2598

Russell, T. O'Neill. DICK MASSEY. Gill (Dublin), 1869. The sufferings and evictions of farmers in the first quarter of the century. 2599

Savage, Marmion W. MY UNCLE THE CURATE. Harper, 1849. A novel of Irish politics in the 1830s. 2600

Sheehan, Patrick A. THE GRAVES AT KILMORNA. Longmans, 1915. Tells of the Fenians and their struggles, mentioning events at Dartmoor prison. 2601

--------. GLENANAAR. Longmans, 1905. Conditions in Ireland in the 1830s, with a family bearing a burden of "inherited shame." 2602

Thynne, Robert. RAVENSDALE. Tinsley, 1873. A Loyalist family during the attempted rebellion led by Emmet. 2603

--------. THE STORY OF A CAMPAIGN ESTATE. Long, 1899. Sympathetic view of the Irish drive for Home Rule and independence. 2604

Trench, W. Stewart. IEME. Longmans, 1871. Explains many aspects of the land question in the latter part of the century. 2605

Trollope, Anthony. CASTLE RICHMOND. Ward & Lock, 1860. Emphasizes the desperation and horror of the famine of 1845-48. 2606

Walsh, Louis J. THE NEXT TIME. Gill (Dublin), 1919. Political unrest from the Catholic Emancipation Bill of '29 to the Rebellion of '48. 2607

III. A. 4. b. Western and Central Europe

1) France

Aubry, Octave. THE EMPRESS-MIGHT-HAVE-BEEN. (tr.) Harper, 1927. The love of the Polish Marie Walewska and Napoleon, as well as his romances with Josephine and Marie Louise of Austria. 2608

Balfour, Andrew. VENGEANCE IS MINE. New Amsterdam Bk. Co., 1899. Napoleon at Elba, the Hundred Days, and the Battle of Waterloo. 2609

Barry, William Francis. THE DAYSPRING. Dodd, 1904. Romance of an Irishman in Paris during the Second Empire. 2610

Beck, Lily Adams. THE THUNDERER. by E. Barrington, pseud. Dodd, 1927. The personal life of Napoleon and Josephine with an account of the Coronation. 2611

Beyle, Marie Henri. THE RED AND THE BLACK. (tr.) by Stendhal, pseud. Richmond, 1898. Depicts France following the fall of Napoleon. 2612

Bickerstaffe-Drew, Francis. DROMINA. by John Ayscough, pseud. Putnam, 1909. A romance concerning the supposed "Lost Dauphin" of France, Louis XVII. 2613

Bill, Alfred H. THE CLUTCH OF THE CORSICAN. Atlantic Monthly, 1925. A picture of the plight of British hostages in France toward the end of Napoleon's power. 2614

--------. HIGHROADS OF PERIL. Little, 1926. The adventures of an American secret agent of exiled Louis XVIII during the First Consulate. 2615

Black, Ladbroke and Robert Lynd. THE MANTLE OF THE EMPEROR. Griffiths, 1906. The early career of Napoleon III (Louis Napoleon)--his joining the Carbonari, his unsuccessful military attempts, and his escape from Ham. 2616

Blake, M. M. GRANTLEY FENTON. Jarrold & Sons, 1902. Novel based on Napoleon's sojourn at Elba. 2617

Blyth, James. A BID FOR LOYALTY. Ward & Lock, 1909. An agent of the Empress Eugenie is entrusted with her jewels in an attempt to save France in the Franco-Prussian War. 2618

Bourchier, M. H. THE ADVENTURES OF A GOLDSMITH. Elkin Mathews, 1898. The involvement of an English goldsmith in a plot against Napoleon. 2619

Bower, Marian. SKIPPER ANNE. Hodder & Stoughton, 1913. Spying for Napoleon during the Chouan Conspiracy. 2620

Braddon, Mary E. ISHMAEL. Harper, 1884. Political developments of 1848 and 1851 and their results, with a good account of the coup of 1851. 2621

Broster, Dorothy K. THE WOUNDED NAME. Doubleday, Page, 1923. A young French Royalist's romance and adventures, chiefly during the Hundred Days. 2622

--------. THE YELLOW POPPY. McBride, 1922. Efforts of Royalists to rebuild power by finding a buried treasure during the Directorate. 2623

Buchanan, Robert. THE SHADOW OF THE SWORD. Appleton, 1875. This novel of Breton shows the effects of war on the common people. 2624

Campbell, A. Godric. FLEUR-DE-CAMP. Chatto, 1905. This story of a French girl reflects many important events during the first fifteen years of the century. 2625

Castle, Agnes and Egerton. WIND'S WILL. Appleton, 1916. Post-war romance of an English officer and a French flower girl. 2626

--------. WOLF-LURE. Appleton, 1917. Vigor, action, and suspense in a tale of castles and counterfeiters. 2627

Chambers, Robert W. (1) LORRAINE. Harper, 1898. (2) ASHES OF EMPIRE. Stokes, 1898. (3) THE RED REPUBLIC. Putnam, 1895. A trilogy telling of Franco-Prussian War events--the Declaration of War, Sedan, the eventual surrender of Paris, and ensuing conditions. 2628

--------. THE MAIDS OF PARADISE. Harper, 1902. Contains excellent descriptions of cavalry charges during the Franco-Prussian War. 2629

Chamson, André. THE MOUNTAIN TAVERN. (tr.) Holt, 1933. Tragic story of a young French officer on his way home after defeat at Waterloo. 2630

Claretie, Jules. AGNES. (tr.) Stock, 1909. A romance during the German siege of Paris (1870-1). 2631

Coleridge, Mary E. THE FIERY DAWN. Longmans, 1901. Based on the Duchess of Berri's Vendean rebellion--an attempt to gain the throne for her son. 2632

Daudet, Alphonse. KINGS IN EXILE. (tr.) Little, 1900. A novel of King Christian II of Illyria and his family in exile in Paris. 2633

--------. THE NABOB. (tr.) Heinemann, 1878. Satirical story of society in Paris during the Second Empire. 2634

--------. ROBERT HELMONT. (tr.) Macmillan, 1896. Horrors and sufferings during the siege of Paris, written from the viewpoint of a recluse. 2635

Delderfield, Ronald Frederick. SEVEN MEN OF GASCONY. Bobbs, 1949. Chronicle of a band of men from Gascony serving in the Napoleonic campaigns. 2636

Dempster, Charlotte L. H. ISEULTE. Harper, 1875. Life of the nobility in the provinces during the Franco-Prussian War. 2637

Doyle, Sir Arthur Conan. (1) THE EXPLOITS OF BRIGADIER GERARD. Appleton, 1896. (2) ADVENTURES OF GERARD (sequel). McClure, 1903. Loosely connected episodes in the adventurous career of a blustering, bragging French officer. 2638

--------. THE GREAT SHADOW. Arrowsmith, 1893. Romance under the shadow of Napoleon's driving ambition; a fine description of the Battle of Waterloo. 2639

--------. UNCLE BERNAC. Appleton, 1897. Northern France during Napoleon's plans for an invasion of

England. 2640

Dumas, Alexandre. THE COUNT OF MONTE CRISTO. (tr.) Routledge, 1888. Imprisoned unjustly on a charge of aiding the exiled Napoleon, Edmond Dantes plots to escape and becomes wealthy and powerful. 2641

--------. THE SHE-WOLVES OF MACHECOUL. (tr.) Little, 1894. Depicts the Vendean rebellion of 1832, led by the Duchess of Berri, who sought to make her son king. 2642

Elwood, Muriel. SO MUCH AS BEAUTY DOES. Liveright, 1941. Romance of Amy Brown and the Duc de Berri, and the way it was affected by the Bourbon restoration. 2643

Endore, Guy. KING OF PARIS. S. & S., 1956. Fictional biography of Alexandre Dumas--as exciting as any of his novels. 2644

Erckmann-Chatrian, <u>pseud.</u> for Emile Erckmann and Alexandre Chatrian. THE PLEBISCITE. (tr.) [same as THE STORY OF THE PLEBISCITE] Scribner, 1871. Conditions of unpreparedness in France before and during the Franco-Prussian War. 2645

Fleischmann, Hector. THE EMPEROR'S SPY. (tr.) Nash, 1913. The story of a woman who acted as a spy for Napoleon during a conspiracy against his life. 2646

Ford, Ford Madox (name originally Ford Madox Hueffer). A LITTLE LESS THAN GODS. Viking, 1928. The hectic Hundred Days of Napoleon's attempt to regain power. 2647

Gavin, Catherine Irvine. MADELEINE. St. Martins, 1957. Romance of a Suez Canal engineer and a lady-in-waiting to the Empress of Napoleon III. 2648

Gennari, Genevieve. THE RIVEN HEART. (tr.) McKay, 1956. Seething France during Napoleon's rule and the subsequent Bourbon restoration. 2649

Gerson, Noel B. EMPEROR'S LADIES. Doubleday, 1959. The marriage of Marie Louise of Austria to Napoleon. 2650

Giono, Jean. HORSEMAN ON THE ROOF. (tr.) Knopf, 1954. Difficult journey through Provence in the midst of a disastrous cholera epidemic. (followed by THE STRAW MAN) 2651

Gonnard, Philippe. EXILE OF ST. HELENA. (tr.) Lippincott, 1909. Portrays the Napoleonic legend in its last phases. 2652

Gorham, Charles. GOLD OF THEIR BODIES. Dial, 1954. A novel based on the life of the artist Paul Gauguin. 2653

Gorman, Herbert Sherman. BRAVE GENERAL. Farrar, 1942. The career of Georges Boulanger, demagogic military and political figure. 2654

Gosselin, Louis L. T. THE HOUSE OF THE COMBRAYS. (tr.) by G. Lenôtre, pseud. Dodd, 1903. The historical background is the Chouan Conspiracy against Napoleon, led by Georges Cadoudal. 2655

Graves, Clotilde Inez Mary. BETWEEN TWO THIEVES. by Richard Dehan, pseud. Heinemann, 1912. The poor government and military leadership and the curtailment of popular rights in Napoleon III's time. 2656

Gribble, Francis. THE DREAM OF PEACE. Chatto, 1904. The retreat into Switzerland of General Bourbaki during the Franco-Prussian War. 2657

--------. A ROMANCE OF THE TUILERIES. Chapman, 1902. A romance of the court of Louis Napoleon with an account of the Revolution of 1848. 2658

Haines, Donald H. THE RETURN OF PIERRE. Paul, 1912. The feelings and experiences of a peasant-soldier in the Franco-Prussian War. 2659

Hall, Moreton. GENERAL GEORGE. Unwin, 1903. The Chouan Conspiracy to assassinate Napoleon and Napoleon's unjust revenge. 2660

Hayes, Frederick W. CAPTAIN KIRKE WEBBE. Hutchinson, 1907. A delightful rascal manages to be at once a French and an English privateer. 2661

Herbert, Alan Patrick. WHY WATERLOO? Doubleday, 1953. Napoleon's activities, from his arrival at Elba to his defeat at Waterloo. 2662

Jacob, Naomi Ellington. FOUNDER OF THE HOUSE. Macmillan, 1936. A Jewish family of art dealers amidst the life of nineteenth century Paris, Vienna, and London. 2663

Johnson, David. PROUD CANARIES. [En. title: SABRE GENERAL] Sloane, 1959. A cavalryman tells of Napoleon's European campaigns from 1806 to 1809. 2664

Kavanagh, Julia. MADELEINE. Appleton, 1848. The heroine, disappointed in love, founds and runs an orphanage. 2665

Knowles, Mabel Winifred. A SPY FOR NAPOLEON. by May Wynne, pseud. Jarrolds Ltd., 1917. Shows conspiracy against the revolutionary government and the spy system of Fouché. 2666

Komroff, Manuel. WATERLOO. Coward, 1936. Napoleon's escape from Elba and his smashing defeat at Waterloo. 2667

Landau, Mark Aleksandrovich. SAINT HELENA, LITTLE ISLAND. (tr.) by M. A. Aldanov, pseud. Knopf, 1924. A story of Napoleon's last illness and death. 2668

Lansworth, Lew X. OVER THE RIVER CHARLIE. Doubleday, 1956. Paris during the Prussian siege of 1870-71. 2669

Leblanc, Maurice. THE FRONTIER. (tr.) Mills & Boon, 1912. A border incident during the Franco-Prussian War. 2670

Lee, Albert. THE EMPEROR'S TRUMPETER. Shaw, 1907. Napoleon's rise and a description of deserted Moscow between its abandonment by the Russians and its burning by the French. 2671

Lenanton, Carola Oman. MAJOR GRANT. by Carola Oman. Holt, 1932. About one of Wellington's spies during the Peninsular War. 2672

Le Poer, John. A MODERN LEGIONARY. Methuen, 1904. A realistic account of French Foreign Legion service in Algeria. 2673

Lovelace, Maud Hart. PETTICOAT COURT. Day, 1930. The court of the Empress Eugenie in the days of Napoleon III. 2674

Lytton, Edward Bulwer, 1st. baron. THE PARISIANS. Dutton, 1873. A picture of the various types of French society. 2675

McAllister, Alister. THE TWO OF DIAMONDS. by Anthony Wharton, pseud. Collins, 1926. Paris during the Second Empire with Napoleon III, Zola, and Flaubert. 2676

Malling, Matilda. A ROMANCE OF THE FIRST CONSUL. (tr.) Heinemann, 1898. About a La Vendée girl who falls in love with Napoleon. 2677

Manceron, Claude. SO BRIEF A SPRING. Putnam, 1958. The "brief spring" is Napoleon's one-hundred-day bid to regain his former power. 2678

Margueritte, Paul and Victor. THE DISASTER. (tr.) Greening, 1898. An account of the Franco-Prussian War in the vicinity of Metz. 2679

--------. STRASBOURG. (tr.) Dutton, 1916. The courage of two Strasbourg families during the Franco-Prussian

War. 2680

Margueritte, Victor. THE FRONTIERS OF THE HEART. (tr.) Stokes, 1913. Pressures in the home of a French girl and her Prussian husband during the Franco-Prussian War. 2681

Marsh, Frances. THE IRON GAME. Fifield, 1909. A story of the Franco-Prussian War of 1870-71. 2682

Murray, David Leslie. TALE OF THREE CITIES. Knopf, 1940. The three cities of the title are Paris, London, and Rome. 2683

Murray, E. C. Grenville. THE MEMBER FOR PARIS. Smith & Elder, 1871. "A tale of the Second Empire." 2684

Neumann, Alfred. ANOTHER CAESAR. (tr.) [En. title: THE NEW CAESAR] Knopf, 1934. A story of Louis Napoleon III, who believed in his destiny as Emperor of the French. 2685

--------. THE FRIENDS OF THE PEOPLE. (tr.) Hutchinson, 1940. The political unrest of Paris during the reverses of 1870 and 1871. 2686

--------. THE GAUDY EMPIRE. (tr.) [En. title: MAN OF DECEMBER] Knopf, 1937. Portrait of Napoleon III and his fall from power, 1856 to 1870. 2687

Ohnet, Georges. THE EAGLE'S TALON. (tr.) Putnam, 1913. Displays the people's discontent with the revolutionary government. 2688

Orcutt, William Dana. THE FLOWER OF DESTINY. McClurg, 1905. Louis Napoleon's escape, marriage, and taking of the Imperial title. 2689

Orczy, Baroness Emmuska. THE BRONZE EAGLE. Doran, 1915. Conflict between Royalists and Bonapartists during the Hundred Days. 2690

--------. CASTLES IN THE AIR. Doran, 1922. Adventures

of a charming rogue in Paris after Napoleon's defeat. 2691

--------. JOYOUS ADVENTURE. Doubleday, 1932. An English gentleman sets out to find the heir to the French throne, who is in hiding in Normandy. 2692

--------. SHEAF OF BLUEBELLS. Doran, 1917. A French noblewoman plots to overthrow Napoleon. 2693

--------. A SPY OF NAPOLEON. Putnam, 1934. Romance and intrigue in the police-state of Napoleon III. 2694

Oxenham, John, pseud. for William Arthur Dunkerley. BROKEN SHACKLES. Lane, 1915. Military tale of Bourbaki's attack on the Prussians and subsequent retreat. 2695

--------. GREAT-HEART GILLIAN. Hodder, 1909. The French army's fateful march to Sedan and the battle which ensued. 2696

--------. OUR LADY OF DELIVERANCE. Hutchinson, 1901. A novel of the Dreyfus case, in which a man falsely convicted of treason was finally cleared. 2697

Pardo Bazán, Emilia. THE MYSTERY OF THE LOST DAUPHIN. (tr.) Funk & Wagnalls, 1906. What became of the son of Marie Antoinette? 2698

Pemberton, Max. THE HUNDRED DAYS. Appleton, 1905. The period of Napoleon's bid to regain power. 2699

--------. THE VIRGIN FORTRESS. Cassell, 1912. Siege, capture, and spying at Metz in the Franco-Prussian War. 2700

Pilgrim, David, pseud. for John Leslie Palmer and Hilary Aiden St. George Saunders. SO GREAT A MAN. Macmillan, 1937. Napoleon's life during the ten months from March, 1808, to January, 1809. 2701

Powers, Anne. THE THOUSAND FIRES. Bobbs, 1957. The battles and adventures of the final years of Napoleon's power. 2702

Praviel, Armand. THE MURDER OF MONSIEUR FUALDÈS. (tr.) Seltzer, 1924. Deals with the murder of an ex-prosecutor and its discovery. 2703

Ralli, Constantine S. THE TYRANNY OF HONOUR. Chapman, 1911. A court trial concerning a contested fortune with a background of the Franco-Prussian War. 2704

--------. THE WISDOM OF THE SERPENT. Griffiths, 1907. The battle of Vionville-Mars la Tour in the Franco-Prussian War is described. 2705

Rawson, Maud Stepney. JOURNEYMAN LOVE. Hutchinson, 1902. The development of culture and politics in rebellious mid-century Paris. 2706

Rayner, Denys Arthur. THE LONG FIGHT. Holt, 1958. A little-known British-French sea battle in the Indian Ocean in 1808. 2707

Reitzel, William. THE PINNACLE OF GLORY. by Wilson Wright, pseud. Macmillan, 1935. The activities of Napoleon during his exile on St. Helena. 2708

Roth, Joseph. THE BALLAD OF THE HUNDRED DAYS. Viking, 1936. Napoleon's return from Elba told from the viewpoint of a laundress infatuated with him. 2709

Rudigoz, Roger. FRENCH DRAGOON. (tr.) Coward, 1959. Adventures of a cavalryman after the French defeat at Leipzig in 1813. 2710

Sabatini, Rafael. THE LOST KING. Houghton, 1937. The mystery of the Lost Dauphin of France, Louis XVII. 2711

Savidge, Eugene Coleman. THE AMERICAN IN PARIS. Lippincott, 1895. The turmoil during the siege of Paris by the Germans. 2712

Scott, Hugh S. THE LAST HOPE. by H. Seton Merriman, pseud. Scribner, 1904. A story of the Lost Dauphin, Louis XVII, and his supposed son. 2713

Seawell, Molly Elliot. THE FORTUNES OF FIFI. Bobbs, 1903. The story of a French actress. 2714

Shackelford, Henry. THE LOST KING. Brentano's, 1903. One theory of the escape of Marie Antoinette's son. 2715

Stacpoole, Henry de Vere. THE DRUMS OF WAR. Duffield, 1910. Competition between Prussia and France at the time of Napoleon III and Bismarck. 2716

Stone, Irving. LUST FOR LIFE. Longmans, 1934. Story of the tortured genius now recognized as a great artist, Vincent Van Gogh. 2717

Strachey, John St. Loe. THE MADONNA OF THE BARRICADES. Harcourt, 1925. A dedicated young couple fights for freedom in the Revolution of 1848. 2718

Wagner, Geoffrey A. SOPHIE. Ward, 1957. A smuggler's daughter becomes wealthy and influential by improper means. 2719

Werfel, Franz. SONG OF BERNADETTE. (tr.) Viking, 1942. Account of fourteen-year-old St. Bernadette and her "beautiful lady," Mary. 2720

Wilkins, William Vaughan. BEING MET TOGETHER. Macmillan, 1944. A young American is an agent for Napoleon and tries to rescue him from St. Helena. 2721

III. A. 4. b. 2) Central Europe (including Germany, the Netherlands, Switzerland, Austria, Hungary, Czechoslovakia, and Poland)

Abrahams, William Miller. IMPERIAL WALTZ. Dial, 1954. Empress Elizabeth of Austria and her marriage to Franz Joseph of Hungary. 2722

Asch, Shalom. SALVATION. (tr.) Putnam, 1934. Story based on the activities of a Jewish rabbi in a small Polish village. 2723

Baum, Vicki. HEADLESS ANGEL. Doubleday, 1948. A German countess who sought happiness in Mexico returns to a reconciliation with her husband. 2724

Beyerlein, Franz Adam. "JENA" OR "SEDAN"? (tr.) Heinemann, 1904. The military life of soldiers from all walks of society. 2725

Bloem, Walter. THE IRON YEAR. (tr.) Lane, 1914. A novel of people and events in the Franco-Prussian War. 2726

Born, Edith de. FELDING CASTLE. [En. title: SCHLOSS FELDING] Knopf, 1959. The upbringing of a young girl in a family of Austrian nobility at the turn of the century. 2727

Brontë, Charlotte. VILLETTE. Tauchnitz, 1853. School life in the nineteenth century in Brussels, Belgium. 2728

Carr, Mildred E. A KNIGHT OF POLAND. Smith & Elder, 1910. Revolt is provoked by the impressment of Poles into the Russian army. 2729

--------. LOVE AND HONOUR. Putnam, 1901. Shows the career of Jerome Bonaparte, Napoleon's younger brother, as ruler of Westphalia. 2730

Castle, Agnes and Egerton. IF YOUTH BUT KNEW! Macmillan, 1906. A romance in Westphalia during the rule of the weak Jerome Bonaparte. 2731

Chatfield-Taylor, H. C. THE CRIMSON WING. Stone, 1902. Adventures of the crown prince, later to become Frederick III, in the Franco-Prussian War. 2732

Cramb, J. A. SCHÖNBRUNN. Putnam, 1918. Napoleon at the height of his power in the period of the Treaty of Schönbrunn (1809). 2733

Franzos, Karl Emil. FOR THE RIGHT. Clarke, 1888. An uneducated rural judge does his best to dispense impartial justice. 2734

Frenssen, Gustav. JÖRN UHL. (tr.) Estes, 1905. German provincial life--the hero is a peasant--in the period of the Franco-Prussian War. 2735

--------. THE THREE COMRADES. (tr.) Estes, 1907. Life in Schleswig-Holstein during the Franco-Prussian War. 2736

Freytag, Gustav. DEBIT AND CREDIT. Ward & Lock, 1856. The changing economic conditions in Germany during the Industrial Revolution. 2737

Frischauer, Paul. A GREAT LORD. Random, 1937. A story of life in Poland during Napoleonic times. 2738

Gasiorowski, Waclaw. NAPOLEON'S LOVE-STORY. (tr.) Dutton, 1905. The part played in his treatment of Poland by the romance of Napoleon and Madame Walewska. 2739

Gregg, Hilda Caroline. A BROTHER OF GIRLS. by Sydney C. Grier, pseud. Blackwood, 1925. The political activities and romantic affairs of an English diplomat in Europe. 2740

--------. (1) THE STRONG HAND. Blackwood, 1920. (2) OUT OF PRISON (sequel). Blackwood, 1922. both by Sydney C. Grier, pseud. Laid chiefly in Germany between 1806 and 1814, these novels depict Napoleon's growing influence. 2741

Grogger, Paula. THE DOOR IN THE GRIMMING. Putnam, 1936. The Catholic peasantry in Styria during the Napoleonic invasion of Austria. 2742

Hartley, M. A SERESHAN. Mills & Boon, 1911. A tale of action including the Vienna revolution and the rebellion of the Hungarians in 1848. 2743

Hatton, Joseph. BY ORDER OF THE CZAR. Munro, 1890. Torture and revenge during the persecution of the Jews in Poland. 2744

Hector, Annie French. MAID, WIFE, OR WIDOW? by Mrs. Alexander, pseud. Munro, 1884. A romance of the Franco-Prussian War. 2745

Heyer, Georgette. AN INFAMOUS ARMY. Doubleday, Doran, 1938. The Battle of Waterloo seen from Brussels with the Duke of Wellington as man of the hour. 2746

Jeans, Alice. THE STRONGER WINGS. Stock, 1909. Shows how higher education and the spread of new ideas led to the uprising in Vienna in 1848. 2747

Jókai, Maurus. THE BARON'S SONS. (tr.) Page, 1900. A widow and her sons in the Revolution of 1848. 2748

--------. THE DAY OF WRATH. (tr.) McClure, 1900. Crime, disease, and poverty leading up to the Magyar Revolution of 1848. 2749

--------. DEBTS OF HONOUR. (tr.) Doubleday, 1900. Tale of the Hungarian insurrection of 1848 and of a family pursued by a curse. 2750

--------. AN HUNGARIAN NABOB. (tr.) Doubleday, 1898. The rich, extravagant way of life of a wealthy Hungarian landowner. 2751

--------. MANASSEH. (tr.) Page, 1901. The simple life and brutal fighting of the Transylvanians in 1848. 2752

--------. THE NAMELESS CASTLE. (tr.) Doubleday, 1898. Based on a report that Marie Antoinette had a daughter who was hidden in a castle in Hungary. 2753

--------. THE NEW LANDLORD. (tr.) Macmillan, 1868. An elderly Hungarian landowner offers passive resistance to the hated Austrians in 1848. 2754

Komroff, Manuel. FEAST OF THE JESTERS. Farrar, 1947. A troupe of French actors who entertained during the Congress of Vienna. 2755

Longard de Longgarde, Dorothea Gerard. A GLORIOUS LIE. by Dorothea Gerard. Long, 1912. Domestic tragedy in Austria during the conflict with Prussia. 2756

Lundegård, Axel. THE STORM BIRD. (tr.) Hodder, 1895. A novel of Vienna in 1848. 2757

Mann, Thomas. THE BELOVED RETURNS. (tr.) Knopf, 1940. The Lotte of Goethe's SORROWS OF WERTHER visits the author after forty years. 2758

Meding, Oskar. FOR SCEPTRE AND CROWN. by Gregor Samarow, pseud. King, 1875. A novel based on events in the Austrian War. 2759

Meredith, George. THE TRAGIC COMEDIANS. Scribner, 1880. A romance based on the later life of Ferdinand Lassalle, a Socialist who agitated for labor unions. 2760

Mundt, Klara. ANDREAS HOFER. (tr.) by Louisa Mühlbach, pseud. Appleton, 1868. An account of the Tyrol during and after the 1809 revolt led by Hofer. 2761

--------. (1) LOUISA OF PRUSSIA AND HER TIMES. (tr.) Appleton, 1867. (2) NAPOLEON AND THE QUEEN OF PRUSSIA (sequel). (tr.) Appleton, 1867. (3) NAPOLEON AND BLÜCHER (sequel). (tr.) Appleton, 1867. all by Louisa Mühlbach, pseud. Include Napoleon's campaigns against Prussia and Russia and his treaty with Alexander of Prussia which resulted in the formation of Westphalia. 2762

Neumann, Robert. A WOMAN SCREAMED. Dial, 1938. The revolt of the Hungarians against Hapsburg rule. 2763

Nordling, John. THE MOONLIGHT SONATA. (tr.) Sturgis & Walton, 1912. Based on the career of Beethoven during his growing deafness. 2764

Openshaw, Mary. THE CROSS OF HONOUR. Laurie, 1910. Warsaw romance of Napoleon and Madame Walewska. 2765

Oxenham, John, pseud. for William Arthur Dunkerley. JOHN OF GERISAU. Hurst, 1902. European wars in the 1860s--Prussia, Austria, Germany, France. 2766

Pemberton, Max. THE GARDEN OF SWORDS. Dodd, 1899. Effect of the Franco-Prussian War on those who remained at home. 2767

Pidoll, Carl von. EROICA. (tr.) Methuen, 1956. Purported narration by a friend of Beethoven telling of the musician's career. 2768

Reuter, Fritz. IN THE YEAR '13. (tr.) Tauchnitz, 1867. A spirited story of rural life showing the German reaction to Napoleon's invading army. 2769

--------. SEED TIME AND HARVEST. (tr.) Low, 1878. Daily life in rural Mecklenburg, and reactions to the Revolution of 1848. 2770

Rosegger, Peter. THE FOREST SCHOOLMASTER. (tr.) Putnam, 1901. Story of a schoolmaster of Napoleonic times in the Alpine forests. 2771

Scott, Hugh S. BARLASCH OF THE GUARD. by H. Seton Merriman, pseud. McClure, Phillips, 1903. About a family in Danzig during the Napoleonic invasion of Russia. 2772

--------. THE VULTURES. by H. Seton Merriman, pseud. Harper, 1902. Foreign secret agents, Polish revolt, and the assassination of Czar Alexander II in 1881. 2773

Seidel, Ina. THE WISH CHILD. Farrar, 1935. Two young cousins in Germany during the Napoleonic era. 2774

Simpson, Helen D. SARABAND FOR DEAD LOVERS. Doubleday, 1935. The story of Sophia Dorothea, Electress of Hanover, divorced and imprisoned for infidelity. 2775

Singer, Isaac B. THE MAGICIAN OF LUBLIN. (tr.) Noonday, 1960. A talented circus performer in Poland. 2776

Skelton, Gladys. BARRICADE. by John Presland, pseud. Philip Allan, 1926. A romance based on the uprising in Vienna in 1848. 2777

Spielhagen, Friedrich. THE HOHENSTEINS. (tr.) Holt, 1870. Follows three generations of the Hohenstein family from 1848. 2778

Strachey, Marjorie. THE NIGHTINGALE. Longmans, 1925. Novel based on the life of the great Polish musician, Chopin. 2779

Sudermann, Hermann. REGINA. (tr.) Lane, 1905. A story of eastern Prussia in which the sins of a father affect the life of his son. 2780

Tautphoebus, Baroness Jemima von. AT ODDS. Lippincott, 1863. Bavaria is the scene for this tale of a romantic triangle. 2781

Thompson, Morton. THE CRY AND THE COVENANT. Doubleday, 1949. Fictional biography of a famous Hungarian obstetrician and early foe of infection, Ignaz Semmelweis. 2782

Westall, William. A RED BRIDAL. Chatto, 1898. Resistance of the Tyroleans, led by Hofer, to the French and Bavarians. 2783

--------. WITH THE RED EAGLE. Chatto, 1897. An English-Irish soldier joins the Tyrolese revolt. (followed by A RED BRIDAL) 2784

Weyman, Stanley J. THE TRAVELLER IN THE FUR CLOAK. Longmans, 1924. Adventures and misadventures of an English diplomat abroad. 2785

III. A. 4. b. 3) Scandinavia and the Baltic

Dixelius, Hildur. THE MINISTER'S DAUGHTER. Dutton, 1926. Colorful novel of people and events in Lapland at the start of the century. 2786

Gulbranssen, Trygve. BEYOND SING THE WOODS. (tr.) Putnam, 1936. Saga of Norwegian farmers on their family estate in the hills. (followed by THE WIND FROM THE MOUNTAINS) 2787

--------. THE WIND FROM THE MOUNTAINS. (tr.) Putnam, 1937. The strength and beauty of rugged Norway shows in this tale of family life. 2788

Hubbard, Margaret Ann. FLIGHT OF THE SWAN. Bruce, 1946. Based on the life of story teller Hans Christian Andersen. 2789

Lagerlöf, Selma. GOSTA BERLING'S SAGA. Amer. Scandinavian Foundation, 1891. A Swedish novel depicting life about 1820. 2790

Moberg, Vilhelm. THE EMIGRANTS. (tr.) S. & S., 1951. A peasant family in Sweden and their voyage to America in 1850. (followed by UNTO A GOOD LAND) 2791

Sorensen, Virginia. KINGDOM COME. Harcourt, 1960. Portrays the deep religious convictions which drove many Scandinavians to emigrate to America. 2792

Wright, Theon. THE KNIFE. Gilbert Press, 1955. The steel-bladed knife introduces civilization to the primitive Eskimos in mid-nineteenth century Greenland. 2793

III. A. 4. c. Southern Europe

1) Iberian Peninsula

Alarcón, Pedro Antonio de. THE THREE-CORNERED HAT. (tr.) Cassell, 1891. Romance in an Andalusian village based on folk tales. 2794

Bailey, H. C. THE YOUNG LOVERS. Methuen, 1918. A story of some of the battles in the Peninsular War. 2795

Champion de Crespigny, Rose. THE SPANISH PRISONER.

by Mrs. Philip Champion de Crespigny. Nash, 1907. A romance, interrupted by the war with England, results in adventure in disguise. 2796

Conrad, Joseph. THE ARROW OF GOLD. Doubleday, 1920. Story of a strange, mysterious woman told by the man who loved her. 2797

Craigie, Mrs. Pearl Mary. THE SCHOOL FOR SAINTS. by John Oliver Hobbes, pseud. Stokes, 1897. An Englishman involved with Marshal Prim and the Carlist outbreak in Spain. (followed by ROBERT ORANGE) 2798

Crockett, Samuel R. THE FIREBRAND. McClure, 1901. Story of Queen Christina during the Carlist Wars. 2799

Daudet, Ernest. RAFAEL. (tr.) Low, 1895. Napoleon and Charles IV of Spain figure in this tale of the Iberian Peninsula. 2800

Forester, C. S. THE GUN. Little, 1933. A story of the Peninsular War and the part played by a particular gun. 2801

Fortescue, John W. THE DRUMMER'S COAT. Macmillan, 1899. A novel concerning the Peninsular War. 2802

Gregg, Hilda Caroline. A YOUNG MAN MARRIED. by Sydney C. Grier, pseud. Blackwood, 1909. A Spanish girl and an English soldier in Spain during the Peninsular War. 2803

Hewlett, Maurice. THE SPANISH JADE. Doubleday, 1908. Romance of an Englishman in Spain. 2804

Heyer, Georgette. THE SPANISH BRIDE. Doubleday, 1941. Romance of an English officer and a Spanish lady. 2805

Lever, Charles. CHARLES O'MALLEY. Little, 1841. Battles, duels, and travels during the Peninsular War. 2806

--------. TOM BURKE OF OURS. Macmillan, 1844. The career of an Irishman in Napoleon's service during victories, conspiracies, and defeats. 2807

Oldmeadow, Ernest J. ANTONIO. Century, 1909. A young monk affected by the suppression of monasteries in Portugal. 2808

Pérez-Galdós, Benito. SARAGOSSA. (tr.) Little, 1899. A novel based on the siege of Saragossa in 1808. 2809

--------. TRAFALGAR. (tr.) Gottsberger, 1884. Strategy of Villeneuve and Nelson in their decisive naval encounter. 2810

Sabatini, Rafael. THE SNARE. Lippincott, 1917. Revolves around Wellington's action against the French in Portugal. 2811

Scott, Hugh S. IN KEDAR'S TENTS. by H. Seton Merriman, pseud. Dodd, 1897. Struggle for power in Spain between Don Carlos and the Queen Regent, Christina. 2812

--------. THE VELVET GLOVE. by H. Seton Merriman, pseud. Dodd, 1901. Political unrest in Spain during the Carlist War is the background for an exciting romance. 2813

Woods, Margaret L. THE KING'S REVOKE. Dutton, 1905. Political affairs in Spain under Napoleon's brother, Joseph Bonaparte. 2814

--------. SONS OF THE SWORD. McClure, 1901. Romance of an Irish girl during the Peninsular War. 2815

--------. THE SPANISH LADY. Cape, 1927. The various effects of a romance between Wellington and a lovely Spanish lady. 2816

III. A. 4. c. 2) Italy and Adjacent Islands

Bailey, H. C. THE PILLAR OF FIRE. Methuen, 1918. England, France, and Italy in the 1850s--Napoleon III, Victor Emmanuel, and Garibaldi. 2817

--------. THE REBEL. Methuen, 1923. Includes accounts of Garibaldi's defeat at Mentana and the Franco-Prussian

War. 2818

Beyle, Marie Henri. THE CHARTERHOUSE OF PARMA. by Stendhal, pseud. Boni & Liveright, 1925. Life of a veteran of Waterloo in Italy in the post-Napoleonic age of petty despots. 2819

Bickerstaffe-Drew, Francis. MAROTZ. by John Ayscough, pseud. Putnam, 1908. Sicily during the time of Victor Emmanuel III and Pope Leo XIII. 2820

Brown, Beatrice Curtis. FOR THE DELIGHT OF ANTONIO. Houghton, 1932. Involvement of an English youth and an aristocratic Venetian in the revolt against Austria. 2821

Conrad, Joseph. SUSPENSE. Doubleday, Page, 1925. The shifting moods of Europe after Napoleon had been imprisoned at Elba. 2822

Crawford, F. Marion. (1) SARACINESCA. Macmillan, 1887. (2) SANT' ILARIO (sequel). Macmillan, 1889. (3) DON ORSINO (sequel). Macmillan, 1892. (4) CORLEONE (sequel). Macmillan, 1898. Panoramic view of social, political, and economic aspects of Roman life in the last half of the century. 2823

Crockett, Samuel R. THE SILVER SKULL. Smith & Elder, 1901. Ferdinand I's rule in the Kingdom of the Two Sicilies after the Congress of Vienna. 2824

Deeping, Warwick. THE LAME ENGLISHMAN. Cassell, 1911. Spirited story of an Englishman in the service of the revolutionist Garibaldi. 2825

Fogazzaro, Antonio. (1) THE PATRIOT. (tr.) Putnam, 1906. (2) THE SINNER. (tr.) [En. title: THE MAN OF THE WORLD] Putnam, 1907. (3) THE SAINT. (tr.) Putnam, 1906. Trilogy dealing with social and religious conditions in Italy and including romance, politics, and domestic affairs. 2826

Giono, Jean. THE STRAW MAN. (tr.) Knopf, 1959. A hussar colonel in the 1848 Italian revolt against Austria. 2827

Gregg, Hilda Caroline. ONE CROWDED HOUR. by Sydney C. Grier, pseud. Blackwood, 1912. Two Englishmen fight along with Garibaldi for Italian freedom. 2828

Hansard, Luke J. THE FLAME IN THE SOUTH. Hutchinson, 1925. Impact of revolutionary activities leading to the unification of Italy. 2829

Hartley, M. BEYOND MAN'S STRENGTH. Heinemann, 1909. Life of a couple in Italy against a background of political developments in early and mid-century. 2830

Hood, Alexander Nelson. ADRIA. Murray, 1902. An Englishman in Venice during the revolt against the Austrians. 2831

Hopkins, Tighe. FOR FREEDOM. Chatto, 1899. Garibaldi and the War of Italian Liberation in 1859. 2832

Hutton, Edward. FREDERIC UVEDALE. Blackwood, 1901. The spiritual life of a youth educated in England and living in Italy. 2833

Kazantzakēs, Nikos. FREEDOM OR DEATH. S. & S., 1956. Emotions flare as Cretans fight to throw off the bondage of Turkey. 2834

Kingsley, Henry. SILCOTE OF SILCOTES. Longmans, 1867. Scenes of battle in the Italian War of Liberation. 2835

Komroff, Manuel. MAGIC BOW. Harper, 1940. Career of the great Italian violinist, Paganini, during the Napoleonic period. 2836

Lampedusa, Giuseppe Di. THE LEOPARD. (tr.) Pantheon, 1960. The fortunes of the Sicilian House of Salina in the latter half of the century. 2837

Lever, Charles. THE DALTONS. Routledge, 1852. Incidents in the Italian fight for independence from Austria. 2838

--------. GERALD FITZGERALD THE CHEVALIER. Harper, 1899. The adventures of a son of the Young Pretender. 2839

Maxwell, Anna. PIETRO THE GARIBALDIAN. Parsons, 1925. The War of Italian Liberation with Garibaldi, Cavour, Mazzini, and Victor Emmanuel as prominent figures. 2840

Meredith, George. VITTORIA. Scribner, 1866. A young opera singer against a background of contemporary political affairs, with a good picture of Mazzini. 2841

Murray, Paul. HEART IS A STRANGER. Harper, 1949. The inevitable complications of a political marriage between rival Vienna and Florence. 2842

Roberts, Cecil. THE REMARKABLE YOUNG MAN. Macmillan, 1954. About Joseph Severn, who nursed Keats during his final illness in Rome. 2843

Scott, Hugh S. THE ISLE OF UNREST. by H. Seton Merriman, pseud. Dodd, 1900. Romance in Corsica during the Franco-Prussian War. 2844

Spender, E. A SOLDIER FOR A DAY. White, 1901. Adventures in the Italian insurrection of 1848. 2845

Thomas, Henry Wilton. THE SWORD OF WEALTH. Putnam, 1906. The Bread Riots and the assassination of King Humbert at the close of the century. 2846

Ward, Mary Augusta. ELEANOR. by Mrs. Humphry Ward. Harper, 1900. Reflects the political, social, and religious thought of the time. 2847

Werfel, Franz. VERDI. (tr.) S. & S., 1925. Venice in the 1880s with Verdi, Wagner, and Boito. 2848

White, William Hale. CLARA HOPGOOD. by Mark Rutherford, pseud. Dodd, 1896. Revolutionary ferment in Italy with Mazzini as a minor character. 2849

Whiting, Mary B. THE TORCHBEARERS. Dent, 1904. Political issues and the Bread Riots of 1898. 2850

III. A. 4. d. Eastern Europe (including Russia and the Balkans), the Near East, and North Africa

Barr, Amelia E. AN ORKNEY MAID. Appleton, 1918. A story of the Crimean War showing the founding of the Red Cross. 2851

Beddoe, David M. THE HONOUR OF HENRI DE VALOIS. Dent, 1905. The background for this romantic novel is the capture of Syria by Ibrahim. 2852

Benson, Edward Frederic. (1) THE VINTAGE. Harper, 1898. (2) THE CAPSINA (sequel). Harper, 1899. Battles, sieges, massacres in the Greek War of Independence, told from the Christian viewpoint. 2853

Bikelas, Demetrios. LOUKIS LARAS. (tr.) Macmillan, 1881. Adventures of a merchant in the bloody Greek War of Independence. 2854

Blech, William James. THE ANGEL. by William Blake, pseud. Doubleday, 1950. The fate of the visionary Emperor Alexander I. 2855

Bryant, Marguerite and George H. McAnnally. CHRONICLES OF A GREAT PRINCE. Duffield, 1924. About Prince Paul d'Arenzano of a small Balkan principality, based on family letters and reports. 2856

Cahan, Abraham. THE WHITE TERROR AND THE RED. Barnes, 1905. Plots against Czar Alexander II and anti-Jewish riots under Czar Alexander III. 2857

Carling, John R. BY NEVA'S WATERS. Little, 1908. "An episode in the secret history of Alexander the First, Czar of all the Russias." 2858

Czajkowski, Michael. THE BLACK PILGRIM. (tr.) Digby & Long, 1900. A tale of the struggle for faith and freedom in the Balkan Peninsula. 2859

Danilevski, Grigovii P. MOSCOW IN FLAMES. (tr.) Brentano's, 1917. Attack on Moscow by Napoleonic forces in 1812. 2860

Delves-Broughton, Josephine. OFFICER AND GENTLEMAN. McGraw, 1951. Story of a father and son in the Crimean War. 2861

Dostoevskii, Fedor. BURIED ALIVE. (tr.) Munro, 1881. The author's own imprisonment is reflected in this novel which is sub-titled, "Ten Years' Penal Servitude in Siberia." 2862

--------. CRIME AND PUNISHMENT. (tr.) Crowell, 1886?. Life amidst the lower stratum of mid-nineteenth century St. Petersburg. 2863

--------. HOUSE OF THE DEAD. (tr.) Dutton, 1911. Penal servitude in Siberia, based on the author's own experiences. 2864

--------. POOR FOLK. (tr.) Roberts, 1894. Realistic account of the living conditions of the masses. 2865

--------. THE POSSESSED. (tr.) Macmillan, 1913. Revolutionary Nihilism in provincial Russia. 2866

Gontcharov, Ivan A. A COMMON STORY. (tr.) Heinemann, 1894. Reflects the unequal class system and the need for social and political reform. 2867

Gordon, Samuel. THE FERRY OF FATE. Duffield, 1906. The persecution of the Jews in Czarist Russia. 2868

Graham, Winifred. THE ZIONISTS. Hutchinson, 1902. Deals with the romance of a Christian and a Jew. 2869

Grant, James. LADY WEDDERBURN'S WISH. Dutton, 1870. Romance against the background of the Crimean War. 2870

--------. LAURA EVERINGHAM. Dutton, 1870. Regimental life and romance in the war in the Crimea. 2871

--------. THE LORD HERMITAGE. Dutton, 1878. The Crimean War is the setting for romance and heroics. 2872

--------. ONE OF THE SIX HUNDRED. Dutton, 1875. A vigorous story of action in the Crimean War. 2873

Gregg, Hilda Caroline. (1) AN UNCROWNED KING. Blackwood, 1896. (2) A CROWNED QUEEN (sequel). Blackwood, 1898. both by Sydney C. Grier, pseud. Two romances of court politics and intrigue in the imaginary kingdom of Thracia in the Balkans. 2874

Hawkins, Anthony Hope. PHROSO. by Anthony Hope, pseud. Stokes, 1897. A melodramatic tale of the adventures of an Englishman on a Greek island. 2875

Jennings, John. BANNERS AGAINST THE WIND. Little, 1954. About Samuel Gridley Howe's part in the fight for Greek independence. 2876

Jókai, Maurus. THE GREEN BOOK. (tr.) Harper, 1897. Court and common life in Russia during the revolutionary 1820s. 2877

--------. THE LION OF JANINA. (tr.) Harper, 1898. An action-jammed story of massacre and bloodshed, telling of the killing of the Janissaries. 2878

Korolenko, Vladimir. IN TWO MOODS. (tr.) Munro, 1892. A sympathetic account of the Nihilist movement of the 1870s. 2879

--------. THE SAGHALIEN CONVICT. (tr.) Unwin, 1892. A novel based on the author's banishment for refusing to take an oath to Alexander III. 2880

Kraszewski, Jósef I. THE JEW. (tr.) Heinemann, 1890. A novel of the insurrection of 1860 written by an author who was exiled in its course. 2881

Lagerlöf, Selma. JERUSALEM. Heinemann, 1903. Tragic story of a Zionist colony in Palestine. 2882

Lambe, John Lawrence. BY COMMAND OF THE PRINCE. Unwin, 1901. Account of a Bulgarian murder trial. 2883

Landau, Mark Aleksandrovich. BEFORE THE DELUGE. (tr.) by M. A. Aldanov, *pseud.* Scribner, 1947. The period of the assassination of Alexander II of Russia. 2884

Law, Margaret Lathrop. AIMÉE. Funk, 1956. A young girl, captured by pirates and sent to the Turkish court, comes to enjoy her life there. 2885

Longard de Longgarde, Dorothea Gerard. THE RED-HOT CROWN. by Dorothea Gerard. Long, 1909. Based on the tragedy which befell Queen Draga of Serbia. 2886

McLaws, Lafayette, *i.e.*, Emily Lafayette McLaws. THE MAID OF ATHENS. Little, 1906. This romantic novel is concerned chiefly with Lord Byron's visit to Athens. 2887

Mayo, *Mrs.* J. R. A DAUGHTER OF THE KLEPHTS. Dutton, 1897. The war of Greek independence. 2888

Merezhkovsky, Dmitri. DECEMBER THE FOURTEENTH. (tr.) Cape, 1923. The accession of Czar Nicholas I amidst revolutionary upheaval and his harsh rule. 2889

Morton, Benjamin A. THE VEILED EMPRESS. Putnam, 1923. A Creole girl is captured by pirates and sent to Turkish Constantinople as a wife to the Sultan. 2890

Murray, David Leslie. TRUMPETER, SOUND! Knopf, 1934. Two English half-brothers, in love with the same dancing girl, serve in the Crimean War. 2891

Oxenham, John, *pseud.* for William Arthur Dunkerley. THE COIL OF CARNE. Lane, 1911. The sufferings of troops in the Crimean War and the ministrations of Florence Nightingale. 2892

--------. HEARTS IN EXILE. Macmillan, 1904. A narrative about political exiles in Siberia in the latter part of the century. 2893

--------. THE LONG ROAD. Macmillan, 1907. Russia's

harsh treatment of her political prisoners in Siberia. 2894

Pemberton, Max. THE GREAT WHITE ARMY. Cassell, 1915. Napoleon's invasion of deserted Moscow and the disastrous retreat of the French army in the brutal Russian winter. 2895

Pickthall, Marmaduke. SAÏD THE FISHERMAN. Methuen, 1903. A good picture of the customs and beliefs of the Orient in this tale of a fisherman turned merchant. 2896

Potter, Margaret Horton. THE GENIUS. Harper, 1906. Based roughly on the life of the composer, Tschaikowsky, with many scenes from Russian life. 2897

Ropes, Arthur R. and Mary E. ON PETER'S ISLAND. Murray, 1901. Secret police versus the underground in the Nihilist movement. 2898

Sladen, Douglas. THE CURSE OF THE NILE. Paul, 1913. The siege and fall of Khartum and the fate of white prisoners. 2899

Stephens, Eve. FAR FLIES THE EAGLE. by Evelyn Anthony, pseud. Crowell, 1955. Based on the eventful life of the idealistic Czar Alexander I to his thirty-ninth year. 2900

Terrot, Charles. THE PASSIONATE PILGRIM. Harper, 1948. One of Florence Nightingale's nurses and her shocking report of field hospitals in the Crimean War. 2901

Tolstoy, Leo. THE COSSACKS. (tr.) Scribner, 1878. Romance of a Russian gentleman and a simple, primitive girl. 2902

--------. WAR AND PEACE. (tr.) Harper, 1886. A classic account of life in Russia and of Napoleon's invasion attempt. 2903

Tur, Eugenia, pseud. THE SHALONSKI FAMILY. (tr.)

Remington, 1882. Country life in Russia at the time of the Napoleonic invasion. 2904

Turgenev, Ivan S. FATHERS AND SONS. (tr.) [En. title: FATHERS AND CHILDREN] Holt, 1872. The old and the new contrasted in this view of Russian social and policital life. 2905

--------. ON THE EVE. (tr.) Macmillan, 1895. The end of the reign of Czar Nicholas I. 2906

--------. RUDIN. (tr.) Macmillan, 1894. Shows the ineffectuality of Liberalism in contemporary Russia. 2907

--------. SMOKE. (tr.) Macmillan, 1896. A novel of character and romance with the portrait of a complex woman. 2908

--------. VIRGIN SOIL. (tr.) Macmillan, 1896. A pessimistic view of social and political thought in Russia. 2909

Underwood, Edna. THE PENITENT. Houghton, 1922. Alexander I and the beginnings of the Russian struggle for national freedom. 2910

Vazov, Ivan. UNDER THE YOKE. (tr.) Heinemann, 1893. A searching novel of the attempted revolt of the Bulgarians from Turkey. 2911

Whishaw, Frederick J. MOSCOW. Longmans, 1906. A story of lovers during the Russian resistance to Napoleon. 2912

Whyte-Melville, George John. THE INTERPRETER. Longmans, 1858. International intrigue during Omar Pasha's Turkish resistance to Russia and the Crimean War. 2913

III. A. 4. e. Overseas Exploration, Enterprise, and Expansion

Conrad, Joseph and Ford Madox Hueffer. ROMANCE. Smith

& Elder, 1903. A land-and-sea adventure story of England and the West Indies. 2914

Daly, Robert Welter. BROADSIDES. Macmillan, 1940. Sea experiences of an Irishman in the British navy during the Napoleonic Wars. 2915

--------. SOLDIER OF THE SEA. Morrow, 1942. Seafaring adventure and naval warfare of the British marines in the Napoleonic Wars. 2916

Forester, C. S. ADMIRAL HORNBLOWER IN THE WEST INDIES. Little, 1958. Hornblower's rousing adventures--including the attempted rescue of Napoleon from St. Helena. 2917

--------. BEAT TO QUARTERS. Little, 1937. The admirable Captain Hornblower engages successfully in naval war off the eastern coast of Central America. 2918

--------. CAPTAIN HORATIO HORNBLOWER. Little, 1939. A volume containing three of the Hornblower stories: BEAT TO QUARTERS; SHIP OF THE LINE; and FLYING COLOURS (see separate listings). 2919

--------. COMMODORE HORNBLOWER. Little, 1945. The Commodore is assigned to enlist Sweden and Russia on the British side in the Napoleonic Wars. 2920

--------. FLYING COLOURS. Little, 1939. Captain Hornblower escapes as he is being taken by the French to a trial for piracy. 2921

--------. HORNBLOWER AND THE ATROPOS. Little, 1953. Among other activities, Hornblower crosses England by canal and attends Nelson's funeral. 2922

--------. LIEUTENANT HORNBLOWER. Little, 1952. Hornblower has the new experience of playing whist for a living. 2923

--------. LORD HORNBLOWER. Little, 1946. A tale of sea battles and ships during the Napoleonic Wars;

Hornblower is raised to the peerage. 2924

--------. MR. MIDSHIPMAN HORNBLOWER. Little, 1950. Hornblower's rise from midshipman to lieutenant. 2925

--------. A SHIP OF THE LINE. Little, 1942. Hornblower commands a ship blockading the Spanish coast in the Napoleonic Wars. 2926

Goudge, Elizabeth. GREEN DOLPHIN STREET. Coward, 1944. The romantic triangle of two sisters in love with the same sailor. 2927

Marryat, Frederick. MR. MIDSHIPMAN EASY. Burt, 1917. Pictures naval life in the early nineteenth century. 2928

Masefield, John. BIRD OF DAWNING. Macmillan, 1933. Race between two clippers for the tea trade between China and England. 2929

Rowland, Henry Cottrell. HIRONDELLE. Harper, 1922. About an Irish lord engaged in slaving and piracy in the War of 1812. 2930

Styles, Showell. FRIGATE CAPTAIN. Vanguard, 1955. Captain Lord Cochrane's exploits during the Napoleonic Wars. 2931

III. B. Asia, Africa, and Oceania in Modern Times (c. 1500-1900

1. Asia in Modern Times

a. India

1) Pre-British to 1600

Eaubonne, Francoise d'. A FLIGHT OF FALCONS. (tr.) McGraw, 1951. The broken heart of a Spanish-Dutch painter who goes to India in the late sixteenth century. 2932

Forrest, R. E. THE RUBY OF RAJAST'HAN. East & West, Ltd., 1914. A romance of Hindustan and Akbar in the sixteenth century. 2933

Steel, Flora Annie. A PRINCE OF DREAMERS. Doubleday, 1908. Interesting story of Indian life and manners under the gifted Emperor Akbar. 2934

Taylor, Philip Meadows. A NOBLE QUEEN. Kegan Paul, 1878. India in the last decade of the sixteenth century under brave Queen Chand Beebee. 2935

III. B. 1. a. 2) Seventeenth and Eighteenth Centuries

Bañkimachandra Chattopadhyaya. CHANDRA SHEKHAR. (tr.) Luzac & Co., 1904. Adventures of a young girl unhappily married to an older man. 2936

Compton, Herbert. A FREE LANCE IN A FAR LAND. Cassell, 1895. Adventures among the Mahrattas of west central India at the end of the eighteenth century. 2937

Gamon, Richard B. WARREN OF OUDH. Macdonald, 1926. India during Warren Hasting's governorship in the mid-eighteenth century. 2938

Gregg, Hilda Caroline. THE GREAT PROCONSUL. by Sydney C. Grier, pseud. Blackwood, 1904. Written as a diary by a member of Warren Hasting's family telling of his work in India. 2939

--------. IN FURTHEST IND. by Sydney C. Grier, pseud. Blackwood, 1894. Travels and experiences during the early years of the East India Company. 2940

--------. LIKE ANOTHER HELEN. by Sydney C. Grier, pseud. Blackwood, 1899. A young lady's experiences in Calcutta during the scandalous period of the Black Hole horrors. 2941

Masters, John. COROMANDEL! Viking, 1955. Barbaric splendor and power reward young Jason Savage's journey to India. 2942

Payne, Robert. BLOOD ROYAL. Prentice-Hall, 1952. Struggle for royal power, as told by an Englishman who married a Persian princess. 2943

--------. YOUNG EMPEROR. [En. title: THE GREAT MOGUL] Macmillan, 1950. India during the time of Shahjahan, prince and emperor, in the first half of the seventeenth century. 2944

Penny, Mrs. F. E. DIAMONDS. Hodder & Stoughton, 1920. Native customs and traditions are reflected in this account of the young East India Company. 2945

Pollard, Eliza F. THE SILVER HAND. Blackie, 1908. About Warren Hastings, the Mahratta Wars, Tippoo Sahib, and an ancient prophecy. 2946

Scott, Sir Walter. THE SURGEON'S DAUGHTER. Munro, 1885. A young man brings his fianceé from Scotland to India and sells her to Tippoo Sultan. 2947

Sell, Frank R. BHIM SINGH. Macmillan, 1926. The Rajput War in India featuring Emperor Aurangzib and his son. 2948

Steel, Flora Annie. MISTRESS OF MEN. Stokes, 1918. The unwanted girl baby who lived to become Empress Nurjahan of India in the early 1600s. 2949

Taylor, Philip Meadows. RALPH DARNELL. by Meadows Taylor. Kegan Paul, 1865. Struggle for control between the British and the native Indians in 1757. (followed by SEETA) 2950

--------. TARA. by Meadows Taylor. Paul, 1863. Uprising of the Mahrattas against the ruling Mohammedans in 1657. (followed by RALPH DARNELL) 2951

--------. TIPPOO SULTAUN. by Meadows Taylor. Kegan Paul, 1840. Conflict for supremacy between England and France, 1788-89. 2952

Tracy, Louis. THE GREAT MOGUL. [En. title: HEART'S

DELIGHT] Clode, 1905. Two Englishmen visit India in the early seventeenth century. 2953

Upward, Allen. ATHELSTANE FORD. Pearson, 1899. The British conquest of India including an account of the infamous Black Hole of Calcutta. 2954

III. B. 1. a. 3) Nineteenth Century

Arnold, William Delafield. OAKFIELD. Longmans, 1853. A young Oxford graduate in India has difficulty adjusting to the realities of life. 2955

Chesney, G. T. THE DILEMMA. Harper, 1876. Efforts of Englishmen to defend their homes in the Indian Mutiny of the 1850s. 2956

Diver, Maud. CANDLES IN THE WIND. Lane, 1909. India during the latter part of the century. 2957

--------. (1) CAPTAIN DESMOND, V. C. Lane, 1907. (2) DESMOND'S DAUGHTER. Putnam, 1916. Both books deal with English life in India in the late 1800s. 2958

--------. THE GREAT AMULET. Lane, 1908. A romance of the Indian border depicting military conflicts, bouts with cholera, and the people themselves. 2959

--------. (1) THE HERO OF HERAT. Putnam, 1913. (2) THE JUDGMENT OF THE SWORD (sequel). Putnam, 1913. Two good stories of exploration and of the Afghan Wars of the 1830s and '40s. 2960

Durand, Henry Mortimer. HELEN TREVERYAN. Macmillan, 1892. The second Afghan War and relations of the British with the people of India. 2961

Forrest, R. E. EIGHT DAYS. Smith & Elder, 1891. The eight days depicted are the period in May, 1857, in which the Sepoy Mutiny started. 2962

--------. THE SWORD OF AZRAEL. Methuen, 1903. An

English officer escapes from the Mutiny of the Sepoys in 1857. 2963

Greenhow, H. M. BRENDA'S EXPERIMENT. Jarrold & Sons, 1896. Indian customs and religion figure in the tale of an English girl married to a Mohammedan. 2964

Gregg, Hilda Caroline. THE ADVANCED GUARD. by Sydney C. Grier, pseud. Blackwood, 1903. The Indian frontier just prior to the Mutiny, with an account of native dungeons and torture practices. 2965

--------. THE WARDEN OF THE MARCHES. by Sydney C. Grier, pseud. Blackwood, 1901. The precarious peace of the frontier is upset when a new commissioner's policies bring war. 2966

Griffiths, Arthur. BEFORE THE BRITISH RAJ. Everett, 1903. Adventures of a soldier in India about 1800. 2967

Hamilton, Lillias. A VIZIER'S DAUGHTER. Murray, 1900. The rugged life of the race of people called Hazaras in Afghanistan in the latter part of the nineteenth century. 2968

Harcourt, A. F. P. JENETHA'S VENTURE. Cassell, 1899. A story of the siege of Delhi depicting most of the important personages in that event. 2969

--------. THE PERIL OF THE SWORD. Skeffington, 1903. Military action at Cawnpore and Lucknow during the Indian Mutiny. 2970

Hockley, William Browne. PANDURANG HÀRI. Chatto, 1891. Account of a Hindu early in the century, giving much information about the Mahrattas. 2971

Hunter, William Wilson. THE OLD MISSIONARY. Frowde, 1895. Sympathetic picture of India in the early nineteenth century. 2972

Irwin, H. C. WITH SWORD AND PEN. Unwin, 1904. Native

customs in India in mid-nineteenth century. 2973

Kaye, Mary Margaret. SHADOW OF THE MOON. Messner, 1957. Story of the Sepoy Rebellion. 2974

Lang, John. THE WETHERBYS. Chapman & Hall, 1853. Satiric comment on English-Indian relations preceding the Mutiny. 2975

MacMunn, George Fletcher. A FREELANCE IN KASHMIR. Dutton, 1914. Kashmir in 1804 is the scene of this tale of romance and adventure. 2976

Masters, John. THE DECEIVERS. Viking, 1952. Thrilling tale concerning the cult of the goddess Kali. 2977

--------. NIGHTRUNNERS OF BENGAL. Viking, 1951. Suspense during the Sepoy Rebellion in the nineteenth century. 2978

Mundy, Talbot. RUNG HO! Scribner, 1914. Vivid account of a young officer's introduction to Indian people and customs. 2979

Oliphant, Philip Laurence. MAYA. Constable, 1908. The daughter of an English officer and her Indian childhood. 2980

Ollivant, Alfred. OLD FOR-EVER. Doubleday, Page, 1923. Experiences during the Afghan War period including an outbreak of cholera. 2981

Pearce, Charles E. LOVE BESIEGED. Paul, 1909. Has as historical background the siege of Lucknow. 2982

--------. RED REVENGE. Paul, 1911. The siege and capture of Cawnpore during the Mutiny in 1857. 2983

--------. A STAR OF THE EAST. Paul, 1912. The Mutiny of 1857 and the events leading up to it. 2984

Scott, Hugh S. FLOTSAM. by H. Seton Merriman, pseud. Longmans, 1896. Based chiefly in India during the rebellious years of the mid-nineteenth century. 2985

Steel, Flora Annie. ON THE FACE OF THE WATERS. Macmillan, 1896. A vivid re-creation of the Mutiny period with emphasis on the siege and capture of Delhi. 2986

Sutherland, Joan. THE EDGE OF EMPIRE. Mills & Boon, 1916. Social life in Kashmir and the expedition of 1895 to Chitral. 2987

Taylor, Philip Meadows. CONFESSIONS OF A THUG. by Meadows Taylor. Bentley, 1839. Incidents of local color told by an Indian officer. 2988

--------. SEETA. by Meadows Taylor. Kegan Paul, 1873. Picture of the Indian Mutiny of 1857 against the English. 2989

Thorburn, Septimus S. HIS MAJESTY'S GREATEST SUBJECT. Appleton, 1897. A political story of the British in India. 2990

Tracy, Louis. THE RED YEAR. Clode, 1908. A vivid, realistic story of the Indian Mutiny of 1857. 2991

Tuttiett, Mary Gleed. IN THE HEART OF THE STORM. by Maxwell Gray, pseud. Appleton, 1891. A novel of India during the Great Mutiny. 2992

Wallis, Henry M. AN OLD SCORE. by Ashton Hilliers, pseud. Ward & Lock, 1906. The righting of a wrong after two generations. 2993

Wentworth, Patricia. THE DEVIL'S WIND. Putnam, 1912. A view of official circles during the Mutiny in the 1850s. 2994

III. B. 1. b. China

Buck, Pearl. IMPERIAL WOMAN. Day, 1956. Compelling story of Tzu-hsi, last and most powerful Empress of China. 2995

--------. PEONY. Day, 1948. Romance of a Chinese bondsmaid and the son of her wealthy Jewish master in the nineteenth century. 2996

Clift, Charmain and George Henry Johnston. THE BIG

CHARIOT. Bobbs, 1953. Tale of excitement with brother against brother during seventeenth century warfare. 2997

Gardner, Mona. HONG KONG. Doubleday, 1958. The Opium War and the Chinese effort to evict foreigners. 2998

Hunter, Bluebell Matilda. THE MANCHU EMPRESS. Dial, 1945. Oriental court splendor and ruthless cruelty under China's last Empress. 2999

Jernigan, Muriel Molland. FORBIDDEN CITY. Crown, 1954. Tzu-hsi, last Empress of China, with a good picture of Peking life. 3000

Mackay, Margaret. VALIANT DUST. Day, 1941. Chinese life in the later nineteenth century is the background for the story of a Scotch family. 3001

Payne, Robert. HOUSE IN PEKING. Doubleday, 1956. Intrigue and romance at the court of Manchu Emperor Ch'ien Lung in the eighteenth century. 3002

Wright, Constance. THEIR SHIPS WERE BROKEN. Dutton, 1938. Opium smuggling in nineteenth century China. 3003

Yaukey, Grace. CHINA TRADER. by Cornelia Spencer, pseud. Day, 1940. An American trader and his wife in a Portuguese-held town in the late eighteenth century. 3004

III. B. 1. c. Japan and Korea

Adams, J. William. SHIBESAWA; or, THE PASSING OF OLD JAPAN. Putnam, 1906. The end of the Shogunate and the beginning of Japan's mingling with the West. 3005

Bennet, Robert Ames. THE SHOGUN'S DAUGHTER. McClurg, 1910. Commodore Perry's trip to Japan when the Shogun, as military dictator, ruled the country, then closed to foreigners. 3006

Blaker, Richard. THE NEEDLE-WATCHER. Doubleday, 1932. Forceful story of a seventeenth century English seaman who, through his knowledge of the compass, became a friend of the Shogun. 3007

Fraser, Mary Crawford. THE STOLEN EMPEROR. by Mrs. Hugh Fraser. Long, 1903. Japan during its feudal era in mid-nineteenth century. 3008

Hayashi, Viscount, ed. FOR HIS PEOPLE. Harper, 1903. Based on an old Japanese play, this story gives a good picture of seventeenth century feudalism. 3009

Lancaster, Bruce. VENTURE IN THE EAST. Little, 1951. The Dutch East India Company in medieval seventeenth century Japan. 3010

Lund, Robert. DAISHI-SAN. Day, 1961. About shipbuilder Will Adams, first Englishman in Japan, who settled there permanently about 1600. 3011

Maclay, A. C. MITO YASHIKI. Putnam, 1889. A novel of Japan in the mid-nineteenth century. 3012

Nagayo, Yoshiro. BRONZE CHRIST. (tr.) Taplinger, 1959. The use in the seventeenth century of a statue of Christ to detect Christians, who were then executed. 3013

Price, Willard de Mille. BARBARIAN. Day, 1941. Shows American trade relations with Japan shortly after Perry's visit. 3014

III. B. 1. d. Other Asiatic Peoples

Landon, Margaret. ANNA AND THE KING OF SIAM. Day, 1944. An English governess to the many children of the King of Siam (Thailand). 3015

Lofts, Norah. SILVER NUTMEG. Doubleday, 1947. Dutch colonial enterprise and life in the East Indies in the mid-seventeenth century. 3016

Morrow, Honoré. SPLENDOR OF GOD. Morrow, 1929. Missionaries in Burma encounter a conflict between Christian and Buddhist philosophies. 3017

Palgrave, W. Gifford. HERMANN AGHA. King, 1872. Oriental splendor provides background for an Englishman's life in the service of an Asian ruler. 3018

III. B. 2. Africa in Modern Times

Abrahams, Peter. WILD CONQUEST. Harper, 1950. The northward trek of the Boers in the 1830s. 3019

Bryden, H. A. THE EXILED SCOT. New Amsterdam Bk. Co., 1899. A Jacobite refugee in the employ of the Dutch East India Company in Africa. 3020

Charters, Zelda. BARBARY BREW. Stackpole Sons, 1937. A young American doctor is captured by pirates and sold as a slave in Tripoli. 3021

Cloete, Stuart. THE FIERCEST HEART. Houghton, 1960. The trip by wagon of a group of Boer farmers seeking a lost freedom in the wilds of South Africa. 3022

--------. THE HILL OF DOVES. Houghton, 1941. Boer families in the Transvaal in 1880. 3023

--------. THE MASK. Houghton, 1957. Features the war between the Boers and the Kaffirs during 1852-54. 3024

--------. THE TURNING WHEELS. Houghton, 1937. The overland journey of the Boers from Cape Colony to the Transvaal. 3025

--------. WATCH FOR THE DAWN. Houghton, 1939. A young Boer tries to build a new life in the unexplored African veldt. 3026

Cobban, J. MacLaren. CEASE FIRE! Methuen, 1900. "A story of the Transvaal War of 1881." 3027

--------. THE RED SULTAN. Rand McNally, 1893. Fast-moving, colorful story of Morocco late in the eighteenth century. 3028

Cripps, Arthur S. (1) A MARTYR'S SERVANT. Duckworth, 1915. (2) A MARTYR'S HEIR (sequel). Duckworth, 1916. Told as first-hand accounts of Jesuit missionary work in Africa in the sixteenth century. 3029

Cullum, Ridgwell. THE COMPACT. Doran, 1909. A romantic triangle in South Africa during the Transvaal War of 1881. 3030

De Kalb, Eugenie. FAR ENOUGH. Stokes, 1935. The Great Trek of the Boers in 1836 and the effect it had on a woman's life. 3031

Divine, Arthur Durham. GOLDEN FOOL. by David Divine, pseud. Macmillan, 1954. The discovery of gold and other background causes of the Boer War. 3032

Doyle, Sir Arthur Conan. THE TRAGEDY OF THE KOROSKO. Smith & Elder, 1898. A pleasure-seeking group of Europeans finds more danger and adventure than expected in a trip to Africa. 3033

Fairbridge, Dorothea. THAT WHICH HATH BEEN. Low, 1913. A story of the Dutch East India Company in Africa about 1700. 3034

Haggard, H. Rider. CHILD OF STORM. Longmans, 1913. Mid-nineteenth century quarrel in Zululand between two Princes. (followed by FINISHED) 3035

--------. FINISHED. Longmans, 1917. Events prior to, during, and after the Zulu War. 3036

--------. MARIE. Cassell, 1912. An exciting, interesting story of the Great Trek in South Africa, as the Boers sought freedom from oppression. (followed by CHILD OF STORM) 3037

--------. SWALLOW. Longmans, 1899. The Great Trek of the Dutch settlers who left Cape Colony to escape unpopular British rule. 3038

Hawes, Charles Boardman. GREAT QUEST. Little, 1921. Adventures of New Englanders in Africa in the 1820s. 3039

Howarth, Anna. KATRINA. Smith & Elder, 1898. The effect of a smallpox epidemic on daily life in mid-nineteenth century South Africa. 3040

--------. NORA LESTER. Smith & Elder, 1902. Relations between English and Dutch farmers in South Africa in the 1890s. 3041

--------. SWORD AND ASSEGAI. Smith & Elder, 1899. The historical setting is the Kaffir risings of 1846 and 1851 in South Africa. 3042

Juta, Rene. CAPE CURREY. Holt, 1920. Cape Town in the 1820s--a romantic story which includes much political history. 3043

Krepps, Robert Wilson. EARTHSHAKER. Macmillan, 1958. An American and a Boer each try to steal a fabulous diamond horde from an African king. 3044

Mason, A. E. W. THE FOUR FEATHERS. Macmillan, 1902. A youth proves he is not a coward in nineteenth century Africa. 3045

Millin, Sarah Gertrude. THE BURNING MAN. Putnam, 1952. An unhappy man's effort to find solace as a missionary to Africa. 3046

--------. KING OF THE BASTARDS. Harper, 1949. Early white settlers in South Africa. 3047

Mitford, Bertram. ALETTA. White, 1900. An Englishman and his Dutch wife just before and during the Boer War. 3048

--------. THE GUN RUNNER. Fenno, 1893. A romance of Zululand in the late 1870s. 3049

--------. THE INDUNA'S WIFE. White, 1898. The wars of the South African colonies at the time of the Great Trek. 3050

--------. THE KING'S ASSEGAI. Fenno, 1894. A story of the Matabele rising, suppressed by the British in 1896. 3051

--------. THE LUCK OF GERALD RIDGELEY. Chatto, 1893. A tale of the Zulu border in the 1870s. 3052

--------. A ROMANCE OF THE CAPE FRONTIER. Heinemann, 1891. Exciting story of the Kaffir Rising in the late 1870s. 3053

--------. THE SIGN OF THE SPIDER. Dodd, 1896. Fighting and romance in South Africa toward the end of the nineteenth century. 3054

--------. 'TWEEN SNOW AND FIRE. Cassell, 1892. Frontier warfare with Kaffirs combined with romance. 3055

--------. THE WORD OF THE SORCERESS. Hutchinson, 1902. Vivid account of Zululand and of fighting with the British. 3056

Ralli, Constantine S. THE STRANGE STORY OF FALCONER THRING. Hurst & Blackett, 1907. Based on the Zulu War of the 1870s. 3057

Roberts, Morley. THE COLOSSUS. Harper, 1899. A story of plans to exploit the wealth of South Africa. 3058

Rooke, Daphne. WIZARDS' COUNTRY. Houghton, 1957. The life, beliefs, and customs of the Tshanini, a Zulu tribe. 3059

Rooney, Philip. GOLDEN COAST. Duell, 1949. A sea yarn of a sailing ship's voyages and encounters with Barbary pirates. 3060

Russell, George Hansby. UNDER THE SJAMBOK. Murray, 1899. The Transvaal just before the South African War. 3061

Sinclair, Kathleen H. THE COVENANT. by Brigid Knight, _pseud._ Crowell, 1943. Differences between English and Dutch factions in South Africa during the Boer War. 3062

--------. WALKING THE WHIRLWIND. by Brigid Knight, pseud. Crowell, 1941. A family in nineteenth century South Africa. 3063

--------. WESTWARD THE SUN. by Brigid Knight, pseud. Crowell, 1942. The discovery of gold and increasing tension between English and Boers. 3064

Skelton, Gladys. DOMINION. by John Presland, pseud. Stokes, 1925. Political career of Cecil Rhodes, premier of Cape Colony. 3065

Slaughter, Frank G. THE DEADLY LADY OF MADAGASCAR. by C. V. Terry, pseud. Doubleday, 1959. Fate of an East India Company ship commissioned to destroy a pirate in the 1700s. 3066

Steen, Marguerite. THE SUN IS MY UNDOING. Viking, 1941. Adventures of an eighteenth century English slave trader, temporarily a prisoner of Barbary pirates. (followed by TWILIGHT ON THE FLOODS) 3067

--------. TWILIGHT ON THE FLOODS. Doubleday, 1949. English colonization and problems on the Gold Coast in the 1890s. 3068

Watt, Lauchlan Maclean. THE HOUSE OF SANDS. Secker, 1913. Experiences of a Scotsman with the Moors of the Barbary coast in the seventeenth century. 3069

Young, Francis Brett. (1) THEY SEEK A COUNTRY. Reynal, 1937. (2) CITY OF GOLD. Reynal, 1939. English colonists in South Africa during the nineteenth century take part in developing the country. 3070

III. B. 3. Oceania in Modern Times

a. Australia and New Zealand

Andrews, Mrs. T. R. STEPHEN KYRLE. Unwin, 1901.

Immigrants to Australia in the 1860s. 3071

Becke, Louis. HELEN ADAIR. Lippincott, 1903. Helen's father is sent to Botany Bay in the 1770s, so she devises a drastic scheme to follow him. 3072

--------and Walter Jeffery. A FIRST FLEET FAMILY. Macmillan, 1896. The voyage of exiled convicts to the new settlements in New South Wales in the late eighteenth century. 3073

Browne, Thomas A. NEVERMORE. by Rolf Boldrewood, pseud. Macmillan, 1892. Excitement in Australia in mid-nineteenth century caused by the discovery of gold. 3074

--------. (1) ROBBERY UNDER ARMS. Macmillan, 1888. (2) THE MINER'S RIGHT. Macmillan, 1890. (3) A COLONIAL REFORMER. Macmillan, 1890. (4) A SYDNEY-SIDE SAXON. Macmillan, 1891. (5) BABES IN THE BUSH. Macmillan, 1900. all by Rolf Boldrewood, pseud. These independent novels give attractive pictures of the life of settlers of Australia in the mid-nineteenth century. 3075

--------. THE SQUATTER'S DREAM. by Rolf Boldrewood, pseud. Macmillan, 1890. Sheep raising in colonial Australia in the 1800s. 3076

--------. WAR TO THE KNIFE. by Rolf Boldrewood, pseud. Macmillan, 1899. Fighting in the Maori War in New Zealand in the 1860s. 3077

Bruce, Robert. BENBONUNA. Long, 1904. Life in the Australian bush in the middle of the nineteenth century. 3078

Close, Robert Shaw. ELIZA CALLAGHAN. Doubleday, 1958. Irish girl escapes an Australian penal colony and makes a good marriage with a founder of Melbourne. 3079

Couvreur, Jessie C. UNCLE PIPER OF PIPER'S HILL. by

Tasma, pseud. Trübner, 1888. Australian life in nineteenth century Victoria. 3080

Cowan, James. THE ADVENTURES OF KIMBLE BENT. Whitcombe & Tomba, 1911. Story of a man who lived for thirteen years with the wild cannibals of the New Zealand bush. 3081

Dark, Eleanor. STORM OF TIME. McGraw, 1950. The flavor of early Australia with its mingling of English settlers, convicts, and aborigines. 3082

--------. THE TIMELESS LAND. Macmillan, 1941. Early difficulties of establishing a stable community in Australia with its many convicts. 3083

Doudy, Henry A. MAGIC OF DAWN. Hutchinson, 1924. Exploration and settlement of Australia in the 1840s. 3084

Dyson, Edward. IN THE ROARING 'FIFTIES. Chatto, 1906. An account of the Australian gold rush of the 1850s. 3085

Eden, Dorothy. SLEEP IN THE WOODS. Coward, 1961. Two girls go husband-hunting in New Zealand in the time when settlers still had to battle savage natives. 3086

Gaskin, Catherine. SARA DANE. Lippincott, 1955. Romance and life of a naval officer and a former prisoner in late eighteenth century Australia. 3087

Goldsmith, Henry. EUANCONDIT. Sonnenschein, 1895. Life in Australia during the 1860s. 3088

Hay, William. HERRIDGE OF REALITY SWAMP. Unwin, 1907. The hardships of convicts banished to uncivilized New South Wales. 3089

Hornung, Ernest William. DENIS DENT. Isbister, 1903. Adventures in the mid-nineteenth century Australian gold fields. 3090

--------. THE ROGUE'S MARCH. Scribner, 1896. Abuses heaped on the convicts at the penal colony at New South Wales. 3091

Kingsley, Henry. THE RECOLLECTIONS OF GEOFFREY HAMLYN. Longmans, 1859. The life of mid-nineteenth century Australia, with much of the story concerning an exiled convict. 3092

Lyttleton, Edith J. PROMENADE. by G. B. Lancaster, pseud. Reynal, 1938. Pioneer life in colonial New Zealand in the nineteenth century. 3093

Nordhoff, Charles and James Norman Hall. BOTANY BAY. Little, 1941. A highwayman, Hugh Tallant, is sent to the penal colony in Australia. 3094

Outhwaite, R. L. and C. H. Chomley. THE WISDOM OF ESAU. Unwin, 1901. Controversy over land ownership in Australia in the later nineteenth century. 3095

Satchell, William. THE GREENSTONE DOOR. Sidgwick & Jackson, 1914. Exciting events in New Zealand during the middle of the nineteenth century. 3096

Simpson, Helen de Guerry. UNDER CAPRICORN. Macmillan, 1938. Life among the upper classes in Australia during the 1830s. 3097

White, Patrick. VOSS. Viking, 1957. Ill-fated trek of the German explorer Voss across the Australian desert. 3098

Whitney, Janet. JENNIFER. Morrow, 1940. Life in an English prison colony in Australia in the early 1800s. 3099

III. B. 3. b. The Philippines, Indonesia, and Other Islands of the Pacific

Becke, Louis and Walter Jeffery. THE MUTINEER. Lippincott, 1898. The mutiny of the seamen on the Bounty and their settling on Pitcairn Island in 1790. 3100

Clarke, Marcus A. H. FOR THE TERM OF HIS NATURAL LIFE. Munro, 1874. A grim account of the almost unbelievably cruel treatment accorded convicts at the penal colony in nineteenth century Tasmania. 3101

Conrad, Joseph. ALMAYER'S FOLLY. Macmillan, 1895. Married life of a civilized European and a semi-savage Malayan in Borneo. 3102

Cronin, Bernard. THE COASTLANDERS. Hodder & Stoughton, 1918. Opposition of older settlers to new ways and developments in nineteenth century Tasmania. 3103

Dick, Isabel. COUNTRY HEART. Crowell, 1946. Girl descended from Tasmanian pioneers marries a Boer War veteran and lives for a time in Africa. 3104

--------. WILD ORCHARD. Crowell, 1945. Emigrants from Victorian England become pioneers in Tasmania in the 1840s. (followed by COUNTRY HEART) 3105

Foreman, Russell. LONG PIG. McGraw, 1958. Thirteen survivors of a nineteenth century shipwreck land on a cannibal isle in the Fijis. 3106

Gerahty, Digby George. BONIN. by Robert Standish, *pseud.* Macmillan, 1944. Life of shipwrecked English seamen on the Bonin Islands, whose ownership was disputed. 3107

Harrison, Samuel Bertram. WHITE KING. Doubleday, 1950. A medical missionary and his work in Hawaii in the second quarter of the nineteenth century. 3108

Hay, William. CAPTAIN QUADRING. Unwin, 1912. The penal colony in nineteenth century Tasmania. 3109

--------. THE ESCAPE OF THE NOTORIOUS SIR WILLIAM HEANS. Unwin, 1918. A romance depicting the convict period of Tasmania. 3110

Hyne, C. J. Cutcliffe. SANDY CARMICHAEL. Lippincott, 1908. Adventures of two fugitives among cannibal-infested Pacific islands in the eighteenth century. 3111

Lyttleton, Edith J. PAGEANT. by G. B. Lancaster, pseud. Century, 1933. The aristocratic families who were the foundation of colonization of Tasmania. 3112

McGinnis, Paul. LOST EDEN. McBride, 1947. The care-free life of one of Cook's sailors who jumped ship at Hawaii. 3113

Melville, Herman. TYPEE. Wiley & Putnam, 1846. Sailors' adventures among the cannibalistic natives of the Marquesas Islands. 3114

Nordhoff, Charles and James Norman Hall. THE BOUNTY TRILOGY. Little, 1936. Contains MUTINY ON THE BOUNTY, MEN AGAINST THE SEA, and PITCAIRN'S ISLAND (see separate listings). 3115

--------. MEN AGAINST THE SEA. Little, 1934. The story of Captain Bligh and his faithful sailors who were set adrift by mutineers in 1789. (followed by PITCAIRN'S ISLAND) 3116

--------. MUTINY ON THE BOUNTY. Little, 1932. Causes and results of the mutiny on the ship Bounty on its return voyage from the South Pacific. (followed by MEN AGAINST THE SEA) 3117

--------. PITCAIRN'S ISLAND. Little, 1934. The mutineers and a group of Polynesians reach Pitcairn's Island and destroy the Bounty. 3118

O'Connor, Richard. OFFICERS AND LADIES. Doubleday, 1958. Adventures during the American occupation of the Philippines in the 1890s. 3119

Oxenham, John, pseud. for William Arthur Dunkerley. WHITE FIRE. Hodder, 1905. Life on a South Sea island in the 1800s. 3120

Teilhet, Darwin Le Ora. MISSION OF JEFFERY TOLAMY. Sloane, 1951. Russian attempt to occupy Hawaii in the early nineteenth century. 3121

III. C. The Western Hemisphere in Modern Times (c.1500-1900)

1. The United States

a. Colonial Period to 1763

Alderman, Clifford L. TO FAME UNKNOWN. Appleton, 1954. A novel of war and romance during the last part of the French and Indian Wars. 3122

Alfriend, Mary Bethell. JUAN ORTIZ. Chapman & Grimes, 1941. Spanish explorer who lived ten years with Indians in Florida, then became a guide for De Soto. 3123

Allen, Hervey. BEDFORD VILLAGE. Rinehart, 1944. Indian-reared Salathiel Albine works to adapt himself to white man's customs. (followed by TOWARD THE MORNING) 3124

--------. THE CITY IN THE DAWN. Rinehart, 1950. An abridgement of Salathiel Albine's adventures as told in THE FOREST AND THE FORT, BEDFORD VILLAGE, and TOWARD THE MORNING, with a concluding chapter, "The City in the Dawn" (see separate listings). 3125

--------. THE FOREST AND THE FORT. Farrar, 1943. Salathiel Albine, raised by Shawnee Indians, returns to the world of the white man. (followed by BEDFORD VILLAGE) 3126

--------. TOWARD THE MORNING. Rinehart, 1948. Pioneer life in Pennsylvania before the Revolution, featuring Salathiel Albine and his common-law wife, Melissa. 3127

Aswell, Mary Louise. ABIGAIL. Crowell, 1959. Lively,

worldly Abigail rebels against the quiet life of her Quaker parents. 3128

Austin, Jane Goodwin. BETTY ALDEN; THE FIRST BORN DAUGHTER OF THE PILGRIMS. Houghton, 1891. Life of the Pilgrims in Massachusetts after the first hard winter was over. 3129

Babcock, William Henry. THE TOWER OF WYE. [same as THE BRIDES OF THE TIGER] Coates, 1901. Early colonists along the Atlantic coast. 3130

Bacheller, Irving. CANDLE IN THE WILDERNESS. Bobbs, 1930. A vivid, picturesque story of Indians and colonists in the early days of New England. 3131

Barker, Shirley. THE LAST GENTLEMAN. Random, 1960. The English loyalty of the New Hampshire governor, Sir John Wentworth. 3132

--------. PEACE, MY DAUGHTERS. Crown, 1949. A novel of the infamous witchcraft trials in Salem with the devil disguised as a shoemaker. 3133

--------. RIVERS PARTING. Crown, 1950. English colonists in the New World find their loyalties divided between their old and new homes. 3134

--------. TOMORROW THE NEW MOON. Bobbs, 1955. Three cousins from the Isle of Man who settled on Martha's Vineyard. 3135

Barr, Amelia E. THE BOW OF ORANGE RIBBON. Dodd, 1888. Contrast between the simple New York Dutch and the dashing British soldiers. (followed by THE MAID OF MAIDEN LANE) 3136

--------. THE HOUSE ON CHERRY STREET. Dodd, 1909. Political controversy in British colonial New York. 3137

--------. A MAID OF OLD NEW YORK. Dodd, 1911. New Amsterdam in the days of Peter Stuyvesant. 3138

Barrett, Wilson and E. A. Barron. IN OLD NEW YORK. Macqueen, 1900. A view of life in colonial New York before the Revolution. 3139

Belden, Jessie Van Zile. ANTONIA. Page, 1901. Story of Dutch colonists in the Hudson River Valley. 3140

Blacker, Irwin R. TAOS. World Pub., 1959. Rebellion of the Pueblo Indians of New Mexico against Spanish oppression in the 1680s. 3141

Bloundelle-Burton, John. THE LAND OF BONDAGE. White, 1904. Adventures of indentured servants in colonial Virginia. 3142

Borden, Lucille Papin. KING'S HIGHWAY. Macmillan, 1941. Story of the Starforths, refugees from Elizabethan England, who seek religious freedom in the New World. 3143

Bowen, Marjorie, pseud. for Gabrielle Campbell Long. MR. WASHINGTON. Appleton, 1915. Washington's career as a soldier in the French and Indian Wars and during the Revolution. 3144

Boyd, Thomas Alexander. SHADOW OF THE LONG KNIVES. Scribner, 1928. Adventures of an Indian-reared scout who attempts to achieve peace between British and Indians. 3145

Breslin, Howard. BRIGHT BATTALIONS. McGraw, 1953. Fighting and romance in the French and Indian Wars. 3146

--------. THE SILVER OAR. Crowell, 1954. A story of colonial America ending with the Boston uprising of 1689. 3147

Buchan, John. SALUTE TO ADVENTURERS. Doran, 1917. A Scotsman who comes to Virginia to manage an estate finds adventure in the wild, new country. 3148

Bynner, Edwin Lassetter. AGNES SURRIAGE. Houghton, 1886. Romance of the collector of the port of Boston and a servant, the daughter of a poor fisherman. 3149

--------. THE BEGUM'S DAUGHTER. Little, 1890. Customs and life in New Amsterdam during the 1689-91 rebellion and the rule of Jacob Leisler. 3150

--------. PENELOPE'S SUITORS. Houghton, 1887. Diary of the romances of Penelope Pelham, later the wife of Massachusetts Governor Buckley. 3151

Cannon, LeGrand. COME HOME AT EVEN. Holt, 1951. Quest of freedom and happiness in America in the Puritan colony of Salem. 3152

Carlisle, Helen G. WE BEGIN. Smith, 1932. A story of Pilgrim founders of our country with emphasis on personalities. 3153

Chalmers, Harvey. DRUMS AGAINST FRONTENAC. R. R. Smith, 1949. The capture of Fort Frontenac by British General Bradstreet and his troops. 3154

Clark, Imogen. THE DOMINE'S GARDEN. Murray, 1901. Social life among the Dutch in colonial New York. 3155

Cochran, Hamilton. SILVER SHOALS. Bobbs, 1945. A tale of hunting for sunken treasure. 3156

Colver, Alice. THE MEASURE OF THE YEARS. Dodd, 1954. First families of Indian Village, now known as Stockbridge, Massachusetts. (followed by THERE IS A SEASON) 3157

--------. THERE IS A SEASON. Dodd, 1957. A girl's elopement with a romantic peddler, and her later, more solid, marriage. 3158

Constantin-Weyer, Maurice. THE FRENCH ADVENTURER. Macaulay, 1931. A fictional account of the famous explorer La Salle. 3159

Cooke, Grace MacGowan and Alice MacGowan. RETURN. Page, 1905. Georgia in the days following its founding by Oglethorpe. 3160

Cooke, John Esten. MY LADY POKAHONTAS. Houghton, 1879. Concerns John Smith and the Indian princess Pocahontas--his problems in settling Jamestown; her marriage and life in England. 3161

Cooke, Rose. STEADFAST. Houghton, 1889. This is the story of a young New England minister. 3162

Coolidge, A. C. PROPHET OF PEACE. Hungerford-Holbrook, 1907. The romance of a Quaker and a Puritan is opposed by relatives. 3163

Cooper, James Fenimore. THE LEATHER-STOCKING TALES: (1) THE DEERSLAYER. Lea & Blanchard, 1841. The famous backwoodsman, Hawkeye, as a youth. (2) THE LAST OF THE MOHICANS. Carey & Lea, 1826. Incidents of the Old French War. (3) THE PATHFINDER. Bentley, 1840. Romance comes to Hawkeye. (4) THE PIONEERS. Colburn & Bentley, 1832. Seventy-year-old Hawkeye in his boyhood home. (5) THE PRAIRIE. Colburn, 1827. The eighty-year-old woodsman goes to the Upper Missouri to escape the advance of civilization. 3164

Cooper, Kent. ANNA ZENGER: MOTHER OF FREEDOM. Farrar, 1946. Struggle for freedom of the press with the first newspaperwoman in a prominent part. 3165

Cross, Ruth. SOLDIER OF GOOD FORTUNE. Banks Upshaw, 1936. Adventures of a French nobleman in the American Southwest. 3166

Crowley, Mary Catherine. THE HEROINE OF THE STRAIT. Little, 1902. Pontiac's Conspiracy with the French against the British. 3167

Devon, John Anthony. O WESTERN WIND. Putnam, 1957. The Mayflower Pilgrims and the settlement of Plymouth. 3168

Dickson, Harris. THE BLACK WOLF'S BREED. Bobbs, 1900. Louisiana in the French colonial period before the outbreak of the Seven Years War. 3169

--------. GABRIELLE TRANSGRESSOR. Lippincott, 1906. Romance of a Turkish prince and a French girl in colonial New Orleans. 3170

--------. THE SIEGE OF LADY RESOLUTE. Harper, 1902. Legend of the rich merchant who wished to become Prince of Louisiana. 3171

Dix, Beulah M. THE MAKING OF CHRISTOPHER FERRINGHAM. Macmillan, 1901. The strictness of the Puritan founders of Massachusetts and their attitude toward Quakers. 3172

--------. MISTRESS CONTENT CRADOCK. Barnes, 1899. A story of some who sought religious freedom in the New World. 3173

-------- and Carrie A. Harper. THE BEAU'S COMEDY. Harper, 1902. A Londoner in the American colonies is falsely suspected of being an Indian spy. 3174

Dodge, Constance. IN ADAM'S FALL. Macrae Smith, 1946. Witch hunt in Puritan Salem. 3175

Dowdey, Clifford. GAMBLE'S HUNDRED. Little, 1939. The romance of a surveyor near Williamsburg, Virginia. 3176

Du Bois, Theodora M. FREEDOM'S WAY. Funk, 1953. A young English gentlewoman is unjustly sent as an indentured slave to America. 3177

Ethridge, Willie Snow. SUMMER THUNDER. Coward, 1959. Colonization of Georgia, an attempted Spanish invasion, and the career of James Oglethorpe. 3178

Flannagan, Roy Catesby. FOREST CAVALIER. Bobbs, 1952. Beginnings of American national feeling in Jamestown in 1676. 3179

Fletcher, Inglis. BENNETT'S WELCOME. Bobbs, 1950. A captain in Charles II's army comes to Carolina as an indentured servant and builds a new life. 3180

--------. CORMORANT'S BROOD. Lippincott, 1959. Friction between British governor and colonists in North Carolina. 3181

--------. LUSTY WIND FOR CAROLINA. Bobbs, 1944. Huguenot settlers find excitement, romance, and opportunity in the New World. 3182

--------. MEN OF ALBEMARLE. Bobbs, 1942. English settlers in colonial North Carolina and a turbulent political battle. 3183

--------. ROANOKE HUNDRED. Bobbs, 1948. The expedition of Grenville's group to Roanoke Island in 1585. 3184

--------. THE SCOTSWOMAN. Bobbs, 1954. Flora MacDonald saves Bonnie Prince Charlie and is forced to fly to the New World. 3185

--------. THE WIND IN THE FOREST. Bobbs, 1957. Conflict between fiercely independent pioneer farmers and plantation owners loyal to England. 3186

Foote, Mary. THE ROYAL AMERICANS. Houghton, 1910. This story spans the period from Montcalm's capture of Oswego to the Revolution. 3187

Forbes, Esther. A MIRROR FOR WITCHES. Houghton, 1928. Compelling story of a fear-crazed girl accused and imprisoned as a witch. 3188

--------. PARADISE. Harcourt, 1937. Story of an estate (named Paradise) twenty miles from Boston. 3189

Forbes-Lindsay, C. H. JOHN SMITH, GENTLEMAN ADVENTURER. Lippincott, 1907. The difficulties and successes of the early settlers in Virginia. 3190

Fraser, Mary Crawford. IN THE SHADOW OF THE LORD. by Mrs. Hugh Fraser. Holt, 1906. A tale of George Washington's parents and of his childhood near Fredericksburg. 3191

Frey, Ruby. RED MORNING. Putnam, 1946. Adventures of Jane Bell in Ohio in 1750, including capture by the Indians. 3192

Fuller, Hulbert. VIVIAN OF VIRGINIA. Page, 1900. Bacon's Rebellion, brought on by the British governor's failure to provide adequate defense against Indians. 3193

Fuller, Iola. GILDED TORCH. Putnam, 1957. La Salle's expedition which resulted in the discovery of the Mississippi. 3194

Garnett, David. POCAHONTAS. Harcourt, 1933. The childhood of Pocahontas, her rescue of John Smith, and her subsequent marriage and life in England. 3195

Gay, Margaret Cooper. HATCHET IN THE SKY. S. & S. 1954. The Detroit area during the French and Indian Wars and the Pontiac Conspiracy. 3196

Gebler, Ernest. THE PLYMOUTH ADVENTURE. Doubleday, 1950. Sympathetic account of the *Mayflower* Pilgrims--their voyage and first winter in the New World. 3197

Gerson, Noel B. DAUGHTER OF EVE. Doubleday, 1958. Indian customs and English life are background for the story of Pocahontas. 3198

--------. FOREST LORD. by Samuel Edwards, *pseud.* Doubleday, 1955. An English nobleman, shanghaied aboard a British ship, comes to America. 3199

--------. THE HIGHWAYMAN. Doubleday, 1955. Melodramatic tale of colonial life during King George's War. 3200

--------. THE IMPOSTOR. Doubleday, 1954. Swords and guns flash as a conspiracy to betray the American colonies is defeated. 3201

--------. KING'S MESSENGER. by Samuel Edwards, *pseud.* Farrar, 1956. A seventeenth century British spy saves the American colonies from the French. 3202

--------. SAVAGE GENTLEMAN. Doubleday, 1950. Life and romance amid the wilderness fighting of the French and Indian Wars. 3203

Gibbs, George. THE LOVE OF MADEMOISELLE. [formerly IN SEARCH OF MADEMOISELLE] Appleton, 1926. Rivalry between French and Spanish colonists in early Florida. 3204

Goodwin, Maud W. THE HEAD OF A HUNDRED IN THE COLONY OF VIRGINIA. Little, 1895. The settling of Virginia and fighting with the Indians, told in autobiographical form. 3205

--------. SIR CHRISTOPHER. Little, 1904. "A romance of a Maryland manor in 1644." 3206

--------. WHITE APRONS. Little, 1896. Story of Bacon's Rebellion, in which women formed a line to delay the enemy. 3207

Gordon, Caroline. THE GREEN CENTURIES. Scribner, 1941. Lives of two pioneer brothers--one is captured by Indians, the other becomes an Indian fighter. 3208

Grant, Dorothy. MARGARET BRENT, ADVENTURER. Longmans, 1944. The fight of a devout Catholic woman for religious freedom in Maryland. 3209

--------. NIGHT OF DECISION. Longmans, 1946. Colonial New York under Stuart-appointed governor Colonel Thomas Dongan. 3210

Gregory, Jackson. LORDS OF THE COAST. Dodd, 1935. California in the rough, ready days of early settlement. 3211

Griffin, Henry Farrand. THE WHITE COCKADE. Greystone, 1941. Adventures of a roving Yankee sea captain and the French Royalist whom he rescues. 3212

Hall, Ruth. THE GOLDEN ARROW. Houghton, 1901. Story of the indomitable Anne Hutchinson, New England religious leader who, banished from one colony, founded another. 3213

Hamilton, Harry. THUNDER IN THE WILDERNESS. Bobbs, 1949. Story of French traders and Indians in the Mississippi Valley. 3214

Hammand, Esther Barstow. ROAD TO ENDOR. Farrar, 1940. A Salem minister attempts to do away with witchcraft. 3215

Harding, Newman. THE ETERNAL STRUGGLE. Long, 1912. Adventure and love in Puritan Massachusetts. 3216

Hawthorne, Nathaniel. THE SCARLET LETTER. Ticknor, Reed and Fields, 1850. Effects of sin in the lives of three people in rigid Puritan Massachusetts. 3217

Hersch, Virginia. SEVEN CITIES OF GOLD. Duell, 1946. Coronado's second expedition in search of gold--to Mexico, Texas, Kansas. 3218

Hinsdale, Harriet. BE MY LOVE. Farrar, 1950. Social life and customs of Boston in colonial times. 3219

Holland, Josiah Gilbert. THE BAY PATH. Scribner, 1857. New England colonial life and character. 3220

Hughes, Rupert. STATELY TIMBER. Scribner, 1939. Adventures of a young man in Puritan New England. 3221

Jennings, John. GENTLEMAN RANKER. Reynal, 1942. An English playboy becomes a man in the army in colonial Virginia. 3222

--------. NEXT TO VALOUR. Macmillan, 1939. A Scotsman who settles in New England becomes involved in the French and Indian Wars. 3223

Johnston, Mary. AUDREY. Houghton, 1902. A girl of the Virginia backwoods loses her family and home at the hands of the Indians. 3224

--------. CROATAN. Little, 1923. The English settlers

on Roanoke Island, attacked by hostile Indians, are aided by friendly ones. 3225

--------. THE GREAT VALLEY. Little, 1926. A minister and his family migrate from Scotland to the Shenandoah Valley. 3226

--------. PRISONERS OF HOPE. Houghton, 1898. Political unrest in Virginia when Britain sent convicts as colonists. 3227

--------. THE SLAVE SHIP. Little, 1924. A vividly told tale of slave traffic between Africa and Virginia. 3228

--------. TO HAVE AND TO HOLD. [En. title: BY ORDER OF THE COMPANY] Houghton, 1900. Lovely English girl flees to the colonies to preserve her honor. 3229

Jordan, Mildred A. ECHO OF THE FLUTE. Doubleday, 1958. A family's experiences in Pennsylvania, with a vivid description of the yellow fever epidemic of 1793. 3230

--------. ONE RED ROSE FOREVER. Knopf, 1941. A romance of the early American glassmaker, German immigrant Baron Stiegel. 3231

Kennedy, John P. ROB OF THE BOWL: A LEGEND OF ST. INIGOES. Lea & Blanchard, 1838. "A story of the early days of Maryland." 3232

Kennedy, Sara Beaumont. THE WOOING OF JUDITH. Doubleday, 1902. A romance of Virginia during the period of British colonization. 3233

Kenyon, Theda. GOLDEN FEATHER. Messner, 1943. Romance of English colonists in Virginia. 3234

Kester, Vaughan. JOHN O' JAMESTOWN. McClure, 1907. Captain John Smith and the first permanent English settlement in America. 3235

King, Grace Elizabeth. LA DAME DE SAINTE HERMINE. Macmillan, 1924. Adjustment of a cultured French girl to wilderness life during the settlement of New Orleans. 3236

Knipe, Emilie Benson and Alden Arthur Knipe. THE SHADOW CAPTAIN. Dodd, 1925. An account of the activities of an Englishman in the town of New York in 1703. 3237

Knowles, Mabel Winifred. THE WITCH-FINDER. by May Wynne, pseud. Jarrolds Ltd., 1923. A tale of witch hunts, trials, and executions in Massachusetts. 3238

Knox, Dorothea H. THE HEART OF WASHINGTON. Neale, 1909. Recounts an early romance of George Washington. 3239

Lauritzen, Jonreed. ROSE AND THE FLAME. Doubleday, 1951. Spaniards and Indians vie for control of the Southwest. 3240

Lee-Hamilton, Eugene. THE ROMANCE OF THE FOUNTAIN. Fisher Unwin, 1905. Ponce de Leon's search for the fountain of youth resulting in the discovery of Florida. 3241

Lide, Alice and Margaret Johansen. DARK POSSESSION. Appleton, 1934. Colonial South Carolina when English settlers and indentured servants faced a primitive life and a hostile land. 3242

Lincoln, Victoria. A DANGEROUS INNOCENCE. Rinehart, 1958. A tangle of romance and jealousy causes involvement in the Salem witchcraft trials. 3243

Lofts, Norah. BLOSSOM LIKE THE ROSE. Knopf, 1939. A crippled boy seeks happiness in the New World. 3244

Lovelace, Maud Hart. THE CHARMING SALLY. Day, 1932. Romance between a Quaker boy and a girl of the first theatrical company to come to the colonies. 3245

--------. EARLY CANDLELIGHT. U. of Minn., 1929. Frontier life on the Upper Mississippi including soldiers, Indians, trappers, and missionaries. 3246

McLaws, Lafayette, i.e., Emily Lafayette McLaws. WHEN

THE LAND WAS YOUNG. Lothrop, 1902. Romance of Antoinette Huguenin and Captain Jack Middleton in the days of Caribbean buccaneers. 3247

MacPhail, Andrew. THE VINE OF SIBMAH. Macmillan, 1906. Adventures of an English captain in his search for a Londoner's daughter in the colonies. 3248

Mann, Helen R. GALLANT WARRIOR. Eerdmans, 1954. Concerns a pioneer woman and her baby who were captured by Indians. 3249

Marsh, George Tracy. ASK NO QUARTER. Morrow, 1945. Yarn of a Newport man who battles Indians, pirates, and poverty. 3250

Mason, Van Wyck. THE YOUNG TITAN. Doubleday, 1959. Stirrings of unity and independence in the New World exemplified in the siege of Louisbourg. 3251

Matschat, Cecile Hulse. TAVERN IN THE TOWN. Farrar & Rinehart, 1942. A story of everyday life and love in Tidewater Virginia. 3252

Miers, Earl Schenck. VALLEY IN ARMS. Westminster, 1943. Struggles of a pioneer couple with Indians and frontier hardships. 3253

Miller, Helen Topping. DARK SAILS. Bobbs, 1945. Oglethorpe leads a group of English settlers to St. Simons Island. 3254

--------. PROUD YOUNG THING. Appleton, 1952. Romantic novel which takes place in Charleston, South Carolina. 3255

Monroe, Forest. MAID OF MONTAUKS. Jenkins, 1902. Contacts of the Montauk Indian tribe with the British in New York. 3256

Montgomery, K. L., <u>pseud.</u> for Kathleen and Letitia Montgomery. MAIDS OF SALEM. Long, 1915. The witch hunt craze, influenced by Cotton Mather, in Salem and

Boston. 3257

Moore, Ruth. A FAIR WIND HOME. Morrow, 1953. This novel concerns Maine and the early history of her seafaring ventures. 3258

Morton, Stanley, pseud. for Stanley and Morton Freedgood. YANKEE TRADER. Sheridan, 1947. A sea captain and trader whose ambitions are wealth and power. 3259

Motley, John Lothrop. MERRY MOUNT. Munroe, 1849. Reflects the cheerlessness and gloom prevalent among the Puritans in the Plymouth colony. 3260

Murfree, Mary Noailles. THE AMULET. by Charles Egbert Craddock, pseud. Macmillan, 1906. Fighting between the English and Cherokees in Tennessee. 3261

--------. A SPECTRE OF POWER. by Charles Egbert Craddock, pseud. Houghton, 1903. The Mississippi Valley during the conflicts between England and France. 3262

--------. THE STORY OF OLD FORT LOUDON. by Charles Egbert Craddock, pseud. Macmillan, 1899. An aspect of the Seven Years War--the Cherokee attack on Fort Loudon. 3263

Murphy, Edward F. BRIDE FOR NEW ORLEANS. Hanover, 1955. The work of priests and nuns with the Casket girls, who came to New Orleans to marry. 3264

Neilson, Winthrop and Frances. EDGE OF GREATNESS. Putnam, 1951. Benjamin Franklin and the day of Braddock's defeat. 3265

Newton, John Edward. THE ROGUE AND THE WITCH. Abelard, 1955. Temporary exile of a Puritan minister accused of witchcraft. 3266

Oemler, Marie. THE HOLY LOVER. Boni & Liveright, 1927. The strict moral principles of John and Charles Wesley and John's reaction to his own great romance. 3267

O'Meara, Walter. THE SPANISH BRIDE. Putnam, 1954. An actress journeys from Castile to frontier New Mexico. 3268

Page, Elizabeth. WILDERNESS ADVENTURE. Rinehart, 1946. Frontiersmen to the rescue of a girl captured by Indians. 3269

Pangborn, Edgar. WILDERNESS OF SPRING. Rinehart, 1958. The rising fortunes of two brothers--one in sailing, the other in medicine. 3270

Paradise, Jean. THE SAVAGE CITY. Crown, 1955. Action-packed novel of New York in the violent 1740s. 3271

Parrish, Randall. A SWORD OF THE OLD FRONTIER. McClurg, 1905. Indian Wars at the time of the Pontiac Conspiracy around Fort Chartres, Illinois, and Detroit, Michigan. 3272

Patterson, Burd Shippen. THE HEAD OF IRON. Walker, 1908. General Braddock's defeat and the British attack on Fort Duquesne. 3273

Pawle, Kathleen. MURAL FOR A LATER DAY. Dodd, 1938. A novel of the founding of New Sweden, a settlement on the Delaware River. 3274

Payson, William Farquhar. JOHN VYTAL. Harper, 1901. What happened to the English settlement at Roanoke? 3275

Pendexter, Hugh. THE RED ROAD. Bobbs, 1927. Events surrounding the battle which resulted in Braddock's defeat. 3276

--------. WIFE-SHIP WOMAN. Bobbs, 1926. Story of a girl who came from France to marry in colonial Louisiana. 3277

Peterson, Henry. DULCIBEL. Winston, 1907. Trials and sentences of a number of people accused of witchcraft in Salem. 3278

Phillips, Alexandra. FOREVER POSSESS. Dutton, 1946. Leisler's Rebellion and daily life on Hudson River Valley estates. 3279

Pier, Arthur S. YOUNG MAN FROM MOUNT VERNON. Stokes, 1940. Fictional account of the youth of George Washington. 3280

Pinckney, Josephine. HILTON HEAD. Farrar & Rinehart, 1941. Tells of a young English surgeon, Henry Woodward, who came to Carolina. 3281

Pound, Arthur. HAWK OF DETROIT. Reynal, 1939. A novel of the founding of Detroit and of the French background of that city. 3282

Pryor, Elinor. THE DOUBLE MAN. Norton, 1957. A British boy brought up as a Cherokee Indian in South Carolina. 3283

Quiller-Couch, Arthur T. LADY GOOD-FOR-NOTHING. Scribner, 1910. Mid-eighteenth century romance of a gentleman and a servant girl. 3284

Rayner, Emma. THE DILEMMA OF ENGELTIE. Cassell, 1912. Incident between New Englanders and Dutch colonists at Christmas, 1702. 3285

--------. DORIS KINGSLEY, CHILD AND COLONIST. Dillingham, 1901. Oglethorpe's colony in Georgia, a haven for religious refugees and poor debtors. 3286

--------. FREE TO SERVE. Small, Maynard, 1897. An English lady becomes a bond-servant in a Dutch home in New York. 3287

--------. IN CASTLE AND COLONY. Stone, 1899. The rivalry between Swedish and Dutch colonies on opposite sides of the Delaware River. 3288

Rees, Gilbert. I SEEK A CITY. Dutton, 1950. Portrays Roger Williams, who sought emotional and religious peace in the New World. 3289

Richardson, John. WACOUSTA. McClurg, 1882. Successes of the Indians under Pontiac in attacking unsuspecting garrisons; their failure against Detroit. 3290

Roberts, Kenneth. BOON ISLAND. Doubleday, 1956. Shipwreck on a small island off the coast of New Hampshire. 3291

--------. NORTHWEST PASSAGE. Doubleday, 1937. Thrilling story of Rogers' expedition against the Indians and his search for an overland route to the Pacific. 3292

Safford, Henry B. TRISTRAM BENT. Coward, 1940. An Englishman raised in Holland spies on the Dutch in the New World. 3293

Sass, Herbert R. EMPEROR BRIMS. Doubleday, 1941. Colorful story of Indian uprising against settlers in South Carolina. 3294

Savage, Les. ROYAL CITY. Hanover House, 1956. Tragic revolt of the Pueblo Indians in Santa Fe in 1680. 3295

Schachner, Nathan. THE KING'S PASSENGER. Lippincott, 1942. An associate of Bacon in the Rebellion of 1676. 3296

Schofield, William Greenough. ASHES IN THE WILDERNESS. Macrae Smith, 1942. A story of King Philip's War, 1675-76. 3297

Schumann, Mary. STRIFE BEFORE DAWN. Dial, 1939. About a young Quaker colonist and the two women who love him. 3298

Scruggs, Philip Lightfoot. MAN CANNOT TELL. Bobbs, 1942. An indentured servant finds love and adventure during Bacon's Rebellion. 3299

Seifert, Shirley. RIVER OUT OF EDEN. Mill, 1940. A young boatman on the lower Mississippi in 1763. 3300

Sessler, Jacob John. SAINTS AND TOMAHAWKS. Pyramid Press, 1940. Dramatic story of Moravian colonists and missionaries. 3301

Seton, Anya. THE WINTHROP WOMAN. Houghton, 1958. About Governor Winthrop's niece from England and her adjustment to colonial life. 3302

Seton, William. ROMANCE OF THE CHARTER OAK. O'-Shea, 1871. The hiding of the Connecticut charter from the hated British governor in an oak tree in Hartford. 3303

Shafer, Donald Cameron. SMOKEFIRES IN SCHOHARIE. Longmans, 1938. A settlement in the Schoharie Valley survives attacks by Indians. 3304

Shaw, Adele Marie. THE COAST OF FREEDOM. Doubleday, 1903. The infamous witch hunts in Massachusetts, during which the governor's wife was accused. 3305

Shaw, Margaret. INHERIT THE EARTH. Bobbs, 1940. Adventures of an English girl who comes to America as an indentured servant. 3306

Simms, W. Gilmore. THE YEMASSEE. Harper, 1835. The grim war between white men and Creek and Cherokee Indians. 3307

Simons, Katherine D. M. ALWAYS A RIVER. by Drayton Mayrant, _pseud_. Appleton, 1956. A Puritan schoolmaster seeks peace in French Huguenot Carolina. 3308

Singmaster, Elsie. HIGH WIND RISING. Houghton, 1942. The hard-working German settlers of Pennsylvania during the French and Indian Wars. 3309

Smith, Alice Prescott. KINDRED. Houghton, 1925. An English spy among the French and the Indians in the Seven Years War. 3310

Smith, Arthur D. Howden. BEYOND THE SUNSET. Brentano's, 1923. Adventures with the Indians in mid-eighteenth century New York. 3311

Smith, Ruel Perley. PRISONERS OF FORTUNE. Page, 1907. Story of the Massachusetts Bay Colony involving pirates and a treasure search. 3312

Snedeker, Caroline Dale. UNCHARTED WAYS. Doubleday, Doran, 1935. The persecution of Quakers in Massachusetts. 3313

Stevens, Sheppard. THE SWORD OF JUSTICE. Little, 1899. Florida during the struggle between French and Spanish. 3314

Stimson, Frederic Jesup. KING NOANETT. by J. S. of Dale, pseud. Scribner, 1897. About Devon settlers in Virginia and Massachusetts. 3315

Stouman, Knud. L. BAXTER, MEDICUS. Greystone, 1941. The studies of an American doctor abroad and his practice in New York. 3316

--------. WITH CRADLE AND CLOCK. Harper, 1946. Practice of medicine in New York City by an English doctor. 3317

Stover, Herbert Elisha. SONG OF THE SUSQUEHANNA. Dodd, 1949. Trading in Pennsylvania during the French and Indian Wars. 3318

Stuart, H. Longan. WEEPING CROSS. Doubleday, 1908. An Indian massacre at Long Meadow, Massachusetts. 3319

Sublette, Clifford. THE BRIGHT FACE OF DANGER. Little, 1926. The vengeful hero joins Bacon's Rebellion. 3320

--------. THE SCARLET COCKEREL. Little, 1925. Rapidly moving tale of the French Huguenot colonization of Carolina. 3321

Swanson, Neil. THE JUDAS TREE. Putnam, 1933. Indian attack on Fort Pitt (Pittsburgh) during the Pontiac Conspiracy. (followed by THE SILENT DRUM) 3322

--------. THE SILENT DRUM. Farrar, 1940. Friction between settlers and traders in the Fort Pitt area. 3323

--------. THE UNCONQUERED. Doubleday, 1947. Frontier

life at the time of the Indian uprising known as the Pontiac Conspiracy. 3324

Taylor, Mary Imlay. ANNE SCARLET. McClurg, 1901. A witch hunt in Salem in which Cotton Mather figures. 3325

Tebbel, John William. CONQUEROR. Dutton, 1951. Story of Sir William Johnson and his dealings with the Indians. 3326

--------. TOUCHED WITH FIRE. Dutton, 1952. La Salle's explorations in the Mississippi Valley. 3327

Thackeray, William Makepeace. THE VIRGINIANS. Lippincott, 1879. About two grandsons of Englishman Henry Esmond who migrate to America. 3328

Tracy, Don. CAROLINA CORSAIR. Dial, 1955. Blood and thunder story of the infamous Blackbeard. 3329

--------. CHESAPEAKE CAVALIER. Dial, 1949. Rise of an English indentured servant. 3330

--------. ROANOKE RENEGADE. Dial, 1954. A story of Raleigh's lost Roanoke colony. 3331

Webster, J. Provand. CHILDREN OF WRATH. Routledge, 1899. Colonists in Virginia near the end of the seventeenth century. 3332

Wellman, Paul I. RIDE THE RED EARTH. Doubleday, 1958. A Frenchman's adventures in Spanish-held Texas and Mexico. 3333

Westley, George Hembert. THE MAID AND THE MISCREANT. Mayhew, 1906. Exploits of an English rogue disapproved of by the Puritan colonists. 3334

Whalen, Will Wilfrid. GOLDEN SQUAW. Dorrance, 1926. The life among Indians of a bride captured on the morning of her marriage. 3335

Whitson, Denton. GOVERNOR'S DAUGHTER. Bobbs, 1953. Romance in New York during the French and Indian

Wars. 3336

Widdemer, Margaret. THE GOLDEN WILDCAT. Doubleday, 1954. Bitter rivalry of the French and British for Indian support. 3337

--------. LADY OF THE MOHAWKS. Doubleday, 1951. Romance of Molly Brant and Colonel Johnson during the French and Indian Wars. 3338

--------. RED CLOAK FLYING. Doubleday, 1950. An Irish girl in exile is loved by two men. 3339

Wilkins, Mary Eleanor. THE HEART'S HIGHWAY. Doubleday, 1900. Unrest and tobacco riots in Virginia following Bacon's Rebellion. 3340

Winwar, Frances. GALLOWS HILL. Holt, 1937. A narrative of Salem during the witchcraft trials. 3341

Zara, Louis. BLESSED IS THE LAND. Crown, 1954. Story of Jews who came as pioneers to New Amsterdam in 1654. 3342

III. C. 1. b. Revolutionary Era (1763-1789)

Adams, Marshall. THEY FOUGHT FOR LIBERTY. Dodge, 1937. Account of a young patriot who returned to America from England at the start of the Revolution. 3343

Alderman, Clifford L. ARCH OF STARS. Appleton, 1950. Effect of the war on people in Vermont. 3344

Allis, Marguerite. NOT WITHOUT PERIL. Putnam, 1941. Life in Vermont of a spirited pioneer woman, Jemima Sartwell. 3345

Atkinson, Eleanor. JOHNNY APPLESEED. Harper, 1915. A warm account of a man whose life became a legend--John Chapman. 3346

Bacheller, Irving. IN THE DAYS OF POOR RICHARD. Bobbs, 1922. Important figures in the Revolution and scenes in both England and America. 3347

--------. THE MASTER OF CHAOS. Bobbs, 1932. The war experiences and romance of a young secretary to General Washington. 3348

Barker, Shirley. FIRE AND THE HAMMER. Crown, 1953. Swift-paced story of Quaker brothers and their Tory activities in Pennsylvania. 3349

Barr, Amelia E. A SONG OF A SINGLE NOTE. Dodd, 1902. A story of New York during the Revolutionary War. 3350

--------. THE STRAWBERRY HANDKERCHIEF. Dodd, 1908. New York at the time of the controversial Stamp Act. 3351

Barry, Jane. THE CAROLINIANS. Doubleday, 1959. Loyalist family in South Carolina shelters a wounded officer of Morgan's Raiders. 3352

--------. THE LONG MARCH. Appleton, 1955. Action-packed report of General Dan Morgan and the Battle of Cowpens. 3353

Beebe, Elswyth Thane. DAWN'S EARLY LIGHT. by Elswyth Thane. Duell, 1943. Williamsburg is the setting for this novel of Revolutionary times. (followed by YANKEE STRANGER) 3354

Bellamy, Edward. THE DUKE OF STOCKBRIDGE. Silver, 1900. The main event here is Shays's Rebellion. 3355

Benét, Stephen Vincent. SPANISH BAYONET. Doran, 1926. Oppression of indentured laborers on a Florida plantation. 3356

Beverley-Giddings, Arthur Raymond. THE RIVAL SHORES. Morrow, 1956. Loyalist refugees in eastern Maryland and Delaware just prior to the outbreak of the war. 3357

Boyce, Burke. MAN FROM MT. VERNON. Harper, 1961.

Portrays George Washington as a man and a soldier. 3358

--------. THE PERILOUS NIGHT. Viking, 1942. Family life on a Hudson River farm with a beautiful girl and her suitors. 3359

Boyd, James. DRUMS. Scribner, 1925. Scots in North Carolina and naval action during the Revolutionary War. 3360

Brady, Cyrus Townsend. THE BLUE OCEAN'S DAUGHTER. Moffat, 1907. Encounters of an American privateer and British frigates result in excitement for a captain's daughter. 3361

--------. THE GRIP OF HONOUR. Scribner, 1900. Features John Paul Jones, revolutionary hero. 3362

Breslin, Howard. SHAD RUN. Crowell, 1955. A fisherman's daughter in the Hudson River Valley at the time the Constitution was ratified. 3363

Brick, John. EAGLE OF NIAGARA. Doubleday, 1955. David Harper, Continental soldier, captured by Indian Joseph Brant. 3364

--------. THE KING'S RANGERS. Doubleday, 1954. A group of woodsmen, led by Colonel Butler, fight for the King in New York State. 3365

--------. THE RAID. Farrar, 1951. Indian raids and captivity spice a vivid account of life in the Hudson River Valley. 3366

--------. THE RIFLEMAN. Doubleday, 1953. Activities of rough-and-ready Tim Murphy, frontiersman. 3367

--------. THE STRONG MEN. Doubleday, 1959. A professional soldier, Baron von Steuben, forms an army from raw colonial volunteers at Valley Forge. 3368

Bristow, Gwen. CELIA GARTH. Crowell, 1959. Absorbing tale of love and war with an orphaned twenty-year-old seamstress as heroine. 3369

Burt, Katherine N. CLOSE PURSUIT. Scribner, 1947. Romantic novel of an English governess on a Tidewater Virginia plantation. 3370

Cannon, LeGrand. LOOK TO THE MOUNTAIN. Holt, 1942. Young newlyweds build a home and future in the New Hampshire mountains. 3371

Carter, Jefferson. MADAM CONSTANTIA. Longmans, 1919. An Englishman's experiences as an American prisoner-of-war. 3372

Chambers, Robert W. (1) CARDIGAN. Harper, 1901. (2) THE MAID-AT-ARMS. Harper, 1902. Stories of the Johnson family showing strained relations between British, colonists, and Indians. 3373

--------. THE LITTLE RED FOOT. Doran, 1921. Indian and Tory warfare in northern New York State. 3374

--------. LOVE AND THE LIEUTENANT. Appleton, 1935. Includes British recruiting of Hessian soldiers in Germany and the Burgoyne campaign. 3375

--------. THE PAINTED MINX. Appleton, 1930. Romance of a Tory actress who waits throughout the War for her colonial lover. 3376

--------. THE RECKONING. Appleton, 1905. Effects of the Revolution on the wealthy landowners of New York State. 3377

Chapman, Ann S. MARY DERWENT. Burt, 1909. A tale of the Wyoming Valley, scene of a devastating Indian massacre. 3378

Chapman, Maristan, _pseud._ for Mary and Stanton Chapman. ROGUE'S MARCH. Lippincott, 1949. Realistic picture of the southern backwoods and account of the Battle of Kings Mountain. 3379

--------. TENNESSEE HAZARD. Lippincott, 1953. Frontier

life in Tennessee at the time of the conspiracy to surrender frontier lands to the Spaniards. 3380

Churchill, Winston. RICHARD CARVEL. Macmillan, 1899. A Maryland patriot is a friend of and a sailor under John Paul Jones. 3381

Coffin, Charles C. DAUGHTERS OF THE REVOLUTION AND THEIR TIMES. Houghton, 1895. The start of the Revolution--the Boston Tea Party and the Battle of Lexington. 3382

Cooke, John Esten. (1) THE VIRGINIA COMEDIANS. Appleton, 1854. (2) HENRY ST. JOHN, GENTLEMAN. Appleton, 1883. Social and cultural life in Virginia in the last half of the century. 3383

Cooper, James Fenimore. RED ROVER. Colburn, 1828. A former pirate fights for his country in the Revolutionary War. 3384

--------. THE SPY. Lea & Carey, 1829. Harvey Birch is the hero in this classic of the Revolution. 3385

Cormack, Maribelle and William P. Alexander. LAND FOR MY SONS. Appleton, 1939. A Scotch-Irish scout and surveyor leaves roadbuilding to join Washington's army. 3386

Crabb, Alfred Leland. JOURNEY TO NASHVILLE. Bobbs, 1957. Description of the journey to and the founding of Nashville. 3387

Crownfield, Gertrude. WHERE GLORY WAITS. Lippincott, 1934. The unhappy romance of Anthony Wayne and Mary Vining. 3388

Davis, Burke. THE RAGGED ONES. Rinehart, 1951. Swift-moving narrative of the attacks upon Cornwallis by Generals Morgan and Greene. 3389

--------. YORKTOWN. Rinehart, 1952. A soldier's experiences during the final years of the Revolution. 3390

Davis, William Stearns. GILMAN OF REDFORD. Macmillan, 1927. Story of Boston on the brink of war as related by a student at Harvard. 3391

Decker, Malcolm. THE REBEL AND THE TURNCOAT. McGraw, 1949. A youth's indecision as to which side he should take in the Revolution. 3392

Degenhard, William. THE REGULATORS. Dial, 1943. A vivid picture of the significant Shays's Rebellion. 3393

De Haven, Aubrey. THE SCARLET CLOAK. Blackwood, 1907. A son searches for his runaway mother during the war. 3394

Devereux, Mary. FROM KINGDOM TO COLONY. Little, 1899. Shows the determination and sacrifices that made the American Revolution successful. 3395

Dodge, Constance. THE DARK STRANGER. Penn, 1940. An immigrant from Scotland seeks his fortune in the New World--land of opportunity. 3396

--------. WEATHERCOCK. Dodd, 1942. Southern aristocrat's struggle to reconcile the justice of his own wealth with the poverty of others. 3397

Eastman, Edward Roe. THE DESTROYERS. Am. Agriculturist Inc., 1946. Attack on Cherry Valley by Tories and Indians. 3398

Eaton, Evelyn. GIVE ME YOUR GOLDEN HAND. Farrar, 1951. An unacknowledged son of George III chooses to be a bonded servant in revolutionary America. 3399

Edmonds, Walter D. DRUMS ALONG THE MOHAWK. Little, 1936. Indian attacks on a farming community's fortress in the Mohawk Valley. 3400

--------. IN THE HANDS OF THE SENECAS. Little, 1947. Attack by Seneca Indians on settlers in Dygartsbush, New York, in 1778. 3401

--------. WILDERNESS CLEARING. Dodd, 1944. Romance

in the Mohawk Valley under threat of attacks from Indians and British alike. 3402

Eggleston, George Cary. A CAROLINA CAVALIER. Lothrop, 1901. Activities of guerrillas in the Carolinas. 3403

Ellsberg, Edward. CAPTAIN PAUL. Dodd, 1941. John Paul Jones battles both with British ships and with a massive, enraged whale. 3404

Erskine, John. GIVE ME LIBERTY. Stokes, 1940. A young Virginian's contacts with Patrick Henry. 3405

Farmer, James Eugene. BRINTON ELIOT: FROM YALE TO YORKTOWN. Macmillan, 1902. A student at Yale joins the American Revolutionary Army. 3406

Fast, Howard. APRIL MORNING. Crown, 1961. A youth attains maturity as a soldier in the colonial militia. 3407

--------. CITIZEN TOM PAINE. Duell, 1943. Activities of a revolutionary writer in England, France, and the United States. 3408

--------. CONCEIVED IN LIBERTY. S. & S., 1939. Perseverance of the determined American army during the cruel winter at Valley Forge. 3409

--------. THE PROUD AND THE FREE. Little, 1950. Little-known revolt of the Eleventh Regiment of the Pennsylvania Line on New Year's Day, 1781. 3410

--------. THE UNVANQUISHED. Duell, 1942. The development of Washington from a Virginia gentleman into a national leader. 3411

Finlay, Lucile. THE COAT I WORE. Scribner, 1947. British sympathizers in Louisiana during the war. 3412

Fleming, Thomas J. NOW WE ARE ENEMIES. St. Martins, 1960. The story of colonial entrenchment and resistance at Bunker Hill. 3413

Fletcher, Inglis. RALEIGH'S EDEN. Bobbs, 1940. A plantation in North Carolina before and during the

Revolution. 3414

--------. TOIL OF THE BRAVE. Bobbs, 1946. The contest between a Continental and a Britisher for a lady's favor in revolutionary North Carolina. 3415

Forbes, Esther. THE GENERAL'S LADY. Harcourt, 1938. Beautiful Tory girl marries an American general to protect her family, then falls in love with a British officer. 3416

Forbes-Lindsay, C. H. DANIEL BOONE. Lippincott, 1908. Adventures of this noted frontiersman in Kentucky. 3417

Ford, Paul Leicester. JANICE MEREDITH. Dodd, 1899. A romance of New Jersey and New York during the Revolution. 3418

Fox, John, Jr. ERSKINE DALE, PIONEER. Scribner, 1920. The two facets of the life of a youth, raised among Indians, who inherits a Virginia estate. 3419

Frederic, Harold. IN THE VALLEY. Scribner, 1890. Life in the Mohawk Valley from the viewpoint of Dutch settlers who hated the British. 3420

French, Allen. THE COLONIALS. Doubleday, 1902. "Chiefly connected with the siege and evacuation of the town of Boston in New England." 3421

Frye, Pearl. GALLANT CAPTAIN. Little, 1955. Compelling tale of the Bon Homme Richard and her gallant captain, John Paul Jones. 3422

Gessner, Robert. TREASON. Scribner, 1944. One of Benedict Arnold's aides learns, to his disillusionment, of his hero's treason. 3423

Giles, Janice Holt. THE KENTUCKIANS. Houghton, 1953. A novel of Kentucky when it was part of Virginia and of the land speculators who operated there. 3424

Gordon, Charles William. THE REBEL LOYALIST. by Ralph Connor, pseud. Dodd, 1935. Adventures of a loyalist among rebels during the struggle between

England and her colonies. 3425

Gray, Elizabeth. THE VIRGINIA EXILES. Lippincott, 1955. The conviction and dignity of the Quaker spirit in the upset times of the Revolution. 3426

Gray, Stanley. HALF THAT GLORY. Macmillan, 1941. A young Virginian who runs away to sea eventually becomes involved in diplomatic relations. 3427

Haines, Edwin Irvine. THE EXQUISITE SIREN. Lippincott, 1938. The Tory wife of Benedict Arnold and her secret love for another. 3428

Haislip, Harvey. PRIZE MASTER. Doubleday, 1959. Adventures of a teen-age midshipman who brings a captured British ship to port. 3429

--------. SAILOR NAMED JONES. Doubleday, 1957. Narrative of John Paul Jones written by a retired Navy captain. (followed by PRIZE MASTER) 3430

Harris, Cyril. RICHARD PRYNE. Scribner, 1941. Suspense-filled tale of a civilian spy for Washington. 3431

--------. TRUMPETS AT DAWN. Scribner, 1938. How war affected social relationships, traditions, and economic balance. 3432

Henri, Florette. KINGS MOUNTAIN. Doubleday, 1950. Pictures leaders of the American and British sides in the Battle of Kings Mountain. 3433

Horan, James David. THE KING'S REBEL. Crown, 1953. A British officer, in sympathy with the struggling colonists, resigns his army commission. 3434

Horne, Howard. CONCORD BRIDGE. Bobbs, 1952. Romance of a girl spy at the start of the War. 3435

Hough, Frank Olney. IF NOT VICTORY. Lippincott, 1939. Exploits of a Quaker boy who becomes a soldier in the Continental Army. 3436

--------. THE NEUTRAL GROUND. Lippincott, 1941.

Efforts of two Westchester County, New York, men to win their neighbors' votes in a political fight. 3437

--------. RENOWN. Lippincott, 1938. A sympathetic portrait of Benedict Arnold. 3438

Hubbard, Lindley Murray. AN EXPRESS OF '76. Little, 1906. "A chronicle of the town of York in the War of Independence." 3439

Jacobs, Helen Hull. STORM AGAINST THE WIND. Dodd, 1944. Tidewater Virginia while colonial resistance to British rule was stiffening. 3440

Jennings, John. THE SEA EAGLES. Doubleday, 1950. The young American Navy during the Revolution--its ships, its men, and the women they left behind. 3441

--------. THE SHADOW AND THE GLORY. Reynal, 1943. A New Hampshire boy runs away to join the army. 3442

Jewett, Sarah Orne. THE TORY LOVER. Houghton, 1901. A novel introducing the hero John Paul Jones. 3443

Johnston, Mary. HUNTING SHIRT. Little, 1931. A frontiersman's two-year search in Indian territory for his sweetheart's stolen necklace. 3444

Karig, Walter and Horace V. Bird. DON'T TREAD ON ME. Rinehart, 1954. The vigorous adventures of John Paul Jones. 3445

Kennedy, John P. HORSESHOE ROBINSON. Putnam, 1835. South Carolina and its strong Tory feelings during the Revolution. 3446

Kennedy, Sara Beaumont. JOSCELYN CHESHIRE. Doubleday, 1901. Life at Hillsboro, N. C., and aboard a British prison ship during the Revolutionary War. 3447

Lancaster, Bruce. THE BLIND JOURNEY. Little, 1953. Secret mission of Benjamin Franklin's messenger from France to America. 3448

--------. GUNS OF BURGOYNE. Stokes, 1939. Burgoyne's defeat at Saratoga. 3449

--------. THE PHANTOM FORTRESS. Little, 1950. The military tactics of Francis Marion, the Swamp Fox, and the romance of one of his men. 3450

--------. THE SECRET ROAD. Little, 1952. Suspense and thrills as General Washington's "secret service" collects information. 3451

--------. TRUMPET TO ARMS. Little, 1944. The forming of individualistic Americans into the army which won our freedom. 3452

Leland, John Adams. OTHNEIL JONES. Lippincott, 1956. A young Cherokee fights with the Swamp Fox, Francis Marion, in Tennessee. 3453

Linington, Elizabeth. THE LONG WATCH. Viking, 1956. A newspaperman is hero in this report of New York's reactions to revolt. 3454

Lynde, Francis. MR. ARNOLD. Bobbs, 1923. Benedict Arnold's activities in Virginia in 1780. 3455

McIntyre, John Thomas. DRUMS IN THE DAWN. Doubleday, Doran, 1932. A romance which touches on the rebelling colonies' need for financial support. 3456

McLean, Sydney. A MOMENT OF TIME. Putnam, 1945. The steadfastness and courage of a New England woman and her family. 3457

Mason, Van Wyck. EAGLE IN THE SKY. Lippincott, 1948. A story of sailors and doctors in the American Revolution. 3458

--------. RIVERS OF GLORY. Lippincott, 1942. Adventures in the naval war of the Revolution, especially the siege of Savannah. (followed by EAGLE IN THE SKY) 3459

--------. STARS ON THE SEA. Lippincott, 1940. Story of

privateering in the opening years of the war. (followed by RIVERS OF GLORY) 3460

--------. THREE HARBOURS. Lippincott, 1938. Naval action during the Revolution in the three harbors of Boston, Bermuda, and Norfolk. (followed by STARS ON THE SEA) 3461

--------. VALLEY FORGE: 24 DECEMBER, 1777. Doubleday, 1950. Touching account of the Christmas of Washington's suffering troops. 3462

Melville, Herman. ISRAEL POTTER. Putnam, 1855. Experiences of an American sailor captured by the British. 3463

Mercer, Charles E. ENOUGH GOOD MEN. Putnam, 1960. Effects of the Revolution on the lives of a small group. 3464

Miller, Helen Topping. CHRISTMAS AT MOUNT VERNON. Longmans, 1957. The Washingtons' first Christmas at home after the close of the war. 3465

--------. SLOW DIES THE THUNDER. Bobbs, 1955. Wartime activities in South Carolina--Charleston and Kings Mountain. 3466

--------. THE SOUND OF CHARIOTS. Bobbs, 1947. Life and war on the Georgia and Tennessee frontiers. 3467

--------. TRUMPET IN THE CITY. Bobbs, 1948. The early phase of the war as it appeared to the residents of Savannah. 3468

Mills, Weymer Jay. THE VAN RENSSELAERS OF OLD MANHATTAN. Stokes, 1907. Romance with New York as background. 3469

Minnigerode, Meade. THE BLACK FOREST. Farrar, 1937. Two generations of pioneers in the area west of the Allegheny Mountains. 3470

Mitchell, S. Weir. HUGH WYNNE, FREE QUAKER. Century, 1897. The Quaker practice of friendship contrasted with the war. 3471

Morrow, Honoré. BEYOND THE BLUE SIERRA. Morrow, 1932. The Mexican settlement of California and the founding of San Francisco. 3472

Muir, Robert. SPRIG OF HEMLOCK. Longmans, 1957. Story of the ill-fated Shays's Rebellion of 1786-87. 3473

Nutt, Frances Tysen. THREE FIELDS TO CROSS. Stephen-Paul, 1947. Staten Island during the Revolution. 3474

Osgood, Grace Rose. AT THE SIGN OF THE BLUE ANCHOR. Clark, 1909. A story of 1776. 3475

Page, Elizabeth. TREE OF LIBERTY. Farrar, 1939. About an American family friendly with Thomas Jefferson. 3476

Paradise, Viola I. TOMORROW THE HARVEST. Morrow, 1952. Story of two women in a small Maine village just after the Revolution. 3477

Parrish, Randall. MY LADY OF DOUBT. McClurg, 1911. A Maryland officer in a British uniform spies for Washington. 3478

--------. PRISONERS OF CHANCE. McClurg, 1908. Set in the lower Mississippi Valley during the French occupation. 3479

Pendexter, Hugh. RED BELTS. Doubleday, 1920. Frontier adventures and Indian fighting during the formation of the state of Tennessee. 3480

Pridgen, Tim. TORY OATH. Doubleday, 1941. Scots settlers in North Carolina at the time of the Revolution. 3481

Quinby, Alden W. VALLEY FORGE. Eaton & Mains, 1906. Contrasts Washington's ill-equipped troops during the harsh winter with the British in comfort in Philadelphia. 3482

Raddall, Thomas. THE GOVERNOR'S LADY. Doubleday, 1960. Governor Wentworth, his ambitious wife, and what befell them because of the Revolution. 3483

Richter, Conrad. FREE MAN. Knopf, 1943. A German immigrant sold as an indentured servant escapes to freedom. 3484

--------. THE LIGHT IN THE FOREST. Knopf, 1953. How a white boy raised by Delaware Indians reacts to rescue. 3485

Ripley, Clements. CLEAR FOR ACTION. Appleton, 1940. An account of the sea battle in which John Paul Jones said, "I have not yet begun to fight." 3486

Rives, Hallie Erminie. HEARTS COURAGEOUS. Bobbs, 1902. The fight for American independence with Patrick Henry as one of the leaders. 3487

Roberts, Kenneth. ARUNDEL. Doubleday, 1930. "A chronicle of the province of Maine and of the secret expedition of Benedict Arnold against Quebec." 3488

--------. OLIVER WISWELL. Doubleday, 1940. The Tory side of the American War for Independence. 3489

--------. RABBLE IN ARMS. Doubleday, 1933. The leadership of Benedict Arnold is emphasized with the American Congress as "villain." 3490

Sabatini, Rafael. THE CAROLINIAN. Houghton, 1925. Vivid story of the conflict between British and colonials in South Carolina. 3491

Safford, Henry B. TORY TAVERN. Penn, 1942. A Tory boy, after three years in the British navy, becomes a spy for the Americans. 3492

Schindall, Henry. LET THE SPRING COME. Appleton, 1953. Colorful story of Virginia at the end of the war. 3493

Schoonover, Lawrence. THE REVOLUTIONARY. Little, 1958. Sea action of John Paul Jones and his Bon Homme Richard, named for Benjamin Franklin. 3494

Scollard, Clinton. THE SON OF A TORY. Badger, 1901.

The siege of Fort Stanwix by the British. 3495

Scott, John Reed. THE MAKE-BELIEVE. Lippincott, 1911. Life in high society circles in colonial Maryland. 3496

Sears, Margaret L. MENOTOMY: A ROMANCE OF 1776. Badger, 1908. Massachusetts in the early stages of the Revolution. 3497

Seifert, Shirley. LET MY NAME STAND FAIR. Lippincott, 1956. Story of Nathanael and Catherine Greene during the Revolution. 3498

--------. WATERS OF THE WILDERNESS. Lippincott, 1941. George Rogers Clark's holding of Kaskaskia and Vincennes during the war. 3499

Simms, W. Gilmore. (1) THE PARTISAN. Harper, 1935. (2) MELLICHAMPE. Harper, 1836. (3) KATHERINE WALTON. Hart, 1851. (4) THE SCOUT. Redfield, 1854. (5) THE FORAYERS. Redfield, 1855. (6) EUTAW. Redfield, 1856. A series of novels picturing South Carolina during the Revolution and presenting major military events, prominent people, outlaw activities, and social functions. 3500

Simons, Katherine D. M. THE RED DOE. by Drayton Mayrant, pseud. Appleton, 1953. Francis Marion, the Swamp Fox of Revolutionary War fame. 3501

Sinclair, Harold. WESTWARD THE TIDE. Doubleday, 1940. The early life of George Rogers Clark and his expedition to Vincennes. 3502

Slaughter, Frank G. FLIGHT FROM NATCHEZ. Doubleday, 1955. Doctor's career after dishonorable discharge from British army. 3503

--------. SANGAREE. Doubleday, 1948. Practice of a doctor on a Georgia plantation after the Revolutionary War. 3504

Spicer, Bart. BROTHER TO THE ENEMY. Dodd, 1958.

Dangerous assignment to enter the British garrison and capture traitor Benedict Arnold. 3505

Stanley, Edward. THOMAS FORTY. Duell, 1947. A young printer, at first undecided, joins the American Army. 3506

Stephens, Robert Neilson. THE CONTINENTAL DRAGOON. Page, 1901. A romance of the area between British and American lines. 3507

--------. PHILIP WINWOOD. Page, 1900. Domestic crisis of an American captain whose wife has Loyalist sympathies. 3508

Stevenson, Burton E. A SOLDIER OF VIRGINIA. Houghton, 1901. The early campaigns of Washington and the defeat of Braddock. 3509

Stimson, Frederic Jesup. MY STORY. by J. S. of Dale, pseud. Scribner, 1917. Purported autobiography of Benedict Arnold. 3510

Stover, Herbert Elisha. EAGLE AND THE WIND. Dodd, 1953. A tale of Pennsylvania during the American Revolution. 3511

--------. MEN IN BUCKSKIN. Dodd, 1950. British-inspired Indian raids in Pennsylvania. 3512

--------. POWDER MISSION. Dodd, 1951. Expedition down the Mississippi for powder for Washington's army. 3513

Swanson, Neil. THE FIRST REBEL. Farrar, 1937. About Scotch-Irish colonists and their insistence on freedom. 3514

--------. THE FORBIDDEN GROUND. Farrar, 1938. Depicts fur trading in and around Detroit. 3515

Taylor, David. FAREWELL TO VALLEY FORGE. Lippincott, 1955. Adventures of two young people who spy for Washington. 3516

--------. LIGHTS ACROSS THE DELAWARE. Lippincott,

1954. Washington's capture of Trenton at Christmas, 1776. 3517

--------. STORM THE LAST RAMPART. Lippincott, 1960. Washington's secret intelligence system in the last phase of the Revolution. 3518

Taylor, Mary Imlay. A YANKEE VOLUNTEER. McClurg, 1899. The early days of the Revolution with Generals Washington, Putnam, and Howe. 3519

Teilhet, Darwin Le Ora. THE ROAD TO GLORY. Funk, 1956. Father Junipero Serra and his missionary work among the Indians in California. 3520

Thompson, Daniel P. THE GREEN MOUNTAIN BOYS. Caldwell, 1840. Contains accounts of land controversies and war in Vermont under the leadership of Ethan Allen. 3521

Thompson, Maurice. ALICE OF OLD VINCENNES. Bobbs, 1901. The patriotism of a lady in old French Vincennes, Indiana. 3522

Thompson, N. P. THE RANGERS. Nichols & Hall, 1851. George Rogers Clark's campaigns in the West. 3523

Tilton, Dwight, pseud. for George Tilton Richardson and Wilder Dwight Quint. MY LADY LAUGHTER. Clark, 1904. Growing tension between British and colonists and the siege of Boston. 3524

Townsend, Frank Sumner. HUGH GRAHAM. Abingdon, 1916. Pioneer life and Indian fighting in western Pennsylvania just before the Revolution. 3525

Turnbull, Agnes. THE DAY MUST DAWN. Macmillan, 1942. Everyday events in a frontier town threatened by Indian attack. 3526

Tyson, J. Audrey. THE STIRRUP CUP. Appleton, 1903. A story of Aaron Burr in New York and Pennsylvania. 3527

Van de Water, Frederic. CATCH A FALLING STAR. Duell, 1949. Romance of Vermont with Ethan Allen as a character. (followed by WINGS OF THE MORNING) 3528

--------. DAY OF BATTLE. Washburn, 1958. The battle of Bennington and the romance of an American soldier with a Tory girl. 3529

--------. THE RELUCTANT REBEL. Duell, 1948. Ethan Allen and the Green Mountain Boys fight for liberty. (followed by CATCH A FALLING STAR) 3530

--------. WINGS OF THE MORNING. Washburn, 1956. The fight for independence in eastern Vermont. (followed by DAY OF BATTLE.) 3531

Van Every, Dale. BRIDAL JOURNEY. Messner, 1950. Occurs in the Ohio River Valley during the seething times near the end of the Revolution. 3532

--------. CAPTIVE WITCH. Messner, 1951. A tale of the western frontier, then Virginia and Kentucky, combining romance and Indian fighting. 3533

--------. THE VOYAGERS. Holt, 1957. The American frontier in the late eighteenth century. 3534

Westcott, Jan. CAPTAIN BARNEY. Crown, 1951. Action-filled story of a noted naval officer, Joshua Barney. 3535

Wheelwright, Jere Hungerford. KENTUCKY STAND. Scribner, 1951. Indian warfare and pioneer life in Kentucky. 3536

White, Helen C. DUST ON THE KING'S HIGHWAY. Macmillan, 1947. Work of Father Garcés and other missionaries among Indians in California and Mexico. 3537

White, Stewart Edward. DANIEL BOONE, WILDERNESS SCOUT. Doubleday, Doran, 1935. Adventures of Long Knife, who first blazed the Wilderness Trail to

Kentucky. 3538

Wiener, Willard. MORNING IN AMERICA. Farrar, 1942. Experiences of an American soldier who served under Charles Lee. 3539

Williams, Ben Ames. COME SPRING. Houghton, 1940. The building of a home in frontier Maine during the Revolution. 3540

Winn, Mary P. and Margaret Hannis. THE LAW AND THE LETTER. Neale, 1907. The coming to New Orleans of young girls as the brides of French soldiers. 3541

Wyckoff, Nicholas E. BRAINTREE MISSION. Macmillan, 1957. Boston in the 1770s and a suggestion to preserve peace by seating representative American colonists in Parliament. 3542

Yerby, Frank. BRIDE OF LIBERTY. Doubleday, 1954. A romantic triangle of two sisters and the man they both love. 3543

Ziegler, Isabelle Gibson. THE NINE DAYS OF FATHER SERRA. Longmans, 1951. Missionary work in early Spanish California. 3544

III. C. 1. c. National Period (1789-1861)

Abbott, Jane Ludlow. RIVER'S RIM. Lippincott, 1950. American patriot's loyalty is suspected because of relatives' leanings in the War of 1812. 3545

Adams, Samuel Hopkins. BANNER BY THE WAYSIDE. Random, 1947. A touring theatrical group in the Erie Canal region. 3546

--------. CANAL TOWN. Random, 1944. A crusading doctor attacks disease in an Erie Canal town--Palmyra, New York. 3547

--------. THE GORGEOUS HUSSY. Houghton, 1934. Peggy O'Neale leads an active life in Washington's political and social circles. 3548

--------. SUNRISE TO SUNSET. Random, 1950. Life in the cotton mill town of Troy, New York, when employees sought better working conditions. 3549

Ainsworth, Edward Maddin. EAGLES FLY WEST. Macmillan, 1946. Story of a newspaperman and pioneer settlements, the gold rush, and the Spanish-Mexican culture in early California. 3550

Aldrich, Bess Streeter. SONG OF YEARS. Appleton, 1939. Romance of the lives and emotions of Iowa pioneers revolving around a family of nine children. 3551

Allen, James Lane. THE CHOIR INVISIBLE. Macmillan, 1897. Story of a hopeless romance in Kentucky after the Revolutionary War. 3552

Allen, T. D., pseud. for Terry D. Allen and Don B. Allen. DOCTOR IN BUCKSKIN. Harper, 1951. Medical missionary to frontier Oregon. 3553

--------. TROUBLED BORDER. Harper, 1954. John McLoughlin, superintendent of Hudson's Bay Company at Fort Vancouver on the Columbia River. 3554

Allis, Marguerite. ALL IN GOOD TIME. Putnam, 1944. A Connecticut clockmaker who foresaw mass production. 3555

--------. BRAVE PURSUIT. Putnam, 1954. Pioneer life in the early days of Ohio statehood showing the status of women. 3556

--------. CHARITY STRONG. Putnam, 1945. Connecticut lady with the convention-defying ambition to be an opera singer. 3557

--------. THE LAW OF THE LAND. Putnam, 1948. Experiences of a Connecticut woman early in the fight for woman suffrage. 3558

--------. NOW WE ARE FREE. Putnam, 1952. Post-Revolution migration of settlers from Connecticut to Ohio. (followed by TO KEEP US FREE) 3559

--------. THE SPLENDOR STAYS. Putnam, 1942. Domestic and political life in Connecticut at the inception of the Monroe Doctrine; centered on the lives of seven sisters. 3560

--------. TO KEEP US FREE. Putnam, 1953. A reconstruction of early life on the Ohio frontier. 3561

--------. WATER OVER THE DAM. Putnam, 1947. The effects of the Farmington, Connecticut Canal on the lives of the people in the area. 3562

Andrews, Robert. GREAT DAY IN THE MORNING. Coward, 1950. Attempt to draw Colorado into the Civil War as a Confederate state and to use her gold for the southern cause. 3563

Arnold, Elliott. TIME OF THE GRINGO. Knopf, 1953. Exciting narrative of New Mexico in the time before the Mexican War. 3564

--------. WHITE FALCON. Knopf, 1955. John Tanner's life with the Ottawa and Chippewa Indians. 3565

Atherton, Gertrude. THE CONQUEROR. Macmillan, 1901. A novel based on the career of Alexander Hamilton, written in a sympathetic vein. 3566

--------. THE DOOMSWOMAN. Continental, 1901. Depicts Spanish life in old California in the 1840s. 3567

--------. REZÂNOV. Cupples, 1906. Manners and trade affairs in San Francisco in 1806, when the Russians were attempting to gain a foothold in California. 3568

--------. THE VALIANT RUNAWAYS. Dodd, 1899. Turmoil in California in the period when Mexican power was declining. 3569

Atkinson, Eleanor. HEARTS UNDAUNTED. Harper, 1917. A girl raised by Indians returns to her white mother and becomes a frontier wife. 3570

Atkinson, Oriana. THE GOLDEN SEASON. Bobbs, 1953. Robust story of Dutch settlers in the Catskill region. 3571

--------. THE TWIN COUSINS. Bobbs, 1951. Family life at an inn on the Susquehanna Turnpike at Catskill, New York. (followed by THE GOLDEN SEASON) 3572

Austin, Mary. ISIDRO. Houghton, 1905. Indians and Spanish settlers in California at the time of the missions. 3573

Babcock, Mrs. Bernie. LITTLE ABE LINCOLN. Lippincott, 1926. The childhood, in Kentucky and Indiana, of Lincoln and his sister, Sarah. 3574

--------. THE SOUL OF ANN RUTLEDGE. Lippincott, 1919. The romance of Ann Rutledge and Abraham Lincoln which influenced him even after her death. 3575

Bacheller, Irving. D'RI AND I. Harper, 1901. A story of America during the War of 1812 featuring vivid descriptions of the St. Lawrence Valley. 3576

--------. EBEN HOLDEN. Lothrop, 1900. Story of a beloved servant in the Adirondacks, with Horace Greeley and Abraham Lincoln as characters. 3577

--------. THE LIGHT IN THE CLEARING. Bobbs, 1917. A tale of the north country in the time of Silas Wright, a governor of New York. 3578

--------. A MAN FOR THE AGES. Bobbs, 1919. Story of a family in New Salem, Illinois, during Lincoln's young manhood. 3579

Baker, Karle Wilson. STAR OF THE WILDERNESS. by Charlotte Wilson, pseud. Coward, 1942. A Cincinnati couple seek their fortune in Texas. 3580

Baldwin, Leland Dewitt. THE DELECTABLE COUNTRY.

Furman, 1939. A young riverman's adventures in the Ohio Valley in "the pursuit of happiness." 3581

Ball, Zachary. PULL DOWN TO NEW ORLEANS. Crown, 1946. Romance with the Ohio and Mississippi Rivers as setting. 3582

Banks, Nancy H. OLDFIELD. Macmillan, 1902. Rural life in Kentucky in mid-century. 3583

--------. ROUND ANVIL ROCK. Macmillan, 1903. A romance of early Kentucky. 3584

Banks, Polan. BLACK IVORY. Harper, 1926. Pirate Jean Lafitte's career as a slave trader in New Orleans. 3585

Barnes, Percy Raymond. CRUM ELBOW FOLKS. Lippincott, 1938. A charming picture of life in a Quaker settlement in New York. 3586

Barney, Helen Corse. FRUIT IN HIS SEASON. Crown, 1951. Quaker pioneers, objecting to slavery, leave Virginia for Ohio. 3587

Barr, Amelia E. THE BELLE OF BOWLING GREEN. Dodd, 1904. The wealthy New York Dutch, who disdained to let the war interfere with their social life. 3588

--------. THE MAID OF MAIDEN LANE. Dodd, 1900. Should New York or Philadelphia be the capital of the young United States? 3589

--------. REMEMBER THE ALAMO. Dodd, 1888. The dramatic attack on the Alamo in the Texan War for independence from Mexico. 3590

--------. SHE LOVED A SAILOR. Warne, 1899. A romance of the administration of President Andrew Jackson. 3591

--------. TRINITY BELLS. Dodd, 1899. Quiet tale of peaceful family life in New York in the early nineteenth century. 3592

Barrett, Monte. SUN IN THEIR EYES. Bobbs, 1944. Life in Texas when there was friction with the Spanish. 3593

--------. TEMPERED BLADE. Bobbs, 1946. Texas at the time of the break from Mexico, with Jim Bowie as hero. 3594

Bartlett, Jenniebelle. CRY ABOVE THE WINDS. Morrow, 1951. Pictures Monterey in the 1830s and deals with Indians, Mexicans, and settlers. 3595

Bartlett, Lanier. ADIOS! Morrow, 1929. Armed resistance of Spanish Californians to acquisition of the area by the United States. 3596

Bartlett, Virginia Stivers. MISTRESS OF MONTEREY. Bobbs, 1933. Social and political controversy in California as reflected in the lives of Governor Fages and his wife. 3597

Bates, Morgan. MARTIN BROOK. Harper, 1901. A report of conditions which resulted in the Abolitionist point of view. 3598

Baume, Frederic E. YANKEE WOMAN. Dodd, 1945. A New England widow sails her husband's ship to California during the gold rush. 3599

Beach, Rex. THE WORLD IN HIS ARMS. Putnam, 1946. A Boston fur-poacher in Alaska. 3600

Bean, Amelia. THE FANCHER TRAIN. Doubleday, 1958. A stirring account of the tragic Mountain Meadow Massacre-the slaughter of an entire wagon train. 3601

Beebe, Ralph. WHO FOUGHT AND BLED. Coward, 1941. Action of the War of 1812 with General Hull near Detroit. 3602

Beecher, Henry Ward. NORWOOD. Fords, Howard & Hulbert, 1866. The gossip and romance of a prosperous small town in New England. 3603

Bell, Sallie. MARCEL ARMAND. Page, 1935. A three-sided romance with one of Jean Lafitte's pirates as hero. 3604

Bennet, Robert Ames. A VOLUNTEER WITH PIKE. McClurg, 1909. A tale of the Louisiana Purchase and Zebulon Pike's journey westward, including the discovery of Pike's Peak. 3605

Benson, Ramsey. HILL COUNTRY. Stokes, 1928. Early Swedish settlers in Minnesota. 3606

Berry, Don. TRASK. Viking, 1960. The customs and beliefs of Oregon Indians discovered by a pioneer travelling through their territory. 3607

Best, Allena. HOMESPUN. by Erick Berry, pseud. Lothrop, 1937. A story of pioneers in such daily occupations as hunting, spinning, and weaving. 3608

Best, Herbert. YOUNG'UN. Macmillan, 1944. Warm, refreshing story of three children left to shift for themselves on a small northern farm. 3609

Binns, Archie. THE LAND IS BRIGHT. Scribner, 1939. A wagon train journeys from Illinois to Oregon and encounters incredible hardships. 3610

--------. MIGHTY MOUNTAIN. Scribner, 1940. A New England Yankee settles in the Washington Territory. 3611

Bird, Robert Montgomery. NICK O' THE WOODS; or, THE JIBBENAINOSAY. Armstrong, 1837. Indian warfare in Kentucky with the capture of hero and heroine and its results. 3612

Birney, Hoffman. EAGLE IN THE SUN. Putnam, 1935. An exciting tale of Santa Fe during the Mexican War. 3613

--------. GRIM JOURNEY. Minton, Balch, 1934. Tale told by a survivor of the terrible sufferings of the Donner Party, caught in mountain snowstorms. 3614

Bischoff, Ilse. PROUD HERITAGE. Coward, 1949. The

life of Gilbert Stuart, who became an outstanding painter. 3615

Blake, Forrester. JOHNNY CHRISTMAS. Morrow, 1948. A story of Indians and Mexicans in the American Southwest in the 1830s and '40s. 3616

Bogue, Herbert Edward. DAREFORD. Clark, 1907. A novel with interesting references to laws just before the Civil War, especially the fugitive slave laws. 3617

Bonner, Geraldine. THE EMIGRANT TRAIL. Duffield, 1910. The overland route to California via Missouri. 3618

Bontemps, Arna. BLACK THUNDER. Macmillan, 1936. The "Gabriel Insurrection": a mob of slaves attempt to capture Richmond about 1800. 3619

Boyd, James. THE LONG HUNT. Scribner, 1930. Realistic story of a rugged frontiersman well-versed in forest-craft. 3620

Boyles, Kate and Virgil D. Boyles. LANGFORD OF THE THREE BARS. McClurg, 1907. Cattle ranching in South Dakota when rustling was prevalent and law enforcement poor. 3621

Brady, Cyrus Townsend. IN THE WASP'S NEST. Scribner, 1902. "A story of a sea-waif in the War of 1812." 3622

Brand, Anna. THUNDER BEFORE SEVEN. Doubleday, 1941. A tale of the Texan revolt against Mexico. 3623

Breslin, Howard. THE TAMARACK TREE. McGraw, 1947. Effects on Vermont residents of a Whig rally addressed by Daniel Webster. 3624

Brigham, Johnson. THE SINCLAIRS OF OLD FORT DES MOINES. Torch Press, 1927. Pioneer life in Iowa in the 1840s. 3625

Bristow, Gwen. DEEP SUMMER. Crowell, 1937. Love blossoms between a northern Puritan girl and a southern aristocrat in Louisiana. (followed by THE HANDSOME

ROAD) 3626

--------. THE JUBILEE TRAIL. Crowell, 1950. Adventures of a quiet New York girl on the Santa Fe Trail after she leaves finishing school. 3627

Brown, Charles B. ARTHUR MERVYN. McKay, 1800. Life in Philadelphia during the yellow fever outbreak of 1793. 3628

Brown, Dee. WAVE HIGH THE BANNER. Macrae Smith, 1942. Davy Crockett, famous frontiersman and hero of the Alamo. 3629

Brown, Joe David. THE FREEHOLDER. Morrow, 1949. An English boy, raised in an orphan asylum, comes to America in quest of freedom and success. 3630

Brown, Katharine Holland. DIANE. Doubleday, Page, 1904. Dealings in runaway slaves in a French community in Mississippi and the Underground Railroad. 3631

--------. THE FATHER. Day, 1928. A father's abolitionist crusading and his daughter's romance are subjects for this lively novel in which Lincoln appears. 3632

Brown, Theron. UNDER THE MULBERRY TREES. Badger, 1909. William Miller's claim that the Second Advent was at hand caused great excitement in the Connecticut countryside. 3633

Brown, William Garrott. A GENTLEMAN OF THE SOUTH. Macmillan, 1903. Heartbreak caused by the so-called code-of-honor which settled differences by dueling. 3634

Burgess, Jackson. PILLAR OF CLOUD. Putnam, 1957. Pioneers blazing a trail from Kansas to the western mountains. 3635

Burgoyne, Leon E. ENSIGN RONAN. Winston, 1955. Youth seeks revenge on Indians but finds romance instead. 3636

Burman, Ben Lucien. STEAMBOAT ROUND THE BEND. Farrar & Rinehart, 1933. Gentle love story of a southern couple against the colorful background of river and bayou country. 3637

Burnett, Frances Hodgson. IN CONNECTION WITH THE DE WILLOUGHBY CLAIM. Scribner, 1899. A rural area of Tennessee before the outbreak of the Civil War. 3638

Burr, Anna. THE GOLDEN QUICKSAND. Appleton, 1936. A young easterner seeks his missing brother in Santa Fe. 3639

Bynner, Edwin Lassetter. ZACHARY PHIPS. Houghton, 1892. Adventures of a Boston boy who joined Aaron Burr's expedition. 3640

Byrd, Sigman and John Sutherland. THE VALIANT. Jason Press, 1955. Stand of the Nez Percé Indians against the inroads of the white man in Oregon. 3641

Cable, George Washington. DR. SEVIER. Scribner, 1884. A tale of life in thriving New Orleans at mid-century. 3642

--------. THE GRANDISSIMES. Scribner, 1880. A novel of the Creole inhabitants of New Orleans. 3643

Caldwell, Taylor (full name: Janet Taylor Caldwell). THE TURNBULLS. Scribner, 1943. An English immigrant becomes a powerful figure in the New York financial world. 3644

--------. THE WIDE HOUSE. Scribner, 1945. Life of a family amidst religious and racial intolerance in upstate New York. 3645

Cameron, Margaret. JOHNDOVER. Harper, 1924. A disillusioned widow, an escaped convicted murderer, and a youth whose Puritan conscience demands justice. 3646

Campbell, Patricia. THE ROYAL ANNE TREE. Macmillan, 1956. A young girl is orphaned soon after her arrival as a settler in Washington territory. 3647

Campbell, Walter Stanley. 'DOBE WALLS. by Stanley Vestal, pseud. Houghton, 1929. Mexicans, Indians, and pioneers figure in this tale of a fort on the Santa Fe Trail in Kit Carson's time. 3648

--------. REVOLT ON THE BORDER. by Stanley Vestal, pseud. Houghton, 1938. Adventure on the Santa Fe Trail at the time of the annexation of New Mexico. 3649

Canfield, Chauncey L. THE CITY OF SIX. McClurg, 1910. California placer miners in the gold rush of '49. 3650

--------. THE DIARY OF A 'FORTY-NINER. Morgan Shepard, 1906. Digging for gold, miners' quarrels, and land disputes in early California. 3651

Cannon, Cornelia James. RED RUST. Little, 1928. A young Swedish farmer experiments to produce a better variety of wheat. 3652

Cannon, LeGrand. A MIGHTY FORTRESS. Farrar, 1937. Inspiring, entertaining story of a New England farmer who became a preacher. 3653

Carhart, Arthur Hawthorne. DRUM UP THE DAWN. Dodd, 1937. About Zebulon Pike's expedition westward. 3654

Carmer, Carl. GENESEE FEVER. Farrar, 1941. A gentleman schoolteacher with strong political ideas. 3655

Carpenter, Edward Childs. CAPTAIN COURTESY. Jacobs, 1906. The struggle for control of California, culminating in victory for the United States. 3656

--------. THE CODE OF VICTOR JALLOT. Jacobs, 1907. New Orleans at the time of the Louisiana Purchase. 3657

Case, Josephine. WRITTEN IN SAND. Houghton, 1945. Yankee General William Eaton leads an invasion of Tripoli in 1805. 3658

Cather, Willa. DEATH COMES FOR THE ARCHBISHOP. Knopf, 1927. The growth and development of the Southwest reflected in the story of the Archbishop of Santa Fe. 3659

--------. MY ANTONIA. Houghton, 1918. An immigrant Bohemian girl is confronted by the trials of rugged frontier life. 3660

--------. SAPPHIRA AND THE SLAVE GIRL. Knopf, 1940. An invalid Virginia lady who "married beneath herself" and her jealousy toward a slave girl. 3661

Catherwood, Mary H. LAZARRE. Bowen-Merrill, 1901. Based on the story of the French Dauphin's supposed escape to America in a temporary state of insanity. 3662

Chambers, Robert W. THE HAPPY PARROT. Appleton, 1929. Lively adventures of a schooner engaged in the slave trade during the War of 1812. 3663

--------. THE RAKE AND THE HUSSY. Appleton, 1930. Vivid and detailed sketches of people and events during the defense of New Orleans. 3664

Chase, Mary Ellen. SILAS CROCKETT. Macmillan, 1935. A four-generation story of Maine seafarers. 3665

Chidsey, Donald Barr. STRONGHOLD. Doubleday, 1948. Love, romance, and murder against a backdrop of the War of 1812 and the Embargo Act. 3666

Churchill, Winston. CONISTON. Macmillan, 1906. Social and political life and developments in Boston and Washington at mid-century. (followed by MR. CREWE'S CAREER) 3667

--------. THE CRISIS. Macmillan, 1901. St. Louis is presented as a forum for the conflicting views which led to the Civil War. 3668

--------. THE CROSSING. Macmillan, 1904. Exploration of the Midwest, wilderness life, and the relations of white men and Indians on George Rogers Clark's expedition. 3669

Cicchetti, Janet. O GENESEE. Lippincott, 1958. Pioneering in New York State with the added hazard of the War of 1812. 3670

Clagett, John. BUCKSKIN CAVALIER. Crown, 1954. Story of a girl captured by Indians. 3671

Clark, Howard. THE MILL ON MAD RIVER. Little, 1948. A story of the brass and clock-making industries in Connecticut. 3672

Cleghorn, Sarah N. A TURNPIKE LADY. Holt, 1907. A novel of daily life in the Vermont country-side during the War of 1812. 3673

Coffin, Robert Peter. JOHN DAWN. Macmillan, 1936. The Maine seacoast and the shipbuilding industry which flourished there. 3674

Coker, Elizabeth Boatwright. DAUGHTER OF STRANGERS. Dutton, 1950. The live-happily-ever-after tale of an octoroon girl on a South Carolina plantation. 3675

Colby, Merle. ALL YE PEOPLE. Viking, 1931. Panoramic picture of American pioneers in the East, South, and West in the year 1810. 3676

--------. THE NEW ROAD. Viking, 1933. The growth of a frontier town in early Ohio. 3677

Colver, Anne. LISTEN FOR THE VOICES. Farrar, 1939. The Concord literary circle, with Emerson, Thoreau, and Alcott. 3678

Comfort, Will. APACHE. Dutton, 1931. A dramatically told story of Mangus Colorado, Apache chief who tried to drive away the white intruders. 3679

Conway, Moncure Daniel. PINE AND PALM. Holt, 1887. Friends from the North and the South differ on the slavery issue, and each agrees to spend a year in the other's home. 3680

Cook, Roberta. THING ABOUT CLARISSA. Bobbs, 1958. Humorous account of two young ladies just returned from a fashionable finishing school. 3681

Coolidge, Dane. GRINGO GOLD. Dutton, 1939. The activities of Mexican bandit Joaquin Murrieta during the California gold rush. 3682

Cooper, Courtney Ryley. THE GOLDEN BUBBLE. Little, 1928. A Kansas City man joins the Colorado gold rush and finds romance as well as success. 3683

--------. THE PIONEERS. Little, 1938. A wagon train led by Kit Carson journeys on the Oregon Trail. 3684

Cooper, James Fenimore. AFLOAT AND ASHORE. Hurd & Houghton, 1867. Seafaring life of an American in the Atlantic and Pacific in the early national period. 3685

Crabb, Alfred Leland. HOME TO KENTUCKY. Bobbs, 1953. Henry Clay's career as a lawyer, closing with his famous Cumberland Gap speech. 3686

--------. HOME TO THE HERMITAGE. Bobbs, 1948. A novel of Andrew Jackson and his wife, Rachel. 3687

Cranston, Paul. TO HEAVEN ON HORSEBACK. Messner, 1952. Story of Narcissa and Marcus Whitman, pioneer missionaries to Oregon, based on a journal she kept. 3688

Cronyn, George W. '49; A NOVEL OF GOLD. Dorrance, 1925. Vivid story of westward expansion speeded by the lust for gold. 3689

Crowley, Mary Catherine. LOVE THRIVES IN WAR. Little, 1903. Brock's taking of Detroit and fighting in the War of 1812. 3690

Crownfield, Gertrude. CONQUERING KITTY. Lippincott, 1935. Exploits of the jilted Kitty Knight, who determined to break men's hearts during the War of 1812. 3691

Culp, John H. THE MEN OF GONZALES. Sloane, 1960.

Thirty-two men who came from Gonzales to aid in the defense of the Alamo. 3692

Curwood, James O. THE COURAGE OF CAPTAIN PLUM. Bobbs, 1908. A young officer is commissioned to investigate a Mormon settlement and report on the marriage problem. 3693

Dana, Richard Henry. TWO YEARS BEFORE THE MAST. Houghton, 1840. Spirited account of a voyage on a merchant sailing vessel. 3694

Daniels, Harriet. MULLER HILL. Knopf, 1943. A mysterious French aristocrat makes a temporary home in New York State. 3695

David, Evan John. AS RUNS THE GLASS. Harper, 1943. Seagoing yarn of a Maine family in the period following the Revolution. 3696

Davidson, Louis B. and Edward J. Doherty. CAPTAIN MAROONER. Crowell, 1952. Mutiny on a whaling ship out of Nantucket. 3697

Daviess, Maria Thompson. THE MATRIX. Century, 1920. Romance of Thomas Lincoln and Nancy Hanks, parents of Abraham Lincoln. 3698

Davis, Dorothy Salisbury. MEN OF NO PROPERTY. Scribner, 1956. Arrival of Irish immigrants in New York and their Americanization. 3699

Davis, Harold Lenoir. BEULAH LAND. Morrow, 1949. A young couple's search for happiness in a journey westward to Oregon. 3700

Davis, J. Frank. THE ROAD TO SAN JACINTO. Bobbs, 1936. Tangled Texas-Mexican politics and the leadership of Houston are the background. 3701

Davis, Julia. CLOUD ON THE LAND. Rinehart, 1951. Adjustment of a girl who opposes slavery in her marriage to a slaveholder. 3702

--------. EAGLE ON THE SUN. Rinehart, 1956. Lucy

MacLeod manages the family plantation while the men fight in the Mexican War. 3703

De Forest, John W. KATE BEAUMONT. Estes, 1871. The South before the Civil War--social life and the attitude toward slavery. 3704

Dell, Floyd. DIANA STAIR. Farrar, 1932. The heroine is a reformer in Boston in the 1840s. 3705

Delmar, Viña. BELOVED. Harcourt, 1956. The romance of Judah Philip Benjamin, lawyer who came to be known as "the brains of the Confederacy." 3706

Derleth, August. BRIGHT JOURNEY. Scribner, 1940. Fur trading in the wild, lovely Northwest Territory, told by a poet-novelist. (followed by THE HOUSE ON THE MOUND) 3707

--------. HILLS STAND WATCH. Duell, 1960. A Wisconsin lead-mining village and a girl discontented with her marriage. 3708

--------. THE HOUSE ON THE MOUND. Duell, 1958. A fur trader's attempt to gain custody of his illegitimate son. 3709

--------. RESTLESS IS THE RIVER. Scribner, 1939. A Hungarian exile who settles in Wisconsin raises grapes for wine. 3710

--------. WIND OVER WISCONSIN. Scribner, 1938. Indian wars in Wisconsin with special emphasis on the natural beauty of the region. 3711

Desmond, Alice Curtis. BEWITCHING BETSY BONAPARTE. Dodd, 1958. About the Baltimore girl whose marriage to Jerome Bonaparte was opposed by his brother Napoleon. 3712

Dickson, Harris. HOUSE OF LUCK. Small, 1916. Speculation in land in lower Mississippi. 3713

Dillon, Mary C. IN OLD BELLAIRE. Century, 1906. A conscientious teacher faces conflict between her own beliefs and those of the people among whom she works. 3714

--------. THE PATIENCE OF JOHN MORLAND. Doubleday, Page, 1909. American politics and politicians under Presidents Monroe, Adams, and Jackson. 3715

--------. THE ROSE OF OLD ST. LOUIS. Century, 1904. St. Louis, Washington, and Paris in the days of the early Chouteaus, Jefferson, and Napoleon. 3716

Dodge, Louis. THE AMERICAN. Messner, 1934. An unsuccessful Illinois farmer seeks fortune in the western gold fields. 3717

Dooley, Sallie May. DEM GOOD OLE TIMES. by Mrs. James H. Dooley. Doubleday, Page, 1906. The life of a slave on a southern plantation as related to his granddaughter. 3718

Dougall, Lily. THE MORMON PROPHET. Appleton, 1899. Joseph Smith--his founding of Mormonism, the persecution of the sect, and Smith's death at the hands of a mob. 3719

Dowdey, Clifford. TIDEWATER. Little, 1943. Virginia landowner who moved his household to the Mississippi Valley. 3720

Downes, Anne Miller. THE PILGRIM SOUL. Lippincott, 1952. Hardships and joys of a pioneer couple settling in the New Hampshire mountains. 3721

--------. THE QUALITY OF MERCY. Lippincott, 1959. A Philadelphia family become pioneers in the wild country beyond the Cumberlands. 3722

Drago, Harry Sinclair. BOSS OF THE PLAINS. by Will Ermine, pseud. Morrow, 1940. A driver on the Great Plains when wagon freighting and Pony Express linked the coasts. 3723

Duffus, Robert. JORNADA. Covici, 1935. A romance is nearly engulfed in the fighting which involves Indians,

Mexicans, and Americans. 3724

Duncan, Thomas W. BIG RIVER, BIG MAN. Lippincott, 1959. Panoramic view of territorial and business growth dealing largely with upper Mississippi lumbering. 3725

Duval, John C. EARLY TIMES IN TEXAS. Steck, 1935. Pioneer life on the frontier and the Texan revolution of 1835-36. 3726

Dye, Eva. CONQUEST. Doubleday, 1922. The expedition of Lewis and Clark and the rush of immigrants into the newly opened West. 3727

Eaton, Evelyn and Edward R. Moore. HEART IN PILGRIMAGE. Harper, 1948. Elizabeth Seton's role as wife and mother and her later founding of the Sisters of Charity. 3728

Edmonds, Walter D. CHAD HANNA. Little, 1940. The rollicking tale of an orphan boy who ran away and joined the circus in the Mohawk Valley. 3729

--------. ERIE WATER. Little, 1933. The building of the Erie Canal and the romance of a carpenter who worked on it. 3730

--------. ROME HAUL. Little, 1929. A farm lad starts as a driver on the Erie Canal and manages to make good. 3731

--------. THE WEDDING JOURNEY. Little, 1947. A husband who gambled away their honeymoon money and the bride who stood by him. 3732

--------. YOUNG AMES. Little, 1942. A country boy who sought success in the big city. 3733

Edwards, E. J. and Jeanette E. Rattray. "WHALE OFF!" Stokes, 1932. American shore whaling, particularly small boat whaling off Long Island. 3734

Eggleston, Edward. THE CIRCUIT RIDER. Scribner, 1874. Ohio at the time of the War of 1812, showing the moral and social influence of the circuit riders. 3735

--------. THE FAITH DOCTOR. Appleton, 1891. A story of faith healing, which had recently become a popular idea in New York. 3736

--------. THE GRAYSONS. Century, 1888. Pioneer life in Illinois, showing Lincoln as a lawyer in a murder trial. 3737

--------. THE HOOSIER SCHOOLBOY. Warne, 1882. A story of early settlers in Indiana reflecting the status of education. 3738

--------. THE HOOSIER SCHOOLMASTER. Judd, 1871. Experiences of an Indiana school teacher who boards with the families of his pupils. 3739

--------. ROXY. Scribner, 1878. Events in a southern Indiana town near the scene of the battle of Tippecanoe. 3740

Eggleston, George Cary. DOROTHY SOUTH. Lothrop, 1902. A romance of Virginia just before the Civil War. 3741

--------. IRENE OF THE MOUNTAINS. Lothrop, 1909. A romance of old Virginia during a political race for governor. 3742

--------. TWO GENTLEMEN OF VIRGINIA. Lothrop, 1908. The "old regime" in Virginia just before the Civil War. 3743

Ehrlich, Leonard. GOD'S ANGRY MAN. S. & S., 1932. A powerful account of John Brown's firm conviction that slavery should be abolished. 3744

Ellerbe, Rose Lucile. ROPES OF SAND. Fischer, 1925. A vivid story of the American settlement of southern California, and a man's search for his Indian son. 3745

Ellis, William D. THE BOUNTY LANDS. World Pub., 1952. Westward movement caused when Revolutionary War veterans were granted land in Ohio. (followed by JONATHAN BLAIR, BOUNTY LANDS LAWYER) 3746

--------. THE BROOKS LEGEND. Crowell, 1958. Surgeon's mate's attempt, after the War of 1812, to acquire an M. D. degree. 3747

--------. JONATHAN BLAIR, BOUNTY LANDS LAWYER. World Pub., 1954. An eastern lawyer on the Ohio frontier. (followed by THE BROOKS LEGEND) 3748

Embree, Charles Fleming. A DREAM OF A THRONE. Little, 1900. A story of the war between the United States and Mexico. 3749

Emmons, Della F. G. SACAJAWEA OF THE SHOSHONES. Binfords, 1943. Sacajawea, the "Bird Woman" of the Lewis and Clark expedition. 3750

Ertz, Susan. NO HEARTS TO BREAK. Appleton, 1937. Elizabeth Patterson, a Baltimore girl, marries Jerome Bonaparte, Napoleon's brother. 3751

Evarts, Hal. FUR BRIGADE. Little, 1928. A fur trapper and his girl in the Indian-dominated early West. 3752

Faherty, William. B., S.J. A WALL FOR SAN SEBASTIAN. Academy Guild, 1962. Missionary, once a soldier, is torn between religious and military methods to aid his town. 3753

Faust, Frederick. THE LONG CHANCE. by Max Brand, pseud. Dodd, 1941. A young frontiersman and a cowardly southerner in the Old West. 3754

Field, Rachel L. ALL THIS, AND HEAVEN TOO. Macmillan, 1938. After innocent involvement in a French murder trial, "Mlle. D" comes to America and begins a new life. 3755

Fierro Blanco, Antonio de. THE JOURNEY OF THE FLAME. (tr.) Houghton, 1933. A Spanish Inspector General's trip through California told in a tale filled with authentic Mexican and Spanish folklore. 3756

Finger, Charles Joseph. WHEN GUNS THUNDERED AT TRIPOLI. Holt, 1937. A rousing tale of American merchant shipping during the Tripolitan War. 3757

Fisher, Anne. OH GLITTERING PROMISE! Bobbs, 1949. A Pennsylvania coal miner becomes a California gold miner. 3758

Fisher, Vardis. CHILDREN OF GOD. Harper, 1939. The beginnings, growth, and quest for peace of the Mormons, 1820-90. 3759

--------. CITY OF ILLUSION. Harper, 1941. The Comstock Lode in Nevada and the brief flourishing of Virginia City. 3760

--------. THE MOTHERS. Vanguard, 1943. Tragic story of the Donner Party told from the viewpoint of mothers involved. 3761

--------. TALE OF VALOR. Doubleday, 1958. The grueling eight thousand mile trip of exploration of Lewis and Clark to the Pacific Northwest. 3762

Fletcher, Inglis. THE QUEEN'S GIFT. Bobbs, 1952. Plantation life after British surrender at Yorktown. 3763

Forbes, Esther. O GENTEEL LADY! Houghton, 1926. The literary circle of Boston and Concord with Longfellow, Emerson, Thoreau, and Whittier. 3764

--------. RAINBOW ON THE ROAD. Houghton, 1954. A light-hearted itinerant portrait painter in Puritan New England. 3765

--------. THE RUNNING OF THE TIDE. Houghton, 1948. Salem, Massachusetts, in the flourishing period of her merchant ships. 3766

Foreman, Leonard L. THE ROAD TO SAN JACINTO. Dutton, 1943. The defense of the Alamo as a step on the road to victory at San Jacinto; Davy Crockett figures. 3767

Forester, C. S. THE CAPTAIN FROM CONNECTICUT. Little, 1941. Fast-sailing yarn of naval encounters between Americans and British in the War of 1812. 3768

Forrest, Williams. TRAIL OF TEARS. Crown, 1959. Forced removal of the Cherokees from their Georgia home to far-off Oklahoma. 3769

Fort, John. GOD IN THE STRAW PEN. Dodd, 1931. The powerful impact of a camp meeting on the people of a poor Georgia community. 3770

Frederick, John. THE BRONZE COLLAR. Putnam, 1925. A French soldier and an English nobleman in Spanish California. 3771

Frost, Elizabeth H. THIS SIDE OF LAND. Coward, 1942. Life on the island of Nantucket in the early 1800s. 3772

Frost, Thomas G. THE MAN OF DESTINY. Grammercy Pub., 1909. This novel is based on the career of Ulysses S. Grant at West Point and in the Mexican and Civil Wars. 3773

Fuller, Edmund. A STAR POINTED NORTH. Harper, 1946. Frederick Douglass, born a slave, escapes to become an Abolitionist leader and noted orator. 3774

Fuller, Iola. THE LOON FEATHER. Harcourt, 1940. Story of Mackinac Island and of the marriage of Tecumseh's daughter to a French trader. 3775

--------. THE SHINING TRAIL. Duell, 1943. The first Black Hawk War results when the Sauk Indians seek to defend their lands. 3776

Furnas, Marthedith. THE FAR COUNTRY. Harper, 1947. Journal kept by a Kentucky storekeeper on his overland trip to California. 3777

Gabriel, Gilbert W. I, JAMES LEWIS. Doubleday, 1932. John Jacob Astor's fur-trading expedition to the Pacific Northwest. 3778

--------. I THEE WED. Macmillan, 1948. The planning of an American refuge for Marie Antoinette, and the French seamstress who was prepared to be her double. 3779

Gaither, Frances. DOUBLE MUSCADINE. Macmillan, 1949. The dramatic story behind a Negro slave's trial for murder. 3780

--------. THE RED COCK CROWS. Macmillan, 1944. An attempted slave rebellion in Mississippi in the 1830s involves a youth sympathetic to the slaves. 3781

Garland, Hamlin. TRAIL-MAKERS OF THE MIDDLE BORDER. Macmillan, 1927. Pioneer life during the westward expansion, the building of railroads, and the Civil War. 3782

Gerson, Noel B. THE CUMBERLAND RIFLES. Doubleday, 1952. Post-Revolution events in Tennessee before the acquisition of statehood. 3783

--------. THE GOLDEN EAGLE. Doubleday, 1953. Fast-moving adventure and romance in the Mexican War. 3784

Giles, Janice Holt. THE BELIEVERS. Houghton, 1957. Story of a husband who accepted the Shaker beliefs and of his wife who could not. 3785

--------. JOHNNY OSAGE. Houghton, 1960. Johnny Fowler, white friend of the Osage Indians, falls in love with a mission worker. 3786

--------. THE LAND BEYOND THE MOUNTAINS. Houghton, 1958. A story of the settling of Kentucky and James Wilkinson's attempts to set up an empire in the west. 3787

Goodrich, Arthur. THE SIGN OF FREEDOM. Appleton, 1916. About a "bound boy" who ultimately finds freedom and achievement as a soldier in the Civil War. 3788

Gorman, Herbert Sherman. THE WINE OF SAN LORENZO. Farrar, 1945. The Mexican War--the battle of the Alamo and the surrender of Santa Anna. 3789

Graham, Shirley. THERE ONCE WAS A SLAVE. Messner, 1947. Frederick Douglass, the slave who escaped, obtained an education, and became a leading Abolitionist. 3790

Grant, Blanch. DOÑA LONA. Funk, 1941. A noble Spanish lady runs a gambling saloon in Santa Fe. 3791

Gray, Elizabeth. JANE HOPE. Viking, 1933. Home life at Chapel Hill, North Carolina, just before the Civil War. 3792

Gray, J. Thompson. A KENTUCKY CHRONICLE. Neale, 1906. Features the settling of Kentucky, particularly the founding and development of Louisville. 3793

Grebenc, Lucile. THE TIME OF CHANGE. Doubleday, 1938. New England farm life for a young widow and her infant son. 3794

Greve, Alice Wheeler. FROM OUT THIS HOUSE. Binfords, 1945. "A novel of the wagon train of 1847 and the tragic Whitman mission." 3795

--------. SHADOW ON THE PLAINS. Binfords, 1944. Indian attacks and massacre on the old Oregon Trail. 3796

Grey, Zane. THE BORDER LEGION. Harper, 1916. A maiden is captured by a band of desperadoes in southern Idaho. 3797

--------. DESERT GOLD. Harper, 1913. Border fighting between the United States and Mexico. 3798

--------. FIGHTING CARAVANS. Harcourt, 1929. Struggle for peace and a pioneer's romance along the old Santa Fe Trail. 3799

Gulick, Grover C. BEND OF THE SNAKE. by Bill Gulick, *pseud.* Houghton, 1950. Vigorous early competition among businessmen in the Washington Territory. 3800

Guthrie, Alfred Bertram. THE BIG SKY. Sloane, 1947. The coming of the white man to the West--his dreams and determination. 3801

--------. THE WAY WEST. Sloane, 1949. Adventures and

hardships of an overland trek from Missouri to Oregon. 3802

Hackney, Louise. WING OF FAME. Appleton, 1934. A story of James Smithson, who provided for the founding of the Smithsonian Institution. 3803

Hall, Rubylea. THE GREAT TIDE. Duell, 1947. A yellow fever epidemic and a torrential hurricane ravage St. Joseph, Florida. 3804

Hallet, Richard M. MICHAEL BEAM. Houghton, 1939. Tale of a frontiersman and his two loves--one for an Indian maid. 3805

Ham, Tom. GIVE US THIS VALLEY. Macmillan, 1952. The hardships of a young couple from Pennsylvania who settle in Georgia. 3806

Hancock, Albert E. BRONSON OF THE RABBLE. Lippincott, 1909. The romance and military exploits of a blacksmith's son who marries a senator's daughter. 3807

Hargreaves, Sheba. THE CABIN AT THE TRAIL'S END. Harper, 1928. An interesting, well-told tale of early pioneers in Oregon. 3808

--------. HEROINE OF THE PRAIRIES. Harper, 1930. Clear picture of a frontier settlement on the Oregon Trail. 3809

Harper, Robert S. TRUMPET IN THE WILDERNESS. Mill, 1940. A young man goes west to make his fortune and becomes involved in the War of 1812. 3810

Harris, Cyril. STREET OF KNIVES. Little, 1950. The story of Aaron Burr's trip to Mexico and his arrest for treason. 3811

Harris, Laura B. BRIDE OF THE RIVER. Crowell, 1956. A plantation girl adjusts to life as the bride of a Mississippi riverboatman. 3812

Harris, Margaret and John. CHANT OF THE HAWK. Random, 1959. A strong novel of mountain men and trappers along the Oregon Trail. 3813

Havighurst, Walter. THE WINDS OF SPRING. Macmillan, 1940. A refreshing story of Wisconsin with a pioneer ornithologist as hero. 3814

Hawkins, Anne. TO THE SWIFT. Harper, 1949. The heroic devotion to duty of the Pony Express riders. 3815

Hawthorne, Nathaniel. THE BLITHEDALE ROMANCE. Houghton, 1852. Story of two girls at Brooks Farm based on incidents in Hawthorne's participation in that experiment in communal living. 3816

--------. THE HOUSE OF THE SEVEN GABLES. Ticknor, Reed & Fields, 1851. Eccentric individuals in the last generation of a decaying family. 3817

Haycox, Ernest. CANYON PASSAGE. Little, 1945. Misplaced loyalty and an Indian uprising on the Oregon-California trail interrupt the course of love. 3818

--------. THE EARTHBREAKERS. Little, 1952. A group of sturdy pioneers cross plains and mountains to settle in the Oregon Territory. 3819

Hazelton, George C., Jr. THE RAVEN. Appleton, 1909. The unhappy life, the romance, and the tragic death of the famed poet, Edgar Allan Poe. 3820

Henkle, Henrietta. DEEP RIVER. by Henrietta Buckmaster, _pseud._ Harcourt, 1944. An anti-slavery mountaineer from Georgia leads in the fight for the Union. 3821

--------. FIRE IN THE HEART. by Henrietta Buckmaster, _pseud._ Harcourt, 1948. Based on the life and career of the famous theater star, Fanny Kemble. 3822

Hepburn, Andrew. LETTER OF MARQUE. Little, 1959. American sailors, impressed into British service, escape and turn privateer. 3823

Hergesheimer, Joseph. BALISAND. Knopf, 1924. A duel

over a girl's love is interrupted by her death, but is fought sixteen years later. 3824

-------. JAVA HEAD. Knopf, 1919. The seafaring traders of Salem, one of whom brings home an Oriental wife. 3825

Hinckley, Helen. THE MOUNTAINS ARE MINE. Vanguard, 1946. A young Mormon girl is involved in a polygamous marriage. 3826

Hogan, Pendleton. THE DARK COMES EARLY. Washburn, 1934. Romance set during the Texans' struggle for independence from Mexico. 3827

Holland, Josiah Gilbert. MISS GILBERT'S CAREER. Scribner, 1860. Life in a Yankee factory town. 3828

Holt, Felix. DAN'L BOONE KISSED ME. Dutton, 1954. Warm story of young love and western Kentucky life. 3829

--------. THE GABRIEL HORN. Dutton, 1951. A tale of settlers of the West, narrated by a little boy. 3830

Hough, Emerson. THE COVERED WAGON. Appleton, 1922. Part of a wagon caravan bound for Oregon is deflected to California by news of gold. 3831

--------. 54-40 OR FIGHT. Bobbs, 1909. The controversy between the young United States and Great Britain over the northwest boundary. 3832

--------. THE MAGNIFICENT ADVENTURE. Appleton, 1916. The Lewis and Clark expedition, Theodosia Burr, and the Louisiana Purchase. 3833

--------. THE PURCHASE PRICE. Bobbs, 1910. Impact of the Slavery Question on mid-century politics and life. 3834

--------. THE WAY OF A MAN. Methuen, 1907. Conflict of political ideals and commercial interests in the South just prior to the Civil War. 3835

Hough, Henry B. LONG ANCHORAGE. Appleton, 1947. New Bedford when the whaling industry was thriving and the textile industry growing. 3836

Howells, William Dean. LEATHERWOOD GOD. Century, 1916. Joseph Dylks claims to be a god in a pioneer Ohio community about 1830. 3837

Hubbard, Elbert. TIME AND CHANCE. Putnam, 1901. This story tells of Capt. John Brown of the Harper's Ferry incident. 3838

Hubbard, Lucien. RIVERS TO THE SEA. S. & S., 1942. A story of steamboating between Pittsburgh and New Orleans--full of action and suspense. 3839

Hueston, Ethel. THE MAN OF THE STORM. Bobbs, 1936. Incorporation of St. Louis, as part of the Louisiana Purchase, into the United States, and adventures of explorer John Colter. 3840

--------. STAR OF THE WEST. Bobbs, 1935. An account of the Lewis and Clark Expedition to the Pacific Northwest. 3841

Hughes, Rupert. THE GOLDEN LADDER. Harper, 1924. A romance of Aaron Burr and his wife, Betty Bowen, telling of his duel with Hamilton. 3842

Hutchens, Jane. TIMOTHY LARKIN. Doubleday, 1942. Missouri family, abandoned by the father, in the decade before the Civil War. 3843

Jackson, Helen Hunt. RAMONA. Little, 1884. The cruelty of the white man in driving the Indian from his land in early California. 3844

Janet, Lillian, pseud. for Janet Cicchetti and Lillian Ressler Groom. TOUCHSTONE. Rinehart, 1947. Romantic triangle in California after the gold rush. 3845

Jennings, John. RIVER TO THE WEST. Doubleday, 1948. A novel of John Jacob Astor's fur business in the

Pacific Northwest. 3846

--------. THE SALEM FRIGATE. Doubleday, 1946. Adventure on the frigate Essex in action against the Barbary pirates. 3847

--------. SHADOWS IN THE DUSK. Little, 1955. Indians and Mexicans take over the government of Santa Fe by force. 3848

--------. THE TALL SHIPS. McGraw-Hill, 1958. About American privateers who harass British shipping in the War of 1812. 3849

--------. TIDE OF EMPIRE. by Bates Baldwin, pseud. Holt, 1952. About a young South Carolinian who has some contact with Jerome Bonaparte and his American wife. 3850

Johnston, Mary. LEWIS RAND. Houghton, 1908. Burr's conspiracy figures in this tale of a French lawyer in Virginia during Jefferson's administration. 3851

--------. MISS DELICIA ALLEN. Little, 1933. Gracious, cultured life on a Virginia plantation before and during the Civil War. 3852

Jones, Idwal. VERMILION. Prentice-Hall, 1947. A celebrated cinnabar mine in California and several generations of owners. 3853

Jones, Madison. FOREST OF THE NIGHT. Harcourt, 1960. A conscientious schoolteacher attempts to bring education to a backward Tennessee frontier village. 3854

Jones, Nard. SCARLET PETTICOAT. Dodd, 1941. Fur trading on the Columbia River. 3855

--------. SWIFT FLOWS THE RIVER. Dodd, 1940. Rugged pioneering in the magnificent Columbia River Valley. 3856

Jordan, Mildred A. ASYLUM FOR THE QUEEN. Knopf, 1948. Pennsylvania is considered as a refuge for the Queen during the French Revolution. 3857

Kane, Harnett T. THE GALLANT MRS. STONEWALL. Doubleday, 1957. The marriage of Anna and Thomas Jackson and his rise to fame in the Civil War. 3858

--------. LADY OF ARLINGTON. Doubleday, 1953. Story of Robert E. Lee's wife, Mary Custis Lee. 3859

--------. NEW ORLEANS WOMAN. Doubleday, 1946. Courageous Myra Clark Gaines, who fought for her mother's reputation and her own inheritance. 3860

--------. PATHWAY TO THE STARS. Doubleday, 1950. The financial success of a Baltimore man in New Orleans. 3861

Kelland, Clarence Budington. HARD MONEY. Harper, 1930. Story of a young Dutchman who establishes a successful bank in New York. (followed by GOLD) 3862

Kelley, Welbourn. ALABAMA EMPIRE. Rinehart, 1957. Adventures of a Scots doctor who came to practice medicine in the young United States. 3863

Kendrick, Baynard Hardwick. THE FLAMES OF TIME. Scribner, 1948. Florida at the time it passed from the Spanish flag to the American. 3864

Kennedy, John P. SWALLOW BARN. Putnam, 1832. Happy, peaceful life of southern hospitality in pre-Civil War Virginia. 3865

Kester, Vaughan. PRODIGAL JUDGE. Bobbs, 1911. Rambling tale with a disreputable judge as hero. 3866

Keyes, Frances Parkinson. THE CHESS PLAYERS. Farrar, 1960. Career of a great chess player of New Orleans who may have been a Confederate agent. 3867

Kirkland, Elithe. DIVINE AVERAGE. Little, 1952. Combines adventure with a study of relations between Texans, Indians, and Mexicans. 3868

--------. LOVE IS A WILD ASSAULT. Doubleday, 1959. Fictional biography of a Texas pioneer woman who married three times and had eighteen children. 3869

Kirkland, Joseph. THE McVEYS. Houghton, 1888. The day-to-day struggles of people who settled on the Illinois plains. 3870

--------. ZURY, THE MEANEST MAN IN SPRING COUNTY. Houghton, 1887. Pioneer life on the Illinois prairie. 3871

Kirkman, Marshall Monroe. THE ROMANCE OF GILBERT HOLMES. Simpkin, 1902. A story with Lincoln and Jefferson Davis as young men. 3872

Knight, Ruth Adams. CERTAIN HARVEST. Doubleday, 1960. The story of Peter Cooper, inventor and industrialist, during the growth of New York. 3873

Krause, Herbert. THE OXCART TRAIL. Bobbs, 1954. Adventures of a young man involved in a killing on the Underground Railroad. 3874

Krey, Laura Lettie. ON THE LONG TIDE. Houghton, 1940. A story of Texas during its struggles for independence and statehood. 3875

Kroll, Harry Harrison. FURY IN THE EARTH. Bobbs, 1945. The effects on people and land of the New Madrid earthquake in the Mississippi Valley. 3876

--------. ROGUE'S COMPANION. Bobbs, 1943. The checkered career of a Mississippi Valley speculator. 3877

Kyne, Peter B. TIDE OF EMPIRE. Cosmopolitan Bk., 1928. A young Irishman's romance in gold rush California. 3878

La Farge, Oliver. THE LONG PENNANT. Houghton, 1933. A privateer's capture of a British ship in the Caribbean in the War of 1812. 3879

Laing, Alexander Kinnan. JONATHAN EAGLE. Duell, 1955. Land and sea exploits in a New England setting. 3880

--------. MATTHEW EARLY. Duell, 1957. A New England

sea captain's pursuit of romance. 3881

Laird, Charlton Grant. THUNDER ON THE RIVER. Little, 1949. Romance of a white captive and an Indian girl during the Black Hawk War in Illinois. 3882

--------. WEST OF THE RIVER. Little, 1953. Absorbing view of fur trading on the upper Mississippi. 3883

Lancaster, Bruce. FOR US, THE LIVING. Stokes, 1940. Pioneer life in Indiana, Illinois, and Kentucky, with young Abe Lincoln as a character. 3884

Lane, Carl D. THE FLEET IN THE FOREST. Coward, 1943. Perry's ships for the Battle of Lake Erie were built in the Pennsylvania forests. 3885

Lane, Elinor Macartney. THE MILLS OF GOD. Appleton, 1901. People and events in Virginia and Europe at the end of the century. 3886

Laughlin, Ruth. THE WIND LEAVES NO SHADOW. McGraw, 1948. The colorful days in New Mexico just before the Mexican War. 3887

Le May, Alan. PELICAN COAST. Doubleday, 1929. Piracy and smuggling in old New Orleans in the early 1800s. 3888

Lewis, Alfred Henry. THE THROWBACK. Cassell, 1906. Ranching in Texas in the 1850s included clashes with Indians. 3889

Lewis, Janet. THE INVASION. Harcourt, 1932. About the Johnston family of Michigan and the Ojibway tribe it married into. 3890

Lewis, Sinclair. THE GOD-SEEKER. Random, 1949. The story of a carpenter in St. Paul and his efforts to organize labor. 3891

Lewisohn, Ludwig. THE ISLAND WITHIN. Harper, 1928. A Jewish family, immigrating from Poland, comes into contact with American civilization. 3892

Lighton, W. Rheem. THE SHADOW OF A GREAT ROCK. Putnam, 1907. A tale of settlers in Nebraska who battled fierce Sioux to establish homes. 3893

Lillibridge, William Otis. WHERE THE TRAIL DIVIDES. Dodd, 1907. Dakota frontier life with cowboys and Indians. 3894

Lincoln, Joseph and Freeman. THE NEW HOPE. Coward, 1941. A Cape Cod privateer slips through the British blockade in the War of 1812. 3895

Linderman, Frank Bird. BEYOND LAW. Day, 1933. Indians and fur traders in the far West. 3896

Lion, Hortense. MILL STREAM. Houghton, 1941. Rhode Island during conflict over home industry or foreign trade. 3897

Lloyd, J. Uri. STRINGTOWN ON THE PIKE. Dodd, 1900. Kentucky just before the Civil War with a superstitious Negro the most notable character. 3898

Lofts, Norah. WINTER HARVEST. Doubleday, 1955. Study of four diverse people in the Donner party. 3899

Longstreth, Thomas. TWO RIVERS MEET IN CONCORD. Westminster, 1946. A novel which reflects Thoreau's strong social and political philosophy. 3900

Loomis, Noel M. THE TWILIGHTERS. Macmillan, 1955. A brutal and bloody story of migrants to Texas slaughtered by bandits. 3901

Lovelace, Maud Hart. THE BLACK ANGELS. Day, 1926. A travelling concert company, the Angel Family Concert Troupe, touring the Midwest. 3902

-------- and Delos Wheeler Lovelace. ONE STAYED AT WELCOME. Day, 1934. Romance and pioneering in Minnesota after the Mexican War. 3903

Lutes, Della. GABRIEL'S SEARCH. Little, 1940. Community life in Michigan among the sturdy pioneers who settled the territory. 3904

Lyle, Eugene P. THE LONE STAR. Page, 1907. The revolt of Texas Americans against Mexico, featuring Houston, Bowie, and Crockett. 3905

Lynn, Margaret. FREE SOIL. Macmillan, 1920. Struggles of free-soilers to build homes in frontier Kansas. 3906

Lytle, Andrew Nelson. THE LONG NIGHT. Bobbs, 1936. A boy's quest to revenge the murder of his father by Alabama gangsters. 3907

Mabie, Mary Louise. THE LONG KNIVES WALKED. Bobbs, 1932. Journey of a covered wagon on the Oregon Trail. 3908

McCarter, Margaret. VANGUARDS OF THE PLAINS. Harper, 1917. The part played by commercial enterprise in the development of the West. 3909

McCoy, Samuel. TIPPECANOE. Bobbs, 1916. An English immigrant to Indiana fights for the United States against Indians at Tippecanoe. 3910

McCulley, Johnston. CAPTAIN FLY-BY-NIGHT. Watt, 1926. Adventure in Mexican California during the second quarter of the nineteenth century. 3911

McCutcheon, George Barr. VIOLA GWYN. Dodd, 1922. A young lawyer comes to Indiana full of hatred and finds love. 3912

McIntyre, Marjorie. THE RIVER WITCH. Crown, 1955. A young girl has her own boat on the Mississippi and Missouri Rivers. 3913

McKee, Ruth E. CHRISTOPHER STRANGE. Doubleday, 1941. A young lawyer, raised and educated in the East, becomes a settler in California. 3914

MacKinnon, Mary Lineham. ONE SMALL CANDLE. Crown, 1956. Touching tale of a second wife's struggle for her husband's love. 3915

McMeekin, Clark, _pseud._ for Dorothy Clark and Isabel

McMeekin. RECKON WITH THE RIVER. Appleton, 1941. An eighty-year-old pioneer woman and her family in the Ohio Valley. 3916

--------. RED RASKALL. Appleton, 1943. An English girl who sails for America is shipwrecked off the coast of Virginia. 3917

McNeilly, Mildred Masterson. EACH BRIGHT RIVER. Morrow, 1950. A courageous southern girl is left alone in rugged Oregon when her fiancé commits suicide. 3918

--------. HEAVEN IS TOO HIGH. Morrow, 1944. A Russian aristocrat, fleeing the wrath of Empress Catherine, finds opportunity in the Pacific Northwest. 3919

Malkus, Alida Sims. CARAVANS TO SANTA FE. Harper, 1928. A young couple is beset by the cultural differences between Spanish grandees and American traders. 3920

Mally, Emma Louise. ABIGAIL. Appleton, 1956. A Yankee abolitionist girl, her Louisiana cousin, and the Underground Railroad. 3921

Malm, Dorothea. THE WOMAN QUESTION. Appleton, 1958. The fight of Susan B. Anthony and Lucy Stone to secure woman suffrage. 3922

Malvern, Gladys. MAMZELLE. Macrae Smith, 1955. Romance of a Louisiana girl in Washington in the company of Dolly Madison, wife of the President. 3923

Manfred, Frederick. LORD GRIZZLY. McGraw, 1954. Hugh Glass, injured by a bear, sought revenge on men he thought had deserted him. 3924

Markey, Gene. THAT FAR PARADISE. McKay, 1960. "Mad" Anthony Wayne and migration from Virginia to the Kentucky wilderness. 3925

Marshall, Edison. YANKEE PASHA. Farrar, 1947. Jason Starbuck's pursuit of romance and adventure. 3926

Masters, Edgar Lee. CHILDREN OF THE MARKET PLACE. Macmillan, 1922. An English youth inherits an estate in Illinois, where he comes to know Stephen Douglas. 3927

Maule, Mary Katherine. PRAIRIE-SCHOONER PRINCESS. Lothrop, 1920. Story of a child orphaned during the crossing of the plains and adopted by a Quaker family. 3928

Meeker, Arthur. FAR AWAY MUSIC. Houghton, 1945. Family life in Chicago in the 1850s. 3929

Meigs, Cornelia. CALL OF THE MOUNTAIN. Little, 1940. A Vermont boy's struggles to make his mountain farm productive. 3930

Melville, Herman. MOBY DICK. Harper, 1851. Classic tale of American whaling; Captain Ahab's mad obsession to kill the white whale which had injured him. 3931

Miller, Caroline. LAMB IN HIS BOSOM. Harper, 1933. Backwoods Georgia is the setting for this tale rich in local color. 3932

--------. LEBANON. Doubleday, 1944. The picturesque backwoods of Georgia and a lovely girl who lived there. 3933

Miller, Helen Topping. BORN STRANGERS. Bobbs, 1949. Pictures two families (the author's ancestors) in nineteenth century Michigan. 3934

--------. HER CHRISTMAS AT THE HERMITAGE. Longmans, 1955. A Christmas celebration of Rachel and Andrew Jackson before his presidential campaign. 3935

Minnigerode, Meade. COCKADES. Putnam, 1927. Based on the legend of the French Dauphin's escape to America after the French Revolution. 3936

Mitchell, S. Weir. FAR IN THE FOREST. Century, 1889.

About the courageous men who wrested their living from the wild forests of Pennsylvania. 3937

--------. THE RED CITY. Century, 1908. Washington's second term as President in Philadelphia, then the capital. 3938

--------. WESTWAYS. Century, 1913. Bitter controversy in a small northern village before the Civil War. 3939

Moberg, Vilhelm. UNTO A GOOD LAND. S. & S., 1954. The Swedish immigrants who came by sailboat, wagon, riverboat, and on foot to settle in Minnesota. 3940

Moore, John Trotwood. HEARTS OF HICKORY. Cokesbury, 1926. Exploits of Davy Crockett and Andrew Jackson in the War of 1812. 3941

Morgan, George. THE ISSUE. Lippincott, 1904. Political and social aspects of the slavery question in the South. 3942

Morrow, Honoré. BLACK DANIEL. Morrow, 1931. Daniel Webster, his second wife, Caroline, and their circle. 3943

--------. ON TO OREGON! Morrow, 1926. A thirteen-year-old boy grows up fast as tragedy strikes his family on their journey to Oregon. 3944

--------. WE MUST MARCH. Stokes, 1925. Narcissa Whitman and a band of pioneer missionaries journey across the Rockies to Oregon. 3945

Mudgett, Helen Parker. THE SEAS STAND WATCH. Knopf, 1944. The recovery of sea trade after the Revolutionary War. 3946

Mulford, Clarence E. BRING ME HIS EARS. McClurg, 1922. The American West of the Missouri River and the Santa Fe Trail. 3947

Murray, Charles A. THE PRAIRIE BIRD. Routledge, 1844. The Indians in the Ohio Valley several years after their defeat by General Wayne. 3948

Myers, John. THE WILD YAZOO. Dutton, 1947. Rough-and-ready pioneer life along the Yazoo River in Mississippi. 3949

Nathan, Leonard. WIND LIKE A BUGLE. Macmillan, 1954. Conflict between Abolitionists and the pro-slavery faction in Kansas. 3950

Neihardt, John G. SPLENDID WAYFARING. Macmillan, 1920. Vivid story of a frontiersman who explored the central overland route to the West. 3951

Nelson, Truman. THE SIN OF THE PROPHET. Little, 1952. The story of a runaway slave who was sent back into slavery. 3952

--------. THE SURVEYOR. Doubleday, 1960. John Brown's political activities in Kansas during its fight over admission as slave or free state. 3953

Nicholson, Meredith. THE CAVALIER OF TENNESSEE. Bobbs, 1928. A novel of Andrew Jackson--his romance, pioneering efforts, and election to the Presidency. 3954

Niles, Blair. EAST BY DAY. Farrar, 1941. Account of the Amistad case--a sailing ship on which a slave crew had seized control. 3955

O'Dell, Scott. HILL OF THE HAWK. Bobbs, 1947. Relations of Kit Carson and a frontiersman in early California. 3956

--------. THE ISLAND OF THE BLUE DOLPHINS. Houghton, 1960. Fate of a young Indian girl after tragedy strikes her tribe. 3957

--------. WOMAN OF SPAIN. Houghton, 1934. A Spanish señorita in early California is wooed by two Americans. 3958

O'Neill, Charles Kendall. MORNING TIME. S. & S., 1949. Post-Revolution life and Wilkinson's conspiracy with the Spanish. 3959

O'Rourke, Frank. THE FAR MOUNTAINS. by Frank O'-Malley, pseud. Morrow, 1959. The decline of Spanish influence in the territory that became New Mexico and Texas. 3960

Orr, Myron David. THE CITADEL OF THE LAKES. Dodd, 1952. Astor's attempt to monopolize the fur trade on Mackinac Island. 3961

--------. MISSION TO MACKINAC. Dodd, 1956. Relations between the English and the French before the outbreak of the War of 1812. 3962

Page, Elizabeth. WAGONS WEST. Farrar & Rinehart, 1930. Based on letters recounting a journey along the Oregon Trail to California. 3963

Parker, Cornelia Stratton. FABULOUS VALLEY. Putnam, 1956. Transformation of a quiet Pennsylvania farming town into a rowdy oil boom town. 3964

Parrish, Anne. A CLOUDED STAR. Harper, 1948. An ex-slave guides a small group northward on the Underground Railroad. 3965

Parrish, Randall. THE DEVIL'S OWN. McClurg, 1917. Exciting tale of the Black Hawk War of 1832 against white settlement of Indian land. 3966

--------. WHEN WILDERNESS WAS KING. McClurg, 1904. A story of the Illinois frontier and the massacre at Fort Dearborn. 3967

Partridge, Bellamy. THE BIG FREEZE. Crowell, 1948. The main historical event is the building of the Croton aqueduct in New York City. 3968

Pearce, Richard Elmo. THE IMPUDENT RIFLE. Lippincott, 1951. A West Point lieutenant campaigns for fair treatment for the Indians in Arkansas Territory. 3969

--------. THE RESTLESS BORDER. Lippincott, 1953. Captain Alexander Prince versus Santa Anna and the

Comanches on the Texas border. 3970

Peattie, Donald Culross. FORWARD THE NATION. Putnam, 1942. The Lewis and Clark Expedition and the Indian Bird Woman, Sacajawea, who guided it. 3971

Peeples, Samuel A. THE DREAM ENDS IN FURY. Harper, 1949. An abused Mexican, Joaquin Murrieta, turns bandit in California during the gold rush. 3972

Pendexter, Hugh. HARRY IDAHO. Bobbs, 1926. Tale of a lost gold mine, Mormon fanatics, Indian allies, and romance. 3973

--------. KINGS OF THE MISSOURI. Bobbs, 1921. The "kings" headed rival fur companies in the trade area around St. Louis. 3974

--------. OLD MISERY. Bobbs, 1924. California in the rough, roaring days following the discovery of gold. 3975

--------. A VIRGINIA SCOUT. Bobbs, 1922. The dangers and thrills of scouting frontier country with capture by Indians. 3976

Pidgin, Charles Felton. BLENNERHASSETT. Clark, 1902. Tells of the Blennerhassett-Burr conspiracy to conquer Texas and establish an independent empire. 3977

Pittman, Hannah D. THE HEART OF KENTUCKY. Neale, 1908. Factually based story of a murderer brought to justice in Kentucky. 3978

Poole, Ernest. THE NANCY FLYER. Crowell, 1949. The thrills of stagecoach driving in New England. 3979

Pope, Edith. RIVER IN THE WIND. Scribner, 1954. A spirited account of the Seminole War in Florida. 3980

Post, Waldron K. SMITH BRUNT. Putnam, 1899. A tale of the naval engagement in which Captain James Lawrence gave his famous command, "Don't give up the ship." 3981

Powers, Alfred. LONG WAY TO FRISCO. Little, 1951.

Tale of California and Oregon centered on a bankrupt miner's contract to deliver fourteen hundred hogs to San Francisco. 3982

Powers, Anne. IRONMASTER. Bobbs, 1951. The political and financial career of an early industrialist. 3983

Prescott, John. JOURNEY BY THE RIVER. Random, 1954. Westward journey of a pioneer wagon train. 3984

Pridgen, Tim. WEST GOES THE ROAD. Doubleday, 1944. The Midwest shortly after the Revolution. 3985

Pryor, Elinor. AND NEVER YIELD. Macmillan, 1942. Mormons in Missouri and Illinois confronted by neighbors' hatred as well as by wilderness hardships. 3986

Pryor, Sara Agnes. COLONEL'S STORY. by Mrs. Roger A. Pryor. Macmillan, 1911. A southern colonel on a hospitable plantation in ante-bellum Virginia. 3987

Putnam, George Palmer. HICKORY SHIRT. Duell, 1949. Two young men fight against each other and against the dangers of Death Valley. 3988

Putnam, Nina. THE INNER VOICE. Sheridan, 1940. This novel of a Quaker in the south gives an insight into the Quaker way of life. 3989

Pyle, Howard. WITHIN THE CAPES. Scribner, 1885. A sailor's adventures at sea and his romance at home. 3990

Quick, Herbert. THE HAWKEYE. Bobbs, 1923. The growth of a new nation, represented here by persevering Iowa pioneers. (followed by THE INVISIBLE WOMAN) 3991

--------. VANDEMARK'S FOLLY. Bobbs, 1922. An Erie Canal boatman searching for his lost mother eventually settles in Iowa. (followed by THE HAWKEYE) 3992

Ratigan, William. ADVENTURES OF CAPTAIN McCARGO. Random, 1956. Picaresque story of a hardy captain on the Great Lakes. 3993

Rayford, Julian Lee. CHILD OF THE SNAPPING TURTLE, MIKE FINK. Abelard, 1951. Frontier and river adventures of a famous scout, trapper, and boatman. 3994

Raynolds, Robert. BROTHERS IN THE WEST. Harper, 1931. Wanderings of two brothers in the Old West in mid-century. 3995

Read, Opie. BY THE ETERNAL. Laird & Lee, 1906. Adventure in New Orleans centering around Andrew Jackson. 3996

Reed, Myrtle. THE SHADOW OF VICTORY. Putnam, 1903. Indian warfare and the massacre at Fort Dearborn. 3997

Reed, Warren. SHE RODE A YELLOW STALLION. Bobbs, 1950. Three generations of a Scottish-American family in Wisconsin. 3998

Richardson, Norval. THE LEAD OF HONOUR. Page, 1910. The setting is Mississippi in the 1830s. 3999

Richter, Conrad. THE FIELDS. Knopf, 1946. Marriage of a pioneer girl to a Boston lawyer in early Ohio. (followed by THE TOWN) 4000

--------. THE TOWN. Knopf, 1950. Pioneer town which has grown gradually from a once dense forest in Ohio. 4001

--------. THE TREES. Knopf, 1940. Pioneers in Ohio clear a homesite in the forest. (followed by THE FIELDS) 4002

Rickert, Edith. OUT OF THE CYPRESS SWAMP. Baker & Taylor, 1902. Pirates, war against the British, and a color-line marriage problem in New Orleans around 1812. 4003

Roark, Garland. RAINBOW IN THE ROYALS. Doubleday, 1950. Sailing ships and seamanship during the California gold rush. 4004

--------. STAR IN THE RIGGING. Doubleday, 1954. "A novel of the Texas navy in their struggle for freedom." 4005

Roberts, Charles H. DOWN THE O-HI-O. McClurg, 1891. Quaker life in the Ohio Valley before the Civil War. 4006

Roberts, Elizabeth Madox. THE GREAT MEADOW. Viking, 1930. Migration of pioneers from Virginia to Kentucky describing the beauty of the country. 4007

Roberts, Kenneth. CAPTAIN CAUTION. Doubleday, Doran, 1934. A young first mate takes command of his ship on the death of his captain early in the War of 1812. 4008

--------. THE LIVELY LADY. Doubleday, 1931. When his ship is captured in the War of 1812, the captain is imprisoned at Dartmoor for a time. 4009

--------. LYDIA BAILEY. Doubleday, 1947. A young couple is caught up in the Haiti Revolution and the Tripolitan War. 4010

Roberts, Walter Adolphe. ROYAL STREET. Bobbs, 1944. Rise of a young man, skilled in fencing and politics, in New Orleans in the 1840s. 4011

Robertson, Constance. FIRE BELL IN THE NIGHT. Holt, 1944. Love of a girl for two men--one who favored the Underground Railroad, one who opposed it. 4012

Robison, Mabel Otis. PIONEER PANORAMA. Denison, 1957. Growing pains of Minnesota in the years from 1853 to 1866. 4013

Roe, Virginia. THE SPLENDID ROAD. Cassell, 1925. Pioneers on the Oregon Trail and in the Sacramento Valley. 4014

Rogers, Cameron. THE MAGNIFICENT IDLER. Doubleday, Page, 1926. Follows the life and career of the great American poet, Walt Whitman. 4015

Rogers, Robert C. WILL O' THE "WASP." Putnam, 1896. A sea story of the War of 1812 against England. 4016

Root, Corwin. AN AMERICAN, SIR. Dutton, 1940. A youth is persuaded by a pretty girl to fight in the War of 1812. 4017

Ross, Zola Helen. LAND TO TAME. Bobbs, 1956. Trouble between Indians and whites over "ceding" tribal lands. 4018

Ryan, Don. DEVIL'S BRIGADIER. Coward, 1954. Two brothers seek revenge for their father's murder in post-Revolutionary politics. 4019

Ryan, Marah Ellis. FOR THE SOUL OF RAFAEL. McClurg, 1906. A romantic triangle involving a Spanish family in California in the 1840s. 4020

Sabin, Edwin Legrand. WHITE INDIAN. Jacobs, 1925. An Englishman becomes a fur trapper and marries an Indian girl. 4021

Sass, Herbert R. LOOK BACK TO GLORY. Bobbs, 1933. Tidewater South Carolina in the seething period before secession. 4022

Savage, Les. DONIPHAN'S RIDE. Doubleday, 1959. A young soldier with Colonel Doniphan's First Missouri Volunteers in the Mexican War of 1846. 4023

Schachner, Nathan. THE SUN SHINES WEST. Appleton, 1943. Romance in Kansas just before the Civil War. 4024

Schaeffer, Evelyn Schuyler. ISABEL STIRLING. Scribner, 1920. A woman's life in New England and Arizona from the 1850s to the 1870s. 4025

Schumann, Mary. MY BLOOD AND MY TREASURE. Dial, 1941. Lovers find themselves on opposing sides in the War of 1812. 4026

Scott, Reva. SAMUEL BRANNAN AND THE GOLDEN FLEECE. Macmillan, 1944. Early days of the California Gold

Rush. 4027

Sedgwick, Catharine Maria. HOPE LESLIE. Harper, 1842. Life on a New England homestead. 4028

Seifert, Shirley. CAPTAIN GRANT. Lippincott, 1946. About Grant's military service and marriage to the start of the Civil War. 4029

--------. PROUD WAY. Lippincott, 1948. Varina Howell during the two years before her marriage to Jefferson Davis. 4030

--------. THOSE WHO GO AGAINST THE CURRENT. Lippincott, 1943. Exploration of the Missouri River and the founding of St. Louis. 4031

--------. THE THREE LIVES OF ELIZABETH. Lippincott, 1952. The heroine's marriages and life in Missouri, in Washington, D. C., and in New York. 4032

--------. THE TURQUOISE TRAIL. Lippincott, 1950. Based on a bride's diary of a trip from Missouri to Mexico during the Mexican War. 4033

Selby, John. ELEGANT JOURNEY. Rinehart, 1944. A Maryland landowner frees his slaves and moves his family to Wisconsin where he founds a town. 4034

Seton, Anya. DRAGONWYCK. Houghton, 1944. Discoveries of a poor New England girl who goes to live with her wealthy New York cousins. 4035

--------. MY THEODOSIA. Houghton, 1941. Romantic life and mysterious death of Aaron Burr's daughter. 4036

Settle, Mary Lee. KNOW NOTHING. Viking, 1960. Antebellum novel of plantation owners in what became West Virginia. 4037

--------. O BEULAH LAND. Viking, 1956. A war veteran claims his bounty land on the Virginia frontier. (followed by KNOW NOTHING) 4038

Shaftel, George Armin. GOLDEN SHORE. Coward, 1943.

Conflict and romance during the American conquest of California. 4039

Shepard, Odell and Willard Odell Shepard. HOLDFAST GAINES. Macmillan, 1946. Tale of an Indian boy raised by a white family during the last part of the eighteenth century. 4040

Sinclair, Harold. AMERICAN YEARS. Doubleday, 1938. Story of a small town, probably patterned on Bloomington, Illinois. 4041

Singmaster, Elsie. I SPEAK FOR THADDEUS STEVENS. Houghton, 1947. About the lawyer and stateman who wielded so much influence in Congress. 4042

Slaughter, Frank G. FORT EVERGLADES. Doubleday, 1951. A doctor in the Florida Everglades during the second Seminole War. 4043

--------. THE GOLDEN ISLE. Doubleday, 1947. A slave trader in Florida kidnaps a doctor to care for the slaves. 4044

--------. THE WARRIOR. Doubleday, 1956. Supposedly written by a blood-brother of the Seminole chief, Osceola. 4045

Small, Sidney. THE SPLENDID CALIFORNIANS. Bobbs, 1928. Spanish settlers in California fight Indians and Mexicans, as well as nature. 4046

Smith, Francis Hopkinson. THE FORTUNES OF OLIVER HORN. Scribner, 1902. Social and artistic life in Washington, New York, and the South. 4047

--------. KENNEDY SQUARE. Scribner, 1911. Life in Maryland with frequent references to literary figures such as Longfellow and Poe. 4048

Snedeker, Caroline Dale. SETH WAY. by Caroline Dale Owen. Houghton, 1917. New Harmony, Indiana: an experiment in communal living. 4049

Snow, Charles H. ARGONAUT GOLD. Macrae Smith, 1936. A wagon train trip westward through Wyoming and Nevada. 4050

Sorensen, Virginia. A LITTLE LOWER THAN THE ANGELS. Knopf, 1942. The Mormons' settlement at Nauvoo, Illinois, and the start of their move to Utah. 4051

Spearman, Frank H. CARMEN OF THE RANCHO. Doubleday, 1937. Romance of a lovely Spanish girl and a Texas scout in early California. 4052

Sperry, Armstrong. NO BRIGHTER GLORY. Macmillan, 1942. Concerns the Northwest when John Jacob Astor was building his fur trading empire. 4053

Spicer, Bart. THE WILD OHIO. Dodd, 1953. Refugees from the French Revolution face hardships in frontier Ohio. 4054

Stanford, Alfred Boller. THE NAVIGATOR. Morrow, 1927. The daring seamen of Salem and the achievements of navigator Nathaniel Bowditch. 4055

Stanley, Edward. THE ROCK CRIED OUT. Duell, 1949. The Blennerhassetts and the treason of Aaron Burr. 4056

Stern, Philip Van Doren. THE DRUMS OF MORNING. by Peter Storme, pseud. Doubleday, 1942. The son of a murdered Abolitionist grows up to continue his father's fight. 4057

Sterne, Emma Gelders. SOME PLANT OLIVE TREES. Dodd, 1937. The colony in Alabama established by Bonapartist refugees from France. 4058

Stevens, Sheppard. IN THE EAGLE'S TALON. Little, 1902. America and Paris before the Louisiana Purchase. 4059

Stevenson, Burton E. THE HERITAGE. Houghton, 1902. The courage of early Ohio settlers defending their new homes against Indians. 4060

Stevenson, Janet. THE ARDENT YEARS. Viking, 1960. The theatrical life and marriage of English actress Fanny Kemble and American Pierce Butler. 4061

Steward, Davenport. RAINBOW ROAD. Tupper, 1953. The discovery of gold in Georgia brings a rush of fortune seekers. 4062

--------. THEY HAD A GLORY. Tupper, 1952. Frontier hardships of a Revolutionary War veteran. 4063

Stewart, George Rippey. EAST OF THE GIANTS. Holt, 1938. New England ship captain's daughter meets a Spanish rancher in California. 4064

--------. ORDEAL BY HUNGER. Holt, 1936. The endurance and perseverance of the Donner wagon train against overpowering hazards. 4065

Stone, Irving. IMMORTAL WIFE. Doubleday, 1944. The heroine is Jessie Benton Fremont, whose husband was once a presidential candidate. 4066

--------. LOVE IS ETERNAL. Doubleday, 1954. A novel about Mary Todd and Abraham Lincoln and the transition from Springfield, Illinois, to Washington, D. C. 4067

--------. THE PRESIDENT'S LADY. Doubleday, 1951. Based on the lives of Rachel and Andrew Jackson. 4068

Stong, Philip. BUCKSKIN BREECHES. Farrar, 1937. Account of a family from Ohio on the Iowa frontier. 4069

--------. FORTY POUNDS OF GOLD. Doubleday, 1951. Two young men from Ohio head west in search of gold. 4070

Stowe, Harriet Beecher. DRED. Houghton, 1896. An attack on the evils and intolerance of slavery. 4071

--------. THE MINISTER'S WOOING. Houghton, 1859. Life and religion in New England at the end of the eighteenth century. 4072

--------. UNCLE TOM'S CABIN. Houghton, 1852. Classic, impassioned tale of the brutality of slavery, which was used for the emancipation cause. 4073

Strachey, Rachel. MARCHING ON. by Ray Strachey, pseud. Harcourt, 1923. The story of a young woman caught up in the Abolitionist movement. 4074

Street, James Howell. OH, PROMISED LAND. Dial, 1940. An orphaned brother and sister in Georgia, Alabama, and Mississippi. 4075

Stuart, Charles Duff. CASA GRANDE: A CALIFORNIA PASTORAL. Holt, 1906. Land disputes in California resulting from the change in government. 4076

Suckow, Ruth. COUNTRY PEOPLE. Knopf, 1924. Three generations of a German family who settled in Iowa. 4077

Summers, Richard Aldrich. VIGILANTE. Duell, 1949. A California politician is the object of the Vigilantes' pursuit. 4078

Swanson, Neil. THE PHANTOM EMPEROR. Putnam, 1934. James Dickson, calling himself Montezuma II, attempted to win a kingdom in the West. 4079

Sweeny, Sarah L. HARVEST OF THE WIND. Caxton, 1935. Pioneer Kansas in the period between the Kansas-Nebraska Bill and the Civil War. 4080

Swift, Hildegarde Hoyt. THE RAILROAD TO FREEDOM. Harcourt, 1932. Harriet Tubman, born a slave in Maryland, escapes and works on the Underground Railroad. 4081

Tate, Allen. THE FATHERS. Putnam, 1938. Decline of a large estate in Virginia just before the Civil War. 4082

Tebbel, John William. VOICE IN THE STREETS. Dutton, 1954. A poor Irishman attains success in New York City. 4083

Teilhet, Darwin Le Ora. STEAMBOAT ON THE RIVER. Sloane, 1952. Eventful journey of a steamboat on the

Sangamon with the youthful Abe Lincoln included. 4084

Terhune, Mary Virginia. CARRINGTONS OF HIGH HILL. by Marion Harland, pseud. Scribner, 1919. An old southern family and its perplexing mystery. 4085

Terrell, John Upton. PLUME ROGUE. Viking, 1942. Pioneers follow the route of Lewis and Clark from St. Louis to the Columbia River. 4086

Tiernan, Mary Spear. HOMOSELLE. Fenno, 1881. Rich picture of southern life on the James River. 4087

--------. SUZETTE. Holt, 1885. Richmond family life in a society founded on slavery. 4088

Titus, Harold. BLACK FEATHER. Macrae Smith, 1936. Action-packed story of a fur trader in Michigan. 4089

Todd, Helen. SO FREE WE SEEM. Reynal, 1936. A courageous mother, deserted by her husband, is left to manage their Missouri farm. 4090

Tracy, Don. CHEROKEE. Dial, 1957. White man's mistreatment of the Cherokees in the Great Smokies. 4091

--------. CRIMSON IS THE EASTERN SHORE. Dial, 1953. The War of 1812 on the eastern coast of Maryland. 4092

Troyer, Howard W. THE SALT AND THE SAVOR. Wyn, 1950. Frontier life in Ohio from the 1840s through the Civil War. 4093

Tupper, Edith S. HEARTS TRIUMPHANT. Appleton, 1906. A romance set in New York with Aaron Burr and Jerome Bonaparte as figures. 4094

Vachell, Horace Annesley. JOHN CHARITY. Dodd, 1901. A story of romance and political activity in England and California in the 1830s. 4095

Valentine, Edward Abram Uffington. HECLA SANDWITH. Bobbs, 1905. The Quakers who settled in Pennsylvania in the 1850s. 4096

Van Every, Dale. THE SCARLET FEATHER. Holt, 1959. Families with different cultural backgrounds adjust to Kentucky pioneer life. 4097

--------. THE SHINING MOUNTAINS. Messner, 1948. The extension of our country's frontiers with the Lewis and Clark Expedition. 4098

--------. THE TREMBLING EARTH. Messner, 1953. The New Madrid earthquake in lead-mining southeastern Missouri. 4099

--------. WESTWARD THE RIVER. Putnam, 1945. An Ohio Valley romance showing international influences in the young American nation. 4100

Venable, Clarke. ALL THE BRAVE RIFLES. Reilly & Lee, 1929. Life in frontier Texas, including fighting at the Alamo and claim jumping. 4101

Ward, Christopher. STRANGE ADVENTURES OF JONATHAN DREW. S. & S., 1932. A wandering New England peddler in the 1820s. (followed by A YANKEE ROVER) 4102

--------. A YANKEE ROVER. S. & S., 1932. An itinerant New England peddler in the Southwest. 4103

Warren, Lella. FOUNDATION STONE. Knopf, 1940. About a southern family from the 1820s through the Civil War. 4104

Warren, Robert Penn. WORLD ENOUGH AND TIME. Random, 1950. Famous Kentucky trial of Jeremiah Beaumont, charged with a Colonel's murder. 4105

Waters, Gladys. FAIRACRES. Waters Press, 1952. Spirited tale of slave running and of the founding of Independence, Missouri. 4106

Watkin, Lawrence Edward. GENTLEMAN FROM ENGLAND. Knopf, 1941. Life in America when freedom and independence were new, exciting possessions. 4107

Weld, John. DON'T YOU CRY FOR ME. Scribner, 1940.

The determination of a wagon train to California, based largely on the Donner party tragedy. 4108

Wellman, Paul I. THE COMANCHEROS. Doubleday, 1952. A New Orleans gambler becomes a Texas Ranger and fights the Comancheros. 4109

--------. THE IRON MISTRESS. Doubleday, 1951. About a famous fighter of the Old West, Jim Bowie, whose favorite weapon was a bowie knife. 4110

Welty, Eudora. THE ROBBER BRIDEGROOM. Doubleday, 1942. Imaginative story of a bandit and a beautiful girl. 4111

Wetherell, June. THE GLORIOUS THREE. Dutton, 1951. The hard trip across the wilderness from Connecticut to Oregon. 4112

White, Stewart Edward. THE BLAZED TRAIL. McClure, 1902. A vivid story of the lumber industry in Michigan. 4113

--------. FOLDED HILLS. Doubleday, 1934. An American man, his Spanish-American wife, and their small son on their southern California ranch. 4114

--------. GOLD. Doubleday, Page, 1913. The wild, rough life in California following the gold strike of '49. (followed by THE GRAY DAWN) 4115

--------. THE GRAY DAWN. Doubleday, Page, 1915. San Francisco in the wild 1850s when decent citizens banded together as Vigilantes. (followed by ROSE DAWN) 4116

--------. THE LONG RIFLE. Doubleday, Doran, 1932. Trapping in the Rockies and life with Blackfoot Indians of a youth who inherited Daniel Boone's rifle. 4117

--------. RANCHERO. Doubleday, 1933. Andy Burnett settles in California and courts a Spanish girl. 4118

--------. THE RIVERMAN. McClure, 1908. Michigan's rugged lumberjacks and the thriving timber business. 4119

--------. STAMPEDE. Doubleday, 1942. Action-packed story of the feud between ranchers and squatters in California. 4120

Whitlock, Brand. THE STRANGER ON THE ISLAND. Appleton, 1933. An outsider's love for a member of a religious sect which practices polygamy. 4121

Whitney, Janet. INTRIGUE IN BALTIMORE. Little, 1951. Irish-educated youth claims his Baltimore estate. 4122

--------. JUDITH. Morrow, 1943. Tangled romances of a young doctor amid Philadelphia's yellow fever epidemic. 4123

Wilder, Robert. BRIGHT FEATHER. Putnam, 1948. The war which resulted from the attempt to force the Seminole Indians to leave their homes. 4124

Williams, Ben Ames. STRANGE WOMAN. Houghton, 1941. A wicked, though beautiful, woman destroys her admirers. 4125

--------. THREAD OF SCARLET. Houghton, 1939. The War of 1812 around the island of Nantucket with an account of a naval engagement. 4126

Williams, Cecil B. PARADISE PRAIRIE. Day, 1953. Saga of Oklahoma in pioneer times. 4127

Williams, Mary Floyd. FORTUNE, SMILE ONCE MORE! Bobbs, 1946. An Australian convict and an English lady's maid in San Francisco. 4128

Wills, Grace E. MURPHY'S BEND. Westminster, 1946. Pioneer settlers in the Susquehanna River Valley early in the nineteenth century. 4129

Willsie, Honoré McCue. BENEFITS FORGOT. Stokes, 1917. A loving mother sacrifices everything for her unappreciative son. 4130

Wilson, Harry Leon. THE LIONS OF THE LORDS. Lothrop, 1903. Brigham Young's Mormon settlement at Salt Lake. 4131

Wilson, William E. ABE LINCOLN OF PIGEON CREEK. McGraw, 1949. Fictional story of the young Abraham Lincoln in Indiana. 4132

Woolson, Constance Fenimore. EAST ANGELS. Harper, 1886. Peaceful Georgia before the Civil War changed its way of life. 4133

Wyckoff, Nicholas E. THE CORINTHIANS. Macmillan, 1960. The two different households of a Mormon, one in Illinois and one in Missouri. 4134

Yates, Elizabeth. HUE AND CRY. Coward, 1953. An organization to catch horse thieves in New Hampshire. 4135

Yerby, Frank. FAIROAKS. Dial, 1957. A vast southern plantation and the controversial slave trade. 4136

--------. THE FOXES OF HARROW. Dial, 1946. Stephen Fox, who rose from poverty to establish a great plantation. 4137

--------. THE TREASURE OF PLEASANT VALLEY. Dial, 1955. A man settles in California during the Gold Rush. 4138

Young, Gordon Ray. DAYS OF '49. Doran, 1925. A man's search for his brother's runaway wife reveals a cross-section of gold-rush California. 4139

Young, Stark. HEAVEN TREES. Scribner, 1926. Luxurious life on a gracious, hospitable Mississippi plantation. 4140

Zelley, Frankie Lee. FAREWELL THE STRANGER. by Saliee O'Brien, pseud. Morrow, 1956. Devora Griggs' fight for her marriage was harder than her fights with Indian raiders. 4141

III. C. 1. d. Civil War Period (1861-1865)

Allen, Hervey. ACTION AT AQUILA. Farrar, 1938. A Civil War romance centering on the battle at Aquila. 4142

Allen, James Lane. THE SWORD OF YOUTH. Century, 1915. A youth, longing to be a soldier, is torn between duty to a dying mother and patriotism. 4143

Allis, Marguerite. THE RISING STORM. Putnam, 1955. Opposing views of slavery held by twin brothers cause conflict; operation of the Underground Railroad. 4144

Andrews, Mary R. S. THE PERFECT TRIBUTE. Scribner, 1906. The character and magnetism of Lincoln win the respect of a dying Confederate officer. 4145

Appell, George Charles. MAN WHO SHOT QUANTRILL. Doubleday, 1957. Curtis Blakeman of the Union Army, who pursued Quantrill's guerrillas. 4146

Ashley, Robert. THE STOLEN TRAIN. Winston, 1953. A story of the Andrews Raiders. 4147

Babcock, Mrs. Bernie. SOUL OF ABE LINCOLN. Lippincott, 1923. Romance of two young people caught up in the swirl of war and influenced greatly by Lincoln. 4148

Babcock, William Henry. KENT FORT MANOR. Coates, 1902. A story of civilian life in and around war-time Washington. 4149

Bacheller, Irving. FATHER ABRAHAM. Bobbs, 1925. Conflict between a northern boy and his southern relatives, with Lincoln introduced as a hero of youth. 4150

Barney, Helen Corse. GREEN ROSE OF FURLEY. Crown, 1953. A Quaker station on the Underground Railroad. 4151

Basso, Hamilton. THE LIGHT INFANTRY BALL. Doubleday, 1959. Deterioration of southern society in the conflict of beliefs and arms. 4152

Bechdolt, Frederick Ritchie. BOLD RAIDERS OF THE WEST. Doubleday, 1940. New Mexico in the wild, rough times when the West was still young. 4153

Beebe, Elswyth Thane. YANKEE STRANGER. by Elswyth Thane. Duell, 1944. Civilian life behind the front lines during hostilities. (followed by EVER AFTER) 4154

Bell, John. MOCCASIN FLOWER. Bk. Masters, 1935. The Sioux uprising near St. Paul in 1862. 4155

Bellah, James Warner. THE VALIANT VIRGINIANS. Ballantine, 1953. Courage of the Virginia cavalry under Early and its battle with Sheridan. 4156

Benadum, Clarence Edward. BATES HOUSE. Greenberg, 1951. Civil War story of a southern girl and a Yankee lawyer. 4157

Bennett, John Henry. SO SHALL THEY REAP. Doubleday, 1944. Two groups of southerners carry on their traditional family feud despite the war. 4158

Benson, Blackwood Ketcham. BAYARD'S COURIER. Macmillan, 1902. Story of a cavalryman's love and adventure. 4159

--------. A FRIEND WITH THE COUNTERSIGN. Macmillan, 1901. Both sides of the war as seen by a Union spy. 4160

--------. OLD SQUIRE. Macmillan, 1903. The adventures of a Negro who takes part in the Gettysburg campaign. 4161

--------. WHO GOES THERE? Macmillan, 1900. A Federal spy, who has lost his memory, serves with the Rebel army. (followed by A FRIEND WITH THE COUNTERSIGN) 4162

Blech, William James. THE COPPERHEADS. by William Blake, pseud. Dial, 1941. Effects of the war on New York City and on the romance of a German immigrant's daughter. 4163

Borland, Hal. THE AMULET. Lippincott, 1957. Young Colorandan delays his wedding to fight for the Confederacy in Missouri. 4164

Boyd, James. MARCHING ON. Scribner, 1927. Experiences of a southern soldier and prisoner-of-war. 4165

Boyd, Thomas Alexander. SAMUEL DRUMMOND. Scribner, 1925. The plight of an industrious Iowa farmer caught in the conflict and aftermath of war. 4166

Bradford, Roark. KINGDOM COMING. Harper, 1933. Southern Negro's viewpoint of plantation life, the Civil War, and post-bellum changes. 4167

--------. THREE-HEADED ANGEL. Harper, 1937. A southern family's struggle for material wealth which was their criterion of success. 4168

Brady, Cyrus Townsend. THE PATRIOTS. Dodd, 1906. Hardships of the final years of the war; Lee's surrender to Grant at Appomattox. 4169

--------. THE SOUTHERNERS. Scribner, 1903. Scene of this Civil War story is Mobile, Alabama. 4170

Branch, Houston and Frank Waters. DIAMOND HEAD. Farrar, 1948. The southern cruiser *Shenandoah* pursues New England whalers. 4171

Brick, John. JUBILEE. Doubleday, 1956. Sherman's famous--or infamous--"March to the Sea." 4172

--------. TROUBLED SPRING. Farrar, 1950. Union soldier returns from Andersonville prison to find his brother married to his sweetheart. 4173

Brier, Royce. BOY IN BLUE. Appleton, 1937. A Union soldier's experiences in the Cumberland Valley and at the Battle of Chickamauga. 4174

Bristow, Gwen. THE HANDSOME ROAD. Crowell, 1938. Concerns two southern women--one an aristocrat, the other from the "poor white" class. 4175

Brooks, Asa Passavant. THE RESERVATION. Brooks, 1908. "A romance of the pioneer days of Minnesota and of the Indian Massacre of 1862." 4176

Brown, Karl. CUP OF TREMBLING. Duell, 1953. Frederick Stowe, son of Harriet Beecher Stowe. 4177

Buckley, R. Wallace. THE LAST OF THE HOUGHTONS. Neale, 1907. The strain and breaking of family ties resulting from opposing loyalties in the war. 4178

Burchell, Sidney Herbert. THE SHEPHERD OF THE PEOPLE. Gay & Hancock, 1924. Social life in the nation's capital during the opening years of the war. 4179

Burnett, William Riley. THE DARK COMMAND. Knopf, 1938. Kansas and Missouri during the war. 4180

Burress, John. BUGLE IN THE WILDERNESS. Vanguard, 1958. Domestic problems of a rural Missouri family are intensified by wartime stress. 4181

Buster, Greene B. BRIGHTER SUN. Pageant, 1954. Escape from a Kentucky plantation via the Underground Railroad. 4182

Cable, George Washington. THE CAVALIER. Scribner, 1903. The Confederate view of the war in Mississippi in the early years. 4183

--------. KINCAID'S BATTERY. Scribner, 1908. New Orleans at the start of the war, with a young artillery officer as hero. 4184

Campbell, Marie. A HOUSE WITH STAIRS. Rinehart, 1950. Story of two girls, one white, one Negro, on a southern plantation. 4185

Campbell, Thomas B. OLD MISS. Houghton, 1929. The happy childhood and tranquil early married life of a Virginia lady is tragically interrupted by the war. 4186

Castor, Henry. THE SPANGLERS. Doubleday, 1948. A Pennsylvania Dutch family and a brief look at unspeakably horrible Andersonville prison. 4187

Chambers, Robert W. AILSA PAIGE. Appleton, 1910. New York during the firing on Fort Sumter and the gay quality of the first wave of war enthusiasm. 4188

--------. SECRET SERVICE OPERATOR 13. Appleton, 1934. An account of the devious methods of obtaining and passing information during the war. 4189

--------. WHISTLING CAT. Appleton, 1932. Two young Texans serve as telegraphers for the Union Army. 4190

Cochran, John Salisbury. BONNIE BELMONT. Cochran, 1907. "Historical romance of the days of slavery and the Civil War" in Ohio. 4191

Coker, Elizabeth Boatwright. LA BELLE. Dutton, 1959. Based on the life of a famous southern beauty who, with her mother, became a camp-follower to Sherman's troops. 4192

Cooke, John Esten. MOHUN. Dillingham, 1869. The Army of North Virginia and wretched condition of Lee's soldiers, ending with the surrender at Appomattox. 4193

--------. SURRY OF EAGLE'S NEST. Dillingham, 1866. A Confederate view of the war, with pictures of Jackson and Jeb Stuart. 4194

Corbett, Elizabeth. FAYE'S FOLLY. Appleton, 1941. Political, social, and romantic events at Faye's Folly, an Illinois farm. 4195

Crabb, Alfred Leland. DINNER AT BELMONT. Bobbs, 1942. A story of captured Nashville. 4196

--------. HOME TO TENNESSEE. Bobbs, 1952. Emphasis is on the strategy of war in an effort to recapture Nashville. 4197

--------. LODGING AT THE SAINT CLOUD. Bobbs, 1946. Tale of occupied Nashville with Yankee soldiers seeking southern spies. 4198

--------. A MOCKINGBIRD SANG AT CHICKAMAUGA. Bobbs, 1949. A tale of embattled Chattanooga, told from the Confederate viewpoint. 4199

--------. PEACE AT BOWLING GREEN. Bobbs, 1955. A novel about life in Kentucky. 4200

Crane, Stephen. THE RED BADGE OF COURAGE. Appleton, 1895. The growth and maturing of an inexperienced soldier in the Civil War, especially at the Battle of Chancellorsville. 4201

Dahlinger, Charles W. WHERE THE RED VOLLEYS POURED. Dillingham, 1907. Battles and campaigns of the war including Centreville, Fredericksburg, and Gettysburg. 4202

Davis, Clyde Brion. NEBRASKA COAST. Farrar, 1939. A farm family moves west to avoid the Civil War and builds a full life in Nebraska. 4203

Davis, Julia. BRIDLE THE WIND. Rinehart, 1953. A Virginia lady achieves reconciliation with her husband after helping a fugitive slave escape. 4204

De Forest, John W. MISS RAVENEL'S CONVERSION FROM SECESSION TO LOYALTY. Harper, 1867. A contemporary novel reflecting American sentiments at the time. 4205

Deland, Margaret. THE KAYS. Harper, 1926. The unpopularity of a pacifist mother and her conscientious objector son. 4206

Demarest, Phyllis Gordon. WILDERNESS BRIGADE. Doubleday, 1957. A Union soldier, an escaped prisoner-of-war, is rescued by and later marries a southern girl. 4207

Devon, Louis. AIDE TO GLORY. Crowell, 1952. Story of General Grant's aide-de-camp and subsequent Secretary of War, John Rawlins. 4208

Dixon, Thomas. THE MAN IN GRAY. Appleton, 1921. Southern view of the war, preceding events, and prominent people, especially John Brown and Robert E. Lee. 4209

--------. THE SOUTHERNER. Appleton, 1925. A novel emphasizing Lincoln's sympathies for the South. 4210

--------. THE VICTIM. Appleton, 1914. The career of

Jefferson Davis from his service in the U. S. Army to his Presidency of the Confederacy. 4211

Doneghy, Dagmar. THE BORDER. Morrow, 1931. A saga of Missouri-Kansas border conflict as it affects a mother and her six small sons. 4212

Dowdey, Clifford. BUGLES BLOW NO MORE. Little, 1937. An intense account of conditions in Richmond between 1861 and 1864. 4213

--------. THE PROUD RETREAT. Doubleday, 1953. Interesting picture of the defeated Confederacy trying to save its treasury. 4214

--------. WHERE MY LOVE SLEEPS. Little, 1945. The fighting around Richmond and Petersburg near the end of the war. 4215

Drago, Harry Sinclair. STAGECOACH KINGDOM. Doubleday, 1943. The Midwest during the Civil War. 4216

Edgerton, Lucile. PILLARS OF GOLD. Knopf, 1941. The Arizona gold rush of the 1860s with good descriptions of the Southwest. 4217

Edmonds, Walter D. THE BIG BARN. Little, 1930. A romantic triangle is the plot in this well-told story of farm life in the Erie Canal region. 4218

--------. CADMUS HENRY. Dodd, 1949. A Confederate youth with aspirations to a cavalry post becomes a balloonist for the army. 4219

Edwards, Amelia A. B. DEBENHAM'S VOW. Hurst & Blackett, 1870. Exciting account of blockade running at Charleston. 4220

Eggleston, George Cary. BALE MARKED CIRCLE X. Lothrop, 1902. Adventures of blockade runners who defied danger for financial gain. 4221

--------. MASTER OF WARLOCK. Lothrop, 1903. A romance of war-torn Virginia in the early part of the hostilities. 4222

--------. THE WARRENS OF VIRGINIA. Dillingham, 1908. Both the North and the South are shown suffering the effects of war. 4223

Eliot, George Fielding. CALEB PETTENGILL, U. S. N. Messner, 1956. About a Union gunboat commander blockading southern ports. 4224

Erdman, Loula. MANY A VOYAGE. Dodd, 1960. The wife of a crusading newspaperman views the troubled Mid-west. 4225

Fairbank, Janet Ayer. BRIGHT LAND. Houghton, 1932. A New England girl who runs away from home finds fulfillment in frontier Illinois. 4226

--------. THE CORTLANDTS OF WASHINGTON SQUARE. Bobbs, 1922. A determined young lady from New York becomes a war nurse against family objections. 4227

Ferrel, Elizabeth and Margaret. FULL OF THY RICHES. Mill, 1944. A Quaker girl and her elderly husband move south, where she falls in love. 4228

Feuille, Frank. THE COTTON ROAD. Morrow, 1954. Running southern cotton to English markets through the Union blockade. 4229

Foote, Shelby. SHILOH. Dial, 1952. Battle of Shiloh as it affects six soldiers--Union and Confederate. 4230

Fox, John, Jr. THE LITTLE SHEPHERD OF KINGDOM COME. Scribner, 1903. A story of the Kentucky mountains and divided loyalties in the war. 4231

Frothingham, Jessie P. RUNNING THE GAUNTLET. Appleton, 1906. Based on the life of William B. Cushing, the naval hero who destroyed the southern ship _Albemarle._ 4232

Gaither, Frances. FOLLOW THE DRINKING GOURD. Macmillan, 1940. The drinking gourd in this tale of an Alabama plantation is the Big Dipper, which guided runaway slaves northward. 4233

Gardiner, Dorothy. THE GREAT BETRAYAL. Doubleday, 1949. Wanton massacre of friendly Indians by Colonel Chivington, whose ruthlessness was caused by ambition to a Congressional seat. 4234

Garth, David. GRAY CANAAN. Putnam, 1947. The loss of a secret Confederate plan and attempts to recover it. 4235

Glasgow, Alice. TWISTED TENDRIL. Stokes, 1928. A novel of the ironic life of John Wilkes Booth and his twisted ideals. 4236

Glasgow, Ellen. THE BATTLE GROUND. Doubleday, Page, 1902. Virginia in the prosperous era before the war and the tragedy brought by the fighting. 4237

Gordon, Caroline. NONE SHALL LOOK BACK. Scribner, 1937. Story of a wealthy Kentucky family and of General Nathan Bedford Forrest of the Confederate Cavalry. 4238

Greene, Homer. A LINCOLN CONSCRIPT. Houghton, 1909. A much-misunderstood conscientious objector receives the friendship of the wise President. 4239

Gruber, Frank. BUFFALO GRASS. Rinehart, 1956. A picture of Kansas near the end of the Civil War. 4240

Harben, Will N. THE TRIUMPH. Harper, 1917. Experiences of an Abolitionist and his family in Georgia. 4241

Harris, Joel Chandler. A LITTLE UNION SCOUT. Duckworth, 1905. A Federal scout proves to be a charming lady in disguise. 4242

Harrison, Constance. THE CARLYLES. Appleton, 1905. Grant's capture of Richmond and Lincoln's visit to the Confederate capital. 4243

Hart, Scott. EIGHT APRIL DAYS. Coward, 1949. Spirit of the Confederate Army during the retreat from Petersburg to Appomattox. 4244

Havill, Edward. BIG EMBER. Harper, 1947. Fresh account

of Norwegian settlers in Minnesota and their fights with the Sioux. 4245

Hawthorne, Hazel. THREE WOMEN. Dutton, 1938. The lives of three women who grew up together on Cape Cod. 4246

Haycox, Ernest. THE LONG STORM. Little, 1946. Action of Copperheads in Oregon as the Civil War has far-flung repercussions. 4247

Heyward, Du Bose. PETER ASHLEY. Farrar, 1932. Concerns traditions of the Old South and the hero's struggle with his conscience at the outbreak of war. 4248

Horan, James David. SEEK OUT AND DESTROY. Crown, 1958. The _CSS Lee's_ attempt to wound the North economically by destroying the New Bedford whaling fleet. 4249

Horsley, Reginald. STONEWALL'S SCOUT. Harper, 1896. A story of the Civil War, including an account of Gettysburg. 4250

Howard, J. Hamilton. IN THE SHADOW OF THE PINES. Eaton & Mains, 1906. A tale about the Great Dismal Swamp in Virginia. 4251

Jacobs, Thornwell. RED LANTERNS ON ST. MICHAEL'S. Dutton, 1940. A well-documented story of Charleston during the War between the States. 4252

Johnston, Mary. CEASE FIRING. Houghton, 1912. Vivid pictures of the disasters and horrors of war. 4253

--------. DRURY RANDALL. Little, 1934. A southern gentleman's search for spiritual peace and happiness. 4254

--------. THE LONG ROLL. Houghton, 1911. A detailed story of the Shenandoah Valley campaign with Stonewall Jackson prominent. 4255

Kane, Harnett T. BRIDE OF FORTUNE. Doubleday, 1948. The first lady of the Confederacy--Mrs. Jefferson Davis. 4256

--------. THE SMILING REBEL. Doubleday, 1955. The Confederacy's seventeen-year-old spy, spirited Belle Boyd. 4257

Kantor, MacKinlay. ANDERSONVILLE. World Pub., 1955. Life and death in and around notorious Andersonville prison. 4258

--------. AROUSE AND BEWARE. Coward, 1936. Two Federal soldiers escape from the infamous Confederate prison of Belle Island. 4259

--------. LONG REMEMBER. Coward, 1955. A panoramic story of the Battle of Gettysburg. 4260

Kelland, Clarence Budington. ARIZONA. Harper, 1939. A woman combines the talents of shooting and cooking to earn a living in the Wild West by baking pies. 4261

Kelly, Eleanor. RICHARD WALDEN'S WIFE. Bobbs, 1950. A southern lady and her household join her husband in pioneer Wisconsin. 4262

Kennedy, Sara Beaumont. CICELY. Doubleday, 1911. A tale of Sherman's March through Georgia with the capture and burning of Atlanta. 4263

Kennelly, Ardyth. THE SPUR. Messner, 1951. John Wilkes Booth reviews his life in the six days between his assassination of Lincoln and his own death. 4264

King, Charles. BETWEEN THE LINES. Harper, 1889. A reliable account of the action of the Army of the Potomac. 4265

--------. THE GENERAL'S DOUBLE. Lippincott, 1897. A story of the Army of the Potomac, stressing McClellan's campaign in Maryland. 4266

--------. NORMAN HOLT. Dillingham, 1901. The military exploits of the Army of the Cumberland. 4267

--------. THE ROCK OF CHICKAMAUGA. Dillingham, 1907. The defense of Chickamauga, where General Thomas won the nickname 'Rock." 4268

Kroll, Harry Harrison. THE KEEPERS OF THE HOUSE. Bobbs, 1940. A rebellious youth discovers he is the illegitimate son of a plantation owner. 4269

Lagard, Garald. LEAPS THE LIVE THUNDER. Morrow, 1955. Most memorable character is Colonel Turpentine, a yellow, whisky-drinking cat. 4270

--------. SCARLET COCKEREL. Morrow, 1948. Love of a surgeon with Mosby's Raiders for a Union general's daughter. 4271

Lancaster, Bruce. NIGHT MARCH. Little, 1958. Two officers attempt to rescue Union soldiers from Libby Prison. 4272

--------. NO BUGLES TONIGHT. Little, 1948. In the process of spying a man learns a cause is more important than an individual. 4273

--------. ROLL, SHENANDOAH. Little, 1956. A soldier, wounded at Appomattox, returns to war as a newspaper reporter. 4274

--------. THE SCARLET PATCH. Little, 1947. Foreign-born volunteers who fought for the survival of the Union. 4275

Lincoln, Joseph Crosby. STORM SIGNALS. Appleton, 1935. Life on Cape Cod during the Civil War portrayed in the story of two sea captains. 4276

Lincoln, Natalie Sumner. THE LOST DESPATCH. Appleton, 1913. Story of a woman in Washington suspected of being a spy and a murderess. 4277

Longstreet, Stephen. GETTYSBURG. Farrar, 1961. Life in the little town of Gettysburg at the time of the famous battle. 4278

--------. THREE DAYS. Messner, 1947. The three days of the title are the time of the Battle of Gettysburg. 4279

Lowden, Leone. PROVING GROUND. McBride, 1946. A

frontier family in Indiana during the war. 4280

Lytle, Andrew Nelson. THE VELVET HORN. McDowell, 1957. Beautifully written story of five young people orphaned shortly before the war. 4281

McCord, Joseph. REDHOUSE ON THE HILL. Macrae Smith, 1938. The personal conflict of a southern sympathizer who loved a Union soldier. 4282

McGehee, Thomasine. JOURNEY PROUD. Macmillan, 1939. Warm story of a southern family which preserved its ideals despite misfortunes. 4283

MacGowan, Alice. SWORD IN THE MOUNTAINS. Putnam, 1910. A story which shows suffering and loyalty in the Cumberland Mountains. 4284

Mackie, Pauline Bradford. THE WASHINGTONIANS. Page, 1903. The intrigues of political life in Washington toward the end of the war. 4285

McLaws, Lafayette, i. e., Emily Lafayette McLaws. THE WELDING. Little, 1907. Political issues in the preliminary stages of the Civil War. 4286

McMeekin, Clark, pseud. for Dorothy Clark and Isabel McMeekin. CITY OF THE FLAGS. Appleton, 1950. Conflicting loyalties in Louisville when Kentucky was still neutral. 4287

McNeilly, Mildred Masterson. PRAISE AT MORNING. Morrow, 1947. International intrigue when the War between the States brings the Russian fleet to American waters. 4288

Mally, Emma Louise. THE MOCKINGBIRD IS SINGING. Holt, 1944. The loves of two young couples in New Orleans and Texas. 4289

Markey, Morris. THE BAND PLAYS DIXIE. Harcourt, 1927. The simultaneous friendship and enmity of two imprisoned Union men who love the same girl. 4290

Mason, Van Wyck. BLUE HURRICANE. Lippincott, 1954.

Melodramatic romance against a background of river war on the Mississippi. 4291

--------. HANG MY WREATH. by Ward Weaver, pseud. Funk, 1941. Fast-moving drama of events leading to the bloody battle of Antietam. 4292

--------. OUR VALIANT FEW. Little, 1956. A tale of the Union naval blockade of Savannah and Charleston. 4293

--------. PROUD NEW FLAGS. Lippincott, 1951. Drama of building the Confederate fleet. 4294

Miller, Helen Topping. CHRISTMAS FOR TAD. Longmans, 1956. Christmas with Lincoln's family in the White House during the Civil War. 4295

--------. NO TEARS FOR CHRISTMAS. Longmans, 1954. Union troops spend Christmas at a Tennessee plantation. 4296

--------. SHOD WITH FLAME. Bobbs, 1946. Romance of three women in love with the same Rebel soldier. 4297

--------. SING ONE SONG. Appleton, 1956. Residents of Kentucky torn between their sympathies for the North and the South. 4298

Miller, May. FIRST THE BLADE. Knopf, 1938. Guerrilla action in Missouri; settlement of the San Joaquin Valley in California. 4299

Minnigerode, Meade. CORDELIA CHANTRELL. Putnam, 1926. Picture of a charming lady of Charleston. 4300

Mitchell, Margaret. GONE WITH THE WIND. Macmillan, 1936. The romance of Scarlett O'Hara against the background of the war and its aftermath. 4301

Mitchell, S. Weir. A DIPLOMATIC ADVENTURE. Century, 1906. Diplomatic relations with France as both sides in the American dispute seek foreign support. 4302

--------. ROLAND BLAKE. Century, 1864. Action and

battles as well as social life in New York and Philadelphia. 4303

Montgomery, James Stuart. TALL MEN. Greenberg, 1927. Action-filled tale of Confederate blockade runners. 4304

Morris, Gouverneur. ALADDIN O'BRIEN. Century, 1902. A northern story of the Civil War. 4305

Morrison, Gerry. UNVEXED TO THE SEA. St. Martins, 1961. Centered around the siege of Vicksburg and Sherman's destructive march to the sea. 4306

Morrow, Honoré. FOREVER FREE. Morrow, 1927. Lincoln's household in the early years of the war harbored a lovely southern spy. (followed by WITH MALICE TOWARD NONE) 4307

--------. GREAT CAPTAIN. Morrow, 1935. Contains a trilogy about Lincoln: FOREVER FREE, WITH MALICE TOWARD NONE, and THE LAST FULL MEASURE (see separate listings). 4308

--------. THE LAST FULL MEASURE. Morrow, 1930. Dramatic account of the last few months of Lincoln's life; the Booth conspiracy and the assassination. 4309

--------. WITH MALICE TOWARD NONE. Morrow, 1928. Lincoln's conflict with Charles Sumner in the last two years of the war. (followed by THE LAST FULL MEASURE) 4310

Murfree, Mary Noailles. THE STORM CENTRE. by Charles Egbert Craddock, pseud. Macmillan, 1905. The romance of a southern gentlewoman and a wounded Union soldier. 4311

Noble, Hollister. WOMAN WITH A SWORD. Doubleday, 1948. About Anna Ella Carroll, whose military advice aided Lincoln's cabinet. 4312

O'Connor, Richard. COMPANY Q. Doubleday, 1957. De-ranked officers are banded together to form a new company. 4313

--------. GUNS OF CHICKAMAUGA. Doubleday, 1955. Story of a Chicago newspaperman discharged from the Union Army. 4314

Oldham, Henry. THE MAN FROM TEXAS. Petersen, 1884. The daring exploits of a Confederate guerrilla general. 4315

O'Neal, Cothburn. UNTOLD GLORY. Crown, 1957. A Tennessee lady makes friends with Union officers to smuggle medical supplies into Memphis. 4316

Palmer, Frederick. THE VAGABOND. Harper, 1903. A romance of Virginia with the war in the background. 4317

Parrish, Randall. MY LADY OF THE NORTH. McClurg, 1904. Adventures of one of General Lee's couriers and action in the Shenandoah Valley. 4318

--------. MY LADY OF THE SOUTH. McClurg, 1909. Romance defies a bitter feud between two families. 4319

--------. THE RED MIST. McClurg, 1914. Adventures of a Confederate spy in Maryland. 4320

Pennell, Joseph Stanley. HISTORY OF ROME HANKS AND KINDRED MATTERS. Scribner, 1944. In learning about his ancestors a young man discovers much about America as well. 4321

Penney, Kate Mayhew. CROSS CURRENTS. Humphries, 1938. Ohio teacher who marries a southerner comes to understand the southern attitude. 4322

Perényi, Eleanor. THE BRIGHT SWORD. Rinehart, 1955. Confederate General John Bell Hood, noble soldier of a lost cause. 4323

Pulse, Charles K. JOHN BONWELL. Farrar, 1952. Vivid story of life in the Ohio Valley. 4324

Reising, Otto. THE QUARREL. by Paul Strahl, pseud. Duell, 1947. A romantic triangle which lasts into the second generation. 4325

Rhodes, James A. and Dean Jauchius. JOHNNY SHILOH. Bobbs, 1959. Based on the adventures of the youngest soldier to bear arms throughout a major war. 4326

Richardson, Norval. THE HEART OF HOPE. Dodd, 1905. The siege of Vicksburg is the main event of this novel. 4327

Roark, Garland. THE OUTLAWED BANNER. Doubleday, 1956. Sea fighting, blockade running, and divided allegiance during the War between the States. 4328

Roberts, Richard Emery. THE GILDED ROOSTER. Putnam, 1947. Conflicts of four people in an unfinished Wyoming fort attacked by the Sioux. 4329

Roberts, Walter Adolphe. BRAVE MARDI GRAS. Bobbs, 1946. Romance and spying in New Orleans seen from a southern viewpoint. 4330

Robertson, Constance. THE GOLDEN CIRCLE. Random, 1951. The turmoil of the war reflected both in politics and in people's lives in Ohio. 4331

--------. SALUTE TO THE HERO. Farrar, 1942. The story of a clever, calculating general who convinced people he was a hero. 4332

--------. THE UNTERRIFIED. Holt, 1946. A story about a group of northerners who dared advocate a peaceful settlement with the South. 4333

Robertson, Don. BY ANTIETAM CREEK. Prentice-Hall, 1960. Tells of the men and strategy of one of the bloodiest battles of the Civil War. 4334

--------. THE THREE DAYS. Prentice-Hall, 1959. Human aspect of the struggle between the blue and the gray at Gettysburg. (followed by BY ANTIETAM CREEK) 4335

Rowell, Adelaide Corinne. ON JORDAN'S STORMY BANKS. Bobbs, 1948. About Sam Davis, Confederate scout, who was hanged as a spy when he was twenty-one. 4336

Sage, William. THE CLAYBORNES. Houghton, 1902. The campaigns at Vicksburg and Richmond. 4337

Schachner, Nathan. BY THE DIM LAMPS. Stokes, 1941. New Orleans and surrounding Louisiana during and following the war. 4338

Schaefer, Jack W. COMPANY OF COWARDS. Houghton, 1957. The "renegade" Company Q has a chance to prove its bravery. 4339

Seabrook, Phoebe H. A DAUGHTER OF THE CONFEDERACY. Neale, 1906. Domestic life in the south during the war. 4340

Seawell, Molly Elliot. THE VICTORY. Appleton, 1906. Family differences caused by divided loyalties. 4341

Seifert, Shirley. FAREWELL, MY GENERAL. Lippincott, 1954. Romance of Flora Cooke and Jeb Stuart and his dramatic military career. 4342

--------. THE WAYFARER. Mill, 1938. A wanderer's adventures with whales, horses, and women. 4343

Shuster, George Nauman. LOOK AWAY. Macmillan, 1939. The struggle to preserve a marriage beset by conflicting loyalties in the war. 4344

Simons, Katherine D. M. THE RUNNING THREAD. by Drayton Mayrant, pseud. Appleton, 1949. An Irish girl falls in love with a southerner during the war. 4345

Sinclair, Harold. THE CAVALRYMAN. Harper, 1958. The army's expedition against the marauding Sioux Indians in the Dakotas. 4346

--------. HORSE SOLDIERS. Harper, 1956. A tingling tale based on the sixteen-day Grierson's Raid. (followed by THE CAVALRYMAN) 4347

Sinclair, Upton. MANASSAS. Macmillan, 1904. Events before and during the early war, including the Underground Railroad. 4348

Slaughter, Frank G. IN A DARK GARDEN. Doubleday, 1946. Young southern surgeon treats the wounded of both sides. 4349

--------. LORENA. Doubleday, 1959. A lovely, courageous girl prepares to defend her home from the dreaded Sherman and his march to the sea. 4350

--------. STORM HAVEN. Doubleday, 1953. Florida cattle drive during the Civil War. 4351

Smith, Chard Powers. ARTILLERY OF TIME. Scribner, 1939. A warm story of family life in upper New York state. (followed by LADIES DAY) 4352

Smith, Francis Hopkinson. THE TIDES OF BARNEGAT. Scribner, 1906. A tale of the everyday life of New Jersey fishermen. 4353

Stern, Philip Van Doren. THE MAN WHO KILLED LINCOLN. Random, 1939. A report of the assassination in a thorough study of John Wilkes Booth. 4354

Sterne, Emma Gelders. NO SURRENDER. Duffield, 1932. Efforts of a southern woman to manage her war-ravaged Alabama plantation. 4355

Stevenson, Janet. WEEP NO MORE. Viking, 1957. Mystery of Elizabeth Van Lew, known as "Crazy Bet." 4356

Stover, Herbert Elisha. COPPERHEAD MOON. Dodd, 1952. Sabotage attempts of deserters from the Union Army. 4357

Street, James Howell. BY VALOUR AND ARMS. Dial, 1944. The naval war on the Mississippi in which the Confederate iron-clad, the *Arkansas*, proved so effective. 4358

--------. CAPTAIN LITTLE AX. Lippincott, 1956. Military exploits of the young son of a Confederate soldier killed at Shiloh. 4359

--------. TAP ROOTS. Dial, 1942. A family in Mississippi maintains its anti-slavery convictions. 4360

Stribling, Thomas S. THE FORGE. Doubleday, 1931. A middle-class Alabama family during and after the war. (followed by THE STORE) 4361

Tiernan, Mary Spear. JACK HORNER. Fenno, 1890. Romance in Richmond during the final year of the war. 4362

Toepfer, Ray Grant. SCARLET GUIDON. Coward, 1958. The common soldier in the war, reflected in the experiences of an Alabama company. 4363

Tracy, Don. ON THE MIDNIGHT TIDE. Dial, 1957. Exploits of two brothers who are blockade runners out of North Carolina. 4364

Wagner, Constance. ASK MY BROTHER. Harper, 1959. Revolves around a cold woman who is deceptively lady-like. 4365

Waldman, Emerson. BECKONING RIDGE. Holt, 1940. Effects of the war on a farming community in the Virginia mountains. 4366

Warren, Robert Penn. BAND OF ANGELS. Random, 1955. Problems of a mulatto girl sold into slavery. 4367

Webber, Everett and Olga. BOUND GIRL. Dutton, 1949. Life of Rebecca Whitman on the border between Missouri and Kansas. 4368

Webster, Henry K. TRAITOR OR LOYALIST. Macmillan, 1904. Concerns the Union blockade on cotton shipments which caused great financial hardship to the South. 4369

Wheelwright, Jere Hungerford. GRAY CAPTAIN. Scribner, 1954. A vivid account of the Army of Northern Virginia. 4370

Whitney, Phyllis A. THE QUICKSILVER POOL. Appleton, 1955. A loveless marriage and its tortuous course. 4371

Williams, Ben Ames. HOUSE DIVIDED. Houghton, 1947.

A long story of Confederate aristocrats related to Lincoln. 4372

Williams, Churchill. THE CAPTAIN. Lothrop, 1903. The story of Grant before his assignment to the Army of the Potomac. 4373

Wilson, William E. THE RAIDERS. Rinehart, 1955. An Ohio River border town is attacked by Confederate Morgan's Raiders. 4374

Winslow, William Henry. SOUTHERN BUDS AND SONS OF WAR. Clark, 1907. South Carolina during the upheavals of war. 4375

Wood, Lydia C. THE HAYDOCKS' TESTIMONY. Headley, 1891. Experiences of Quakers in the South as they follow their teachings against war and slavery. 4376

Yerby, Frank. CAPTAIN REBEL. Dial, 1956. A New Orleans gambler runs the Union blockade. 4377

Young, Stark. SO RED THE ROSE. Scribner, 1934. Mississippi plantation social life before and even during the war. 4378

Zara, Louis. REBEL RUN. Crown, 1951. Capture of a train by Federal troops in an effort to cut communications. 4379

III. C. 1. e. Reconstruction and Expansion (1865-1900)

Adams, Andy. THE LOG OF A COWBOY. Houghton, 1903. An accurate account of a cattle drive from Texas to the Blackfoot Agency in Montana. 4380

--------. THE OUTLET. Houghton, 1905. A cattle drive in the 1880s, as a rancher delivers the cattle he has sold. 4381

Adams, Henry. DEMOCRACY. Holt, 1880. A novel of politics in the nation's capital. 4382

Adams, Samuel Hopkins. TENDERLOIN. Random, 1959.

New York's rowdy tenderloin area in the Gay Nineties as seen by a reporter for _The Police Gazette_. 4383

Aldrich, Bess Streeter. A LANTERN IN HER HAND. Appleton, 1928. Strong novel of a pioneer mother who embodied the love and devotion which built our country. 4384

--------. THE LIEUTENANT'S LADY. Appleton, 1942. Experiences of a soldier's young wife at an army outpost on the Missouri River, based on an actual diary. 4385

Alexander, Holmes Moss. AMERICAN NABOB. Harper, 1939. A story of Virginia and West Virginia in the rebuilding period following the Civil War. 4386

Anderson, Ada Woodruff. THE HEART OF THE ANCIENT FIRS. Little, 1908. Life in the Northwest after the completion of the Northern Pacific Railway. 4387

Andrews, Annulet. MELISSA STARKE. Dutton, 1935. The adjustment of southerners to the new standards which came to prevail after the war. 4388

Arthur, Herbert. FREEDOM RUN. by Arthur Herbert, _pseud._ Rinehart, 1951. Californians repel a Russian invasion after the U. S. purchase of Alaska. 4389

Atherton, Gertrude. SENATOR NORTH. Lane, 1900. Washington in the late 1890s showing political discussions during the Spanish-American War. 4390

Aydelotte, Dora. ACROSS THE PRAIRIE. Appleton, 1941. A story of small town people and events in Kansas in the 1890s. 4391

--------. LONG FURROWS. Appleton, 1935. A narrative of everyday life in a midwestern rural community in the 1890s. 4392

--------. MEASURE OF A MAN. Appleton, 1942. Country storekeeper and prominent citizen of a small Illinois town near the end of the century. 4393

--------. RUN OF THE STARS. Appleton, 1940. Friction between the ranchers who want free range and the "nesters" who fence their farmland. 4394

--------. TRUMPETS CALLING. Appleton, 1938. A good story of Oklahoma homesteading in the newly-opened Cherokee Strip. 4395

Bandelier, A. F. THE DELIGHT MAKERS. Dodd, 1890. The life and activities of the Pueblo Indians of New Mexico, based on ethnological study. 4396

Barber, Elsie Oakes. HUNT FOR HEAVEN. Macmillan, 1950. Community settled in Pennsylvania by a church group from Chicago. 4397

Barnett, Donald R. A CROSS OF GOLD. Dorrance, 1939. Frontier Montana during the second half of the nineteenth century. 4398

Bean, Amelia. THE FEUD. Doubleday, 1960. Exciting account of early Arizona's Graham-Tewksbury feud. 4399

Beebe, Elswyth Thane. EVER AFTER. by Elswyth Thane. Duell, 1945. Romance which takes place in Virginia, New York, England, and Cuba. 4400

Beer, Thomas. SANDOVAL. Knopf, 1924. A charming scoundrel from the deep south fascinates New York society. 4401

Bindloss, Harold. THE CATTLE-BARON'S DAUGHTER. Stokes, 1906. The west in the 1870s, when homesteaders were fencing in parts of former grazing lands. 4402

Binns, Archie. YOU ROLLING RIVER. Scribner, 1947. The town of Astoria on the Pacific coast at the mouth of the Columbia River. 4403

Birney, Hoffman. THE DICE OF GOD. Holt, 1956. A novel based on Custer's Seventh Cavalry and its stand at the Little Big Horn. 4404

Bisno, Beatrice. TOMORROW'S BREAD. Liveright, 1938.

Experiences of a Russian Jewish immigrant in late nineteenth century Chicago. 4405

Blake, Forrester. WILDERNESS PASSAGE. Random, 1953. Westward expansion into Utah--wagon trains, fur trappers, and the struggling Mormon settlers. 4406

Bojer, Johan. THE EMIGRANTS. (tr.) Appleton, 1925. Trials of Norwegian settlers in the Red River Valley, North Dakota. 4407

Borland, Hal. THE SEVENTH WINTER. Lippincott, 1959. A cattleman's struggle against fierce weather in pioneer Colorado. 4408

Breneman, Mary Worthy, pseud. of Mary Worthy Thurston and Muriel Breneman. THE LAND THEY POSSESSED. Macmillan, 1956. Americanization of homesteaders from the Ukraine. 4409

Bretherton, Vivien. ROCK AND THE WIND. Dutton, 1942. A girl from Cornwall comes to love her new home in wide, wild America. 4410

Brink, Carol. BUFFALO COAT. Macmillan, 1944. A story of the doctors of Opportunity, Idaho, in the 1890s. 4411

Brooks, Mansfield. THE NEWELL FORTUNE. Lane, 1906. A young American investigates the origin of his inherited fortune, and becomes involved in the slave trade. 4412

Brown, Dee. YELLOWHORSE. Houghton, 1956. The cavalry on the western frontier uses a balloon against the Sioux. 4413

Buck, Charles Neville. THE CODE OF THE MOUNTAINS. Watt, 1915. Life in both Kentucky and the Philippines during the Spanish-American War. 4414

Burnett, William Riley. ADOBE WALLS. Knopf, 1953. "A novel of the last Apache rising." 4415

--------. MI AMIGO. Knopf, 1959. A story of one of the

Southwest's most notorious killers, Billy the Kid. 4416

--------. SAINT JOHNSON. Dial, 1930. A man's desire to become sheriff of Tombstone, Arizona, is thwarted by his thirst for revenge. 4417

Busch, Niven. DUEL IN THE SUN. Morrow, 1944. A vigorous western story of a part-Indian orphan girl. 4418

Cable, George Washington. JOHN MARCH, SOUTHERNER. Scribner, 1894. Financial schemes and political quarrels in a southern town suffering from Civil War ravages. 4419

Caldwell, James Fitz James. THE STRANGER. Neale, 1907. A schoolteacher from the North in the Reconstruction South. 4420

Caldwell, Taylor (full name: Janet Taylor Caldwell). THIS SIDE OF INNOCENCE. Scribner, 1946. Family discord when an adventuress married to one brother falls in love with another. 4421

Carson, Katharine. MRS. PENNINGTON. Putnam, 1939. Small-town life in Kansas during a chautauqua program one summer. 4422

Carter, Isabel Hopestill. SHIPMATES. Scott, 1934. A sea captain's wife scorns security ashore to sail with her husband. 4423

Cheney, Brainard. LIGHTWOOD. Houghton, 1939. Difficulties facing southerners trying to hold and rebuild their lands after the war. 4424

Chester, George Randolph. GET-RICH-QUICK WALLINGFORD. Burt, 1907. A fast-talking swindler aspires to profit at others' expense. 4425

Chevalier, Elizabeth. DRIVIN' WOMAN. Macmillan, 1942. A Virginia belle, a river boat gambler, and the rising tobacco industry in the post-Civil War era. 4426

Christie, Robert. THE TREMBLING LAND. Doubleday,

1959. Psychological novel of a man of the west who flees a revenging gun for twenty years. 4427

Churchill, Winston. MR. CREWE'S CAREER. Macmillan, 1908. The powerful political influence of great financial concerns such as railroads. 4428

Clark, Walter Van Tilburg. THE OX-BOW INCIDENT. Random, 1940. Rough-and-ready cowboy life in Nevada about 1885. 4429

Coburn, Walt. BARB WIRE. Century, 1931. Conflict between cattle ranchers, who wanted open range, and sheep raisers, who built fences. 4430

Coker, Elizabeth Boatwright. INDIA ALLAN. Dutton, 1953. Colorful narrative of South Carolina and the hated carpet-bag government. 4431

Constant, Alberta. OKLAHOMA RUN. Crowell, 1955. Pioneer life at the opening of the Oklahoma Territory. 4432

Cooke, David C. POST OF HONOR. Putnam, 1958. An isolated fort in the Wild West faces an Indian uprising. 4433

Coolidge, Dane. THE FIGHTING DANITES. Dutton, 1934. Conflict between the U. S. government and the Mormons in Utah. 4434

--------. HIDDEN WATER. McClurg, 1910. Conflict between cattlemen and sheepmen for grazing rights in Arizona. 4435

--------. LONG ROPE. Dutton, 1935. Long Rope Bowman backs up his boast of being the best cowboy in the West. 4436

Cooper, Courtney Ryley. THE LAST FRONTIER. Little, 1923. The opening of the West and the building of the Kansas-Pacific Railroad. 4437

--------. OKLAHOMA. Little, 1926. The Oklahoma land rush in 1889 when the Territory was opened to homesteaders. 4438

Corbett, Elizabeth. THE FAR DOWN. Appleton, 1939. The family of a Civil War veteran after his death. 4439

--------. THE LANGWORTHY FAMILY. Appleton, 1937. Family life in the Midwest toward the end of the nineteenth century. 4440

--------. MR. AND MRS. MEIGS. Appleton, 1940. A sympathetic, entertaining story of family life. 4441

--------. SHE WAS CARRIE EATON. Appleton, 1938. Quiet story of domestic life in a small midwestern town. 4442

Corcoran, William. GOLDEN HORIZONS. Macrae Smith, 1937. Early settlers in western Kansas. 4443

Corle, Edwin. BILLY THE KID. Duell, 1953. A story which essays to understand the youthful desperado who committed twenty-one murders. 4444

Crabb, Alfred Leland. BREAKFAST AT THE HERMITAGE. Bobbs, 1945. A novel of Nashville's rebuilding with emphasis on beauty in architecture. 4445

--------. REUNION AT CHATTANOOGA. Bobbs, 1950. Yankee ex-soldiers return as peacetime visitors to Grandma Blevins and her family in post-war Kentucky. 4446

--------. SUPPER AT THE MAXWELL HOUSE. Bobbs, 1943. A novel of recaptured Nashville and of the opening of a new restaurant. 4447

Croy, Homer. LADY FROM COLORADO. Duell, 1957. An Irish girl goes to the West as a washerwoman. 4448

Cullum, Ridgwell. THE ONE WAY TRAIL. Jacobs, 1911. Frontier life on a Montana ranch. 4449

--------. THE WATCHERS OF THE PLAINS. Jacobs, 1909. Indian uprising in the Nebraska and Dakota region in the 1870s. 4450

Cunningham, John M. WARHORSE. Macmillan, 1956. "A novel of the Old West; ranch life in Montana." 4451

Davis, Clyde Brion. JEREMY BELL. Rinehart, 1947. Experiences of two boys working in a southern lumber camp. 4452

Deasy, Mary. THE CORIOLI AFFAIR. Little, 1954. Tragic romance of a dashing river captain and a young Irish girl. 4453

Derleth, August. STILL IS THE SUMMER NIGHT. Scribner, 1937. The strong love of a Wisconsin family for their small home town on the rolling Sac Prairie. 4454

Dixon, Thomas. THE CLANSMAN. Doubleday, Page, 1905. The rise to strength of the Ku Klux Klan--the Invisible Empire. (followed by THE TRAITOR) 4455

--------. THE LEOPARD'S SPOTS. Wessels, 1908. First book in a series about racial conditions in the South following the Civil War. (followed by THE CLANSMAN) 4456

--------. THE TRAITOR. Doubleday, 1907. The decline and dissolution of the Ku Klux Klan. 4457

Dowdey, Clifford. SING FOR A PENNY. Little, 1941. The financial success and social failure of a man who put fortune ahead of all else. 4458

Downing, J. Hyatt. HOPE OF LIVING. Putnam, 1939. A courageous wife takes over the management of a Dakota farm. 4459

--------. SIOUX CITY. Putnam, 1940. An ambitious young man during the growth of Sioux City. 4460

Drago, Harry Sinclair. MONTANA ROAD. Morrow, 1935. Settlement of the Dakota Territory and efforts of the Indians to save their land. 4461

--------. SINGING LARIAT. by Will Ermine, pseud. Morrow, 1939. A Civil War veteran finds bitter fighting as he tries to stop the sale of whisky and guns to the Indians. 4462

Ducharme, Jacques. THE DELUSSON FAMILY. Funk, 1939. Warm, simple account of a French-Canadian family in New England. 4463

East, Fred. GHOST GOLD. by Tom West, pseud. Dutton, 1950. Shooting-packed search for $40,000 stolen from the Sagebrush Bank. 4464

Elwood, Muriel. AGAINST THE TIDE. Bobbs, 1950. The marriage of a California rancher and a Spanish girl. 4465

Erdman, Loula. THE EDGE OF TIME. Dodd, 1950. A young married couple homestead in the Texas panhandle before the advent of the railroad. 4466

--------. THE FAR JOURNEY. Dodd, 1955. A young mother's journey by covered wagon to join her husband in Texas. 4467

Ertz, Susan. THE PROSELYTE. Appleton, 1933. Marriage in London of a Mormon missionary and the romantic crisis caused by the doctrine of polygamy after the couple returns to Utah. 4468

Evans, Muriel. WAGONS TO TUCSON. by Ed Newsom, pseud. Little, 1954. A wagon train journey through Indian lands to Tucson. 4469

Evarts, Hal. THE SHAGGY LEGION. Little, 1930. Colorful, realistic picture of the far West and the diminishing of the buffalo herds. 4470

---------. TUMBLEWEEDS. Little, 1923. The opening and settling of the Cherokee Strip of Oklahoma. 4471

Fairbank, Janet Ayer. THE SMITHS. Bobbs, 1925. Parallels the rise of a family with the growth of a city, Chicago. 4472

Faralla, Dana. CIRCLE OF TREES. Lippincott, 1955. Immigrants from Denmark survive a disastrous first year in building a home in Minnesota. 4473

Fast, Howard. THE AMERICAN. Duell, 1946. Based on the career of an Illinois politician, John Peter Altgeld. 4474

--------. FREEDOM ROAD. Duell, 1944. Thought provoking novel of race relations and the Ku Klux Klan in the South. 4475

--------. THE LAST FRONTIER. Duell, 1941. Cheyenne Indians, treated unfairly on an Oklahoma reservation, defy the army and return to Montana. 4476

Ferber, Edna. CIMARRON. Grosset, 1929. The growth of a town in the newly opened Oklahoma Territory. 4477

--------. SARATOGA TRUNK. Doubleday, 1941. Society life of a Texan and an adventuress in New Orleans and Saratoga. 4478

--------. SHOW BOAT. Doubleday, 1926. Pictures a passing aspect of American theater--a Mississippi River showboat. 4479

Ferber, Richard. THE HOSTILES. Dell, 1958. The resistance of the Sioux to reservation life before the Battle of the Little Big Horn. 4480

Fergusson, Harvey. THE CONQUEST OF DON PEDRO. Morrow, 1954. A New York businessman finds health, marriage, and success in New Mexico. 4481

Fish, Rachel Ann. RUNNING IRON. Coward, 1957. Southern settlers adjust to life in wild, raw Wyoming Territory. 4482

Foote, Mary. THE CHOSEN VALLEY. Houghton, 1892. Two men engaged in a system of irrigation in the west. 4483

--------. COEUR D'ALÉNE. Houghton, 1894. Based on the Coeur d'Aléne labor riots of 1892 in the west. 4484

Ford, James Lauren. HOT CORN IKE. Dutton, 1923. A

picture of New York City in the tale of a street peddler and minor politician. 4485

Ford, Paul Leicester. THE HONORABLE PETER STERLING. Holt, 1894. The power and influence of politics, honest and corrupt, in a democratic society. 4486

Foreman, Leonard L. THE RENEGADE. Dutton, 1942. A white man raised by the Sioux finds his loyalties divided at the Battle of the Little Big Horn. 4487

Fox, John, Jr. CRITTENDEN. Scribner, 1905. Participation in the Cuban War helps a southerner find his own courage and his loyalty to the United States. 4488

--------. THE KENTUCKIANS. Scribner, 1898. Political rivalry between the Cumberland mountaineers and the lowland landowners. 4489

--------. THE TRAIL OF THE LONESOME PINE. Scribner, 1908. Hill folk and town folk differences in Kentucky and Virginia during the process of industrialization. 4490

Frederic, Harold. THE LAWTON GIRL. Scribner, 1890. Political, social, and commercial life in a small manufacturing town. 4491

--------. SETH'S BROTHER'S WIFE. Scribner, 1887. New York State country life--farming, journalism, voting. 4492

French, Alice. EXPIATION. by Octave Thanet, pseud. Scribner, 1890. Reconstruction in Arkansas. 4493

Gabriel, Gilbert W. BROWNSTONE FRONT. Century, 1924. Revealing picture of New York in the 1890s. 4494

Garland, Hamlin. THE MOCCASIN RANCH. Harper, 1909. Hardships of immigrant settlers who built homes on the wild Dakota prairie. 4495

--------. A SPOIL OF OFFICE. Arena Pub., 1892. The politics of Iowa, Kansas, and Nebraska in the 1870s. 4496

Garth, David. FIRE ON THE WIND. Putnam, 1951. Action-packed story of the timber country of Michigan. 4497

Giles, Janice Holt. HANNAH FOWLER. Houghton, 1956. A tender love story of pioneer settlers in Kentucky. 4498

Glasgow, Ellen. THE DELIVERANCE. Doubleday, Page, 1904. Post-bellum life on a large Virginia tobacco plantation. 4499

--------. THE ROMANCE OF A PLAIN MAN. Macmillan, 1909. The story of a "plain man" of Virginia who dares defy society to love a woman of the "aristocracy." 4500

--------. THE VOICE OF THE PEOPLE. Doubleday, Page, 1900. The rich scenery of Virginia is the setting for this story of political ambition. 4501

Glidden, Frederick. AND THE WIND BLOWS FREE. by Luke Short, pseud. Macmillan, 1945. Free enterprise of cattlemen in early Oklahoma prior to statehood. 4502

Gordon, Armistead. OMMIRANDY. Scribner, 1917. Story of an ex-slave who remained with his former master after the war. 4503

Grey, Zane. HERITAGE OF THE DESERT. Harper, 1910. Mormons, Navajos, and cattle thieves on the Arizona desert. 4504

--------. RIDERS OF THE PURPLE SAGE. Harper, 1912. The Mormon settlements in Utah. 4505

--------. TRAIL DRIVER. Harper, 1936. A cattle drive from Texas to Kansas in 1871. 4506

--------. THE U. P. TRAIL. Harper, 1918. Indian massacre, captures, and escapes punctuate this story of the building of the Union Pacific Railroad. 4507

--------. WESTERN UNION. Harper, 1939. A story of the development of the American West. 4508

--------. YOUNG FORESTER. Harper, 1910. A story of

the then new science of forestry--the conservation of our national resource. 4509

Guthrie, Alfred Bertram. THESE THOUSAND HILLS. Houghton, 1956. The hard work of a cowboy to achieve his dream--a ranch of his own. 4510

Hagedorn, Hermann. THE ROUGH RIDERS. Harper, 1927. Exciting story of Theodore Roosevelt in the Spanish-American War. 4511

Haines, William W. THE WINTER WAR. Little, 1961. Fighting with Sioux and Cheyenne warriors in Montana's severe winter after Custer's defeat. 4512

Haldeman-Julius, Emanuel and Marcet. DUST. Brentano's, 1921. The drudgery of Kansas pioneers in a loveless marriage building a farm from empty prairie. 4513

Hall, Oakley M. WARLOCK. Viking, 1958. A partly factual story of the western frontier about Wyatt Earp and Tombstone, Arizona. 4514

Hancock, Albert E. HENRY BOURLAND. Macmillan, 1901. The suffering of the South due to poor government planning after the war. 4515

Harris, Bernice. JANEY JEEMS. Doubleday, 1946. White and Negro mountaineers in rural North Carolina. 4516

Harris, Corra May. CIRCUIT RIDER'S WIFE. Altemus, 1910. A wife relates the trying ministry of her husband in a widely scattered congregation. 4517

Harris, Frank. THE BOMB. Kennerley, 1908. The violent Haymarket Riot in Chicago in 1886, typifying the labor problems of the period. 4518

Harris, Leon F. and Frank Lee Beals. LOOK AWAY, DIXIELAND. Speller, 1937. A soldier returns to find that the war has destroyed his home. 4519

Harris, Margaret and John. ARROW IN THE MOON. Morrow, 1954. A young easterner becomes involved with love, Indians, and adventure in Nebraska and adjoining territories. 4520

--------. MEDICINE WHIP. Morrow, 1953. A western adventure story set in Wyoming. 4521

Hatcher, Harlan H. THE PATTERNS OF WOLFPEN. Bobbs, 1934. Growing industrialism changes the life of a family descended from Kentucky pioneers. 4522

Havighurst, Walter. THE QUIET SHORE. Macmillan, 1937. The growth and development of the Lake Erie area from swamp to farming to industrial use. 4523

Haycox, Ernest. ACTION BY NIGHT. Little, 1943. The war waged against cattle rustlers by ranchers. 4524

--------. THE ADVENTURERS. Little, 1954. Suspense-filled story of colonists in the Pacific Northwest. 4525

--------. BUGLES IN THE AFTERNOON. Little, 1944. The personal conflict and love of a member of General Custer's force. 4526

--------. RIM OF THE DESERT. Little, 1941. The bitter range warfare between ranchers and nesters in the Old West. 4527

--------. TROUBLE SHOOTER. Doubleday, 1937. A western thriller built around the growth of the Union Pacific Railroad. 4528

Henry, Will. NO SURVIVORS. Random, 1950. Custer's battles with Indians come to a climax in the tragedy at the Little Big Horn. 4529

Herbst, Josephine. PITY IS NOT ENOUGH. Harcourt, 1933. The tragic life of a young man who went into the south as a carpetbagger. 4530

Hooker, Forrestine. WHEN GERONIMO RODE. Doubleday, 1924. Compelling story of the struggle between white men and Indians. 4531

Horgan, Paul. A DISTANT TRUMPET. Farrar, 1960. A soldier and his bride live on an army post in Arizona

Territory under threat of Apache warfare. 4532

Hough, Emerson. THE GIRL AT THE HALF-WAY HOUSE. Appleton, 1900. A former army captain becomes a frontier settler. 4533

--------. NORTH OF 36. Appleton, 1923. The struggle of a young lady in Texas to rebuild her father's ranch by a cattle drive to Abilene, Kansas. 4534

Howard, Elizabeth Metzger. BEFORE THE SUN GOES DOWN. Doubleday, 1946. All levels of society in a small Pennsylvania town in the 1880s. 4535

Howells, William Dean. THE RISE OF SILAS LAPHAM. Ticknor, 1885. A climbing Boston family attempts to break into high society. 4536

--------. THE VACATION OF THE KELWYNS. Harper, 1920. A tale of New England life in the middle 1870s. 4537

Hueston, Ethel. CALAMITY JANE OF DEADWOOD GULCH. Bobbs, 1937. Account of a woman of the lusty gold rush era in the Black Hills country. 4538

Hulme, Kathryn. ANNIE'S CAPTAIN. Little, 1961. The transition from graceful sailing ships to the new steamships in a sea captain's life. 4539

Idell, Albert. BRIDGE TO BROOKLYN. Holt, 1948. A warm tale of family life including the excitement over the completion of the Brooklyn Bridge. (followed by THE GREAT BLIZZARD) 4540

--------. CENTENNIAL SUMMER. Holt, 1943. New York during the centennial year of 1876. (followed by BRIDGE TO BROOKLYN) 4541

--------. THE GREAT BLIZZARD. Holt, 1948. The story of the Rogers family in the blizzard of March, 1888, in New York. 4542

--------. STEPHEN HAYNE. Sloane, 1951. Coal mining and the development of organized labor. 4543

Irwin, Will. YOUTH RIDES WEST. Knopf, 1925. A picture of a Colorado mining camp in the 1870s. 4544

Isham, Frederic S. BLACK FRIDAY. Bobbs, 1904. Bank failures caused by wild speculation in farming land in the expanding West. 4545

Janvier, Thomas Allibone. SANTA FE'S PARTNER. Harper, 1907. Memories of a small territorial New Mexican railroad town. 4546

Jewett, Sarah Orne. A COUNTRY DOCTOR. Houghton, 1884. A New England country doctor whose unconventional ward becomes a doctor. 4547

Johnston, Mary. MICHAEL FORTH. Harper, 1919. Economic, domestic, and religious adjustments of southerners during the Reconstruction. 4548

Kelland, Clarence Budington. GOLD. Harper, 1931. The daughter of a banker puts money management before romance. 4549

--------. VALLEY OF THE SUN. Harper, 1940. Pioneering in the desert country of Arizona. 4550

Kennelly, Ardyth. GOOD MORNING, YOUNG LADY. Houghton, 1953. The paradoxical loves of a delightful young girl--first for a bandit, then for a professor. 4551

--------. THE PEACEABLE KINGDOM. Houghton, 1949. The second wife and children of a polygamous tailor in Salt Lake City in the 1890s. (followed by UP HOME) 4552

--------. UP HOME. Houghton, 1955. Story of Mormons in Salt Lake City in the 1890s showing the special problems of a man's "second family." 4553

Kenyon, Theda. BLACK DAWN. Messner, 1944. Ancient family animosity recurs in the aftermath of the war. 4554

Keyes, Frances Parkinson. BLUE CAMELLIA. Messner,

1957. The pioneers of the rice industry in Louisiana. 4555

Kinkaid, Mary H. THE MAN OF YESTERDAY. Stokes, 1908. The closing years of the century in the Indian Territory. 4556

Krey, Laura Lettie. AND TELL OF TIME. Houghton, 1938. Unrest following the Civil War causes trouble to a young couple on a Texas plantation. 4557

Lane, Rose Wilder. FREE LAND. Longmans, 1938. Hardships of early settlers on the plains of the Dakotas. 4558

--------. LET THE HURRICANE ROAR. Longmans, 1933. The endurance of western pioneers who lived in a dugout and forced a living from a hostile country. 4559

Lanham, Edwin. THE WIND BLEW WEST. Longmans, 1935. The honest courage of pioneers and the greed of slick promoters. 4560

Laut, Agnes C. FREEBOOTERS OF THE WILDERNESS. Moffat, 1910. The dishonest activities of men attempting to steal timber in the West. 4561

Le May, Alan. THE SEARCHERS. Harper, 1954. The five-year search for a girl captured by Comanches. 4562

Leonard, Jonathan. BACK TO STAY. Viking, 1929. Small New England community in the 1870s. 4563

Liddon, Eloise S. SOME LOSE THEIR WAY. Dutton, 1941. Romance of an English actress who comes to Alabama. 4564

Lipsky, Eleazar. LINCOLN McKEEVER. Appleton, 1953. A New York lawyer, living in the west, undertakes a land grant case complicated by racial differences. 4565

Lockridge, Ross Franklin. RAINTREE COUNTY. Houghton, 1948. A long novel of the Fourth of July, 1892, in Indiana, interspersed with flashbacks. 4566

Lockwood, Sarah. FISTFUL OF STARS. Appleton, 1947. A young couple in a Wisconsin lumber and mining community. 4567

Loomis, Noel M. A TIME FOR VIOLENCE. Macmillan, 1960. Conflict between ranchers and outlaws in the Texas panhandle in the 1880s. 4568

Lott, Milton. DANCE BACK THE BUFFALO. Houghton, 1959. The Plains Indians attempt to bring back their old way of life through ceremonial dancing. 4569

--------. THE LAST HUNT. Houghton, 1954. A western story about the last of the buffalo hunters. 4570

Lovelace, Maud Hart. GENTLEMEN FROM ENGLAND. Macmillan, 1937. The experiences of a group of Englishmen who came to Minnesota to make a fortune raising beans. 4571

MacDonald, William Colt. CALIFORNIA CABALLERO. Covici, 1936. When American settlers were beginning to outnumber the Spanish in California. 4572

MacLeod, Le Roy. THE YEARS OF PEACE. Century, 1932. Life in a farming village in the Wabash River Valley of Indiana. 4573

McMeekin, Clark, pseud. for Dorothy Clark and Isabel McMeekin. THE OCTOBER FOX. Putnam, 1956. Picture of a Kentucky family dominated by the father. 4574

--------. TYRONE OF KENTUCKY. Appleton, 1954. The task of rebuilding a war-torn farm confronts a Confederate veteran and his bride. 4575

Mann, E. B. GUNSMOKE TRAIL. Morrow, 1942. Cattle rustling, shady dealings, and murder in the Old West. 4576

--------. TROUBLED RANGE. Morrow, 1940. An eastern belle wins her man in the West. 4577

--------. WITH SPURS. Morrow, 1937. Fast-moving, action-packed western. 4578

Markey, Gene. KENTUCKY PRIDE. Random, 1956. Two Civil War veterans vie for an estate and a lady. 4579

Matschat, Cecile Hulse. PREACHER ON HORSEBACK. Farrar, 1940. Based on reminiscences of a circuit rider's wife. 4580

Meeker, Arthur. PRAIRIE AVENUE. Knopf, 1949. Plush living and fast tempo of Chicago stressing the period from 1885 to 1896. 4581

Meigs, Cornelia. RAILROAD WEST. Little, 1937. Tells of some of the difficulties encountered in building the Northern Pacific Railroad. 4582

Miller, Helen Topping. AFTER THE GLORY. Appleton, 1958. Reluctant reunion of brothers who fought on opposing sides in the Civil War. 4583

--------. CHRISTMAS WITH ROBERT E. LEE. Longmans, 1958. A short book telling of the Lee family's first Christmas after the surrender at Appomattox. 4584

--------. MIRAGE. Appleton, 1949. Romantic novel of Texas two decades after the Civil War. 4585

-------- and John Dewey Topping. REBELLION ROAD. Bobbs, 1954. Rebuilding a run-down plantation after the Civil War. 4586

Moore, John Trotwood. THE BISHOP OF COTTONTOWN. Winston, 1906. Social conditions in a southern cotton mill town with accounts of child labor and attempted lynching. 4587

Murfree, Mary Noailles. WHERE THE BATTLE WAS FOUGHT. by Charles Egbert Craddock, pseud. Houghton, 1884. Romance in a Tennessee town close to a great Civil War battlefield. 4588

Myrick, Herbert. CACHE LA POUDRE. Paul, 1905. "The romance of a tenderfoot in the days of Custer." 4589

Norris, Kathleen. CERTAIN PEOPLE OF IMPORTANCE.

Doubleday, 1922. The story of the Crabtree family's move from New England to California. 4590

Nyburg, Sidney. THE GATE OF IVORY. Knopf, 1920. A man's great love brings him to assume a woman's guilt and that of her husband. 4591

Ogden, George W. THE LAND OF LAST CHANCE. McClurg, 1919. A story of the Oklahoma Territory when it was first opened. 4592

--------. SOONER LAND. Dodd, 1929. The difficulties of homesteaders fighting to retain their land. 4593

Ogley, Dorothy and Mabel Cleland. IRON LAND. Doubleday, 1940. The mining of iron ore in Minnesota. 4594

Older, Cora. SAVAGES AND SAINTS. Dutton, 1936. The rebuilding of a Catholic mission at Santa Lucia, California. 4595

O'Rourke, Frank. ACTION AT THREE PEAKS. Random, 1948. Life on a frontier army post in the American West. 4596

Oskison, John. BLACK JACK DAVY. Appleton, 1926. A story of pioneers in Oklahoma. 4597

--------. BROTHERS THREE. Macmillan, 1935. Concerns three Oklahoma brothers—a merchant, a cattleman, and a scholar. 4598

Overton, Gwendolen. THE HERITAGE OF UNREST. Macmillan, 1901. Unjust government policy toward the Apache Indians in the Southwest. 4599

Page, Thomas Nelson. RED RIDERS. Scribner, 1924. A lad of the home guards, too young for war service, fights later against carpetbaggers. 4600

--------. RED ROCK. Scribner, 1899. Struggle to rebuild a southern plantation in the days of the carpetbaggers and the Ku Klux Klan. 4601

Parkhill, Forbes. TROOPERS WEST. Farrar, 1945. An

unbiased account of Indian-white relations in Wyoming after Custer's Last Stand. 4602

Parmenter, Christine. A GOLDEN AGE. Crowell, 1942. The story of a happy family in a small Massachusetts town. 4603

Parrish, Randall. BOB HAMPTON OF PLACER. McClurg, 1906. The battle which ensued when Custer attempted to confine three thousand unwilling Sioux to a reservation. 4604

--------. MOLLY McDONALD. McClurg, 1912. Romance and Indian fighting on the Great Plains. 4605

Paterson, Arthur. SON OF THE PLAINS. Macmillan, 1895. The dangerous journey along the Santa Fe Trail before the advent of the railroad. 4606

Payne, Robert. THE CHIEFTAIN. Prentice-Hall, 1953. The Nez Percé Indians of Oregon and their Chief Joseph. 4607

Payne, Will. MR. SALT. Houghton, 1903. The financial panic of 1893. 4608

Pettibone, Anita. JOHNNY PAINTER. Farrar, 1944. A fourteen-year-old lad is left to make his own way in the Washington Territory. 4609

Pierce, Ovid W. ON A LONESOME PORCH. Doubleday, 1960. A Carolina family rebuilds its home and life after the Civil War. 4610

Prebble, John. THE BUFFALO SOLDIERS. Harcourt, 1959. Men of three races figure in this tale of western action just after the Civil War. 4611

Quick, Herbert. THE INVISIBLE WOMAN. Bobbs, 1924. Political and cultural growth of the midwest farming area in the 1890s. 4612

Rayner, Emma. VISITING THE SIN. Small, Maynard, 1900. Revenge in the Kentucky and Tennessee mountains. 4613

Reiners, Perceval. ROSES FROM THE SOUTH. Doubleday,

1959. Husband-hunting in West Virginia's White Sulpher Springs and in New York City. 4614

Richter, Conrad. THE SEA OF GRASS. Knopf, 1936. A novelette of romance on the southwestern frontier. 4615

Ripley, Clements. GOLD IS WHERE YOU FIND IT. Appleton, 1936. Rivalry of farming, fruit growing, and mining as industries in early California. 4616

Roberts, Walter Adolphe. CREOLE DUSK. Bobbs, 1948. A New Orleans doctor fights the yellow fever epidemic in Panama. 4617

Roe, Vingie E. THE GREAT TRACE. Macrae Smith, 1948. The bitter rivalry between two leaders of a wagon train hampers the difficult journey. 4618

Rølvaag, Ole E. GIANTS IN THE EARTH. (tr.) Harper, 1927. Norwegian pioneers on the wild Dakota frontier. (followed by PEDER VICTORIOUS) 4619

--------. PEDER VICTORIOUS. (tr.) Harper, 1929. Second generation of Norwegians in the Dakotas. 4620

Ross, Lillian. THE STRANGER. Morrow, 1942. The story of a California pioneer couple who met through a matrimonial agency. 4621

Ross, Zola Helen. CASSY SCANDAL. Bobbs, 1954. Anti-Chinese race riots, a raging fire, and a short-lived marriage. 4622

--------. GREEN LAND. Bobbs, 1952. The Pacific Northwest during the development of the railroads. 4623

Rucker, Helen. CARGO OF BRIDES. Little, 1956. A group of young women sails to Washington State to marry bachelors. 4624

Sandoz, Mari. MISS MORISSA. McGraw, 1955. The resolute heroine fights prejudice against women doctors in Nebraska. 4625

Santee, Ross. BUBBLING SPRING. Scribner, 1949. Stagecoaches, Indian fights, buffalo hunts, and cattle drives in the Old West. 4626

Schaefer, Jack W. SHANE. Houghton, 1949. Soft-spoken Shane helps a Wyoming homesteader defend his property. 4627

Seawell, Molly Elliot. THROCKMORTON. Appleton, 1890. Virginia just after the Civil War. 4628

Sedges, John, pseud. THE TOWNSMAN. Day, 1945. An English immigrant settles in a little town in Kansas. 4629

Selby, John. ISLAND IN THE CORN. Farrar, 1941. The financial decline of a wealthy family. 4630

Seton, Anya. THE TURQUOISE. Houghton, 1946. A girl from the Southwest who tries to find happiness in gay New York. 4631

Shiel, M. P. CONTRABAND OF WAR. Richards, 1899. International politics and finance during the Spanish-American War. 4632

Sims, Marian. BEYOND SURRENDER. Lippincott, 1942. Rebuilding a half-ruined plantation with the aid of a few loyal ex-slaves. 4633

Sinclair, Bertrand W. RAW GOLD. Dillingham, 1908. The quest for gold by unscrupulous men in the wild Northwest. 4634

Sinclair, Harold. THE YEARS OF GROWTH. Doubleday, 1940. A small Illinois town in the second half of the last century. 4635

Slaughter, Frank G. THE STUBBORN HEART. Doubleday, 1950. Doctor's wife converts their plantation into a hospital for whites and Negroes. 4636

Smith, Chard Powers. LADIES DAY. Scribner, 1941. Novel of romance and social developments in upstate New York. 4637

Sorensen, Virginia. MANY HEAVENS. Harcourt, 1954.

Romance of a Mormon couple at the turn of the century. 4638

Stephenson, Howard. GLASS. Kendall, 1933. Contrasts farm and town in late nineteenth century Ohio. 4639

Stewart, Catherine. THREE ROADS TO VALHALLA. Scribner, 1948. Violence, romance, and tragedy in Florida following the Civil War. 4640

Straight, Michael W. CARRINGTON. Knopf, 1960. The fixing of blame for the Fetterman Massacre by the Sioux in 1866. 4641

Street, James Howell. TOMORROW WE REAP. Dial, 1949. Inroads of a northern lumber company in Mississippi in the 1890s. 4642

Stribling, Thomas S. THE STORE. Doubleday, 1932. The transformation of the Old South during the Reconstruction Era. 4643

Swain, Virginia. THE DOLLAR GOLD PIECE. Farrar, 1942. A cattle baron in Kansas City in 1887. 4644

Synon, Mary. THE GOOD RED BRICKS. Little, 1921. Politics, horse racing, and prize fighting in Chicago in the 1890s. 4645

Tarkington, Booth. THE GENTLEMAN FROM INDIANA. Mc-Clure, 1900. A crusading newspaperman in an Indiana town. 4646

Taylor, Ross. BRAZOS. Bobbs, 1938. Adventures of a young cowboy, his term in jail, and his work on the railroad. 4647

--------. THE SADDLE AND THE PLOW. Bobbs, 1942. Problems of a young married couple raising horses in Texas. 4648

Thomason, John. GONE TO TEXAS. Scribner, 1937. Romance and adventure in Texas during post-Civil War years. 4649

Tippett, Thomas. HORSE SHOE BOTTOMS. Harper, 1935.

How wage cuts and labor troubles paved the way for labor unions in the Illinois mining district. 4650

Tolbert, Frank Xavier. THE STAKED PLAIN. Harper, 1958. A renegade Texas blacksmith and gunsmith joins the Comanches. 4651

Tourgée, Albion W. BRICKS WITHOUT STRAW. Fords, 1880. Social and political conditions in the south during Reconstruction. 4652

--------. (1) A FOOL'S ERRAND. Fords, 1879. (2) THE INVISIBLE EMPIRE. Fords, 1883. Reconstruction in the south as seen by a Union officer who settled there. 4653

Towne, Charles H. GOOD OLD YESTERDAY. Appleton, 1935. Family life in New York in the Gay Nineties. 4654

Train, Arthur Cheney. TASSLES ON HER BOOTS. Scribner, 1940. Graft, politics, and the career of Boss Tweed in New York. 4655

Turnbull, Agnes. ROLLING YEARS. Macmillan, 1936. Three generations of a family in a Scottish community in Pennsylvania, 1870-1910. 4656

Van de Water, Frederic. THUNDER SHIELD. Bobbs, 1933. Thunder Shield, the hero, is a white boy adopted by Cheyennes. 4657

Warren, Charles M. ONLY THE VALIANT. Macmillan, 1943. Pioneer life and cavalry warfare against the Apaches. 4658

--------. VALLEY OF THE SHADOW. Doubleday, 1948. U. S. Cavalry company attacks Deesohay and his Apaches. 4659

Waters, Frank. THE WILD EARTH'S NOBILITY. Liveright, 1935. A young man who had lost everything in the Civil War builds a new life in Colorado. 4660

Watts, Mary Stanbery. THE NOON-MARK. Macmillan, 1920.

Warm, realistic account of life in a small midwestern city. 4661

--------. VAN CLEVE. Macmillan, 1913. Events of the Spanish-American War and life at the time. 4662

Weekley, Robert S. THE HOUSE IN RUINS. Random, 1958. Attacks on the Federal Army of occupation by Rebels who refused to accept Lee's surrender. 4663

Wellman, Manley Wade. CANDLE OF THE WICKED. Putnam, 1960. Two men seek land between Fort Scott, Kansas, and Independence, Missouri, in 1873. 4664

Wellman, Paul I. ANGEL WITH SPURS. Lippincott, 1942. General Jo Shelby and his ex-Confederates who go to fight in Mexico. 4665

--------. THE BOWL OF BRASS. Lippincott, 1944. Two Kansas communities will stop at nothing to acquire county seat status. 4666

--------. BRONCHO APACHE. Doubleday, 1950. One of Geronimo's defeated band escapes, returns to Arizona, and becomes a ruthless marauder. 4667

Westcott, Edward Noyes. DAVID HARUM. Appleton, 1898. David Harum is a shrewd Yankee banker. 4668

Wharton, Edith. AGE OF INNOCENCE. Appleton, 1920. The smug Four Hundred in New York in the 1870s. 4669

--------. THE BUCCANEERS. Appleton, 1938. High society life in New York and Newport. 4670

Whipple, Maurine. THE GIANT JOSHUA. Houghton, 1941. Warm story of a Mormon household in the Dixie Mission in Utah. 4671

White, Leslie Turner. LOG JAM. Doubleday, 1959. A tale of the logging industry in the 1870s. 4672

White, Stewart Edward. THE ROSE DAWN. Doubleday, 1920. California when large ranches were succumbing to small farms fed by irrigation. 4673

--------. THE WESTERNERS. McClure, 1901. An unscrupulous half-breed is the central figure in this story of wars with the Sioux. 4674

--------. WILD GEESE CALLING. Doubleday, 1940. The forests of the Pacific Northwest come alive in this tale of a lumberjack. 4675

White, William Allen. A CERTAIN RICH MAN. Macmillan, 1909. A Civil War veteran attains wealth and heroism. 4676

--------. IN THE HEART OF A FOOL. Macmillan, 1918. Kansas in the second half of the nineteenth century. 4677

Whitlock, Brand. J. HARDIN & SON. Appleton, 1923. Small town life in Ohio. 4678

Whitney, James H. FATHER BY PROXY. Exposition, 1955. Factually based story of Reconstruction days in Florida. 4679

Williams, Ben Ames. OWEN GLEN. Houghton, 1950. Laid in a small Ohio town among Welsh coal miners. 4680

--------. THE UNCONQUERED. Houghton, 1953. Politics and romance in post-war New Orleans. 4681

Wilson, Margaret. THE ABLE McLAUGHLINS. Harper, 1923. Struggle between justice and charity in a Scottish community in the Middle West. 4682

Wise, Evelyn V. LONG TOMORROW. Appleton, 1938. The work of a Catholic priest in a prejudiced Minnesota hamlet. 4683

Wister, Owen. RED MEN AND WHITE. Harper, 1896. Relations with Indians in the West featuring General George Crook. 4684

--------. THE VIRGINIAN. Macmillan, 1902. A cultured Virginian becomes a cowboy and courts a teacher from Vermont. 4685

Woods, Edith E. THE SPIRIT OF THE SERVICE. Macmillan, 1903. Naval service in the Spanish-American War. 4686

Wylie, Ida Alexa Ross. HO, THE FAIR WIND. Random, 1945. Martha's Vineyard in the days of camp meetings and whaling ships. 4687

Yerby, Frank. PRIDE'S CASTLE. Dial, 1949. The story of Pride Dawson, a robber-baron of the 1870s. 4688

--------. THE VIXENS. Dial, 1947. A southern aristocrat who had fought for the Union returns home. 4689

Young, Gordon Ray. IRON RAINBOW. Doubleday, 1942. The building of railroads across the American West. 4690

III. C. 1. f. Survey Novels (which include more than two periods)

Arnold, Elliott. BLOOD BROTHER. Duell, 1947. The Apaches after the Gadsden Purchase and the friendship of Cochise and a government scout. 4691

Babson, Naomi. I AM LIDIAN. Harcourt, 1951. Account of our country from Massachusetts to Montana charmingly told as memories of her youth by a ninety-year-old lady. 4692

Delmar, Viña. THE BIG FAMILY. Harcourt, 1961. Various members of the John Slidell family played important parts in America's history over the years from the Revolution to the Civil War. 4693

Ferber, Edna. AMERICAN BEAUTY. Doubleday, 1931. The slow decadence of a fine old Connecticut farm and family through two centuries. 4694

Johnson, Gerald White. BY REASON OF STRENGTH. Minton, 1930. A North Carolina family from the War of Independence through the War between the States. 4695

McMeekin, Clark, *pseud.* for Dorothy Clark and Isabel McMeekin. SHOW ME A LAND. Appleton, 1940. Sixty years in a woman's life, filled with fun, romance, and fine horses, and showing Virginia and Kentucky in the nineteenth century. 4696

Sandburg, Carl. REMEMBRANCE ROCK. Harcourt, 1948. A long epic novel depicting American history from the Pilgrims' landing until after the Civil War. 4697

Seton, Anya. THE HEARTH AND EAGLE. Houghton, 1948. A Yankee family from the colonial period to the Reconstruction. 4698

Steele, Wilbur. DIAMOND WEDDING. Doubleday, 1950. A hardy Coloradan who married a gentle New England woman. 4699

Watson, Virginia C. MANHATTAN ACRES. Dutton, 1934. Ten generations of a New York family during the growth of Manhattan. 4700

Zara, Louis. THIS LAND IS OURS. Houghton, 1940. American history from 1755 to 1835 in the life of one Andrew Benton. 4701

III. C. 2. Latin America

a. Colonial Period to 1800

Allen, Dexter. COIL OF THE SERPENT. Coward, 1956. Reign and military successes of Nezahual. (followed by VALLEY OF EAGLES) 4702

--------. VALLEY OF EAGLES. Coward, 1957. Nezahual, monarch of Tezcuco, at the time of Cortez. 4703

Baggett, Samuel Graves. GODS ON HORSEBACK. McBride, 1952. The conquest of Mexico by Cortez with scenes from Aztec life. 4704

Baron, Alexander. THE GOLDEN PRINCESS. Washburn, 1954. The Spanish conquest of Mexico and relations with the Indians. 4705

Batchellor, D. O. THE UNSTRUNG BOW. Sherman & French,

1910. Experiences of an Englishman in Pizarro's conquest of Peru. 4706

Behn, Aphra. OROONOKO. Pearson, 1871. The capture, revolt, and death of a young Negro chief kidnapped from his home into slavery. 4707

Bloundelle-Burton, John. A GENTLEMAN ADVENTURER. Melrose, 1895. The efforts of William Paterson and his party to make the Isthmus of Darien an English colony. 4708

Clagett, John. CRADLE OF THE SUN. Crown, 1952. Juan de Moncada escapes the Inquisition and resists the Spanish invasion of Yucatan. 4709

Cochran, Hamilton. WINDWARD PASSAGE. Bobbs, 1942. Swashbuckling tale of the pirate Henry Morgan and his raid on Panama. 4710

Craine, Edith Janice. THE VICTORS. Duffield, 1933. The struggles of the Incas during the Spanish conquest of Peru. 4711

Dixon, Thomas. THE SUN VIRGIN. Liveright, 1929. The culture of the Incas is reflected in this romance of Pizarro in Peru. 4712

Douglas-Irvine, Helen. FRAY MARIO. Longmans, 1939. Adventures and misadventures of a Spanish vagabond in Chile. 4713

Duguid, Julian. A CLOAK OF MONKEY FUR. Appleton, 1936. Early Spanish colonizers search avidly for the fabled treasure of gold in South America. 4714

--------. FATHER COLDSTREAM. Appleton, 1938. A Jesuit priest is the hero of this novel of eighteenth century Paraguay. 4715

Eliot, Ethel. ROSES FOR MEXICO. Macmillan, 1946. Account of the Virgin Mary's appearance to Juan Diego at Guadalupe. 4716

Foulke, William D. MAYA: A STORY OF YUCATAN.

Putnam, 1900. Sixteenth century Yucatan as revealed by explorations, early legends, and contemporary accounts. 4717

Friedenthal, Richard. THE WHITE GODS. Harper, 1931. Cortez's conquest of Mexico and his romance with the Indian girl, Marina. 4718

Green, Gerald. SWORD AND THE SUN. Scribner, 1953. The struggle between the Pizarros and Diego de Almagro for control of Peru. 4719

Griffith, George. THE VIRGIN OF THE SUN. Pearson, 1898. A tale of the conquest of Peru and the Incas by Pizarro and de Soto. 4720

Hays, Hoffman Reynolds. TAKERS OF THE CITY. Reynal, 1946. Bishop Bartolomé de las Casas opposes the conquistadors' exploitation of native Mexican Indians. 4721

Hudson, Charles Bradford. THE CRIMSON CONQUEST. McClurg, 1907. The bloody conquest of the Incas of Peru by the Spanish under Pizarro. 4722

Locke, Charles O. LAST PRINCESS. Norton, 1954. The Spanish conquest of Peru as it appeared to the native Incas. 4723

Maass, Edgar. DON PEDRO AND THE DEVIL. Bobbs, 1942. Don Pedro goes with Pizarro to win a kingdom in the New World. 4724

Madariaga, Salvador de. THE HEART OF JADE. Creative Age, 1944. A bright tapestry of Aztec civilization in Mexico during Montezuma's time. 4725

Maltby, A. QUEEN--BUT NO QUEEN. Sisleys, 1907. Philip II of Spain in Yucatan before his marriage with Queen Mary of England. 4726

May, Stella Burke. THE CONQUEROR'S LADY. Farrar & Rinehart, 1930. The conquest of Chile by Pedro de Valdivia is the focal point of this novel. 4727

Millar, George Reid. ORELLANA DISCOVERS THE AMAZON. [same as CROSSBOWMAN'S STORY OF THE FIRST EXPLORATION OF THE AMAZON] Heinemann, 1954. First-person narration of the momentous discovery in the mid-sixteenth century. 4728

Minnigerode, Meade. THE TERROR OF PERU. Farrar & Rinehart, 1940. A young Peruvian adventurer and his pursuit of a lovely Spanish girl. 4729

Niles, Blair. DAY OF IMMENSE SUN. Bobbs, 1936. A novel about the Peruvian people at the time of the Spanish conquest. 4730

--------. MARIA PALUNA. Longmans, 1934. Love of an Indian maiden for a caballero during the Spanish conquest of Guatemala. 4731

Shellabarger, Samuel. CAPTAIN FROM CASTILE. Little, 1945. A colorful account of the Spanish conquest of Mexico. 4732

Smith, Arthur D. Howden. CONQUEROR. Lippincott, 1933. Cortez obtains the aid of an Indian girl in conquering the Aztecs of Mexico. 4733

Spence, Hartzell. BRIDE OF THE CONQUEROR. Random, 1954. Aristocratic and beautiful Doña Eloisa in sixteenth century Peru. 4734

--------. VAIN SHADOW. McGraw, 1947. A rich, colorful account of Francisco de Orellana, discoverer of the Amazon River. 4735

Stucken, Eduard. THE GREAT WHITE GODS. (tr.) Farrar, 1934. Spanish conquest of Aztec Mexico by Cortez. 4736

Thorpe, Francis Newton. THE SPOILS OF EMPIRE. Little, 1903. Concerns the Spanish Conquest of Mexico. 4737

Wallace, Lew. THE FAIR GOD. Houghton, 1873. Pictures Mexican life and culture at the advent of Cortez. 4738

III. C. 2. b. Nineteenth Century: Revolutions and Republics

Baerlein, Henry. THE HOUSE OF THE FIGHTING COCKS. Harcourt, 1923. Story of a Spanish student in Mexico under Maximilian. 4739

Beals, Carleton. TASTE OF GLORY. Crown, 1956. About Bernardo O'Higgins, liberator of Chile in the early nineteenth century. 4740

Blest-Gana, Alberto. MARTIN RIVAS. (tr.) Chapman & Hall, 1916. Mid-century life in the Republic of Chile--social, economic, and political. 4741

Brand, Charles Neville. MEXICAN MASQUERADE. by Charles Lorne, pseud. Dodge, 1938. Mexico in the mid-nineteenth century when Napoleon III set up Maximilian as Emperor. 4742

Conrad, Joseph. NOSTROMO. Harper, 1904. Adventure story of a wealthy Englishman includes exciting episodes and daring men. 4743

Cook, G. Oram. RODERICK TALIAFERRO. Macmillan, 1903. The shaky government of Maximilian, made Emperor of Mexico by Napoleon III of France. 4744

Davis, Richard Harding. SOLDIERS OF FORTUNE. Scribner, 1897. A mining engineer in a small South American republic seething with revolution. 4745

Dombrowski, Katharina von. LAND OF WOMEN. Little, 1935. Violence and Indian customs in Paraguay under Francisco Solano López. 4746

Escragnolle Taunay, Alfredo de. INNOCENCIA. (tr.) by Sylvio Dinarnte, pseud. Chapman & Hall, 1889. Love and cruelty in the backlands of Brazil. 4747

Gorman, Herbert Sherman. THE BREAST OF THE DOVE. Rinehart, 1950. Romance and tragedy in Mexico while Maximilian was Emperor. 4748

--------. CRY OF DOLORES. Rinehart, 1947. The struggle

of the Mexicans to throw off the rule of Spain in 1810. 4749

Harding, Bertita. PHANTOM CROWN. Bobbs, 1934. Attempt of Maximilian and Carlotta, backed by Napoleon III, to rule Mexico. 4750

Henderson, Daniel M. A CROWN FOR CARLOTTA. Stokes, 1929. Tragic romance and adventures of Maximilian and Carlotta in Mexico. 4751

Hudson, William Henry. GREEN MANSIONS. Knopf, 1916. A poetic interpretation of life in the tropical forests of Venezuela. 4752

Jeffries, Graham Montague. FLAMES OF EMPIRE. by Peter Bourne, pseud. Putnam, 1949. Concerning the ill-starred Emperor Maximilian of Mexico. 4753

Jennings, John. CALL THE NEW WORLD. Macmillan, 1941. A court-martialed West Point graduate joins the South American struggle for freedom in the nineteenth century. 4754

La Farge, Oliver. SPARKS FLY UPWARD. Houghton, 1931. Social classes in mid-century Central America. 4755

Lyle, Eugene P. THE MISSOURIAN. Doubleday, Page, 1905. The Mexican War with emissaries from the defeated Confederacy and France as figures. 4756

Marchal, Lucien. SAGE OF CANUDOS. (tr.) Dutton, 1954. Incident involving a "holy city" in the Brazilian hinterlands. 4757

Niles, Blair. PASSENGERS TO MEXICO. Farrar, 1943. Ill-fated French attempt to rule Mexico through Maximilian. 4758

Pilling, William. PONCE DE LEON. Laurie, 1910. Argentina in the early nineteenth century, depicting the end of Spanish influence there. 4759

Pollock, Alyce and Ruth Goode. DON GAUCHO. McGraw, 1950. The pampas of Argentina are the scene of vigorous fighting. 4760

Raynolds, Robert. PAQUITA. Putnam, 1947. Light-hearted romance of a noble Spanish lady in Mexico. 4761

Rundell, E. Ralph. COLOR OF BLOOD. Crowell, 1948. Argentina under dictator Juan Manuel de Rosas. 4762

Sabran, Jean. VENGEANCE OF DON MANUEL. (tr.) by Bernard Deleuze, _pseud._ Putnam, 1953. An adventure story about Spanish colonial days in Chile. 4763

Strabel, Thelma. STORM TO THE SOUTH. Doubleday, 1944. Two cousins involved in emotional conflict and political revolution in Spanish California and Peru. 4764

Teilhet, Darwin Le Ora. LION'S SKIN. Sloane, 1955. Californian William Walker attempts to gain control over Nicaragua. 4765

--------. RETREAT FROM THE _DOLPHIN._ Little, 1943. The Chilean Revolution and the good ship _Dolphin._ 4766

Verissimo, Erico. TIME AND THE WIND. (tr.) Macmillan, 1951. A family in southern Brazil during the period from 1740 to 1895. 4767

White, Edward Lucas. EL SUPREMO. Dutton, 1916. About the dictator of Paraguay from 1814 to 1840, Rodríguez de Francia. 4768

White, Leslie Turner. LOOK AWAY, LOOK AWAY. Random, 1943. A group of southerners attempts to settle in Brazil after the American Civil War. 4769

Williams, Joel, _pseud._ THE COASTS OF FOLLY. Reynal, 1942. South Americans plot to gain their independence in the early nineteenth century. 4770

III. C. 3. Canada

a. French and British Colonial Periods (to 1867)

Altrocchi, Julia. WOLVES AGAINST THE MOON. Macmillan, 1940. The development of a fur trade by a Canadian and his French-Indian wife, with glimpses of Ottawa Indian life. 4771

Barr, Robert. IN THE MIDST OF ALARMS. Stokes, 1894. A romantic tale of a rural area with the Fenian attempt to capture Canada as background. 4772

Bedford-Jones, Henry. STAR WOMAN. Dodd, 1924. Rivalry between English and French for the fur trade of the rich Hudson's Bay territory. 4773

Campbell, Grace MacLennan. THE HIGHER HILL. Duell, 1944. Homey tale of life in Ontario during the War of 1812. 4774

Campbell, Wilfrid. A BEAUTIFUL REBEL. Doran, 1909. Attack of the Americans on Canada during the War of 1812 and the Battle of Queenstown Heights. 4775

Capes, Bernard. LOVE LIKE A GIPSY. Constable, 1901. Canada and England during the American War of Independence. 4776

Cather, Willa. SHADOWS ON THE ROCK. Knopf, 1931. Delicate, sensitive reflections of events in Quebec under Frontenac. 4777

Catherwood, Mary H. THE LADY OF FORT ST. JOHN. Houghton, 1891. Rivalry between the forts of Port Royal and St. John and the heroism of Lady La Tour. 4778

--------. THE ROMANCE OF DOLLARD. Century, 1889. French Captain Dollard and a handful of loyal followers battle an overwhelming Iroquois force. 4779

--------. THE WHITE ISLANDER. Century, 1893. A good picture of Indians and their treatment of captives. 4780

Chambers, Robert W. THE DRUMS OF AULONE. Appleton, 1927. A French girl's experiences reflect Mme. de Maintenon's anti-Huguenot influence in the French court. 4781

Cody, Hiram Alfred. THE KING'S ARROW. Doran, 1922. Tory loyalists who flee to Canada during the American Revolution. 4782

Cooney, Percival John. KINSMEN. Doran, 1916. Rebellion against a quasi-feudal overlord in Upper Canada. 4783

Costain, Thomas B. HIGH TOWERS. Doubleday, 1949. Account of an attempt to build a French empire in America featuring the Le Moyne family of Montreal. 4784

Crowley, Mary Catherine. A DAUGHTER OF NEW FRANCE. Little, 1901. "Account of the gallant Sieur Cadillac and his colony on the Detroit." 4785

--------. IN TREATY WITH HONOUR. Little, 1906. French Canada's fight for responsible government in the 1830s. 4786

Curwood, James O. THE BLACK HUNTER. Cosmopolitan Bk., 1926. The disputed Canadian frontier when both France and England were colonizing. 4787

--------. THE PLAINS OF ABRAHAM. Doubleday, 1928. Vivid account of French-Canadians orphaned by an Indian massacre. 4788

De La Roche, Mazo. BUILDING OF JALNA. Little, 1944. Philip Whiteoak and his bride migrate to Ontario in mid-nineteenth century. 4789

--------. MORNING AT JALNA. Little, 1960. A mother and her four children in Canada during the American Civil War. 4790

Eaton, Evelyn. QUIETLY MY CAPTAIN WAITS. Harper, 1940. Canada under the French regime. 4791

--------. RESTLESS ARE THE SAILS. Harper, 1941.

Exciting trip by land and sea to warn Louisbourg of attack. 4792

--------. THE SEA IS SO WIDE. Harper, 1943. Three Acadians, exiled from Nova Scotia, settle in Williamsburg, Virginia. 4793

Elson, John M. THE SCARLET SASH. Dent, 1925. A novel of life during the War of 1812, including an account of the Battle of Queenstown Heights. 4794

Elwood, Muriel. DEEPER THE HERITAGE. Scribner, 1946. Eighteenth century life in Montreal and eastern Canada. 4795

--------. HERITAGE OF THE RIVER. Scribner, 1945. Indian warfare, political intrigue, and romance in Montreal. 4796

--------. TOWARDS THE SUNSET. Scribner, 1947. The children and grandchildren of French-Canadian pioneers. 4797

--------. WEB OF DESTINY. Bobbs, 1951. The Marquis de Montcalm and Sir William Johnson appear in this tale of Canada. 4798

Fraser, Hermia H. TALL BRIGADE. Binfords, 1956. Adventures of a brigade leader for the early Hudson's Bay Company. 4799

French, Maida P. BOUGHS BEND OVER. Doubleday, 1944. Loyalists who seek refuge in Canada face difficulties establishing a home in the forests. 4800

Freuchen, Peter. LEGEND OF DANIEL WILLIAMS. Messner, 1956. An escaped slave's experiences in Canada. 4801

Gaspé, Philippe Aubert de. THE CANADIANS OF OLD. (tr.) [pub. later as: CAMERON OF LOCHIEL] Appleton, 1890. A story of French settlers in Canada in the mid-eighteenth century. 4802

Gibbs, George. FLAME OF COURAGE. Appleton, 1926. Intrigues and romance of members of the French court in Canada during the Seven Years War. 4803

Goodridge Roberts, Theodore. BROTHERS OF PERIL. by Theodore Roberts. Page, 1905. Land and sea adventures when British fishermen were struggling for control of Newfoundland. 4804

Gordon, Charles William. THE ROCK AND THE RIVER. by Ralph Connor, pseud. Dodd, 1931. Romance of a young Canadian boy and an American girl just prior to the War of 1812. 4805

--------. THE RUNNER. by Ralph Connor, pseud. Doubleday, 1929. Fighting between Americans, English, Indians, and Canadians in the War of 1812. 4806

Harris, Cyril. ONE BRAVER THING. Scribner, 1942. English loyalist doctor and family exiled to Nova Scotia at the end of the American Revolution. 4807

Haworth, Paul Leland. THE PATH OF GLORY. Little, 1911. A story of the conquest of Canada including Wolfe's military victory on the Plains of Abraham. 4808

Isely, Bliss. BLAZING THE WAY WEST. Scribner, 1939. Early French fur traders and explorers. 4809

Jennings, John. STRANGE BRIGADE. Little, 1952. The settlement of the Canadian West. 4810

Kirby, William. THE GOLDEN DOG. Page, 1897. Quebec in the 1740s was the scene of colonizing and fur trading. 4811

Lancaster, Bruce. BRIGHT TO THE WANDERER. Little, 1942. Loyalist refugees engaged in the political conflict over the Family Compact. 4812

Laut, Agnes C. HERALDS OF EMPIRE. Appleton, 1902. "Being the story of one Ramsay Stanhope, lieutenant to Pierre Radisson in the Northern fur trade." 4813

--------. LORDS OF THE NORTH. Heinemann, 1901. Pictures pioneer life, fur trading, and a woman captured by Indians. 4814

--------. THE STORY OF THE TRAPPER. Appleton, 1902. The exploits and adventures of a fur trapper who wanders across the continent. 4815

Lyman, Olim L. THE TRAIL OF THE GRAND SEIGNEUR. New Amsterdam Bk. Co., 1903. Refugees from revolutionary France who seek a new life in America, settling near Lake Ontario. 4816

Lyttleton, Edith J. GRAND PARADE. by G. B. Lancaster, pseud. Reynal, 1943. Four generations of a prominent colonial Halifax family. 4817

McCulloch, John H. THE MEN OF KILDONAN. Doubleday, Doran, 1926. Travels and trials of settlers who migrated from Scotland to Canada. 4818

McDowell, Franklin D. THE CHAMPLAIN ROAD. Macmillan, 1939. Jesuit missionaries and martyrs among the Hurons in Canada. 4819

McIlwraith, Jean. A DIANA OF QUEBEC. Smith & Elder, 1912. Romance of Quebec late in the century with Nelson as one of the main characters. 4820

McLennan, William and Jean McIlwraith. THE SPAN O' LIFE. Harper, 1899. Jacobite activities in Canada and the capture of Louisbourg. 4821

Marquis, Thomas G. MARGUERITE DE ROBERVAL. Fisher Unwin, 1899. Canada as a French colony; the explorations of Cartier. 4822

Merwin, Samuel. THE ROAD TO FRONTENAC. Doubleday, 1901. A party travelling through French Canada is captured by Indians. 4823

Niven, Frederick. MINE INHERITANCE. Macmillan, 1940. Evicted Scots crofters settle in the Red River region. 4824

O'Grady, P. W. and Dorothy Dunn. DARK WAS THE WILDERNESS. Bruce, 1945. Features the North American martyrs--Jogues, Brébeuf, Lalemant, and Goupil. 4825

Parish, John C. THE MAN WITH THE IRON HAND. Houghton, 1918. French-Canadian expansion into the Mississippi Valley. 4826

Parker, Gilbert. THE POMP OF THE LAVILETTES. Appleton, 1897. A rousing tale of adventure and rebellion under Papineau in 1837. 4827

--------. THE POWER AND THE GLORY. Harper, 1925. The northern explorations of Robert La Salle. 4828

--------. THE SEATS OF THE MIGHTY. Appleton, 1896. A colonial romance ending with the fall of Quebec. 4829

--------. THE TRAIL OF THE SWORD. Appleton, 1896. Fighting among French, Indians, and British in New France and New England. 4830

--------. WHEN VALMOND CAME TO PONTIAC. Macmillan, 1895. A romance of a Canadian village, with a supposed son of Napoleon as chief character. 4831

Parrish, Randall. BEYOND THE FRONTIER. McClurg, 1915. Rivalry between La Salle and Governor La Barre in colonial Canada. 4832

Patterson, Frances Taylor. WHITE WAMPUM. Longmans, 1934. Fictional account of the life of an Indian girl converted to Catholicism. 4833

Quiller-Couch, Arthur T. FORT AMITY. Scribner, 1904. Fighting among British, French, Americans, and Indians in the Ticonderoga-Quebec area in the 1750s. 4834

Raddall, Thomas. HIS MAJESTY'S YANKEES. [abridged version: SON OF THE HAWK] Doubleday, 1942. Effects on Nova Scotia of the American War for Independence. 4835

--------. ROGER SUDDEN. Doubleday, 1945. Rivalry between French and English in the colonization of Nova Scotia. 4836

Ritchie, Cicero T. WILLING MAID. Abelard-Schuman, 1957. Struggle for supremacy in Nova Scotia among British,

French, Indians, and Acadians. 4837

Roberts, Charles G. D. (1) THE FORGE IN THE FOREST. Silver, 1897. (2) A SISTER TO EVANGELINE. Silver, 1900. (1) The settlement of the Acadians and (2) their expulsion, both accounts influenced by Longfellow's poem Evangeline. 4838

--------. THE PRISONER OF MADEMOISELLE. Page, 1905. Romance of a Yankee sea captain and a French girl in Acadia. 4839

Smith, Alice Prescott. MONTLIVET. Houghton, 1906. English and French rivals band together to fight the Indians. 4840

Smith, Arthur D. Howden. THE DOOM TRAIL. Brentano's, 1922. Fur trade rivalry with the French diverting English trade goods to their own use. 4841

Spicer, Bart. THE TALL CAPTAINS. Dodd, 1957. Soldiers, farmers, townsfolk, and politicians in the final days of New France. 4842

Stone, Grace. THE COLD JOURNEY. Morrow, 1934. A group of captured villagers is marched through the wilderness to French settlements in the north. 4843

Sullivan, Alan. THE FUR MASTERS. Coward, 1947. Competitive fur trading in the early nineteenth century as seen by a Hudson's Bay Company man. 4844

--------. THREE CAME TO VILLE MARIE. Coward, 1943. A romance of three settlers to New France. 4845

Vaczek, Louis C. RIVER AND EMPTY SEA. Houghton, 1950. A canoe trip to Hudson's Bay through the Canadian wilderness. 4846

Wharton, Anne Hollingsworth. A ROSE OF OLD QUEBEC. Lippincott, 1913. Mary Thompson and Captain Nelson in Quebec and London, 1780-1790. 4847

White, Stewart Edward. CONJURER'S HOUSE. McClure, 1903.

Rivalry as the Hudson's Bay Company tries to gain control of the fur trade. 4848

III. C. 3. b. The Dominion of Canada (1867-1900)

Cameron, William Bleasdell. THE WAR TRAIL OF BIG BEAR. Duckworth, 1927. The connection of Big Bear and other Cree Indians with the rebellion of 1885 and the Frog Lake Massacre. 4849

Campbell, Grace MacLennan. THE THORN-APPLE TREE. Duell, 1943. Romance of Scotch-Canadian pioneers. 4850

Cody, Hiram Alfred. FIGHTING-SLOGAN. Doubleday, Doran, 1926. Romance and rivalries when the Fenians rebelled against England. 4851

Constantin-Weyer, Maurice. THE HALF-BREED. Macaulay, 1930. About a man who sometimes disagreed violently with government policy. 4852

Cotes, Sara Jeannette. THE IMPERIALIST. by Mrs. Everard Cotes. Constable, 1904. Life and business interests in a Canadian town in the 1870s. 4853

De La Roche, Mazo. MARY WAKEFIELD. Little, 1949. A family of English immigrants at their estate, Jalna. 4854

Hatton, Joseph. UNDER THE GREAT SEAL. Cassell, 1893. Poor management of political affairs under the Lorne government in Newfoundland. 4855

Jarvis, W. H. P. THE GREAT GOLD RUSH. Murray, 1913. The rush to the Klondike after the discovery of gold. 4856

Keith, Marian. THE SILVER MAPLE. Revell, 1906. A Scots lumberman joins the expedition to assist Gordon in fighting Riel's second rebellion. 4857

MacGregor, Mary E. M. A GENTLEMAN ADVENTURER. Doubleday, Doran, 1924. A young Scotsman in the service of the Hudson's Bay Company is stationed at remote outposts. 4858

Mackie, John. THE PRODIGAL'S BROTHER. Jarrold & Sons, 1899. The Northwest Province during the Red River Rebellion of 1885. 4859

White, Stewart Edward. THE SILENT PLACES. Hodder, 1904. Two Hudson's Bay Company men and their journey through untamed wilderness. 4860

Young, Samuel H. THE KLONDIKE CLAN. Revell, 1916. The Klondike Gold Rush of the 1890s. 4861

III. C. 4. The Caribbean Area

Alderman, Clifford L. SILVER KEYS. Putnam, 1960. Sir William Phips' expedition from Maine to the Caribbean in search of sunken treasure in the late seventeenth century. 4862

Atherton, Gertrude. THE GORGEOUS ISLE. Doubleday, 1908. A popular nineteenth century winter resort in the West Indies. 4863

Best, Herbert. DIANE. Morrow, 1954. Plantation owner's death is avenged by his daughter, who takes over management of the estate. 4864

Bloundelle-Burton, John. THE HISPANIOLA PLATE. Cassell, 1895. Sir William Phips' quest for a lost Spanish treasure. 4865

Bontemps, Arna. DRUMS AT DUSK. Macmillan, 1939. Toussaint L'Ouverture and the Negro uprising in Haiti during the French Revolution. 4866

Brown, Wenzell. THEY CALLED HER CHARITY. Appleton, 1951. Pirates, pursued by the British, take refuge in the Virgin Islands in the seventeenth century. 4867

Carpentier, Alejo. KINGDOM OF THIS WORLD. Knopf, 1957. Haiti in the period of King Henri Christophe. 4868

Castor, Henry. THE YEAR OF THE SPANIARD. Doubleday, 1950. The historic year of 1898 when the United States won Cuba, Puerto Rico, and the Philippines from Spain. 4869

Devereux, Mary. LAFITTE OF LOUISIANA. Little, 1902. About Jean Lafitte, the French pirate who operated largely in the Gulf of Mexico. 4870

Emerson, Peter Henry. CAÓBA, THE GUERILLA CHIEF. Scribner, 1897. A romance of the Cuban Rebellion against Spain in the late nineteenth century. 4871

Galván, Manuel de Jesus. THE CROSS AND THE SWORD. (tr.) Ind. U. Press, 1954. Early Spanish settlement of the Caribbean area. 4872

Hearn, Lafcadio. YOUMA. Harper, 1890. A story of the Negro insurrection on Martinique in 1848 and of a slave who remained loyal. 4873

Hergesheimer, Joseph. THE BRIGHT SHAWL. Knopf, 1922. A romantic American youth, inflamed by Cuba's struggle against Spain, joins the revolution. 4874

Husband, Joseph. CITADEL. Houghton, 1924. A privateer captain faces slavery and death to rescue his lady. 4875

Jeffries, Graham Montague. DRUMS OF DESTINY. [En. title: BLACK SAGA] by Peter Bourne, pseud. Putnam, 1947. A Scotch doctor in Haiti during the revolt of the slaves. 4876

Jesse, F. Tennyson. MOONRAKER; or, THE FEMALE PIRATE AND HER FRIENDS. Knopf, 1927. Contains a rousing sea tale and a story of Toussaint L'Ouverture. 4877

Lancaster, Bruce and Lowell Brentano. BRIDE OF A THOUSAND CEDARS. Stokes, 1939. The effect on Bermuda of the blockade runners during the U. S. Civil War. 4878

Mackintosh, Elizabeth. THE PRIVATEER. by Gordon Daviot, pseud. Macmillan, 1952. Exciting tale of naval action in the Caribbean in the days of privateer Henry Morgan. 4879

Martineau, Harriet. THE HOUR AND THE MAN. Moxon, 1841. Toussaint L'Ouverture's part in the rebellion on Haiti and his betrayal. 4880

Mason, Van Wyck. CUTLASS EMPIRE. Doubleday, 1949. Henry Morgan's flight from England, and his bloody career as pirate of the Caribbean. 4881

Raddall, Thomas. PRIDE'S FANCY. Doubleday, 1946. A yarn of privateering between Nova Scotia and the Caribbean. 4882

Roberts, Walter Adolphe. SINGLE STAR. Bobbs, 1949. Revolutionary days in Cuba in the 1890s. 4883

Rowland, Henry Cottrell. IN THE SHADOW. Appleton, 1906. An Oxford-educated Negro leads a rebellion in Haiti. 4884

Simons, Katherine D. M. THE LAND BEYOND THE TEMPEST. by Drayton Mayrant, pseud. Coward, 1960. The Sea Venture, on an expedition to take supplies to Jamestown, is stricken by a storm off Bermuda. 4885

Slaughter, Frank G. BUCCANEER SURGEON. by C. V. Terry, pseud. Hanover, 1954. A ship's surgeon of Spanish and English ancestry on the Spanish Main. 4886

Smith, Herbert Huntington. HIS MAJESTY'S SLOOP, DIAMOND ROCK. by H. S. Huntington, pseud. Houghton, 1904. British defense of an island near Martinique during the Napoleonic War. 4887

Smith, Minna Caroline. MARY PAGET. Macmillan, 1900. England and Bermuda at the time of James I. 4888

Street, James Howell. MINGO DABNEY. Dial, 1950. Guerrilla warfare in the Cuban revolt against Spanish rule. 4889

Taylor, Angeline. BLACK JADE. McBride, 1947. Romantic novel of Haiti at the end of the eighteenth century. 4890

Taylor, James G., Jr. DARK DAWN. Mohawk, 1932. Adventure during the Negro uprising in Haiti in 1791. 4891

Vandercook, John W. BLACK MAJESTY. Harper, 1928. Romanticized life of Henri Christophe, the slave who became King of Haiti. 4892

Webb, Barbara. ALETTA LAIRD. Doubleday, 1935. Romance in the Bermudas during the American Revolution. 4893

Yolland, G. UNDER THE STARS. White, 1907. The Jamaica Insurrection of 1865. 4894

Index

(Reference is to entry numbers.)